THE W EFFECT

Publication of this book has been made possible in part by the generous support of the following individuals:

Alida Brill and Steven Scheuer

Barbara Grossman and Michael Gross

Betty Prashker

Mary Ann and Robert Roncker

Jenny Warburg/The Bydale Foundation

THE W EFFECT

BUSH'S WAR ON WOMEN

Edited by Laura Flanders

with research by Phoebe St. John and Livia Tenzer

The Feminist Press
at the City University of New York

Published by the Feminist Press at the City University of New York
The Graduate Center, 365 Fifth Avenue
New York, NY 10016, www.feministpress.org

First Feminist Press edition, 2004

09 08 07 06 05 04 5 4 3 2

Library of Congress Cataloging-in-Publication Data

The W effect : Bush's war on women / edited by Laura Flanders with research by Phoebe St. John and Livia Tenzer.— 1st Feminist Press ed.
p. cm.
ISBN 1-55861-471-0 (pbk.)
1. Women—Social conditions—21st century. 2. Women—United States—Social conditions—21st century. 3. Women's rights. 4. Women and war. 5. Women—Government policy—United States. 6. War on Terrorism, 2001—-Social aspects. I. Flanders, Laura.
HQ1155.W44 2004
305.42'0973'0905—dc22

2004003185

NOTE: The Feminist Press at CUNY does not support or oppose any political candidate or party. Our informational materials are strictly for educational purposes and suggest no endorsement, bias, or preference. Citizens make their electoral decisions based on a broad range of information. Nothing in this publication is meant to suggest that a person's vote should be cast on the basis of a single issue or event.

Text design by Dayna Navaro
Printed on acid-free paper in Canada by Transcontinental Printing

TABLE OF CONTENTS

WOMEN TAKE ACTION

WHAT'S ON THE HORIZON

INTRODUCTION

Feigning Feminism, Fueling Backlash

LAURA FLANDERS

George W. Bush campaigned for the presidency of the United States declaring that "W is for Women." At the Republican Party convention in 2000, his supporters wore that slogan emblazoned on buttons pinned to their chests. As one female delegate from Texas told me, "Bush's agenda puts women front and center. For women, George has nothing but respect."

While women's advocates looked on skeptically, George W. Bush came into office and seemed to make good on his "W is for women" promise. The president appointed a number of high-visibility women to his cabinet and inner circle. His administration advanced some socially-conscious-sounding initiatives, a "Family Time Flexibility Act," for example, and an education policy called "No Child Left Behind." After September 11, 2001, images of burqa-clad women in Afghanistan flooded the media, providing a backdrop to George W.'s drive to war. To judge by Bush's rhetoric, the U.S. bombing of Afghanistan was motivated, not by revenge for the strikes on the United States but by a wish to liberate women and girls from the sexist Taliban. "The fight against terrorism is also a fight for the rights and dignity of women," declared the First Lady Laura Bush in a special radio broadcast. As the attention shifted to another military operation, the President made it a point to mention Saddam Hussein's Baath Party's grim record of abuse and rape of women as he laid out his case for the U.S. invasion and occupation of Iraq.

Is W for women? As the essays in this collection show, beneath the masterful media spin, a very different reality has been emerging. Contributor Richard Goldstein has called this ploy "stealth misogyny." While the president dresses his cabinet and his policies up in women-friendly clothing for political reasons (women were far more likely than men to vote for Bush's Democratic opponent in 2000), the effects of his actions are quite the opposite. Pandering to anti-tax extremists, his budgets have left state and federal treasuries without the funds to pay for basic public services. Religious radicals in government jobs are issuing regulations and promulgating laws that would leave the most vulnerable Americans with more limited, not expanded, choices in life. Bush's cabinet secretaries turn out to be media decoys. Each trails a long conservative résumé, in many cases betraying the very causes—affirmative action, women's rights, civil rights—which helped them advance. (For more on Bush's women, see *Bushwomen: Tales of a Cynical Species* by this author.) The "flexibility" in the Flexibility Act turned out to be all the employers'—to pay overtime, as has been required for over seventy years, or to "offer" time-off instead (at the employer's convenience). W's No Child Left Behind Act actually left millions of children behind when the law imposed new mandates on state school systems, while his budget failed to cover the cost.

More than any Republican administration before his, Bush's has gone to some lengths to appeal to women voters. But women's rights advocates agree that W's administration's male—and female—members are doing their best to reverse the gains that women have made, not just in the last decade, but over much of the twentieth century. Coinciding with several simultaneous global trends (including globalized trade, the rise of agribusiness, and the growth of a new information and "service" economy), the Bush era is shaping up to be a crunch moment for human equality. Far from advancing towards greater fairness, we are witnessing an exacerbation of the power divide between the world's rich and poor—closely represented by its male and female populations.

The Bush administration's actions in the wake of 9/11 have widened this already deep divide. The wealthiest and most militarized government on the planet will reward its friends, but its enemies are "evil" in Washington's eyes, and the only acceptable solution to that "evil" is a military one. The administration's go-it-alone response to the 9/11 attacks has fuelled a fury which, in some places, is directed against all things American—including rights for women and the enterprise known as feminism. And for all the talk of "security," the vast majority of the world's people find their lives not more secure but more perilous, not only because of threats from abroad, but also because of the rise of radicals in their own countries, who would spread fundamentalist religion in the name of national resistance.

Rejecting the national laws and international mechanisms developed over the last century to advance peace, ecology, and equal opportunity, W is coming to stand not for Women, but for War. Feigning feminism, Bush is fueling backlash. That's the W effect, but only part of it. There's more to it, as this book shows.

The Bush era began at the start of a new century that seemed to promise new gains for women. From winning the vote to securing rights in the workplace, to legal abortion, available birth control, and the wider acceptance of homosexuality—indeed, the broad array of male and female gender roles and sexualities—the struggle for women's rights had transformed the world in the preceding one hundred years. (The term "feminism" was first used in France in the 1880s.) On the international front, human rights laws were expanding to include reproductive rights and to recognize rape as a war crime. World development and health organizations were coming to realize just how heavily the world's well-being relies on well women, especially in developing nations and areas plagued by the spread of disease. As the twenty-first century began, the world was undergoing massive transformation; the process wasn't slowing, but not surprisingly, along with all the gains, there was negative fallout. Why, for example, do the Islamic extremists of the Taliban embrace gender apartheid? "Perhaps," writes Barbara Ehrenreich, in an essay republished here,

> The answer lies in the way that globalization has posed a particular threat to men. Western industry has displaced traditional crafts—female as well as male—and large-scale, multinational-controlled agriculture has downgraded the independent farmer to the status of a hired hand. From West Africa to Southeast Asia, these trends have resulted in massive male displacement, and frequently, unemployment. At the same time, globalization has offered new opportunities for Third World women—in export oriented manufacturing, where women are favored for their presumed "nimble fingers" and more recently, as migrant domestics working in wealthy countries.

Women appeal to employers too, because women can be paid less than men, as Rhonda Perry of the Missouri Rural Crisis Center points out in this book. Women in developing countries are estimated to occupy between 60 and 90 percent of the jobs in the labor-intensive stages of the clothing industry as well as in the production of food crops for export. From Wal-Mart, the consumer retailer, to Dole Foods, the global food corporation, suppliers tend to hire a largely female work force and work them longer hours for less pay in unhealthy conditions. There are jobs, indeed, but globalization's "benefits" are double-edged.

Against this backdrop, sexual politics helped bring George W. Bush to office. The former governor of Texas had two significant credentials for the job. He was the eldest son of a former President George Herbert Walker Bush, and he was the "dragon slayer," so dubbed by his supportors when he unseated a popular Democratic governor in a bitter battle in 1994. The dragon was Ann Richards, one of the Democratic Party's female stars.

His sights set on the presidency, Bush campaigned to end the two-term Clinton/Gore era. The economy had been doing well—the national Treasury was predicting years of surpluses—so candidate Bush couldn't target the Clinton/Gore economic policies. Instead, he tapped into its biproduct, a sense of social discomfort and cultural dislocation. Affluent Americans had enlarged their houses, their stock portfolios, and their cars—and Hollywood promoted their lifestyle as the standard to which all should aspire. U.S. corporations had consolidated and expanded their reach—their influence over political priorities at home and abroad grew in direct proportion to their mushrooming campaign gifts. Beneath the numbers lay a social malaise. The benefits of the 1990s boom settled mostly in the upper reaches of the economy. Although affluent Americans thrived, extreme poverty persisted, working-class wages stagnated, and manufacturing jobs—disproportionately men's jobs—accelerated their exodus overseas.

Bush didn't run against the Democratic incumbency on money; he ran against the mores, or morality of this group, something he called "values." The consumer media didn't fully understand all that was wrapped up in the word, but Bush's supporters did. "The administration I'll bring is a group of men and women who are focused on what's best for America, honest men and women, decent men and women, women who will see service to our country as a great privilege and who will not stain the house," George W. Bush told Iowans in January 2000. After six years of sex scandals and impeachment investigations, the word "stain" summoned just one image to the public mind: White House intern Monica Lewinsky's tainted dress.

Bush vowed to restore what he called "civility" to Washington, meaning sexual order, among other kinds. What his administration actually installed were anti-tax, pro-religious extremists, men—and women—who had served in previous Republican administrations, or worked for the Christian Right, or labored in associated Right-Wing think tanks. The "values" Bush's people brought to the job were ideological: economically libertarian—against taxes, environmental restrictions, workplace regulations, and pretty much any function for government outside of policing and the military—and socially controlling. As Nina Easton explains here, "The Christian right's sway within the Republican party . . . made it an influential power broker in the neck-and-neck 2000 presidential race."

Once in office, Bush made good on his commitments to the tax-cutters, issuing tax reductions worth $3 trillion mostly to wealthier Americans and, not coincidentally, to the Religious Right. Almost the first thing the President did after his inauguration was cut off funds for organizations that so much as mention available abortion services overseas, reinstating the so-called global gag rule. While a handful of carefully selected women—like Elaine Chao, the wife of Mitch McConnell, a Republican House leader—sailed through confirmation by the Senate (Chao became secretary of labor), further down the bureaucratic ladder, where public confirmation is not required, the Bush transition team named controversial activists to powerful government positions. Kay Coles James, the former dean of Pat Robertson's Regent University, an adamant anti-abortion, anti-affirmative action activist, became director of the U.S. Office of Personnel Management, overseeing hiring and firing and discrimination complaints for the entire federal workforce. Bill Berkowitz's article in this collection runs down the list of anti-feminist, anti-government, Independent Women's Forum (IWF) leaders who have found good government jobs. Nancy Pfotenhauer, the IWF's president and CEO, was chosen to serve on the National Advisory Committee on Violence against Women (the IWF actively opposed the Violence against Women Act and helped to get key provisions of it repealed in federal court). To the President's Council of Economic Advisors, Bush appointed Diana Furchtgott-Roth, a former fellow of the right-wing American Enterprise Institute, who in the 1990s co-authored a book denying the existence of the glass ceiling and the gender gap in wages, and dismissing claims that discrimination against women persists in the U.S. workplace.

Even as he publicly proclaimed his commitment to equality for all Americans, Bush tried to shut down the Department of Labor's network of regional women's bureaus (women's rights activists defeated that effort.) In the name of budget-cutting, he stopped money for the program that monitored discrimination in federal agencies, and forced cut backs at the Equal Employment Opportunity Commission even as the number of complaints of discrimination in the workplace hit a multi-year high.

Similar strategies were deployed by W. on the international level. Steve Benen, here, in an article originally written for Americans for the Separation of Church and State, reports on the activities of Tommy Thompson, secretary of Health and Human Services, and John Klink, the men W.'s administration chose to lead delegations to United Nations conferences on children's rights, population, and development. Klink, formerly the Vatican's representative at the UN, provoked an international firestorm during the conflict in the former Yugoslavia when he opposed making the "morning after" birth control pill available for women who had been raped by enemy troops. Klink opposes condom use even to prevent AIDS.

After the attacks of September 11, 2001, the conventional wisdom is that "everything changed." Suddenly the president was saying things like "You're either with us or you're with the terrorists" and suggesting that the nation had a God-driven destiny to wage what he at one point called "a crusade." To some, his unilateralism came as a shock. It shouldn't have. There had been many hints of the same attitude on the campaign trail. He didn't trumpet his ideology—he did not come out for the reversal of *Roe v. Wade* or the end of the division between church and state—but he signaled his intentions clearly enough. When asked during an early debate to name the philosopher he most respected, Bush answered, "Jesus Christ." As a candidate, he visited Bob Jones University, a Southern college that was infamous for its ban on interracial dating, and its defiance of federal civil rights mandates. Bob Jones's founders believed that God's law supercedes man's law, but when a reporter asked what role religion would have in the Oval Office, the candidate fudged: "Some may accept the answer, and some may not . . . I really don't care. It's me. It's just what I'm all about." Mainstream, overwhelmingly secular reporters generally accepted his God talk as a personal, not a political, thing. By his own account, GW was completely transformed by Jesus Christ on the eve of his fortieth birthday. (His reputation until that point was as a drinker and brawler. Bush was arrested twice before he graduated college, once for drinking and driving, once for property damage.) "Christ changed my heart," said Bush. People would either understand his conversion or they wouldn't: "If they don't know, it's going to be hard to explain," candidate Bush told a reporter.

With hindsight, it's easy to hear a preview of "You're either with us or you're with the terrorists." As New York Firefighter, Brenda Berkman told the women of New York in a speech published for the first time here, coverage of the attacks on the United States reinforced old gender stereotypes about patriotism and heroics. On the international front, the so-called "war on terror" made it that much easier for unilateralism to acquire a heroic glow.

Butch is back, declares Richard Goldstein in his delightful essay "Bush's Basket" (originally published in the *Village Voice*). "All men must cope with the complications of feminism. I would argue that the demand for sexual equality is a major reason for the global rise of fundamentalism. Bush owes his fortune to this movement in America, but his appeal goes far beyond the Christian right. He represents a model that invites female initiative and counsel but not control. . . . [Bush] embodies the primal uncertainty many men feel in face of sexual change."

Consider the language now in vogue: the legislation that is the cornerstone of the Bush administration's strategy to counter terrorism is called the USA PATRIOT Act. The men now in charge of deciding U.S. policy abroad once drew up a strategic document they called "Project for New American Century." As several of the contributors to *The W Effect* suggest, Bush's cowboy persona represents an undisguised desire for the United States to wield untrammeled power in the world, and for power in the home to return to men—preferably Christian, white, straight men. There is an advantage to the administration in pushing the hot buttons of a fearful American public. According to Bob Woodward's account, *Bush at War*, in war council discussions over what to include in Bush's September 20, 2001, speech to Congress and the American people, Defense Secretary Donald Rumsfeld suggested mentioning the possibility that nuclear weapons might be used against the United States because "it's an *energizer* for the American people." An *energized* public is more likely to go along with their president.

The cornerstone of President Bush's strategy for curbing the spread of terrorism and chemical, nuclear and biological weapons is war. Since coming into office, the W administration has rejected decades of arms control based on mutual deterrence, walked away from the cold war Nuclear Non-Proliferation Treaty, and abandoned the nuclear nations' promise: "No first strike." In the name of defending democracy, Attorney General John Ashcroft's Justice Department detained hundreds of American residents without charge. Thousands of foreign nationals have lingered for years now, in legal limbo, in Guantanamo Bay, without civil legal representation and without prisoner of war protections as required by the Geneva Convention.

Talk to women's rights advocates and they'll say that Bush's approach to the war on terror is no surprise. For all the high-octane talk about international threats, the administration's approach to trouble abroad is entirely in keeping with its approach to problems back home. Ideological, unilateral, ambitious, deceptive, punitive, Bush's buck-the-global-consensus attitude to the war on terror is entirely consistent they say, with his administration's "blame the victim" agenda at home. Witness the administration's approach to poverty: work harder, longer (the renewed Temporary Assistance for Needy Families Act mandates longer work hours for needy mothers), or marry. The second of these two solutions is another "crusade": While the Bush administration claims not to be able adequately to fund its own "Leave No Child Behind" public education program, it has billions of dollars to spend on promoting abstinence and heterosexual marriage, with no evidence that such promotion programs work. The President also has personal and political energy to spare to "defend the sanctity of traditional marriage" while he has none to spend on educating sexually active adults about sexually transmitted disease. Global AIDS activists call the Bush administration's disparagement of condoms something akin to a human rights crime (see Doug Ireland, "Bush's War on the Condom.")

Like Saddam Hussein's nonexistent nukes, many threats turn out to have been manufactured and Americans' fears manipulated. But the social dislocation and economic disease Butch Bush appeals to is very real. The most militarized nation in the world possesses unparalleled military strength, but economically it is divided. At the time of this writing, the *Wall St. Journal* carries this front page story: "The Gap in Wages Is Growing Again for U.S. Workers." The article begins, "The data show that young workers—who currently have fewer job prospects than a few years ago—and men, in particular, are feeling the brunt" (January 23, 2004). In addition, the world is teetering on a political, as well as an ecological, brink. The divide between those who have what they need to sustain rewarding lives and those who do not has gone from a wealth gap to a poverty canyon. In many parts of the developing world local farmers can no longer sell their crops—U.S. corporations' crops are cheaper at the market. Desperate people, as the cliché goes, are more inclined to do desperate things—to those who are close to them, as domestic violence experts have told us, and to perceived targets even very far away.

The Bush era presents us with a critical choice: are the people of the planet going to craft a new social contract for contemporary times, one that would address the new imbalances in the world and bestow rights and responsibilities accordingly, in the interests of mutual security and support. Or are we going to adopt a "with us or against us" war strategy where bullets and bombs substitute for treaties and talks. Are we going to privatize the problems of poverty, alienation, lack of opportunity, criminality—and blame the mother, the school student, the worker, the unemployed youth, the immigrant for his or her failure to "succeed"? Are we going to lower the floor ever further for wages, community health, and environmental sustainability? As Indian feminist Vandana Shiva suggests in her powerful essay here, profit-hungry corporations and the international financial organizations have set impossible rules for global agriculture and trade. Their rules have brought us to a brink in the international arena; tax cutters and anti-government activists have done the same thing at home.

Privatizing the problem, the contributors to this book suggest, isn't good for sustaining life on earth or the planet's ecology but it is good for protecting the status quo. Those like Kay Coles James, Nancy Pfotenhauer, and Diana Furchtgott-Roth, who hold the individual alone accountable for the quality of his or her life, work to ensure that any larger picture—of institutional bias, say, or historical injustice—is left out. A public that sees no power structure at work is unlikely to challenge that power to change.

Women's rights advocates know all this already. Indeed, it has been the essence of the feminist fight. To reveal the political conditions that contextualize our personal lives—that is the struggle feminists, regardless of what they call themselves, have been engaged in from the start. To read or watch the most powerful media, one would think that Bush's second-wave sexism is occurring in a post-feminist moment. And there's some truth to that. As Sharon Lerner points out in "A New Kind of Abortion

War," "for the most part pro-choice groups have been playing catch-up, putting out fires rather than igniting their own public relations offensives." The biggest women's rights organizations continue to be dominated by relatively affluent white women. They still struggle, as Dorothy Roberts notes, to set their priorities to match the majority of women's needs. In the arena of international relations and even on the labor front, something similar has been happening—women's rights activism contributed to changing global economic and cultural conditions, and then found itself wrapped up in dealing with fallout.

Consumer media, of course, sideline much of what is actually going on. A study by the White House Project found that women accounted for only 11 percent of all guest appearances on Sunday talk shows in 2000 and 2001, and only 10 percent when guests included presidential and vice-presidential candidates. Where they appeared, women spoke less and were less often invited back. Women accounted for only 7 percent of repeat guests—and the situation worsened after September 11, 2001. In the immediate aftermath of the attacks on the US, guest appearances by women dropped 39 percent. In the most powerful media, where the public debate was framed, one gender was utterly marginalized. Women's rights advocates and international activists with an expertise in conflict resolution or the reconstruction of post-conflict societies—were virtually invisible.

As feminist media critic Jennifer Pozner reminds, it is "one of journalism's most entrenched conventions: news is what the powerful say and do, not what the public experience. . . . The news-follows-power principle not only eschews diversity, its self-perpetuating cycle prevents change."

While the so-called women's movement has many flaws, it is also true that the more isolationist G. W. Bush has become, the more women work and think trans-nationally—see the articles here by Felicity Hill and the anti-war statement by Paola Bachetta et al. And the more that the W team impose gag orders and attempt to shut the public and the press out of their decision-making, the more journalists like veteran White House correspondent Helen Thomas and groups like the anti-war outfit Code Pink speak up.

Even Bush's anointed "warriors" complain. Ideology is bad for armies, Bush's hand-picked occupiers in Iraq have said. Members of Lieutenant General Jay Garner's team in Baghdad blamed political blinders for the chaos in Iraq after the invasion of 2003. Secretary of Defense Donald Rumsfeld insisted on vetting the experts chosen to be sent to the region. The process "got so bad that even doctors sent to restore medical services had to be anti-abortion," one of Garner's team told *Newsweek* in October 2003.

The Bush warriors suffered their greatest propaganda gaffe so far when Jessica Lynch, the woman they tried to make into an icon of their war, refused to go along with their manufactured story and told the truth. It bothered her, Lynch told TV journalist Diane Sawyer "that they used me as a way to symbolize all this stuff . . ." Sawyer asked if Lynch, a young soldier injured and hospitalized in Iraq, went down shooting, "like Rambo," as the initial reports had claimed. "No, I went down praying on my knees," Lynch told the country. Lynch says that a Native American solider, Private Lori Peistewa, a single mother with two daughters from an economically deprived community in the southwest, was the one who went down shooting. She was the hero, if hero there was, although the blonde, blue-eyed Lynch better fit the Pentagon's preferred image.

Despite all of this, it may be true that W treats some women with respect. George W. Bush may indeed have some women on his mind; what he's most interested in are votes. The second Bush (George Herbert Walker being the first) slipped into office in 2001 after a contested election, in which he lost the popular vote by half a million ballots—and the women's vote by a dramatic 10 percent. To win a comfortable electoral majority in 2004 Bush must shrink the GOP's gender gap. It's not impossible. The so-called women's vote is a by no means homogeneous. In fact, while the Democratic Party has come to rely on women voters to provide it with a winning edge, fissures have been opening up. Women, much to the Democrats' distress, do not vote as a group, and their votes are not tied predictably to "women's issues"—such as legal abortion—which Democratic candidates typically stress. Research by pollster Anna Greenberg reveals that religious women and Southern women vote solidly Republican. Blue-collar women can be drawn to the GOP too—as they were by anti-government, "Contract with America" candidates in the congressional races of 1994. Married women are more likely than single women to vote Republican. The women's vote is racially determined, too. For years, the majority of white women have voted Republican. For Al Gore, African American made the difference — if it hadn't been for the loyalty of African American women, who voted 94 percent Democratic, Al Gore would not have won the "women's vote" as he did – he would have lost it, by one point.

"If only because of the gender gap," writes contributor Richard Goldstein, "Bush must appear to embrace women's concerns." Hence the legislative happy talk and the brouhaha about appointing a handful of women to high office; there's just one hitch. As Molly Ivins has said, "in politics, you have to dance with them that brung you." In Bush's case, that has meant Christian Right ideologues and the corporate interests wrapped up in what used to be called the military-industrial complex. Stealth misogyny will only cover up so much. Reality is not so hard to make out. Once, mostly women had insecure, poorly protected, mostly non-unionized "service" work; now most workers, male and female, have jobs like that. Once it was only women who had to fight for their privacy from government snooping into their families and personal decisions; with the passage of the PATRIOT ACT, government spying is every American's concern. At one time, the U.S. propped up oppressive regimes and groups—such as Taliban—so long as the rights they violated were mostly women's and girls. We have since learned that violators of women's rights often don't stop there.

It's just possible that the Bush era will prompts us to review, not just our relationship to women's rights, but our understanding of human interdependence. National security is impossible without global security, says Yifat Susskind of the international women's group MADRE. Security is either global and human, or it is not at all. If that's an idea that gains popularity after Bush, the W era could be said to have one positive effect, after all.

WINNER TAKES ALL

A Mean-Spirited America: Today, I Fear My Own Government More Than I Do Terrorists

JILL NELSON

MSNBC.com, 5.3.03

These days, a sense of apprehension and foreboding lurks in the back of my head and the pit of my stomach. It's a gut-wrenching reminder that something very bad has happened and is about to happen anew. It is an anticipation of the next insult and injury in an America that has been defined under the Bush administration by a profound meanness of spirit.

The evidence of this overwhelming meanness of spirit is everywhere, abroad and at home. Even the administration's efforts to justify the war in Iraq as one of liberation and declare victory cannot mask the human costs to American troops and their families. How many thousands of Iraqis are dead? Where are the ridiculously named "weapons of mass destruction" that Bush used to justify this invasion? Witness the looting of priceless antiquities, kitsch and cash from Iraqi museums and Saddam Hussein's palaces and homes, allowed and participated in not only by Iraqis but members of the American armed forces and their "embedfellows," the media.

Yet to question this war and its aftermath is characterized as at worst treason and at best anti-American cynicism. And woe unto those who criticize Halliburton, Kellogg Brown & Root and the rest of the corporate sponsors of the Bush administration as they line up at the trough of government contracts to rebuild Iraq and control its oil. Now, the armed forces in Iraq have turned to shooting Iraqi demonstrators, the very people they supposedly came to "liberate" with democracy.

UNDER SIEGE AT HOME

Here on the home front, our e-mail communications, bookstore purchases, and even our public library withdrawals are open to government surveillance. The attorney general lengthens the arm of government repression every day, seeking the right to revoke an American's citizenship if he alone decides their words or deeds fall within his definition of treason. Slowly chipping away at our civil and democratic rights.

The Internal Revenue Service announces that it will scrutinize the returns of the poorest taxpayers, those claiming the earned income tax credit. This is a credit offered to taxpayers who earn under $35,000 for a family of four, and it averages less than $2000. The Bush administration wants to spend $100 million to go after these working-poor Americans in search of fraud rather than concentrate on corporations who, according to some estimates, defraud the government by tens of billions of dollars every year.

And what of the move in many states to curtail or severely cut back Medicaid benefits to the 50 million people that program currently insures, a move that will result in the loss of insurance, cuts in benefits, and an increasingly unhealthy population? And unemployment, and the awful school system, and systemic poverty, and gun violence? The list goes on.

This as President Bush crisscrosses the country like a snake-oil salesman in an effort to sell his tax-cut program, one that will again reward the wealthiest Americans and increase the tax burden on the poor and middle class. This after already pushing through a tax cut two years ago that failed to stimulate the economy but succeeded in resurrecting a deficit that, at the end of the Clinton administration a year before, was a surplus.

LIVING IN FEAR

Meanwhile, here in our great democracy, Americans go along with the program or remain silent, too afraid of the Muslim bogeymen thousands of miles away to recognize the Christian ones in our midst. Fearful that we will be verbally attacked, or shunned, or lose our livelihoods if we dare question the meanness that characterizes our government and, increasingly, defines our national character.

I do not feel safer now than I did six, or twelve, or twenty-four months ago. In fact, I feel far more vulnerable and frightened than I ever have in my fifty years on the planet. It is the United States government I am afraid of. In less than two years the Bush administration has used the attacks of 9/11 to manipulate our fear of terrorism and desire for revenge into a blank check to blatantly pursue imperialist objectives internationally and to begin the rollback of the Constitution, the Bill of Rights, and most of the advances of the twentieth century.

RECIPE FOR CHANGE

It is none too early to begin organizing for the 2004 elections. Each of us must take a hard look at the changes that have been wrought by this administration internationally and domestically and ask ourselves: Is this the democracy we cherish? We must hold our elected officials accountable and make them take a stand against what increasingly looks like fascism. If they will not, we must vote them out of office.

Three years ago, before the bloodless coup d'etat that made George W. Bush president, America was a far-from-perfect nation. Yet there was the possibility, almost gone now, that our country might evolve into a place that lived up to its loftiest democratic rhetoric. Today, I live in an America that makes my stomach hurt and fills me with terror. A nation run by greedy, frightened, violent bullies. It is time to take our country back before it is too late.

The Power and the Glory: Who Needs the Christian Coalition When You've Got the White House? The Religious Right's Covert Crusade

NINA J. EASTON

The American Prospect, Vol. 13 no. 9, 5.20.02

Gary Bauer, Christian-right leader and 2000 presidential candidate, fully appreciates the political perils of the discussion we're about to enter into this early spring morning. Jerry Falwell and Pat Robertson publicly breached the same territory shortly after the September 11 terrorist attacks, when they suggested that liberals and gays were responsible for America's cursed fortunes. Both earned the public's ire and a dressing-down from the president of the United States.

But Bauer is a creature of Washington; politics are what make his "heart beat faster," as he put it. A Georgetown law graduate who served President Ronald Reagan as undersecretary of education, the former head of the Family Research Council seems confident that he can describe the Christian right's views about 9/11—and President Bush's divinely inspired mission in its wake—in a way that won't horrify the secular press.

"People like me," he began, picking his words cautiously, "believe that God's hand has been on America from the very beginning—the Founders believed that—and that our success as a nation is attributed at least in part to God's blessings. Evangelicals believe that no leader rises without God allowing that leader to rise. No nation rises and falls without God permitting that nation to rise and fall.

"If you believe that God may be taking his hand off of America because we have moved away from him, then what the scriptures say is that we as Christian leaders must be on our knees asking for forgiveness for how we have failed. And we should be asking God what we as Christian leaders ought to be doing—not suggesting that somebody else's sins or somebody else's failures are the cause."

In this period of divine destiny, Bauer added, with evil striking a fallen America, evangelicals believe that George W. Bush is a man chosen by

God for a reason. "There is a very strong feeling in the evangelical world that this hotly contested election, the longest election night in history, lasting for months, [meant that] somehow God was working to put into the White House a man whose life had been transformed by accepting Christ," Bauer said. "Then, when 9/11 happened, there was this sense that God had blessed us again to have in the Oval Office such a man when such a horrible thing had happened. You'll often hear in evangelical churches: 'Can you imagine if Al Gore were president and this had happened to our country?!'

"God," Bauer concluded, "put George Bush there for a time like this."

If that's the case, one might justifiably wonder where He's thought to put the Christian right. Ralph Reed's once-vaunted Christian Coalition—the grass-roots pressure group that Republican presidential candidates of the 1990s courted and liberal foes feared—now mostly exists in name only. The Family Research Council, known for channeling the frustrations of God-fearing folk through the corridors of Capitol Hill, has lost nearly a third of its budget and laid off some of its Washington-based staff. For a decade, the movement's leaders insisted that Christian conservatives were just like everyone else (only, maybe, a bit holier). Then, just days after the terrorist attacks, Falwell and Robertson revealed a hatefulness starkly at odds with the nation's mood of unity.

The institutions of the Christian right have indeed fallen on hard times. Not one of them has amassed the staying power of Washington's influential liberal network (like the Sierra Club, for instance). But if it looks like the Christian right has dropped off the political map, perhaps that's only because the territory has grown so familiar. A populist movement once identified with interest groups and their leaders can increasingly be identified with the Republican Party itself. Fully 28 percent of Republican voters fit the category "religious right," making theirs the largest piece of the GOP pie. And at the new Christian right's very center, as Bauer's comments suggest, is George W. Bush.

According to conservative evangelicals, Bush is carrying out a divinely inspired mission. Not coincidentally, the same constituency also considers Bush the trusted guardian of its political interests. Who needs Ralph Reed and the Christian Coalition when you have the Republican Party and the president of the United States?

Using the Republican Party to pursue a Christian-right agenda, of course, was the endgame of strategists like Reed. He taught his organizers how to rise through the ranks of the GOP, how to speak in political parlance instead of "Christianeze," how to run for office with party support. During the 1990s, the Christian Coalition trained some 16,000 potential political leaders, many of whom have gone on to become state legislators, mayors, and school-board members. "We took a system that was scary and complex and had an unseemly taint, and made it understandable and friendly, something people want to participate in," said D.J. Gribbin, one of the key architects of the coalition's state network.

Reed's career is in some respects emblematic of the Christian right's evolution. After leaving the Christian Coalition in 1997, he formed an Atlanta-based Republican consulting firm. Three years later, he played a central role in galvanizing conservative evangelicals to quash the primary candidacy of John McCain, thereby securing Bush's nomination. In 2001, Reed was elected chairman of Georgia's GOP.

"The influence of Christian conservatives within the GOP has made them less visible, distinctive, and independent, but it has also made them a critical component of the Republican coalition," political analysts John Green of the University of Akron and Kimberly H. Conger of Ohio State University wrote in the February issue of Campaigns & Elections. The pair found that Christian activists still hold strong positions in eighteen state GOP parties, the same number as in 1994, and moderate influence in twenty-six states, twice the 1994 number. The movement is especially well integrated into the GOP firmament in Midwestern and Southern states.

The Christian right's sway within the Republican party, along with its far-reaching grass-roots base, made it an influential power broker in the neck-and-neck 2000 presidential race. During the primary, mainstream pundits scoffed at candidate Bush for naming Jesus as his favorite philosopher. But if that was a political calculation on Bush's part (as much as heartfelt response), it was quite possibly among the savviest of his campaign. From that moment on, the powerful Republican evangelical bloc has remained solidly at his side. Republican evangelical voters—80 percent of whom voted for Bush, compared to only 65 percent for Bob Dole in 1996—were crucial to getting Bush into office.

Unlike his father, Bush was quick to make good on that support. Shortly after his inauguration last year, Bush cut off funds for organizations providing abortion services overseas (the announcement perfectly coincided with a "march for life" in downtown Washington). As director of the U.S. Office of Personnel Management, overseeing the entire federal workforce, Bush appointed the former dean of the government school at Pat Robertson's Regent University, Kay Coles James, who also happens to be one of the nation's most articulate anti-abortion advocates. And most notably, to the U.S.'s top law enforcement post he named John Ashcroft, a Pentecostal whose insistence on holding daily prayer sessions in his Justice Department office has earned him the scorn of Beltway pundits and the adulation of the Christian right. Ashcroft's attempt to overturn Oregon's assisted-suicide law was similarly popular with evangelical activists.

Bush scored still more points by crafting a compromise on stem-cell research and borrowing pro-life language in calling on the Senate to ban human cloning. "Life is a creation, not a commodity," he said, to a rumble of applause.

Significantly, however, although the Christian right's support for the Bush administration is strong, it is not unconditional. Bush's effort to direct federal resources toward faith-based charities, stymied by Constitutional provisions that call for strict separation between social programs and proselytizing, lost as much conservative religious support as it captured. And many evangelicals are frustrated that the president hasn't taken a more vigorous pro-Israel stance in the Middle East war.

Exactly how far is the administration willing to tilt in order to maintain evangelical support? Anyone who thinks that in his pursuit of a worldwide war on terrorism Bush has forgotten who was responsible for his narrow election—and who could be responsible for returning the Senate to Republicans next fall—would do well to consider a little-noticed scene from this spring's Beltway dramas. It occurred on the same evening that the Democratic-controlled Senate Judiciary Committee dealt the right a major defeat by voting to reject the appellate nomination of U.S. District Court Judge Charles W. Pickering.

That night, at the Willard Inter-Continental Hotel on Pennsylvania Avenue, a couple of blocks from the White House, presidential adviser Karl Rove assured 250 Christian-right activists that, despite the Pickering setback, the president remained determined to satisfy their craving for a like-minded Supreme Court nominee. "This is about the future," Rove said of the party-line judiciary committee vote. "This is about sending George W. Bush a message that, 'You send us someone that is a strong conservative, you're not going to get him.' Guess what? They sent the wrong message to the wrong guy." After this macho applause line, Rove urged "coordination" between the political efforts of the White House and Christian-right groups, according to a tape leaked to *The Washington Post.* Said Rove, "We'll win if we work together far more often than the other side wants us to."

Overturning *Roe v. Wade* has become the signature concern of the Christian right, and probably the one uppermost in the minds of those who heard Rove's speech. Conservative evangelicals are furious that Republican-appointed Supreme Court justices have helped keep abortion legal. When the time comes to fill a vacancy on the high court, they will demand that a paper trail be followed on any appointee to assure themselves that he or she is staunchly anti-abortion. "Another [Supreme Court Justice David] Souter," warned Bauer, pointedly referring to Bush Senior's appointee, "is not going to be tolerated."

Christian-right groups are already gearing up to wage war with liberals over Bush's first Supreme Court appointment. The Christian Coalition is soliciting money for its own Judicial Task Force, calling the next couple of months "a watershed in American history." Concerned Women for America, a far more robust group with a daily radio show and 500,000 members, has just hired lobbyist Thomas Jipping—historically an important figure in judicial battles—to run its judicial operations. The Traditional Values Coalition also has a judicial monitoring project.

But no anti-abortion Supreme Court nominee is likely to be confirmed without a Republican Senate. And in order to capture the Senate, the Republicans require not only money but an energized grass-roots base—something the Christian right is best equipped to provide. Political analyst Charles Cook described the Senate races as "a perfectly level playing field." In the 1990s, conservative Christian activists enjoyed their greatest electoral successes in similarly tight races. Especially in Southern states, say conservative Christian leaders, there is latent anger to be tapped, sparked by a widespread perception that White House nominees who are also evangelical Christians—Pickering and Ashcroft among them—are automatically pegged by liberal lawmakers as unfit for public office.

The campaign year has already begun for Christian-right groups. Of particular interest are Republican Representative Jim Talent's efforts to unseat Jean Carnahan in Missouri, and Republican John Thune's challenge to incumbent Senator Tim Johnson in South Dakota. Bauer's political action committee (PAC), called the Campaign for Working Families, will spend about $1 million on congressional races. The Family Research Council, meanwhile, ran a half-million-dollar ad campaign comparing Senate Majority Leader Tom Daschle with Iraqi dictator Saddam Hussein. The ad, which ran in South Dakota newspapers and was sponsored by the group's PAC, placed photos of Hussein and Daschle side by side, asking what the two men have in common. Both, the ad asserted, oppose drilling for oil in Alaska's Arctic National Wildlife Refuge. What that cause has to do with the council's stated agenda of promoting marriage and family as the "seedbed of virtue" is anyone's guess. But the group is also attacking Senate Democrats for allegedly stalling on the consideration of Bush's Court of Appeals nominations.

Bauer, who commands a network of 100,000 activists around the country, many of them former supporters of his presidential campaign, observed that "events drive movements like these." One event that will drive today's Christian right is next fall's election, because of its potential to determine whether the Christian right can tip the five-to-four balance on the Supreme Court. "They believe that this is their moment," said

Ralph Neas, the movement's archenemy and president of People for The American Way.

Arguably the most influential of today's Christian-right activists is James Dobson, who reaches an estimated 7.5 million listeners a week with his Colorado-based "Focus on the Family" radio show. Dobson specializes in dispensing family advice. But like Reed, he understands that the Christian right runs on emotional energy, especially anger. And he is adept at transforming that anger into politics.

When Bush names his first Supreme Court nominee, he'd better know where Dobson stands. "If Pat Robertson wages a protest, it doesn't light up the congressional switchboard. The only person taking Pat Robertson seriously is Tim Russert," said Michael Cromartie, vice president of the Ethics and Public Policy Center. But Dobson, Cromartie says, can make real trouble for lawmakers who cross his agenda.

California legislators learned that in January, when they were considering legislation, modeled on the Vermont law that would legalize "civil unions" between two people of either gender. Dobson turned the bill into a cause célebre on his radio show, and Sacramento was inundated with angry calls and letters. The legislation stalled. Later, he urged listeners to repudiate Secretary of State Colin Powell for encouraging sexually active youngsters to use condoms. The president added a paragraph to a speech making clear that the White House supports abstinence.

Strangely, Dobson doesn't consider himself a political activist. He founded the Family Research Council as a lobby arm, then separated himself from it four years later, remaining only a board member. "He feels very strongly that when he talks about things like abortion and gay rights he is not involved in politics, that in fact he is engaged in a moral argument," Bauer said. "For years, he has tried to make this distinction, because his critics accuse him of trying to be a political broker within the Republican Party. Jim never wanted to be and never tried to be what Pat Robertson tried to be in the Republican Party."

In fact, Dobson is very much a political player. And the California episode reflects a central truth about today's Christian conservatives: A huge and politically astute army of activists is at the ready, available to follow a compelling general, should George Bush lose or forsake his position as their leader. Warned Bauer: "If there is a failure or betrayal on [conservative Christian] issues, there will be a challenge within the Republican Party. It will rise up. The movement is too large, and that vote is too big a part of the Republican Party not to create a leader if it feels it's being taken for granted or told to get to the back of the bus."

TeamBush to Abused Women: Fuhgedaboutit!

BILL BERKOWITZ

***WorkingForChange,* 10.25.02**

In late August, Attorney General John Ashcroft made two appointments to the Department of Justice's National Advisory Committee on Violence Against Women. The Advisory Committee, co-chaired by the Departments of Justice and Health and Human Services, provides practical and general policy advice concerning the implementation of legislation related to violence against women. Strangely enough, both of the women Ashcroft nominated, Nancy Ptotenhauer and Margot Hill, opposed the legislation when it was passed in 1994—and since renewed in 2000—that the committee oversees.

Ptotenhauer, the president and Chief Executive Officer of the Independent Women's Forum (IWF), has been a busy Bush administration appointee over the past several months. In March, President Bush tapped her to be a delegate to the United Nations Commission on the Status of Women. In May, despite or because of her lobbying against CAFE (Corporate Average Fuel Economy) standards, she was named to the Sec. of Energy's Advisory Board and in June, despite or because of her disbelief there is a gender wage gap, she was picked to be a member of Sec. of Labor Elaine Chao's Committee on Workplace Issues.

Before taking the helm at IWF in 2001, Ptotenhauer served on the organization's Board of Directors, was the Senior Economist for the Republican National Committee and was the Chief Economist for President George H.W. Bush's Council on Competitiveness. After leaving the White House in 1992, she served as Executive Vice President for the conservative Citizens for a Sound Economy (CSE) and hosted her own daily morning talk show.

Most recently, according to her official IWF bio, Ptotenhauer served as Director of the Washington Office for Koch Industries, "the second-largest privately held company in the country" which is described as a diversified energy company with operations in 44 states and estimated revenues in excess of $38 billion annually.

Hill, a Boston police detective, sits on IWF's national advisory board.

In an IWF press release Ptotenhauer said that she looked forward to serving and she appreciated having the "unique opportunity to work with the Administration in changing the attitudes and perceptions surrounding domestic violence, sexual assault, and stalking." And that's the rub. Despite the fact that IWF has long opposed strict enforcement of and even the need for a Violence Against Women Act, Ptotenhauer and Hill will take their seats on the National Advisory Committee.

THE INDEPENDENT WOMEN'S FORUM

What is the Independent Women's Forum? Who runs the show at their Washington, DC-based offices and what are they about?

Media Transparency, a website tracking the money behind conservative politics, says that IWF, which has a $1.3 million yearly budget, is "neither Independent nor a Forum. Not independent because it is largely funded by the conservative movement. Not a forum because it merely serves up women who mouth the conservative movement party line." Between 1994 and 2001 IWF received more than $2.4 million in grants from such right-wing foundations as Castle Rock Foundation (Coors Family), the Lynde and Harry Bradley Foundation, John M. Olin Foundation, and the Sarah Scaife Foundation. (For more on IWF, see: mediatransparency.org.)

IWF's Mission Statement is straightforward enough: "to affirm women's participation in and contributions to a free, self-governing society."

Here are the fine points:

"The Independent Women's Forum speaks for those who:

- "Believe in individual liberty and responsibility for self-governance, the superiority of the market economy, and the imperative of equal opportunity for all.
- "Respect and appreciate the differences between, and the complementary nature of, the two sexes.
- "Affirm the family as the foundation of society.
- "Believe women are capable of defining and asserting their interests and concerns in private and public life, and reject the false view that women are the victims of oppression.
- "Believe political differences are best resolved at the ballot box, and therefore oppose court imposition of what the democratic process rejects.
- "Endorse individual recognition and reward based on work and merit, without regard to group membership or classification."

Here's how Chris Black opened his May 2002 Chicago Tribune piece on IWF: "The conservative women at the Independent Women's Forum are cheering the return of the guy. From their standpoint, the terrorist attacks on the United States turned the feminist tide and brought back traditional values, a retreat to home and hearth, and an appreciation for the manly man."

Black points out that although IWF only has 1,600 members and prints only 16,000 copies of its journal, *The Women's Quarterly*, the organization is "enjoying stature and influence in Washington far beyond its modest membership."

This is not surprising considering the high powered and well-connected conservative women that sit on IWF's Board of Directors and Advisory Board. Grace Paine Terzian, publisher of *The Women's Quarterly*, told Black that "We increasingly gain notice and respect. More of our type of people are in town now with the Bush administration. It is a good time for us. The common-sense ideas we have always promoted are now being played out in the administration."

Founded in 1992, as a direct response to the Clarence Thomas hearings, IWF's Board of Directors (including Directors Emeritae) consists of Chairman, R. Gaull Silberman, Vice Chairman, Heather R. Higgins, Carol Crawford, Kimberly O. Dennis, Wendy Lee Gramm (economist and wife of Sen. Phil Gramm), Nancy Mitchell Ptotenhauer, Sally C. Pipes, Directors Emeritae: Lynne V. Cheney, wife of the vice president, Midge Decter, Elizabeth Lurie, Kate O'Beirne, Washington Editor for *The National Review*, and Louise V. Oliver, former Vice President of Government Relations at the Heritage Foundation.

The Advisory Board, whose chair is Christina Hoff Sommers, Ph.D., author of *The War Against Boys* and *Who Stole Feminism* and currently a Resident Scholar at the American Enterprise Institute, is also stocked with a dazzling array of Washington insiders, including Elaine Chao, Secretary of Labor and wife of Sen. Mitch McConnell (R-Ky); Linda Chavez, President Bush's first choice to be labor secretary who currently runs the Washington, D.C.-based Center for Equal Opportunity; Mary Ann Glendon, Professor of Law at Harvard University and a member of The President's Council on Bioethics; Arlene Holen, an Associate Director of the Congressional Budget Office, and a number of resident scholars from various conservative Washington, D.C. think tanks.

Charlotte Hays, the editor of the *Quarterly*, is an ex-lefty who, explains Black, "did a 180-degree ideological turn to the right after she got mugged in New Orleans in the 1970s." The *Quarterly*'s articles are all over the anti-feminist map. Black writes: IWF vehemently opposes affirmative action, it "rails against Title IX, the 1972 law that bans sex discrimination in educational institutions receiving government money. . . . They take no position on abortion because members are divided on the subject. But other favorite targets are the Take Our Daughters to Work Day and military women in combat. They debunk 'feminist myths' and say reports of rape, wage discrimination, domestic violence and gender bias in schools are either flat-out wrong or wildly exaggerated."

THE FUTURE OF VAWA

In an early September Alert, Endabuse.org, part of the Family Violence Prevention Fund, pointed out that IWF "has a long history of opposing domestic violence prevention tools such as the Violence Against Women Act (VAWA), and fueling backlash against those working to help battered women." According to the Alert, former IWF President Anita K. Blair said in 2000 that VAWA "is not helpful and, in fact, often harms individuals and families caught in violent relationships." She added VAWA funds programs that "remain unproven and may make dangerous situations worse."

Another committee appointee, Oliver J. Williams, Executive Director of the Institute on Domestic Violence in the African American Community, told Endabuse.org that "Honest, reasoned debate is good and can make us stronger. But it will be a challenge if we have someone on the Committee who won't let the truth come to light. It may be more difficult to reach common ground with someone who minimizes the issue. If Pfotenhauer has a closed mind and an agenda to undo the Violence Against Women Act, I would find her appointment troubling."

The Alert maintains that IWF members and their supporters "have frequently accused battered women's advocates of using incorrect statistics and misleading the public about the prevalence and severity of domestic violence. IWF leaders and members often claim that women are the perpetrators of domestic violence as frequently, or more frequently, than are men."

Endabuse.org also cites an article written by Betsy Hart that appeared in *The Women's Quarterly* in 2000, entitled "Violence Against Tax Payers." Hart criticizes VAWA and battered women's advocates. "How is it that Congress could take such interest groups—and their false array of data so seriously? Why reward them with $1.5 billion and a Violence Against Women Act? Perhaps it is because feminist organizations have become a powerful political force, their interests long ago diverged from the common good—and in this case, even from the interests of the victims they claim to represent." The article continues, "The Violence Against Women Act will do nothing to protect women from crime. It will, though, perpetuate false information, waste money and urge vulnerable women to mistrust all men."

Family Violence Prevention Fund President Esta Soler said that "The IWF has been working to block progress on measures that can prevent domestic violence and help victims for many years. They distort the facts, disseminate misleading information, support the backlash against our movement and undermine our efforts to end abuse. It was simply wrong for Attorney General Ashcroft to appoint the head of an organization that minimizes domestic violence to the federal Advisory Council on Violence Against Women."

Will Ptotenhauer and her organizational colleague, Margot Hill, step up to the challenge, cast off their ideological garb and become genuine advocates on behalf of abused and battered women? Doubtful, but only time will tell. One thing is for sure. In Washington these days, the foxes continue to be appointed to guard the social-policy henhouses.

Hardly Sporting: Don't Gut Title IX Until You Know What It Does

LYNN SANDERS

***Slate*, 10.1.02**

Editor's Note: In June 2002, the Bush administration's Department of Education set up a fifteen-member Commission on Athletic Opportunity to review the impact of Title IX of the Education Amendments of 1972. The commission members—who included Ted Leland, athletic director at Stanford University; Cynthia Cooper, former coach of the the WNBA's Phoenix Mercury; Bob Bowlsby, athletic director at the University of Iowa; and Graham Spanier, president of Penn State University—were predominantly anti-Title IX or neutral. Their selection signaled a serious effort by the Bush team to undermine a law that has long served to prevent gender discrimination in federally funded schools.

True to expectation, the commission's report included recommendations that, if implemented, would dramatically lower the standards for school compliance with Title IX. Two members—Julie Foudy, current president of the Women's Sports Foundation, and Donna De Varona, former president of the foundation and two-time Olympic gold medalist—refused to sign this document, instead issuing a minority report that details the commission's lack of effort to "focus on critical issues, [and] compile all of the evidence necessary to fully address the state of gender equality in our nation's schools. . . ."

In July 2003 the Bush administration backed away from the commission's proposed changes—largely in response to outcry from women's groups, parents, and athletes around the country. However, activists and female athletes remain cautious about future reform of the law that gives girls and women equal opportunity in sports.

The girls' field-hockey team in Charles McGrath's town has a new hazing ritual featuring forced simulated oral sex with bananas. Rooting around for the cause of this particular element of the decline of Western civilization,

McGrath—writing recently in the *New York Times Magazine*—came up with a sure-fire suspect: Title IX. In his story, McGrath misleadingly described Title IX as "the landmark 1972 law that required universities and colleges to grant equal financing and resources to male and female athletics."

Like almost everyone else, McGrath is wrong about Title IX, because the law isn't limited to gender equity in sports. To be sure, something approaching hysteria about the impact it would have on sports did start almost immediately after Nixon signed the law in 1972, with members of Congress getting their tightie-whities in a bunch about what would happen to football if school athletic budgets had to be shared with girls. But it wasn't until 1975 that the then-Department of Health, Education, and Welfare issued regulations clarifying that Title IX would also prohibit sex discrimination in athletics. Parity in sports was an afterthought. So, before conservatives call for Title IX's demise and liberals prepare to ward off their attacks, we need to get a grip on what the law does and doesn't do.

Title IX outlawed sex discrimination in *all* areas of education. The statute reads: "No person in the United States shall, on the basis of sex, be excluded from participation in, be denied the benefits of, or be subjected to discrimination under any education program or activity receiving Federal financial assistance." In non-legalese, this means schools can't discriminate on the basis of sex in student admissions, scholarships, recruitment, courses, or any aspect of employment, as well as in providing opportunities for boys and girls to participate in sports.

Since Title IX became law in 1972, girls cannot be discouraged from taking science classes or prevented from joining the math club. Boys may sign up for cooking classes. Law schools and medical schools were forced to stop using quotas limiting the number of women students and could no longer refuse to admit women by claiming they'd get pregnant and waste their education—routine practices before the law's implementation. Title IX litigation has addressed fairness in testing and scholarships, employment discrimination against teachers, bias against pregnant students, and sexual harassment in elementary schools.

For instance: In 1989, a federal court found that the New York State Department of Education's exclusive reliance on SAT scores to award state merit scholarships—which are supposed to reward high-school performance—discriminated against girls, because the test failed to reflect girls' better grades in high school. In a 1998 case, a federal court in Kentucky ruled that dismissing pregnant students from the National Honor Society violated Title IX. In a case involving a fifth-grader, the Supreme Court ruled in 1999 that school officials who were informed of student-on-student sexual harassment and did nothing could be sued. Most famously, Title IX has also produced dramatic increases in the numbers of girls and women participating in high-school and college athletics by requiring schools to show that they meet the athletic needs of female students, that they are expanding to meet those needs, or that organized sports roughly reflect the proportions of male and female students in the school.

Title IX has thus ensured that schools are places where students of both genders can pursue courses of study, play on teams as they wish, be rewarded on an equitable basis for good scholarship, and study without being harassed by teachers or peers. All reasonable goals, it seems, but the law is nevertheless under attack.

The Bush administration is celebrating Title IX's thirtieth anniversary with a series of town-hall meetings, soliciting public input about how equal opportunity in athletics should be measured. The administration is responding to the claim that Title IX is a quota system that hurts boys: Critics claim it requires schools to create sports teams and fill them with girls who don't really want to play, wasting resources better spent on more interested boys.

The Bushies' focus on sports is portentous for two reasons. First, it obscures what's at stake in challenging Title IX: Sports are just a fraction of the educational programs the law has shaped. Second, focusing on sports reduces the debate about Title IX to the grossest of stereotypes about girls' and boys' natural inclinations and interests—stereotypes almost palatable when the claim is that girls are less physically aggressive, but alarming when they go further to allege that girls can't do math. Simply put, the problem with the administration's reconsideration of Title IX is that it focuses solely on the impact of the law on sports today, but it jeopardizes other Title IX programs tomorrow.

The administration can limit the debate over Title IX to sports without risking a public outcry because most Americans also believe it is limited to athletics. I've been quizzing friends and colleagues about Title IX ever since I read "Shaming Young Mothers," in which McGrath's colleague, Nicholas Kristof, also mischaracterized the law as limited to sports. In my informal poll, I found not a soul who could describe the law any more accurately than the staff of the *New York Times*. Perhaps as a result of its great success, we have simply forgotten how much Title IX has mattered off the athletic field.

When the topic is sports, stereotypes about girls' and boys' natural interests and inclinations abound. Critics of Title IX see uninterested women being forced onto the playing field, pushing eager young men to the sidelines. To most of us, Title IX has wrought Brandi Chastain on the plus side, but on the minus side, throngs of would-be boy gymnasts and wrestlers, who claim that Title IX has shut them out. To the degree that Title IX seems to disrupt the natural order of things—boys like frogs and snails and sports; girls like sugar and spice and well, *not* sports—the law seems misguided.

A more accurate understanding of Title IX's aims and impact would look beyond sports to the huge increases in the numbers of women lawyers, doctors, executives, engineers, and scientists in our midst. To be sure, Title IX codified social change: Women were already making their way onto college campuses and into graduate schools before the law was passed. But it is indisputable that Title IX had an immediate and massive impact on the gender contours of higher education. And lest you believe that the need for the law has passed, it bears noting that in 2000, the Department of Education received 396 complaints of sex discrimination alleging a violation of Title IX—but only twenty-one of these complaints alleged discrimination in intercollegiate athletics. Without Title IX, these wrongs would be much harder to remedy.

In the two town-hall meetings held thus far—in Atlanta and Chicago—Title IX has been both celebrated and criticized. The celebration is strange, given that the agenda of the meetings is to cast doubt upon the law. But everyone, especially male coaches, insists that women's increased participation in athletics is the greatest thing since the invention of the jockstrap. In Atlanta, Grant Teaff, the former head football coach at Baylor, declared Title IX "outstanding legislation."

Except, Teaff and other critics go on to say, for the fact that it's a quota system, focused on outcomes and not opportunities. Perhaps not surprisingly, women lawyers and coaches who defend Title IX—pointing to NCAA statistics showing how much less female coaches earn, and how much more is spent on recruitment and scholarships for male athletes—are promptly called quota queens.

Quota is a dirty word in American politics, and no one wants to have to fend off the charge that they're for them. But the issue here is really *whose* quota system is being challenged. Any numeric reference point refers to a quota. So, when a football coach argues that he should be able to field a team of ninety-five (male) players, he's also seeking a quota. Before Title IX, quotas were routinely used to limit, not expand, opportunities for women. So after Title IX, it's perhaps inevitable that whenever slots on men's teams are "lost," someone cries "quota."

In the town-hall meetings, it's also clear that the argument won't end with the issue of quotas on the playing field. Challenges to Title IX's implementation in both athletics and academics have been mounted for years by the Independent Women's Forum, a conservative organization that has the ear of the administration and a prominent role in today's Title IX debates. In June, IWF affiliate Jessica Gavora warned of "quota creep" from sports to other areas of education. Gavora—who advises and writes speeches for Attorney General John Ashcroft (and who's also the daughter-in-law of anti-Clinton attack-dog Lucianne Goldberg)—claims it is wrong to suggest that both sexes are "equally interested in and capable of playing lacrosse, excelling in physics, becoming electrical engineers or scoring 1600 on the SAT." Similarly, in the town-hall meeting in Atlanta, Gavora's IWF colleague Christine Stolba sounded an alarm about "quotas in every arena of higher education, including the classroom."

But again, there are quotas and there are quotas. Apparently statistical arguments about gender equity on campus are entirely palatable when the claim is that men and not women are at risk. Without a glimmer of worry about self-coronating as a quota queen, Stolba ominously remarked that "the underrepresented sex on campus will no longer be women, but men." One wonders: Does she think dismantling Title IX would get more boys to stay in school? And what if the lower numbers of boys on campus simply manifest boys' natural distaste for learning? Then shouldn't we let nature take its course?

Participating in sports may build character (the prevalence of banana fellatio notwithstanding), but participating in higher education builds life-chances off the playing field. Americans who get more years of schooling get more of everything else too: They make more money, stay healthier, and vote more. When women receive more education, it offsets the fact that their pay still lags behind men's. Since Title IX became law, women have made great strides off, as well as on, the playing field. To scale it back now would be . . . bananas.

Orphaned by the Drug War

BOBBI MURRAY

AlterNet, 9.26.02

Editor's Note: All too often criminal justice issues are cast as men's issues. Men still hugely outnumber women in U.S. jails and prisons, but as Bobbi Murray's story reveals, the war on drugs and mandatory minimum sentences have dramatically increased the number of U.S. women behind bars. Most of the increase has been among nonviolent offenders, and sometimes, as in this case from Texas, the incarcerated and their families are victims of corrupt police practices encouraged by a political climate that supports efforts to get "tough on crime." In 1999, when Tom Coleman wrongly arrested almost a tenth of Tulia's black community, George W. Bush was on the campaign trail, but he was still Governor of Texas. Coleman was named Texas Lawman of the Year.

Murray's story, written in September 2002, has a relatively happy ending. In September of 2000, the New York-based William Moses Kunstler Fund for Racial Justice, the NAACP Legal Defense and Education Fund, the Drug Policy Alliance, the Tulia Legal Defense Project and other local civil rights organizations teamed up to investigate the Tulia drug sting and to bring it to national, media attention. On August 22, 2003, Texas Governor Rick Perry pardoned thirty-five people arrested in the Tulia sting. Officer Tom Coleman was indicted on charges of corruption. The men and women whose lives Murray profiles here will never be the same; many lost their jobs and their livelihoods while they were in prison. Their struggle against the drug war continues, but the Tulia case is an example of activists working together to expose a wrong and get it righted. Now the civil rights groups who worked on the case are meeting with families of the former prisoners and town leaders to prevent similar injustices from happening again.

"I live a sad life," says Mattie White. "Every time I think it's going to be okay, it's not, and I just get sad again."

And there is no happy ending in sight for Mattie, who at fifty-one is raising her granddaughter Roneisha, eight, and grandson Cashawn, five, while their mother, Kizzie White, twenty-five, serves a twenty-five-year sentence in a Gatesville, Texas, prison. Kizzie was arrested in 1999 for selling cocaine as part of a large-scale and now highly controversial sting operation in Tulia, Texas. Cashawn's father was also arrested as part of the same bust, and is now serving an eighty-year sentence. Her kids ended up with Mattie.

A TALE OF INJUSTICE

Kizzie was one of forty-six defendants—thirty-seven of them black—who were rounded up in a mass arrest that netted roughly one out of every eight residents of Tulia's small African American community. There are an estimated three hundred black residents in Tulia. Three of Mattie's kids were arrested: Kizzie, Kareem (sentenced to sixty years), and Donnie (sentenced to twelve years). "I just couldn't believe it—all these people locked up like this," says Mattie White, who manages the Tulia 46 Relief Fund. "Ain't no fifty people selling drugs, ain't no thirty people selling drugs (in Tulia)."

And Mattie has no doubts of her daughter's innocence. To her knowledge, Kizzie never used or sold drugs. "They didn't find no drugs," she says of the bust.

The massive drug sweep was based on the word of one officer, Tom Coleman, who is now accused of being corrupt, and a tiny bag of cocaine. The ACLU—which, along with the NAACP of Texas, filed a civil rights complaint with the U.S. Department of Justice in October 2000—called the eighteen-month-long Tulia sting "a blatant, racially-motivated act of police and prosecutorial misconduct."

Reform advocates see Tulia as a high-relief example of the way the war on drugs is prosecuted nationally. "Drug abuse cuts across class and race lines, but drug enforcement is located in low-income communities of color," says Marc Mauer, assistant director of the Washington, D.C.-based prison reform organization and author of the book, *Race to Incarcerate.*

MOM IS IN JAIL

Like Kizzie, most women of color in prison are doing time for minor non-violent drug offenses, which account for the rapidly growing rate of female incarceration. A Sentencing Project report shows that the number of women incarcerated for drug offenses rose a breathtaking 888 percent from 1986 through 1996, fueled by the escalating war on drugs. Drug offenses accounted for nearly half of all female convictions. And 80 percent of these female inmates had children.

Significantly, a large percentage of women sentenced for drug offenses are African American and Latina; in New York, a staggering 91 percent of those sentenced to prison for drug offenses are black or Latina, as are 54 percent in California.

And they are overwhelmingly poor. According to sociologist Dorothy Ruiz, "Eighty percent of imprisoned women report incomes of less than $2000 in the year before the arrest and 92 percent report incomes under $10,000." Kizzie, who worked at a meat processing plant making a paltry $8 an hour until a month before her arrest, was actually better off than most others.

A vast majority of women convicted for drug offenses are involved with holding and using small amounts of narcotics, while others get caught for conspiracy, that is, being involved with men who use and sell. Both men and women can serve long sentences thanks to mandatory minimum sentencing, but women usually end up serving more time for lesser offenses. Kizzie, for example, was imprisoned on charges of delivering cocaine on three occasions and marijuana on one. According to Mattie, her daughter would be facing fifty-two years behind bars but for the judge's decision to run the sentences concurrently.

"The only way you can escape mandatory minimum is by cooperating, and that means giving someone else up," says Monica Pratt, of Families Against Mandatory Minimums. But a woman is more likely to be a low-level user than a drug kingpin and therefore has little to trade for a lighter sentence, while her boyfriend who may be more deeply involved can cut a better deal.

When women are imprisoned, it also affects three generations of family: the grandmother, mother and children. Rather than turn the kids over to the child welfare system, the grandmother often steps forward to take care of kids.

LIVING WITH GRANDMA

Mattie still lives in Tulia, a seven-hour drive from her daughter, and juggles two physically demanding part-time jobs—as a prison guard and an in-home care worker for infirm women—while she raises two active young children.

"It's a stressful job for grandmas to raise grandkids—the kids think they can get away with everything," she says. Mattie admits that she sometimes lets some things slide because she feels sorry for the kids, who only see their mother two or three times a year. Compassion and the sheer exhaustion of cooking, cleaning and otherwise caring for the children makes it hard to keep constant tabs on the children. "We teach them right from wrong, though," White says firmly.

Mattie is one of thousands of African American grandmothers being squeezed by a cruel effect of the war on drugs: the spiraling incarceration rate for African American women, who make up fully half of the female prison population. With the mothers behind bars, grandmothers become the primary guardians of the children left behind. Fifty-three percent of the children of incarcerated parents are cared for by their grandmothers. The result is a crushing emotional, physical and financial burden imposed on older women of color, the enormity of which is only beginning to be assessed.

"Female incarcerations place three generations at risk and destroy families, leaving lasting scars on children as well as putting an enormous financial and health burden on grandmother caregivers," Ruiz writes in a recent paper published in the Western Michigan University, School of Social Work Journal. These grandmothers often suffer from number of health problems, such as depression, insomnia, hypertension, back pain, and stomach pain, caused by physical and emotional stress. Mattie suffers from high blood pressure, and was hospitalized twice in June with a stomach ailment that doctors linked to stress. The women also tend to suffer social isolation as they juggle their various responsibilities. But the grandmothers often tend to under-emphasize their health problems to avoid being seen as too infirm to take care of kids who often have nowhere else to go.

The financial burden is often severe, as well. Many have worked low-wage jobs all their lives and, unlike surrogates in the foster care system, do not receive monetary support from the government. The arrangement can be precarious for both the caretakers and the children. Mattie talks about shuffling grandkids between other relatives while she works (her husband is also out of the house on the job). She often worries about the health of granddaughter Roneisha, who doesn't get to sleep until after Mattie gets home after ten at night. "She's a sick little girl," she frets.

In Mattie's eyes, the entire White family is a victim of the drug war and its agents. "He (Coleman) messed up a bunch of people's lives, not only the ones in prison, but their children and the grandparents that are looking after them," she says.

A BLEAK FUTURE

Unless Kizzie is cleared of all charges, her release from prison won't put an end to the White family's problems. If she can't find a job, she will be ineligible for welfare. Persons with felony convictions for drug use or sale permanently lose all welfare benefits under changes instituted to welfare laws in 1996. As a result, grandmothers often retain responsibility for kids during a lengthy transition period after the mothers leave prison.

If the family lives in public housing, there is a substantial risk of losing their home if the returning ex-offender is still addicted—one offense by a relative and the whole family, including the grandmother and the children can be thrown out. "It's a complex problem. They're using drugs, and some of these women are terrible mothers. But it's not the kids' faults. The long-term goal should be to reunite the kids with a drug-free mother," Mauer says.

Pratt points out that there is virtually no drug rehabilitation until the last few months in prison, and, at the federal level, it is left to the discretion of prison officials. "So you go to prison, going cold turkey, not learning any new behavior patterns, drug treatment at the very end of your sentence, if at all. What support do you have to stay clean?" Pratt asks.

But there is hope in Kizzie's case, at least. Randy Credico, of the William Moses Kunstler Fund for Racial Justice, which is involved with the Tulia 46, says Kizzie could be released from prison if state officials find evidence of official misconduct. Texas Attorney General John Cornyn opened a state investigation into the bust in August.

Credico says, "The Attorney General could vacate the sentences, or could take over the cases and drop them and give them a new trial in a new city." The defendants could also receive a pardon or clemency, but that would require them to admit guilt, which Credico says is highly unlikely.

For now, Mattie White continues her balancing act. Her grandkids are getting more used to not having their mom around. "They stopped asking me when she was coming home, will she be back before my birthday, that kind of thing," she says. "But when they see other kids' parents getting out, they feel sad."

Better Safe . . . ?

PATRICIA J. WILLIAMS

***The Nation*, 3.11.02**

In my last column, I called the expansion of profiling that has occurred since September 11 "equal opportunity." I meant it ironically, but a surprising number of people took me literally. So I want to make clear that I don't consider this upgraded frisking any kind of opportunity, nor do I think that its expansion is really the same as equality. I am also aware, as was pointed out to me, that there are people in the world who might appreciate a good cavity search, confident that this is all for their benefit. And while I understand that we have all become subject to "nothing more than" the same ministrations that visitors to maximum security prisoners go through, the fact that some think this is the best of all possible worlds strikes me as fatuous.

The billions of dollars currently being pumped into police and surveillance budgets represent an unprecedented investment in a heavily patrolled world. Such an extraordinary buildup will inevitably exacerbate questions about the limits of state force; it will require the greatest vigilance to prevent our turning into not just a police state but one big global military base. Specific categories of us will probably continue to bear a special burden—black women in airports are, according to some figures, searched more than anyone else because I, as Typical Black Everywoman, meet the description of a drug courier better than you—as in You, profiled *Nation* reader and Typical Ungendered White Person.

Blacks and Latinos are the profiled shape of the "war on drugs," even though the majority of actual drug abusers are young white people like Governor Jeb Bush's poor daughter, Noelle. The "war on terror" promises to be even more sweeping. For the time being, our new international, militarized police force has increased its scrutiny, from black women in airports and black men in cars, to include Middle Eastern men anywhere, Asian people who look vaguely Filipino, as well as ample Minnesota housewives actually armed with sets of silver fondue forks.

Is this better or worse? I think it's a misuse of data, often creating a false sense of security. The kind of profiling that seems to inform the majority of stops and searches is usually based on statistical relations so vague as to be useless. Such profiling, premised on diffuse probabilities about looks and dress, ethnicity or nationality, class or educational status, begs for more analysis. Otherwise it can be defeated on the one hand by guards and gatekeepers whose interpretation of looks or class status is skewed by selective and subjective prejudice and on the other hand by travelers committed to the art of disguise.

The attacks on the Pentagon and the World Trade Center were carried out by deeply rational and well-trained operatives whose tactics defied easy profiling. They looked—and were—well educated; they dressed professionally. The fact that the FBI actually had information that some of them had been involved in terrorist networks counted less in the real world than that they looked good. After all, it is true that in a very large sense sleek, well-dressed professionals commit fewer crimes than the hungry, grumpy lower classes. I have this painful recurring dream of the security guards at Logan on September 11, carelessly waving all eighteen men through, while strip searching long lines of black women having bad hair days.

I worry that we're doing the same thing with shoes: Richard Reid was able to board an airplane because he played against the expectation embedded in profiles. He looked odd enough to have been stopped and questioned, but ultimately looks had little to do with what made him dangerous. Although they were suspicious, security officials did not discover his criminal record, surely better evidence of his propensities than whether he wore a ponytail. He was finally allowed on board; he was a British citizen, and British citizens were not the subject of any profile. They searched his bag but not his shoes, because shoes were not at that point the subject of any profile. Now that we know thick-soled sneakers can be turned into weapons of mass destruction, airports spend a lot of time removing and examining them. It's likely to catch copycats, I suppose, which is not a problem to be ignored, but does anyone really believe that Al Qaeda would use shoes again? In other words, while there is, after Richard Reid, a marginal relation between shoes and bombs, the actual odds of it ever happening precisely like that again are slim to nonexistent. Indeed, what distinguishes professional operatives who calculatedly sow terror is that they take the time to play against type.

So I worry when I hear about plans to expand profiling as we now seem to practice it. I worry when I hear about plans to have our thumbprints taken, our irises scanned, our DNA plotted. How can we be putting all this work into appearances when appearances bear no necessary relation to intent? The risk of this is not just one of diminished dignity or privacy. The problem ought to have been made clear to us in the wake of "accidents" like Amadou Diallo. The problem ought to be apparent in recent news stories about the CIA having flown an unmanned surveillance craft over a street in Afghanistan. It had a night vision camera on it that caught in its scope a group of men conversing who fit a profile because one of their number was unusually tall, as is Osama bin Laden. After some consultation at the remote site where the CIA officers and their telemonitors were located, the CIA decided to bomb the group. The men were killed, but as of this writing, the CIA admits it still doesn't know who the men were. Civilians on the ground claimed that the men were townspeople scavenging for scrap metal.

This death by actuary. This profiled guilt. This trial by night vision drone. Our superlative technology permits us to listen, scan, survey and X-ray anybody and everybody in the world. But a sea of data alone won't help us if there is no higher wisdom in the final analysis. Good "intelligence" means more than eyes and ears—there must be a heart and a brain, or we will never achieve the global stability we all so desperately desire.

WAR

Raising the Voices of Afghan Women: An Interview with Masuda Sultan

PHOEBE ST. JOHN

1.9.04

Editor's note: Masuda Sultan is program coordinator of Women for Afghan Women, an organization of Afghan and non-Afghan women in the New York area who are committed to ensuring the human rights of women in Afghanistan.

TELL US A BIT ABOUT YOURSELF. YOU'RE AFGHAN? YOU'RE HOW OLD? WHERE DID YOU GROW UP?

I was born in Afghanistan, in Kandahar. During the Soviet invasion, my parents decided when I was about four and a half to flee the country—there were tanks around the city and my father had received some death threats. We left, we came to Brooklyn, New York, and I grew up in Brooklyn and Queens. I'm now twenty-five years old.

WHO DID YOU VOTE FOR IN 2000?

(*Laughs*) I'm embarrassed to say it! I voted for President Bush!

IT SOUNDS LIKE THE LAST FEW YEARS HAVE BEEN QUITE A JOURNEY FOR YOU!

I think I was very politically unaware in some ways. Thinking about family values, conservative values—which I grew up with, and believed in—the impression I had of President Bush was that he would restore certain "family values" to this country. And that was a mistake on my part, I think.

DID YOU HEAR LAURA BUSH ADDRESS THE NATION IN 2001 TO THE EFFECT THAT THE AFGHAN WAR WAS A WAR TO LIBERATE WOMEN AND PREVENT THE SPREAD OF TERRORISM AND TALIBAN RULE? WHAT DID YOU THINK? DID YOU BELIEVE HER?

I didn't hear the radio address, but I read it. The first thing I thought was, why is she saying this now? In her address she said that civilized people throughout the world are speaking out in horror. The Taliban took control of Kandahar towards the end of '94, and as you know the brutality had been going on for quite a few years, something that the Feminist movement in this country knew about and campaigned against. So the timing of it, of course, was questionable to me. That being said, it was good that she finally said something, but using the goal of liberating

Afghan women as a justification for this war is just not true. While the end of Taliban brutality was a welcome by-product of the war, and a triumph for human rights, it clearly wasn't the main reason for war; if that was our goal we would have gone in sooner. Besides, during the civil war, women were living under similar oppression and the U.S. did nothing. It's very clear to me, as I think it is to everyone else, that the United States was attacked on 9/11 and we wanted to go and get the people who did it. It was retaliation.

DID YOU SUPPORT THE BOMBING? ON WHAT GROUNDS?

Yes. I'm a New Yorker and this was my home as well, so when 9/11 happened I could understand the desire to respond.

My feeling was that if we were going to respond with military action, as I expected us to, the imperative was to go about it in the right way. I was hoping that there would be less aerial strikes and more of a ground offensive, so that we could be more accurate in our hunt. And I did write to President Bush and a few members of Congress to articulate my concerns about innocent Afghans being caught up in this. So it was a complicated feeling for me. I can't say I really supported the bombing a hundred percent or was against it completely. I'm not a pacifist. I felt that at least if Al Qaeda and the Taliban were gone from Afghanistan, ordinary people could begin to take their lives back.

YOU TRAVELED TO AFGHANISTAN IN LATE 2001 WITH A DOCUMENTARY FILM CREW. WHAT DID YOU FIND WHEN YOU GOT THERE?

I had been very worried about the family I had just connected with a few months earlier, on another visit to the country. When I got there in December I very quickly found out about the awful tragedy that my family members had been through, and I literally could not believe it.

The story that surviving relatives told me was that, living in Kandahar city next to some Taliban-controlled buildings, my relatives became afraid when the war began, hearing bombings every night, and gunfire. So the whole extended family, about forty people, decided to flee. They went to a tiny farming village, literally in the middle of the desert, to be safe. And one night, as they had just gone to bed, there were—it's still very hard to talk about. They heard loud sounds and one of my cousins, she was six months pregnant, went to the doorway to see what was going on. Children no more than eight or nine explained to me that they saw her literally be sliced in half by some kind of shrapnel. Everyone started running out of their homes. It was dark, and as they were running—women and children just fleeing for their lives, anywhere and in any direction—they were being shot at from above.

I later found out that it was American gunships shooting at them. These girls showed me their gunshot wounds. Some of them fell on the spot and died. Some hid in irrigation ditches and stayed there not knowing what to do. It's in the documentary, "Ground Zero to Ground Zero."

But it was really difficult to hear, especially as an American, because I knew this could not have been the intended target. My first reaction, still needing for all this to sink in, was to think, "Have they apologized? What have they done?" I was so naïve. These women looked at me and said, "No. We haven't heard anything." I mean, the next day, the survivors literally had to take body parts off the ground, put them on a tractor and take them back into the city to bury them. Some of my relatives had to be taken to Pakistan, because they couldn't get proper treatment in Afghanistan. The bills, and everything—it was just overwhelming for all of them. And our government didn't even so much as say, "We're sorry," or "We're here to find out just what happened."

SO, YOU'VE KEPT CONTACT WITH FAMILY MEMBERS, AND IN SEPTEMBER 2003 IN KANDAHAR YOU MET WITH WOMEN FROM ALL OVER THE COUNTRY FOR A CONFERENCE ON WOMAN AND THE CONSTITUTION. WHAT'S YOUR TAKE ON THE SITUATION FOR AFGHAN WOMEN THROUGHOUT THE COUNTRY NOW? WE HEARD A LOT ABOUT WOMEN SHEDDING THEIR BURQAS AND NO LONGER BEING CONFINED TO THEIR HOMES.

Well, Kabul has become this NGO bubble. Rents are approaching New York City prices, there are UN vehicles, 4 by 4s, and SUVs all over town, and restaurants are catering to internationals working there. So the environment of Kabul has physically changed a lot and some women have slowly started to take off their burqas, more than two years into this. But there are many women in Kabul who still wear the burqa.

Outside of Kabul I would say very, very little has changed for Afghan women. In Kandahar you don't even see women on the street, for one thing, because of the lack of security. There's also of course the cultural component: Women tend not to be allowed to go out of their homes. But security is the number one concern of Afghan women and men. Without that, nothing can happen for them. And they have said, "Why do you focus on the burqa? That will come off in time. What we really want is to come out of our homes, to go to school, to work and be able to feed our children, and we will do it with the burqa on. We will take it off when we're ready."

COULD YOU TELL ME A LITTLE MORE ABOUT MAJOR CHALLENGES WOMEN IN AFGHANISTAN ARE FACING NOW, AND HOW BUSH ADMINISTRATION POLICIES ARE HELPING OR HURTING THEIR CHANCES OF OVERCOMING THEM?

As far as security goes, Afghan people—men, women, the President—have been calling for the extension of peacekeepers outside of Kabul. It's been said so many times that it's just really frustrating to see it fall on deaf ears. NATO recently agreed to expand peacekeeping to Kunduz and to one other city, so that was a success, however the actual expansion has been very slow, and in fact, the chief of NATO who was in Afghanistan for four years warned of disastrous consequences if it wasn't properly expanded. The UN recently threatened to pull out unless something was done about security.

The desire for peace and security is an incredible driving force for most Afghans. We've talked to the State Department, to Congress, and to anyone and everyone who would listen to this concern, and what we have been told is that the United States is resistant to provide more resources for the expansion of these troops. And I personally feel the U.S. is capable of pushing for this expansion. If we want to do it, we can certainly have it done. Further, while the U.S. has been leading in terms of reconstruction dollars, we absolutely need to increase reconstruction aid to Afghanistan, and in particular, to women.

WHAT OTHER CHALLENGES WOULD YOU HIGHLIGHT?

The constitution was just ratified, and it does call for equality for men and women, which is a huge success, however it also says that "no law can be contrary to the provisions and beliefs of the sacred religion of Islam" and identifies Hanafi jurisprudence as what shall apply when there's no other provision in the constitution or laws on an issue. So this is going to mean that the implementation of the constitution and the battle for women's rights is going to be waged in the courts, in a judicial system that is in shambles. Because how do you reconcile women's equality with the extremist views of Islam that exist in Afghanistan?

Another challenge concerns the elections coming up in Afghanistan, scheduled for June. Unless Afghan women actually feel secure enough to come out and cast their votes, we will not really know what more than half the population wants. I believe that it is in the interest of the U.S. and the UN to encourage women to vote by providing proper security and facilities, because women tend to vote for moderate candidates, not the extremists who don't want them to vote in the first place. Once candidates understand that they will have to win the women's vote as well as the men's, the will certainly change their tune. So either the extremists will have to change, or moderates will be elected. This is a better outcome for everyone.

How could the U.S. government help this situation, aside from supporting the extension of peacekeepers?

The Afghan diaspora has to be more included in the reconstruction. The Afghans in America and Europe enjoy a unique position, in that they can understand the culture and religion of Afghanistan and they can also communicate with the Afghans there. What I have heard from people in Afghanistan is that highly paid consultants come in from the West to design these elections and to consult with Afghans, but that they have outright insulted them at times and don't really understand the culture.

Also, because of the way USAID functions, and the way aid is distributed, there are amazing grassroots women's organizations doing groundbreaking work inside Afghanistan, that do not have support from the U.S. government. Instead, these large international aid agencies with large overheads are able to get these grants. I know it's a challenge, but more of this money absolutely has to be granted to the women who will be around when the international aid agencies pack up to move on to the next crisis. This means spending some of that money to make sure Afghan women's organizations can be trained and learn how to work with USAID.

How important is the treatment of women and girls to the development of Afghan society in general? What about to the war on terrorism?

I think we learned on 9/11 that women's progress in Afghanistan is tied, not only to the progress of Afghanistan as a country, but really to the world. The Taliban and Al Qaeda's policies towards women constituted complete brutality and oppression. The American feminist movement actually understood this, and this is something that I am still learning: that any regime that oppresses its women will be destructive in other ways, and ultimately is not the kind of regime that we should be dealing with.

There are some very brave, strong women in Afghanistan. Can you describe the women's conference on the new constitution, then in the drafting phase, that took place in September 2003?

Women for Afghan Women had this dream of hosting its third annual conference in Kandahar, and at first it seemed really crazy because of the security situation. But we felt it was really important to have a conference outside of Kabul, because as I said, Kabul is an NGO bubble and the rest of Afghanistan is not getting the resources it needs. So we went ahead and planned for a Kandahar conference, bringing together forty-five women from all over the country. It was a tremendous struggle to organize, not only because of the security situation but also the logistical problems, the lack of infrastructure, airplanes, phones.

We intentionally chose women who normally did not go to these types of conferences, grassroots leaders who were doing work related to human rights in their villages, cities and towns. Some of them were illiterate, they were of different ethnicities and spoke different languages; almost none spoke English. It was a four-day conference, based around a series of workshops looking at concepts of the constitution and women's rights in Islam, and aimed at devising a list of articulated demands for women in the new Afghan constitution. The document they came up with was the Afghan Women's Bill of Rights.

At night, the women would play Afghan tambourines, dancing and rejoicing. It was really an incredible experience. They told us about their lives and the struggles that they had experienced. Women had lost children during the war or their children had been kidnapped by the Taliban; all kinds of things had happened to them, and they were so eager to participate and have a voice in the future of their country. It was truly a dream come true for me, organizing for women's voices to be in the new Constitution of Afghanistan, and doing so in the city my family and I once called home.

AT THE CONSTITUTIONAL LOYA JIRGA IN DECEMBER 2003, A YOUNG WOMAN SPOKE OUT AGAINST "WARLORD" RULE AND "WARLORDISM." WHAT DO YOU KNOW ABOUT HER?

Yes, Malalai Joya. I was floored when I read that. I thought it was incredibly brave of her to speak out and also I was worried about her as I think all of us were. Essentially she said that criminals, who have committed abuses against Afghans, should be taken to court and tried for their crimes. I think it's a very straightforward, standard, and reasonable! Taxi drivers, NGO workers and ordinary Afghans I've spoken to say the same thing: Malalai Joya had the courage to say this in public and voice the concerns of all Afghans. But a group of extremists got up and started marching toward her. They were stopped, and Malalai Joya had to go into the protection of the UN, and received death threats. And I'm concerned that while now in Kabul she's under the protection of the UN, what happens when she has to go back home, and face extremists in her home village? That's something that I think a lot of us working on Afghan issues take for granted—that women can maybe speak in certain circumstances, but ultimately they will have to go back home and face what there is to face.

WHAT COULD AMERICANS WHO CARE ABOUT AFGHANISTAN DO TO HELP WOMEN LIKE HER?

Our organization is part of the Policy Council for Afghan Women, which is a group of organizations looking to influence U.S. policy in Afghanistan. In the latest military and aid package to Iraq and Afghanistan, 87 billion dollars in all, President Bush's office did not request one dollar to be earmarked for Afghan women. It was Congresswoman Maloney, here in New York City, who along with other members of Congress eventually secured 60 million dollars to be earmarked for them. I'm still learning about the complicated processes in Washington, D.C., and understanding that it's not really over until it's over. But in any case it says a lot about what can be done from here.

In this country, every single person's voice should matter, and unless we raise our voices, they won't matter. Joining organizations like ours is one way to do this. If people are interested and committed to making a difference, there are many groups that can help them do this. And a little bit of money goes a long way in Afghanistan, so that's a good way to help too.

WE'RE CALLING IT THE "W EFFECT"—WHEN BUSH SAYS ONE THING AND DOES ANOTHER IN THE AREA OF WOMEN'S RIGHTS. HOW WOULD YOU CHARACTERIZE THE W EFFECT IN AFGHANISTAN?

I think it is easy to speak about concern, and President Bush has voiced his support for the Afghan people, but when it comes to action he's fallen short. For example, the lion's share of the 87 billion dollar military and aid package went to military operations, especially in Iraq. Afghans are not fooled that easily.

It seems to me that this war and the reconstruction are being carried out on the cheap by President Bush and his administration. They seem to have adopted the view that as long as they talk about democracy and initiate some policies and show some interest, then that will be enough. Afghanistan has suffered over twenty-three years of war, and it is almost in complete ruin, and I honestly think this administration needs to make more of a commitment to Afghanistan. Their focus has been on doing the very least that they can do to keep things together, instead of seeing the Afghan people as citizens of the world and partners in the war against terror.

TELL US BRIEFLY ABOUT WOMEN FOR AFGHAN WOMEN.

We are a non-profit organization based in New York City. We were formed before 9/11 and we are an Afghan-led group of Afghan and non-Afghan women. We support grassroots organizations in Afghanistan and essentially function to empower Afghan women economically and politically both in Afghanistan and NYC, serving as a megaphone for their voices.

THANK YOU, MASUDA!

Call Me American: A Young Man Contemplates Going to War

RUSSELL MORSE

Pacific News Service, **9.14.01**

When Clinton was sending troops to Kosovo and I had just turned 18, I said I would head to Mexico if Uncle Sam came for me. When I saw footage of the World Trade Center crumbling on Tuesday, I decided I would go to war if they wanted me.

I went from flag burner to flag waver in a matter of minutes. Brad Pitt in *Fight Club* told it pretty well. "We have no Great War. We have no Great Depression. Our Great War is a spiritual one. Our Great Depression is our lives."

I spoke to my mother on the phone Thursday night and she told me, "Your generation will be defined by how you respond to all of this... We became known for the anti-war movement. Drugs. Free love. I won't pretend like I wasn't a part of it, but can you imagine? Our fathers saved the world and that is how we responded."

As a generation, we've been searching for meaning. We've been looking for a reason to care about something. Our parents united in protest against Vietnam. Our grandparents came together to fight fascism. We couldn't find anything better than sweatshops and Starbucks to be upset about.

But now we understand that we are Americans. We understand the significance of our privilege because until it was threatened, we didn't know it could be any other way. We want to protect it. We may not know who we're fighting yet, but this is our Great War.

In all likelihood, though, it won't come to that. Every time I tell someone I'll go if I'm drafted, they say, "We don't fight wars like that anymore." It's true.

For one, we don't know who the enemy is. Most likely, it's not a country, state or people. The perpetrators have no real military or territorial objectives. So while our grandfathers fought a real enemy—Nazi

Germany and its allies, who sought world domination—we fight an enemy not directly associated with a government or even a war. I don't want to kill some guy with the misfortune of being a citizen of a scapegoat country. America is rightfully angry, and my fear is that that anger will be misdirected. Civilians in another country will be killed, just as they were killed here. And that idea stifles some of my patriotism. If I join the army, I'll probably end up doing airport security until I'm thirty-five, rummaging through baby strollers with an M-16 on my back. But I'm ready. I don't know that I've ever called myself an American before. I was too busy griping about what young people in this country gripe about—poverty, injustice, racism, and an inflated military budget (which doesn't seem like such a bad idea now). All that's been swept aside.

There are, however, people in my classes at San Francisco State that have used this as an opportunity to talk about how America had it coming. True, we've bombed and slaughtered all over the globe, but the only reason these kids are in a position to say this stuff is 'cause they're white, upper middle class college students—they won't be the ones sent off to fight. They're lofty, Orange County-expatriate idealists. All they know how to do is rebel in the unoriginal mode of the neo-hippie faux revolutionary.

I don't believe that we should scapegoat a nation. I don't believe that we should kill civilians. I'm not in favor of military expansion. But now I am down with America. I'm down with the cops and the firemen. I'm down with the soldiers. I'm down with the National Guard. And to a certain extent, I'm down with George W.

I can't say a part of me isn't wishing this happened a year or so ago, when my man Clinton was still in office. There are a thousand reasons I dislike Bush, which I will not list. But there is one reason I embrace him—like it or not, he's our man. And Tuesday night was his inauguration. The attacks have served to legitimize his presidency.

As our president addressed the nation, a friend of mine got excited, nodding his head and pumping his fist. He is first-generation Salvadoran, but Tuesday night, he became as American as John Wayne. When CNN ran footage of Palestinians celebrating, he shouted at the screen. "You won't be laughin' when the bomb lands on your nose, fool."

Wednesday was not exactly like December 8, 1941. Young men were not lining up at recruiting offices. But they were waving flags on freeway overpasses and cheering police officers in the street.

In my entire life, I've never seen young people cheer the police.

Sneak Attack: The Militarization of U.S. Culture

CYNTHIA ENLOE

Ms., 12.01/1.02

Things start to become militarized when their legitimacy depends on their associations with military goals. When something becomes militarized, it appears to rise in value. Militarization is seductive.

But it is really a process of loss. Even though something seems to gain value by adopting an association with military goals, it actually surrenders control and gives up the claim to its own worthiness.

Militarization is a sneaky sort of transformative process. Sometimes it is only in the pursuit of *de*militarization that we become aware of just how far down the road of complete militarization we've gone. Representative Barbara Lee (D.-Calif.) pulled back the curtain in the aftermath of September 11 attacks when she cast the lone vote against giving George W. Bush carte blanche to wage war. The loneliness of her vote suggested how far the militarization of Congress—and its voters back home—has advanced. In fact, since September 11, publicly criticizing militarization has been widely viewed as an act of disloyalty.

Whole cultures can be militarized. It is a militarized U.S. culture that has made it easier for Bush to wage war without most Americans finding it dangerous to democracy. Our cultural militarization makes war-waging seem like a comforting reconfirmation of our collective security, identity, and pride.

Other sectors of U.S. culture have also been militarized:

Education. School board members accept Jr. ROTC programs for their teenagers, and social studies teachers play it safe by avoiding discussions of past sexual misconduct by U.S. soldiers overseas. Many university scientists pursue lucrative Defense Department weapons research contracts.

Soldier's girlfriends and wives. They've been persuaded that they are "good citizens" if they keep silent about problems in their relationships with male soldiers for the sake of their fighting effectiveness.

Beauty. This year, the Miss America Pageant organizers selected judges with military credentials, including a former Secretary of the Navy and an Air Force captain.

Cars. The Humvee ranks among the more bovine vehicles to clog U.S. highways, yet civilians think they will be feared and admired if they drive them.

Then there is the conundrum of the flag. People who reject militarization may don a flag pin, unaware that doing so may convince those with a militarized view of the U.S. flag that their bias is universally shared, thus deepening the militarization of culture.

The events of post-September 11 have also shown that many Americans today may be militarizing non-U.S. women's lives. It was only after Bush declared "war on terrorists and those countries that harbor them" that the violation of Afghan women's human rights took center stage. Here's the test of whether Afghan women are being militarized: if their well-being is worthy of our concern only because their lack of well-being justifies the U.S.'s bombing of Afghanistan, then we are militarizing Afghan women—as well as our own compassion. We are thereby complicit in the notion that something has worth only if it allows militaries to achieve their missions.

It's important to remember that militarization has its rewards, such as newfound popular support for measures formerly contested. For example, will many Americans now be persuaded that drilling for oil in the Alaskan wilderness is acceptable because it will be framed in terms of "national security"? Will most U.S. citizens now accept government raids on the Social Security trust fund in the name of paying for the war on terrorism?

Women's rights in the U.S. and Afghanistan are in danger if they become mere by-products of some other cause. Militarization, in all its seductiveness and subtlety, deserves to be bedecked with flags wherever it thrives—fluorescent flags of warning.

Working-Class Women as War Heroes

FARAI CHIDEYA

***AlterNet,* April 3, 2003**

Private Jessica Lynch is a hero, the kind who in her hopefully long life will never escape her youthful fame. The baby-faced nineteen-year-old fought off Iraqis in an ambush, endured broken bones, gunshot and stab wounds, and went eight days without food. This movie played in real time has all the elements that make fast-paced war flicks like *Behind Enemy Lines* box office magic. Her face, frozen with what must have been shock, pain and relief during her rescue, is already one of the most haunting images of the war.

Lynch is linked in more ways than one to Shoshanna N. Johnson, a thirty-year-old mother from El Paso, Texas. Johnson, who left her two-year-old daughter with her parents when she deployed, joined the army to get training to be a chef. She ended up one of the first American prisoners of war in Iraq. Lynch—well, she wanted to be a kindergarten teacher.

How did a chef-in-training and a future teacher end up toting guns in the desert? Both of these female war heroes come from hometowns fighting their own battles, economic ones. Lynch comes from the you-can't-make-this-stuff-up town of Palestine, in Wirt County, a farm community in western West Virginia of 5,900 people, 99 percent of them white. Wirt has a 15 percent unemployment rate; 20 percent live below the poverty line; and the average income per person is $14,000.

El Paso County is huge by comparison—nearly 700,000 people—but no more prosperous. Seventy-eight percent of El Pasans are Latino, and 24 percent live below the poverty line. The border city, hit hard by the impact of NAFTA, has a per capita income of just $13,000.

The folks in Wirt and El Paso are separated by half a country, but they have a lot in common. In both places, the economy has collapsed. The military is probably one of the best games in town. Jessica Lynch's family says she joined to get an education, something she probably couldn't have gotten otherwise. Now that she's a hero, a group of colleges have stepped forward to offer her a scholarship.

Wouldn't it be great if people like Lynch and Johnson didn't have to go to war to get a job or an education? At the same time that Americans are protesting against the war, thousands this week protested in favor of affirmative action, which faces its latest Supreme Court challenge. Working-class women and African Americans like Lynch and Johnson will be among those to lose if affirmative action is ended. But affirmative action, as useful as it is, only gives a fraction of Americans the chance they deserve. Schools in working-class neighborhoods are becoming more like truly impoverished ones. In other words, they've become places where too many bright students lose hope.

Yale graduate and notably lackluster student George W. Bush got the benefits of an affirmative action program called "legacy admission," i.e., preference for the kids of alums (particularly the rich ones). For all his hawkishness, Bush went AWOL from his National Guard duty during the Vietnam War, 1972–1973. His father was a war hero. But these days rich men (and women) don't fight.

That's left to the working class. A *New York Times* article titled "Military Mirrors Working-Class America" notes, "With minorities overrepresented and the wealthy and the underclass essentially absent, with political conservatism ascendant in the officer corps and Northeasterners fading from the ranks, America's 1.4 million-strong military seems to resemble the makeup of a two-year commuter or trade school outside Birmingham or Biloxi far more than that of a ghetto or barrio or four-year university in Boston."

Don't get me wrong—I'm not saying money's the only reason people join the military. A lot of enlistees are following their dreams of serving their country. Others, like a twenty-seven-year-old interviewed in the *Times* article, like to blow things up (though not necessarily people). And some, like a friend of mine who spent ages 17–20 in the military, think it's a great way to grow up and find your mission in life.

There are a few other options for young Americans seeking a way to give to their country, earn money for college and get skills; in particular, the service corps like City Year and AmeriCorps. In these programs, young Americans the same age as Lynch can spend a year or two giving back to a local community—working on buildings, serving the elderly, even helping teach kindergarten. With school budgets being slashed, there's plenty of need and plenty of room for young recruits to lend a hand.

But these programs are still modest compared to the size and stability of the military. Before the motto an "Army of One," the Navy boasted the slogan, "It's Not Just a Job, It's an Adventure." Some people just want a job. What they get is far more uncertain.

Reading, Tracing, and Locating Gender in 9/11 Detentions

IRUM SHEIKH

The Subcontinental, Fall 03

The detention of (primarily) Muslim men in the aftermath of 9/11 has had a heavy impact on women, as wives, mothers, sisters, daughters, organizers, lawyers, social workers, and community leaders. Most of the female relatives of detainees were housewives; their lives took a sharp turn when their breadwinner husbands were gone overnight. Some became the breadwinners and assumed household responsibilities. Some became social workers and provided comfort to other women in similar situations. Some organized and spoke eloquently as community leaders about the government's unjust policies. Others spoke at press conferences and rallies and gave interviews to newspapers and television stations and made telephone calls to community, religious, and civil and human rights organizations. The oral histories that I present in this essay identify a variety of roles that women played during and after 9/11 detentions.

Many human and civil rights organizations reports have indicated a heavy concentration of male detainees. For example, a Migration Policy Institute report released in July 2003, noted that more than 90 percent of the 406 detainees included in their analysis were males.[1] Another report by the Department of Justice's Office of the Inspector General, issued in June 2003, noted that all of its 762 case studies of detainees involved men.[2] My own research confirms this trend, as only two of the more than forty detainees I have interviewed over the past two years have been female.

The primary reason for this heavy concentration of male detainees is the government's enforcement of policies that selectively and deliberately target Muslim men. Starting November 9, 2001 the Department of Justice (DOJ) ordered the questioning of 5,000 men ages 18–33 who came from countries connected to Al Qaeda.[3] On January 25, 2002, the Deputy Attorney General launched the Absconder Apprehension Initiative. The purpose of the program was to locate 314,000 individuals who had final deportation or removal orders against them. Most notably, on June 5, 2002, Attorney General Ashcroft announced the Special Registration program, requiring men with certain visas from predominately Muslim countries to register and submit fingerprints and photographs. By August 2002, the DOJ had institutionalized these racial profiling practices into its legal apparatus.[4]

Even in cases where enforcement officers found female family members in violation of immigration laws, they disregarded them for enforcement purposes, and concentrated their efforts on males. The result of the DOJ's male-centered crackdown is that traditional discourse about 9/11 policies has been masculine. But if we scrutinize this story through the lens of gender, we find that women have played significant roles, sometimes as victims, sometimes as activists and leaders, often inspired to action by the inequity of the new DOJ and INS policies. Take, for example, Uzma Naheed, a Pakistani living in New Jersey, who, along with her husband, Ansar Mahmood, had an expired visa.

In October 2001, FBI and INS officers came to investigate Uzma in connection to her brother, who had been arrested in the previous week. After the initial questioning at home, the officers wanted to take her to police station. Uzma was breast-feeding her young son and felt uncomfortable leaving him behind. Her husband, Ansar, volunteered to go with the INS officers. They promised that he would be home the next day since he only had an expired visa. Ansar spent the next four months in solitary confinement at the Special Housing Unit of the Metropolitan Detention

Center (MDC) in Brooklyn, New York, for an expired visa. Uzma was never arrested for her equally expired visa.

Uzma was among the first women relatives of detainees to step forward and speak out about the way male family members were placed in solitary confinement. In December 2001, she received a letter from her husband stating his specific whereabouts in the MDC. She went to the jail to see him and was told that he was not there, but she showed the letter to the security guards and argued with them. By the end of the day, she was allowed to see her husband, chained and shackled, in a visiting booth across a glass door. Through this meeting, she learned about jail conditions and transmitted that information to media and human and civil rights organizations. With the help of other community members, she organized and participated in numerous protests in front of the MDC. As a result, Uzma's husband and brother were allowed weekly calls and lawyer visitation privileges. Uzma continued to talk to the media and speak at protests and rallies. She was open about her undocumented status, taking the line that the DOJ has already snatched everything from her by sending her husband and brother to jail—"What else they could they do?" They decided to depart voluntarily in April 2002. Ansar Mahmood was deported in May 2002 to Pakistan.[5]

Women who were arrested felt that they were treated as terrorists only because of their ethnic and religious backgrounds. Aisha, an eighteen-year-old woman from Pakistan with an expired visa, was arrested in upstate New York in October 2001. Her husband, Tosueef, was initially arrested on the suspicion of anthrax possession and taken to the local police station. After the initial interrogation, four or five FBI agents came to search Tosueef 's home at 1 A.M. They also questioned Aisha about anthrax. Gharam Masala,[6] a child's sketch of a car on a windy road with "danger" written at the end, and a medicine bottle with a slightly different name "made her suspicious." She was taken to the local police station without handcuffs around two in the morning and questioned about Osama Bin Laden, trips to Afghanistan, anthrax again, and her opinion about the attacks on the World Trade Center.

The next morning, local newspapers and television stations published and aired a story including her, her husband, and their mutual friend, Ansar Mahmood.[7] The mayor shut down the water supply since it was suspected that these three persons had put anthrax in the local reservoir. Aisha was strip-searched and was asked to squat and cough. Later she was placed in the local jail where other female inmates ridiculed her for being a Muslim. They told her that they had seen her story on television. Without knowing the details of the case, Aisha angrily told them "I did not do anything." She spent the next four months in five different jails in New York, some of those days in solitary confinement. Many fellow inmates felt that Aisha should not be deported since her violations were not serious. They encouraged her to fight her case, but Aisha had had enough. She wanted to go back to Pakistan and be with her family as soon as possible. At her last court hearing, she cried and requested to be sent home immediately. She was deported two weeks after the court hearing.

Beyond being detained, the crisis of 9/11 led many women to become leaders. Shokeria Yagi, an Afghani American, naturalized citizen, was in Jordan with her three sons when her husband was arrested from Albany, New York, in October 2001 and placed in the MDC in solitary confinement. Her in-laws did not want her to return to the United States in an anti-Muslim environment, but nonetheless she left Jordan and came back to Albany with her three sons to find her husband. She called the INS, lawyers, enforcement officials, politicians, community organizers, and civil rights organizations. Within a week, Ali was moved from solitary confinement into the general population of the MDC.

Working full time, taking care of her children as a single mother, and fighting for the release of her husband, Shokeria has evolved from a housewife into an activist and community leader.[8] Speaking in front of 20,000 people in October 2002 at a peace march in New York she said, "I am here to fight for my husband's rights . . . I am here to fight for my children's rights. My father and brother died in Afghanistan trying to run away from the civil war there. I was orphaned at ten. I do not want that to happen to my children or to the children in Iraq. I want my husband home."[9] In August 2003, she appeared on CBS's "60 Minutes" and informed the general public about the abusive conditions in which most of the Muslim detainees were kept after 9/11.[10]

Wives, mothers, and daughters in many families shaped themselves into human shields to protect their men, in the face of post-9/11 detentions. They handled the media and worked closely with community, and human and civil rights organizations to organize protests and bring people together. In the end, their hard work and determination raised awareness of the issue from a local to national level. Yet the contributions of these women have remained unnoticed. Only after listening to their individual stories one by one was I able to trace the patterns of courage, fire, pain, and resistance, to locate scattered experiences, and to make sense of their significance through gender discourse.

Notes

This article is dedicated to Founder Regional Foundation, which provided me funding for my research.

1. Migration Policy Institute, *American's Challenge: Domestic Security, Civil Liberties, and National Unity After September 11, 2003.* Appendix A

2. Office of the Inspector General, "The September 11 Detainees: A Review of the Treatment of Aliens Held on Immigration Charges in Connection with the Investigation of the September 11 Attacks" April 2003 (released June 2, 2003)

3. Memorandum for Regional directors, from Michael A. Pearson, INS Executive Associate Commissioner, Office of Field Operations, dated 10-23-01, *The Subcontinental*, 77

4. Information for this timeline is available from the American Immigration Lawyers Association website at www.aila.org.

5. Based on a personal interview with Uzma Naheed and Ahmar (Uzma's brother) in Lahore, Pakistan March 2003. Her husband Ansar Mahmood and her three children were also interviewed in Karachi in April 2003.

6. A Pakistani spice generally used for cooking.

7. Ansar Mahmood was taking photographs close to the water reservoir when a security guard suspected him of terrorism and called the police. FBI and local police went to Ansar's workplace, a local pizza store. Aisha's husband, Tosueef, and Ansar worked together and were friends. Tosueef was arrested along with Ansar in the evening on suspicion of anthrax dissemination. Aisha was arrested at night in her home. Ansar is still in jail fighting his deportation. (Based on personal interviews with Aisha, Tosueef, and Ansar over the last year.)

8. Personal interview conducted with Shokeria Yagi, Albany December 2002.

9. Ferguson, Sarah, "A Peace Movement Emerges" *Village Voice*, October 7th, 2002

10. CBS, "Guilty Until Proven," "60 minutes," aired in August 2003.

Upstanding Native Women

PATRISIA GONZALES

***Column of the Americas* by Patrisia Gonzales and Roberto Rodriguez, Universal Press Syndicate, 11.7.03**

An Indian woman had to die in war for folks to figure out how to honor native women. Lori Piestewa, a Hopi single mother of two, was honored in Arizona this summer as the first Native American female soldier to die in war. But many Native American women died in wars against the Indians, and many are courageously raising their children as single parents as Piestewa did.

In her memorial, Aztec dancers participated in recognition that she was also Mexican. Her family wanted all her heritage honored. And the long-standing battle over naming places found victory when Squaw Peakin Phoenix was renamed Piestewa Peak. Native American activist Winona LaDuke notes that the renaming represents the right of Native Americans to take control of their place names and words. LaDuke spoke recently of many native "women of consequence." These are the women fighting nuclear dumping, genetic engineering and other social ills. Many tribes have special names for warriors or those who defend their people in various ways. In indigenous America, "upstanding women" are often in the front of physical confrontations in Bolivia, Ecuador and Chiapas, where they have been raped to bring the male warriors out of cover.

Lori Piestewa and Jessica Lynch were roommates at Fort Bliss military base and close friends everywhere else thereafter. Then they (along with thirteen members of the U.S. Army's 507th Maintenance Company) were ambushed last March after they took a wrong turn. Lynch, who was hospitalized and cared for by Iraqi doctors and was eventually found by soldiers, emerged as the symbol of American strength and heroism. An Afro-Latina was also captured. But how many know her name? Now, former POW Shoshanna Johnson, who was shot in both legs, is in the news because the army granted her 30 percent disability benefits; Lynch was awarded 80 percent. Lynch became the public hero with book and movie deals, while the women of color (a strong contingent in the military) are footnotes.

Piestewa's death will be remembered for changing the "s-word," as many Native Americans call it. Abenaki storyteller and historian Marge Bruchac notes that the word (squaw) is the derivative of an Algonquian word that originally meant woman. However, it became used by white settlers and frontiersman as a profane reference to vagina.

Bruchac is a lone voice among Native Americans, arguing that there are occasions when the word should be preserved, such as to recognize the historical memory of a female. The meanings of words change with who has the power to use them, and who has the power to tell the stories.

About the time of the peak's renaming, I stopped at a farmer's market in Whittier, California. One type of bread caught my eye—"Frontier Squaw Bread." I asked the vendor why the bread was called this. "Because it's made from wheat, molasses and cinnamon. It goes down slow, and it's sweet and sticky all over," he replied. I told him that usage was offensive to many native folks. He replied he knew that but no harm was meant by it. I responded, but how you used that word is exactly why it's offensive. Then he started raising his voice in self-justification as he spoke in a tone that sounded like he was feeling unjustly made responsible for history.

A lady with teased hair piped in: "It's an old frontier recipe. Well, I've seen it in the history books." Nothing like official California history to justify comfort zones. I asked my mother-in-law not to buy the bread, and I later told her what he said. Since she mostly speaks Spanish, she didn't understand the whole exchange. But, being a woman of consequence herself (having raised seven children), she knew you don't eat bread named that way.

I went home fuming, perhaps because of peaks and Tomahawk and

Apache bombs that co-opt native names and words (and the stories that will be told) in wars against other peoples. Despite some national coverage, few people knew that Piestewa's father fought in 'Nam and that her grandfather fought in World War II.

However, a romanticized and fictionalized account of Jessica Lynch's rescue had saturated the media to boost morale for the war. Piestewa's tale as part of a warrior ethic rooted in native cultural roles, family tradition, as well as patriotism (and economic necessity) will be among those told in a forthcoming documentary on the native warrior ethic by Ojibwe scholar and journalist Patty Loew.

Yes, Lynch got a movie. But Piestewa got a mountaintop.

Hidden Casualties: An Epidemic of Domestic Violence When Troops Return from War

JON ELLISTON AND CATHERINE LUTZ

Southern Exposure **31.1 (Spring 03)**

After a spate of wife killings at Fort Bragg, domestic abuse in military families is under new scrutiny—but the Defense Department still turns a blind eye on key causes.

One novel way news reporters have tried to pinpoint the start of major U.S. military engagements is to monitor pizza deliveries at the Pentagon. It's been called the "Domino's theory": When the generals and their staffs go into imminent-war mode, they stay at their posts late into the night, and the pizza orders shoot up.

There are more grim indicators that a military operation is nigh. As the war in Afghanistan began in October 2001, for example, "We could literally tell what units were being deployed from where, based on the volume of calls we received from given bases," says Christine Hansen, executive director of the Connecticut-based Miles Foundation, which has assisted more than 10,000 victims of military-related domestic violence since 1997. The calls were from women who were facing threats and physical abuse from their partners—the same men who were supposedly being deployed on a mission to make America safer. "Then the same thing happened on the other end, when they came back," Hansen adds.

Hansen and other domestic violence workers say that such patterns of abuse are signs of how issues of gender, power and control are magnified in the military, making domestic violence an even more extensive and complicated problem than it is among civilians. And while recent events have sparked an unprecedented amount of official soul-searching about domestic violence in military families, those key issues have rarely entered the discussion.

It took the rapid-fire deaths of four women to turn national attention to this oft-overlooked form of domestic terror. The problem forced its way into the headlines last July, following a spate of murders by soldiers stationed at Fort Bragg in Fayetteville, North Carolina. In the space of just five weeks, four women married to soldiers were killed by their spouses, according to the authorities. Marilyn Griffin was stabbed 70 times and her trailer set on fire, Teresa Nieves and Andrea Floyd were shot in the head, and Jennifer Wright was strangled. All four couples had children, several now orphaned as two of the men shot themselves after killing their wives. The murders garnered wide attention because they were clustered over such a short period, and because three of the soldiers had served in special operations units that fought in Afghanistan. (The throat-slitting murder of Shalamar Franceschi a few months before by her husband, a just-released Fort Bragg soldier, might also have been added to the tally, but wasn't.)

The murders have raised a host of questions—about the effects of war on the people who wage it, the spillover on civilians from training military personnel to kill, and the role of military institutional values. On the epidemic of violence against women throughout the United States and on the role of gender in both military and civilian domestic violence, however, there has been a deafening silence.

ANOTHER KIND OF CASUALTY

The military maintains that violence against spouses is no more prevalent in the armed forces, arguing that it uses different criteria than civilian authorities for identifying domestic violence, including severe verbal abuse. "People have been throwing some wild figures around," says Lt. Col. James Cassella, a Defense Department spokesman. "My understanding is that it's kind of an apples and oranges comparison." But the military's method may actually underestimate the problem, since it ignores violence against a legion of non-married partners, an especially important omission, considering that one recent study found that single men represent nearly 60 percent of soldiers using a gun or knife in attacks on women. And there is no way to independently corroborate the figures the military releases on domestic violence cases that are handled through military judicial processes, since they are shielded, as civilian police records are not, from public view. The cited studies did attempt to control, however, for the most important demographic differences—the apples and oranges—in military and civilian populations.

Mary Beth Loucks-Sorrell, interim director of the North Carolina Coalition Against Domestic Violence, a state-wide umbrella group based in Durham, is convinced that women partnered with soldiers face disproportionate risks of domestic abuse, a conclusion reached through years of fielding reports from abused women (and occasionally men). Reports from military communities are not only more frequent but the level of violence they describe is more extreme, she says. Some soldiers also terrorize their partners in unique ways, reminding the women of the sniper and bare-handed killing skills they acquire in training. Her anecdotal accounts are backed up by studies that found military men are more likely to use weapons than are civilians, and more likely to strangle their wives until unconscious.

On hearing of the four murders, many people in the general public and media asked whether the soldiers might have suffered from post-combat trauma or simply, as the military suggested, from the stress of deployment and its disruption of family life. In both these views, the soldier's home front violence is the traumatic outcome of "what he saw" in combat, rather than the much more significant trauma of what he did—and indeed, what he is trained to do.

Stan Goff, a veteran of several of special operations units who today is a militant democracy activist in Raleigh, scoffs at the "TV docudrama version of war" underlying this view. "Go to Afghanistan," he says, "where you are insulated from outside scrutiny and all the taboos you learned as a child are suspended. You take life more and more with impunity, and discover that the universe doesn't collapse when you drop the hammer on a human being, and for some, there is a real sense of power. For others, for all maybe, it's PTSD [post-traumatic stress disorder] on the installment plan."

HIDDEN IN PLAIN SIGHT

In the Pentagon's approach to the problem and in virtually all media accounts, gender has been left hidden in plain sight. Not only does the military remain by reputation the most "masculine" occupation available, but people in Fayetteville, and in the armed forces generally, consider Special Forces and Delta Force, where three of the four men worked, the Army's toughest units. Special operations units are some of the last in the military to exclude women, and they also specialize in unconventional warfare, which is combat that often follows neither the letter nor the spirit of the rules of war. As a sign in a Special Forces training area says: "Rule #1. There are no rules. Rule #2. Follow Rule #1." Such a macho, above-the-law culture may provide not a small part of the recipe for domestic violence. Combine this with a double standard of sexuality, one in which, as many soldiers and their wives told us, infidelity is to be expected on Special Forces deployments—where the men operate with unusual autonomy and are often surrounded by desperately poor women—whereas the infidelity of wives, reactive or not, real or imagined, gets punished with violence.

If there was a common thread that tied the murdered women's lives together, it was the one identified by Christina DeNardo, a *Fayetteville Observer* reporter: All four of them, DeNardo reported, had expressed a desire to leave their marriages, a situation that domestic violence workers have identified as the most dangerous time for women in abusive relationships. That is when the control these men tend to insist on in their relationships appears about to dissolve. Christine Hansen, of the Miles Foundation, says that military personnel are controlled from above at work more than most U.S. workers, and many come home looking to reassert control, often with violence. The anxieties about control, and consequently the violence, flare up most before and after military deployments, Hansen says, as soldiers lose and then try to reinstate control. That's why her foundation got a spike in calls before and after the Afghanistan deployments.

The Pentagon says it is waging a determined campaign to curtail risks to military spouses and non-married partners. In a widely disseminated directive issued in November 2001, Deputy Secretary of Defense Paul Wolfowitz declared that "domestic violence is an offense against the institutional values of the military." But some analysts have countered that domestic violence, rape, and male supremacism itself are not anomalies or sideshows to war; instead, they lie near the center of how it is prosecuted and narrated. Like gender and control issues, military culture's institutionalized promotion of violence, and its effect on life at home, has gone unaddressed by the military brass.

When the subject of how military service might promote violence against women is raised, it proves to be a touchy one. In 1996, Madeline Morris, a Duke University law professor argued in the *Duke Law Journal* that military organizational norms are "conducive to rape." Those norms, she wrote, include "elements of hypermasculinity, adversarial sexual beliefs, promiscuity, rape myth acceptance, hostility toward women, and possibly also acceptance of violence against women." Morris's thesis, which was bolstered by a good deal of military and academic research, was hotly contested by conservative commentators, but it launched little actual dialogue about the potential ties between military values and domestic violence.

Still, a few rare reporters and commentators have pointed out the obvious costs of training millions of men to kill. "There is nothing equal to the military as the incubator of violence," Alexander Coburn argued in a *New York Press* column after the Fort Bragg murders. He placed the killings in the context of the war against terrorism, in particular a Special Forces search and destroy mission that left dozens of Afghan civilian noncombatants dead, wounded, and roughed up. "The villagers of Hajibirgit paid the price," he wrote. "The four murdered women in Fort Bragg paid another installment."

DOWNPLAYING THE VIOLENCE

"Army accepts role in 4 domestic killings," read a headline in the Raleigh *News and Observer* on Nov. 8, 2002, when the Pentagon concluded a special investigation that was supposed to connect the dots. In the face of intense questioning about how they would account for the cluster of killings and seek to ward off such tragedies in the future, Defense Department officials dispatched a nineteen-member epidemiological team to Fort Bragg to get to the bottom of it all. Staffing the team were behavioral specialists from the Army and the Centers for Disease Control.

The team's investigative report concluded that "marital discord" and family problems exacerbated by the stress of deployment, were the main aggravating factors. The report, Hansen says, "diminishes the violence these women suffer" by failing to pay much attention to victims and their search for security. It likewise fails to look at the factors that make military women especially vulnerable to abuse, which include their financial insecurity as individuals, their geographical and social isolation from family and friends, and, most importantly, their living cheek by jowl with men trained in extreme violence and in the idea of their superiority as men and as soldiers.

The special investigation was just the latest in a long line of commissions established over the course of the many gendered military scandals of the last fifteen years, from Tailhook to Aberdeen to the dozens of women cadets raped at the Air Force Academy. Such investigations have neither stemmed the problem nor prompted the military to recognize the fundamental role of gender in crimes like the Fort Bragg killings. This would entail seeing the murders as a piece of the larger, epidemic problem of violent abuse by men within the military, including rape of female (and some male) soldiers and civilians, lesbian and gay bashing, and brutal hazing rituals.

And it would also require much greater involvement and investment in protecting military families. A relatively new Army program provides $900 a month plus health care for the few abused women whose husbands are removed from the force for domestic violence. But Fort Bragg has no domestic violence shelter, though for many years the base was donating a paltry $10 a day to a local shelter when military wives fled there. Tellingly, both enforcement of domestic violence laws and information about such proceedings appear to be woefully inadequate. When domestic violence is confirmed by military authorities, case review committees staffed by officers often recommend such meager "punishments" as anger management or stress reduction courses, or treatment for alcohol abuse. Even severe felony assaults often result in non-judicial sanctions such as demotion or extra work assignments. Of the 1,213 reported domestic violence incidents known to military police and judged to merit disciplinary action in 2000, the military could report only twenty-nine where the perpetrator was court-martialed or sent to a civilian court for prosecution. The military claims to have no data on the disciplinary outcome of the much larger number of domestic incidents—12,068 reported to family services in that year. They also have no record of the outcome of 81 percent of the police cases.

This poor record-keeping and apparent reluctance to prosecute offenders can be explained in part by the military's institutional interests in burying certain potentially controversial aspects of its domestic violence problem. The first is public relations. To recruit and retain a 1.4 million-person force, including women and married men, remains a monumental task that would only be made harder by widespread knowledge of the extent of the violence. Second, there are financial motives. Each soldier costs more than a hundred thousand dollars to recruit and train, money that goes down the drain if a soldier is discharged or imprisoned. Finally, there is the continuing, if waning, power of a belief, still widespread in the pre-volunteer and mostly unmarried force, that "If the army had wanted you to have a wife, it would have issued you one." Protecting women from domestic violence in this environment falls even farther down the list of missions to be accomplished than it does in the civilian sector.

AFTERMATH

In the aftermath of the tragic string of murders, some attitude and policy shifts have buoyed the hopes of battered women in Fayetteville. Some women who have been trying to get help for years noted there were some at least temporary changes made on post in the wake of the killings, including a greater urgency about sending women to court in town to get protective orders. And both before and since the murders, many women have successfully left their abusive husbands.

In other ways, however, life in Fayetteville goes on as usual in the months since the murders. Women married to abusive soldiers have been calling the Fayetteville newspaper and domestic violence shelters around the country in sharply higher numbers since the Fort Bragg killings were reported. They have spoken out about the frequent failure of commanders to take their calls for help seriously. And they have complained that they were often sent to military chaplains, some of whom advised them that suffering is a woman's lot or that their husbands were just "working off some excess energy" through violence.

The difficulties women have in leaving their abusers are well known. Military wives have additional disincentives. The unemployment rate for military wives is extremely high—hovering around 20 percent for those living at Fort Bragg—and those who do find employment are often stuck in the minimum wage retail jobs that are the main work available in the satellite economy around most large posts. If military wives report abuse, they risk not only retribution from their husbands, as do women in the civilian world, but loss of their total family income, health care and other benefits, and even their housing and neighbors if their husband is discharged.

The local domestic violence shelter continues to take in the refugee women and children who come to its door. One of the first shelters to be established in North Carolina by a group of feminists, prominently including some wives of soldiers, the Care Center struggles to keep its head above water, particularly given the torrent of people sent there for anger management classes by the courts in lieu of jail time. Virtually every weekday night, from two to four dozen people come for the multi-hour sessions, similar versions of which are also run on post.

In other quarters around town, there is defiance or denial. One woman whose husband worked at Fort Bragg with one of the killers reported that his unit had great sympathy for him. "They were all convinced that he was the victim," the woman said, "that she [the murdered wife] started it all."

The people in Fayetteville most affected by these recent events are, of course, the hundreds of battered women still living in daily fear of their partners or ex-partners. Surprisingly, their stories often focus less on the violence itself (though some continue to live with scars, neurological damage, and other permanent signs of their abuse) than on the failures of the Army and others in the community to help them when they sought rescue. Other women noted the stark contrast of the severity with which the military judicial system deals with soldiers who attack and injure other soldiers of equal rank. These women's main refrain, repeated over and over again: "He was never held accountable for what he did to me."

"WITH US OR AGAINST US"

The celebration of soldiers over the last several decades, grown more fervent since the war on terror began, has hampered attempts to address the problem by further elevating violent masculinity to a place of honor in the culture. In good times, critical views of military practice are not well received; in the intimidating, "with us or against us" atmosphere fostered by the Bush administration since 9/11, they may be considered tantamount to treason. Hansen, who has received death threats since her foundation appeared in news stories about the murders, notes that some civilian judges have been even more reluctant than before to convict soldiers of domestic violence, when doing so would trigger the Lautenberg amendment, a 1996 law that prohibits convicted abusers from owning firearms.

Wartime, it appears, is the hardest time to take stock of the real causes of military-related domestic violence. The idea that the soldier makes an unrecompensable sacrifice creates a halo effect, so that the murderers are painted as victims of the horrors of combat, while scant attention is paid to the women they killed or the failures of the system to protect them. As Stan Goff, the special operations veteran, told us, soldiers living in this climate can turn to their wives and say, "The culture's worshiping me. Why aren't you?" While they may have provided a wake-up call of sorts, the Fort Bragg murders, and the official response to them, have resulted in little that will change the situation of militarism's hidden casualties: The thousands of women who live in fear—in wartime and peacetime—and struggle each day, as Hansen says, "trying to provide for the safety of themselves and their children."

A Cautionary Tale from Kosovar Women to Women in Post-War Iraq

IGO ROGOVA

***Kosova Women's Network Newsletter*, 4.03**

This newsletter is being released as another war came to an end, the war in Iraq. It is clear by now that the dictatorship of Saddam Hussein vanished under the heavy bombing of the American and British forces. Many rejoiced the day when a government that persecuted and discriminated [against] its own people disappeared. The big question is what comes next. To us as women's rights activists, the big concern is what will happen to women in a post-war Iraq. And, as women's groups that work in a post-conflict area, run mainly by a UN administration, we have a briefly recounted but very complex story to tell to the women of Iraq.

Kosovar women started to get organized in the early 1990s and worked very closely with the local parallel ("underground") government that resisted the persecution of the Kosovar Albanian population by the authoritarian regime of Slobodan Milosevic. When war started in ex-Yugoslavia, we became part of the regional women's networks that raised their voices against the war and provided help to women and refugees in those very hard times. When the war came to Kosova, women's rights activists became refugees themselves, but never stopped working with and for women, this time in refugee camps in Macedonia and Albania.

We greeted joyfully the decision that put Kosova under a UN administration. The UN was to us the revered international organization that developed and passed key documents that stipulated women's rights and promoted their integration in all levels of decision-making. But when we returned home, we were, unfortunately, disappointed by the UN Mission in Kosova (UNMIK). We were eager to work with the international agencies in developing effective strategies for responding to the pressing needs of Kosovar women, but most of those agencies did not recognize that we existed and often refused to hear what we had to say on decisions that affected our lives and our future. Some of the international staff came to Kosova thinking and assuming that this is an extremely patriarchal society where no women's movement can flourish. And there were those who wanted us to do all the groundwork for them: find staff and offices, set up meetings and provide translations, but were not interested in listening to us and acknowledging our special expertise. They had their own fixed ideas and plans and their ready-made programs that they had tried in other countries, and they did not want to change their plans to respond to the reality of our lives.

Instead of dedicating all our energy to helping women and their families put together lives shattered by war, we had to spend efforts in fighting to be heard and in proving to UNMIK that we knew what was best for us, that women in Kosova were not just victims waiting to be helped—they could help themselves, as they did in the past, and they could be key and effective actors in building their own future.

But we did not give up. We raised our voice. We met with UN officials, wrote letters, went to meetings to present our ideas, knowledge, and expertise. We talked to donors and built alliances with those international organizations in Kosova and abroad that genuinely saw and related to us as partners in the common efforts to advance women's cause in our country. This is part of an ongoing multilayered struggle that women's groups in Kosova have been engaged in during the last four years, a struggle to be part of the decision-making process from day one, a struggle to get better organized and become more effective, a struggle to take the place we deserve in shaping our lives and the future of our society.

We urge and encourage women in Iraq to organize, raise their voice and be part of the rebuilding of their country.

We saw how the international media portrayed the women of Iraq. They showed only the women with black scarves. Women had no voice in the media, as if they are not part of Iraq. The same thing happened with Kosovar women's image during the war. International media didn't show intellectual women on TV. It was as if they don't exist. We know there are strong, organized, intellectual women in Iraq, as there were strong, organized, intellectual women in Kosova or in any other country in the world.

But if the UN takes over the civic administration in Iraq, it is time that they change the principle of their work. Sympathetic and knowledgeable international people must concentrate their work in cooperating with local experts, giving space, resources, and a deep hearing and recognition also to the women's local NGOs.

Baghdad Burning: Girl Blog from Iraq

www.riverbendblog.blogspot.com

Editor's Note: The Riverbend weblogger has been reporting since August 2003 on the effects of the U.S. incursion and ongoing presence in Baghdad. She describes herself as an Iraqi raised abroad during childhood, who returned to Baghdad in her early teens. "Most of my friends are of different ethnicities, religions, and nationalities. I am bilingual," she states, explaining the fact that she writes in English and is conversant with Western and other cultures. "But no matter what—I shall remain anonymous. I wouldn't feel free to write otherwise. . . . You know me as Riverbend, you share a very small part of my daily reality—I hope that will suffice."

SATURDAY, 8.23.03
WE'VE ONLY JUST BEGUN . . .

Females can no longer leave their homes alone. Each time I go out, E. and either a father, uncle, or cousin has to accompany me. It feels like we've gone back fifty years ever since the beginning of the occupation. A woman, or girl, out alone, risks anything from insults to abduction. An outing has to be arranged at least an hour beforehand. I state that I need to buy something or have to visit someone. Two males have to be procured (preferably large) and "safety arrangements" must be made in this total state of lawlessness. And always the question: "But do you have to go out and buy it? Can't I get it for you?" No you can't, because the kilo of eggplant I absolutely have to select with my own hands is just an excuse to see the light of day and walk down a street. The situation is incredibly frustrating to females who work or go to college.

Before the war, around 50 percent of the college students were females, and over 50 percent of the working force was composed of women. Not so anymore. . . . Before the war, I would estimate (roughly) that about 55 percent of females in Baghdad wore a hijab—or headscarf.

I am female and Muslim. Before the occupation, I more or less dressed the way I wanted to. I lived in jeans and cotton pants and comfortable shirts. Now, I don't dare leave the house in pants. A long skirt and loose shirt (preferably with long sleeves) has become necessary. A girl wearing jeans risks being attacked, abducted or insulted by fundamentalists who have been . . . liberated!

The whole situation is alarming beyond any description I can give. Christians have become the victims of extremism also. Some of them are being threatened, others are being attacked. A few wannabe Mullahs came out with a "fatwa," or decree, in June that declared all females should wear the hijab, and if they didn't, they could be subject to "punishment." Another group claiming to be a part of the "Hawza Al Ilmia" decreed that not a single girl over the age of fourteen could remain unmarried—even if it meant that some members of the Hawza would have to have two, three, or four wives. This decree included females of other religions. In the south, female UN and Red Cross aides received death threats if they didn't wear the hijab. This isn't done in the name of God—it's done in the name of power. It tells people—the world—that "Look—we have power, we have influence."

Don't blame it on Islam. Every religion has its extremists. In times of chaos and disorder, those extremists flourish. Iraq is full of moderate Muslims who simply believe in "live and let live." We get along with each other—Sunnis and Shi'a, Muslims and Christians, and Jews and Sabi'a. We intermarry, we mix and mingle, we live. We build our churches and mosques in the same areas, our children go to the same schools . . . it was never an issue.

Someone asked me if, through elections, the Iraqi people might vote for an Islamic state. Six months ago, I would have firmly said, "No." Now I'm not so sure. There's been an overwhelming return to fundamentalism. People are turning to religion for several reasons. The first and most prominent reason is fear. Fear of war, fear of death, and fear of a fate worse than death (and yes, there are fates worse than death). If I didn't have something to believe in during this past war, I know I would have lost my mind. If there hadn't been a God to pray to, to make promises to, to bargain with, to thank—I wouldn't have made it through.

Encroaching Western values and beliefs have also played a prominent role in pushing Iraqis to embrace Islam. Just as there are ignorant people in the Western world (and there are plenty—I have the emails to prove it . . . don't make me embarrass you), there are ignorant people in the Middle East. In Muslims and Arabs, Westerners see suicide bombers, terrorists, ignorance, and camels. In Americans, Brits, etc., some Iraqis see depravity, prostitution, ignorance, domination, junkies, and ruthlessness. The best way people can find to protect themselves, and their loved ones against this assumed threat is religion.

Finally, you have more direct reasons. Sixty-five percent of all Iraqis are currently unemployed for one reason or another. There are people who have families to feed. When I say "families," I don't mean a wife and two kids . . . I mean around sixteen or seventeen people. Islamic parties supported by Iran, like Al-Daawa and SCIRI [Supreme Council for the Islamic Revolution in Iraq], are currently recruiting followers by offering "wages" to jobless men (an ex-soldier in the army, for example) in trade of "support." This support could mean anything—vote when the elections come around, bomb a specific shop, "confiscate," abduct, hijack cars . . . So concerning the anxiety over terror and fundamentalism—I would like to quote the Carpenters—worry? "We've only just begun . . . we've only just begun . . . "

SUNDAY, AUGUST 24, 2003
WILL WORK FOR FOOD . . .

Over 65 percent of the Iraqi population is unemployed. The reason for this is that Bremer made some horrible decisions. The first major decision he made was to dissolve the Iraqi army. That may make sense in Washington, but here we were left speechless. Now there are over 400,000 trained, armed men with families that need to be fed. Where are they supposed to go? What are they supposed to do for a living? I don't know. They certainly don't know.

The story of how I lost my job isn't unique. I'm a computer science graduate. Before the war, I was working in an Iraqi database/software company located in Baghdad as a programmer/network administrator (yes, yes . . . a geek). Every day, I would climb three flights of stairs, enter the little office I shared with one female colleague and two males, start up my PC and spend hours staring at little numbers and letters rolling across the screen. It was tedious, it was back-breaking, it was geeky and it was . . . wonderful.

I loved my job. At 8 A.M. I'd walk in lugging a backpack filled with enough CDs, floppies, notebooks, chewed-on pens, paperclips, and screwdrivers to make Bill Gates proud. I made as much money as my two male colleagues and got an equal amount of respect from the manager. . . .

What I'm trying to say is that no matter *what* anyone heard, females in Iraq were a lot better off than females in other parts of the Arab world (and some parts of the Western world—we had equal salaries!). We made up over 50 percent of the working force. We were doctors, lawyers, nurses, teachers, professors, deans, architects, programmers, and more. We came and went as we pleased. We wore what we wanted (within the boundaries of the social restrictions of a conservative society).

During the first week of June, I heard my company was back in business. It took several hours, seemingly thousands of family meetings, but I finally convinced everyone that it was necessary for my *sanity* to go back to work. They agreed that I would visit the company (with my two male bodyguards) and ask them if they had any work I could possibly take home and submit later on, or through the Internet.

One fine day in mid-June, I packed my big bag of geeky wonders, put on my long skirt and shirt, tied back my hair and left the house with a mixture of anticipation and apprehension.

We had to park the car about a hundred meters away from the door of the company because the major road in front of it was cracked and broken with the weight of the American tanks as they entered Baghdad. I half-ran, half-plodded up to the door of the company, my heart throbbing in anticipation of seeing friends, colleagues, secretaries . . . just generally something familiar again in the strange new nightmare we were living.

The moment I walked through the door, I noticed it. Everything looked shabbier somehow—sadder. The maroon carpet lining the hallways was dingy, scuffed, and spoke of the burden of a thousand rushing feet. The windows we had so diligently taped prior to the war were cracked in some places and broken in others . . . dirty all over. The lights were shattered, desks overturned, doors kicked in, and clocks torn from the walls. Everyone was standing around, looking at everyone else. The faces were sad and lethargic and exhausted. And I was one of the only females. . .

I continued upstairs, chilled to the bone, in spite of the muggy heat of the building which hadn't seen electricity for at least two months. My little room wasn't much better off than the rest of the building. The desks were gone, papers all over the place . . . but A. was there! I couldn't believe it—a familiar, welcoming face. He looked at me for a moment, without really seeing me, then his eyes opened wide and disbelief took over the initial vague expression. He congratulated me on being alive, asked about my family, and told me that he wasn't coming back after today. Things had changed. I should go home and stay safe. He was quitting—going to find work abroad. Nothing to do here anymore. I told him about my plan to work at home and submit projects . . . he shook his head sadly. I stood staring at the mess for a few moments longer, trying to sort out the mess in my head, my heart being torn to pieces. My cousin and E. were downstairs waiting for me—there was nothing more to do, except ask how I could maybe help? A. and I left the room and started making our way downstairs. We paused on the second floor and stopped to talk to one of the former department directors. I asked him when they thought things would be functioning, he wouldn't look at me. His eyes stayed glued to A.'s face as he told him that females weren't welcome right now—especially females who "couldn't be protected." He finally turned to me and told me, in so many words, to go home because "they" refused to be responsible for what might happen to me.

Ok. Fine. Your loss. I turned my back, walked down the stairs and went to find E. and my cousin. Suddenly, the faces didn't look strange—they were the same faces of before, mostly, but there was a hostility I couldn't believe. . . . I cried bitterly all the way home—cried for my job, cried for my future and cried for the torn streets, damaged buildings and crumbling people.

I'm one of the lucky ones . . . I'm not important. I'm not vital. Over a month ago, a prominent electrical engineer (one of the smartest females in the country) named Henna Aziz was assassinated in front of her family—two daughters and her husband. She was threatened by some fundamentalists from Badir's Army [a Shi'a extremist group] and told to stay at home because she was a woman, she shouldn't be in charge. She refused—the country needed her expertise to get things functioning—she was brilliant. She would not and could not stay at home. They came to her house one evening: men with machine-guns, broke in and opened fire. She lost her life—she wasn't the first, she won't be the last.

THURSDAY, 1.15.04
SHARI'A AND FAMILY LAW

On Wednesday our darling Iraqi Puppet Council decided that secular Iraqi family law would no longer be secular—it is now going to be according to Islamic Shari'a. Shari'a is Islamic law, whether from the Quran or quotes of the Prophet or interpretations of modern Islamic law by clerics and people who have dedicated their lives to studying Islam.

The news has barely been covered by Western or even Arab media and Iraqi media certainly aren't covering it. It is too much to ask of Al-Iraqiya [the Pentagon-funded Iraqi TV station] to debate or cover a topic like this one—it would obviously conflict with the Egyptian soap operas and songs. This latest decision is going to be catastrophic for females—we're going backwards.

Don't get me wrong—pure Islamic law according to the Quran and the Prophet gives women certain unalterable, nonnegotiable rights. The problem arises when certain clerics decide to do their own interpretations of these laws (and just about *anyone* can make themselves a cleric these days). The bigger problem is that Shari'a may be drastically different from one cleric to another. There are actually fundamental differences in Shari'a between the different Islamic factions or "methahib." Even in the same methahib, there are dozens of different clerics who may have opposing opinions. This is going to mean more chaos than we already have to deal with. We've come to expect chaos in the streets . . . but chaos in the courts and judicial system too?!

This is completely unfair to women specifically. Under the Iraqi constitution, men and women are equal. Under our past secular family law (which has been in practice since the '50s) women had unalterable divorce, marriage, inheritance, custody, and alimony rights. All of this is going to change. I'll give an example of what this will mean. One infamous practice brought to Iraq by Iranian clerics was the "zawaj muta'a," which when translated by the clerics means "temporary marriage." The actual translation is "pleasure marriage"—which is exactly what it is. It works like this: a consenting man and woman go to a cleric who approves of temporary marriage and they agree upon a period of time during which the marriage will last. The man pays the woman a "mahar," or dowry, and during the duration of the marriage (which can be anything from an hour, to a week, a month, etc.) the man has full marital rights. Basically, it's a form of prostitution that often results in illegitimate children and a spread of STDs.

Sunni clerics consider it a sin and many Shi'a clerics also frown upon it . . . but there are the ones who will tell you it's "halal" and Shari'a, etc. Secular Iraqi family law considers it a form of prostitution and doesn't consider a "pleasure marriage" a legitimate marriage. In other words, the woman wouldn't have any legal rights and if she finds herself pregnant—the child, legally, wouldn't have a father. . . .

Another example is in marriage itself. By tribal law and Shari'a, a woman, no matter how old, would have to have her family's consent to marry a man. By Iraqi law, as long as the woman is over eighteen, she doesn't need her family's consent. She can marry in a court, legally, without her parents. It rarely happened in Iraq, but it *was* possible. According to Iraqi secular law, a woman has grounds to divorce her husband if he beats her. According to Shari'a, it would be much more difficult to prove abuse.

Other questions pose themselves—Shari'a doesn't outlaw the marriage of minors (on condition they've hit puberty). Iraqi secular law won't allow minors to marry until the age of at least sixteen (I think) for women and the age of eighteen for men.

By Iraqi civil law, parents are required to send their children to complete at least primary school. According to Shari'a, a father can make his son or daughter quit school and either work or remain at home. So what happens when and if he decides to do that? Does Shari'a apply or does civil law apply?

Women are outraged . . . this is going to open new doors for repression in the most advanced country on women's rights in the Arab world! Men are also against this (although they certainly have the upper hand in the situation) because it's going to mean more confusion and conflict all around.

During the sanctions and all the instability, we used to hear fantastic stories about certain Arab countries like Saudi Arabia, Kuwait, Oman, and Qatar, to name a few. We heard about their luxurious lifestyles—the high monthly wages, the elegant cars, sprawling homes and malls . . . and while I always wanted to visit, I never once remember yearning to live there or even feeling envy. When I analyzed my feelings, it always led back to the fact that I cherished the rights I had as an Iraqi Muslim woman. During the hard times, it was always a comfort that I could drive, learn, work for equal pay, dress the way I wanted, and practice Islam according to my values and beliefs, without worrying whether I was too devout or not devout enough.

I usually ignore the emails I receive telling me to "embrace" my new-found freedom and be happy that the circumstances of all Iraqi women are going to "improve drastically" from what we had before. They quote Bush (which in itself speaks volumes) saying things about how repressed the Iraqi women were and how, now, they are going to be able to live free lives.

The people who write those emails often lump Iraq together with Saudi Arabia, Iran, and Afghanistan and I shake my head at their ignorance but think to myself, "Well, they really need to believe their country has the best of intentions—I won't burst their bubble." But I'm telling everyone now—if I get any more emails about how free and liberated the Iraqi women are *now* thanks to America, they can expect a very nasty answer.

WEDDINGS, WOMBS, AND WHOOPEE

Roe in Rough Waters

JENNIFER BAUMGARDNER

***The Nation*, 2.10.03**

Desiree was a high school senior from Buffalo who already had a 1-year-old daughter when she came to spend the night with me. She wore jeans and a huge sweatshirt, but anyone could see she was pregnant. Desiree was at twenty-one weeks and had never been to New York City. In fact, she didn't know one person here, nor did she have money for a hotel, which is why the clinic called me. I picked her up at the end of her first day of the three-day procedure. She had been counseled about the abortion and her options. Laminaria, tubes of sterile seaweed, had been placed in her cervix in order to dilate it overnight. We ate Mexican food and then she fell asleep by the light of MTV. At 7 the next morning, we headed back to the clinic and she continued her abortion. As we entered Parkmed Eastern Women's Center, a scary nun and toothless old man divebombed Desiree, surrounding her like autograph-seekers, begging her not to kill her baby.

Most women I have hosted are facing situations similar to Desiree's. (I host through Haven, a loose coalition of women who provide a place to stay for people in town for what are always later-term abortions.) The women find out they are pregnant too late to get an abortion in their hometown, or they can't raise the money. The abortion starts out costing $300, but by the time they get through the dangerously sticky red tape of Medicaid (if they are lucky enough to be in a state where Medicaid pays for procedures), it's $500—or $2,000. (The New York Abortion Access Fund—NYAAF, founded by a recent college grad and run by a half-dozen young women—contributed to forty abortions last year, almost all of which cost between $995 and $3,000.) Often the woman herself has almost no money or spent it getting to New York, and the clinician has to call around to various funds that will pick up part of the cost of an abortion. It can take days and a half-dozen calls for the clinician to get the money together. Haven and these funds are a sort of underground railroad for abortions—the irony being that abortion is legal and a woman's right.

This month, abortion has been legal for thirty years. The terrain has become increasingly complex. The same moment the planets aligned so that conservatives had a monopoly on government, the Alan Guttmacher Institute announced that abortion rates had declined—dramatically. In 1992 the AGI predicted that 43 percent of American women would have an abortion before the age of 45. Basically, the abortion rate was pushing 50 percent. A decade later, the number was one in three. Due to population growth, this still means just over 1.3 million abortions per year, but it's the lowest abortion rate in twenty-nine years. Six percent are medical abortions (RU–486); the rest are surgical.

The fact that the abortion rate has dropped is that rare thing: good news for both those who wave gory photos of 21-week-old fetuses and those who wave signs that read George, Get Out of My Bush! After all, pro-choicers want women to have the tools that make the need for abortion minimal. "We'd prefer women have adequate contraception to control reproduction," says Lauren Porsch, a 23-year-old staffer at Physicians for Reproductive Choice and Health and founder of NYAAF. "It's cheaper, easier on the woman, less painful all around." (Most pro-choicers see abortion ideally as a backup, since 54 percent of women getting abortions report that they were using birth control the month they got pregnant. Desiree was on the pill when she got pregnant.)

The decline coincided with the approval of emergency contraception in 1998 (the AGI estimates that 51,000 abortions were averted by the use of EC in 2000 alone, and Planned Parenthood distributed 459,000 doses to women in 2000) and eight years of President Clinton, who vetoed almost every piece of antichoice legislation that crossed his desk. Ironically, though, the downtrend in unwanted pregnancies is poised to be reversed. If successful, the Republican agenda is sure to pave the way for more late-term abortions like Desiree's.

Until recently, it was more likely the Bush Administration would do something sneaky, like remove crucial information about condoms from the Centers for Disease Control website, rather than launch overt assaults on choice. Meanwhile, it was the Democrats' role, with their slim majority in the Senate, to keep bans and restrictions at bay after they passed the House. And they succeeded. As Ken Connor, president of the Family Research Council, put it colorfully in the *New York Times*, the 107th Senate was "a veritable graveyard of pro-life legislation." As of January 7, though, when the 108th Congress convened, the Senate has been primed to become a veritable "pro-life" birthing center.

En route to swift delivery is a ban on "partial-birth" abortions, [This bill was signed into law on November 5, 2003. See p. 81, Voss.—ed.] a ban on human embryonic cloning, the Child Custody Protection Act, the Abortion Non-Discrimination Act and the Unborn Victims of Violence Act. Each bill is notably uninterested in protecting the woman's rights, worrying instead about the fetus, the pregnant woman's parents (if she's a minor) and the religious healthcare worker. (This value system was reinforced on January 14, when George W. Bush declared National

Sanctity of Human Life Day for the following Sunday.) There isn't a lot of reason to believe that these proposals, which have all passed in the House before, won't clear the new Senate in the near future.

"These are the worst threats I have ever seen in thirty years of this work," says Gloria Feldt, the president of Planned Parenthood Federation of America (PPFA). Within days of winning back the Senate and keeping the House, Republicans made their first moves on reproductive freedom. Mississippi's Trent Lott, then poised to become Senate majority leader, promised a ban on late-term abortions, a gift to conservative Christians in his party. After Lott was forced to resign due to his sudden endorsement of affirmative action on Black Entertainment Television, Dr. Bill Frist of Tennessee stepped into his cowboy boots. Dr. Frist, a dashing cardiovascular surgeon from a state that flunks *NARAL*'s contraceptive-access report card, is just as conservative as Lott and brings with him the added ammo of being a doctor, as he made clear during the "partial birth" abortion wars of 1998 (soon to be reprised). "As a physician," he remarked at the time of President Clinton's veto of a ban on D&X (intact dilation and extraction, or so-called partial birth) procedures, "I believe that partial-birth abortions cannot and should not be categorized with other medical procedures—or even other abortions. . . . For the sake of women, their children and our future as a society, we must put a stop, once and for all, to partial-birth abortion." His press release urges the Senate to "listen to the facts"—facts on which he, the only M.D. in the bunch, presumably has a grip. As a heart surgeon, though, Dr. Frist is not a medical expert on matters of reproduction any more than a gynecologist is well versed in angioplasty. The American College of Obstetricians and Gynecologists (representing 95 percent of the field) believes a ban of the D&X abortion procedure to be "inappropriate" and "dangerous."

Recently, Dr. Frist did the Sunday morning talk-show circuit, confidently discussing a ban on D&X procedures as if it were already in the bag. But as PPFA's Gloria Feldt points out, "The Republicans could overreach and fail." Advocates "out in the field are not despairing at all; they are angry." Feldt also notes that the general public is "connecting the dots in terms of the Administration's war on women." As far as the D&X ban goes, Feldt believes that the 2000 *Stenberg v. Carhart* Supreme Court decision (which held that bans on abortion procedures without an exception for the health of the mother are in violation of *Roe*) is helpful. "There will be an argument within the Republican leadership between those who will want a bill that they know to be constitutional and those who will want to be more extreme," Feldt told me. "They may kill their own chances and not make it constitutional. This type of legislation gives us the opportunity to lay the case for laws to codify principles of *Roe*."

Planned Parenthood reports that Dr. Frist has voted to "limit or deny access to the constitutional right to abortion services of women in the military, women federal employees, low-income women, women in prison and young women. He never missed an opportunity to vote to make abortion a right that more and more women cannot exercise." It will come as no surprise, then, that Frist is a big-time proponent of abstinence-only sex education, voting for a $75 million budget to lobby teenagers not to have sex in lieu of acknowledging that many do and providing them with information and contraception. This, when poor teenagers have an abortion rate that is rapidly rising.

Dr. Frist and the anti-sex education crowd are clearly speaking to an imaginary teen population. There is a direct relationship between poverty and abortion, and an utter ignorance about sex and procreation is epidemic. This especially has an impact on later-term abortions. "The women I see can't get any healthcare to determine how pregnant they are and often don't know their own cycle. Sometimes, by the time they get their Medicaid straightened out and can come in, they are at twenty-seven weeks," says a counselor at Parkmed Eastern Women's Center, sighing. "Last week I told a woman with six children living in a shelter that she is having number seven."

The reproductive rights movement needs to amplify the voices of the women affected by Republican bans on Medicaid for abortions, bans that result in the death of more-developed fetuses and untold hardships for the women and their families. Instead, we have too frequently reached out to a stereotypical "young woman" who is clueless, ungrateful and often in need of a "wake-up call." In fact, of the ninety-seven funds under the National Network of Abortion Funds, many are staffed by younger women. Both Haven and NYAAF are run by 23-year-olds, NOW-NYC by a 27-year-old. Planned Parenthood's VOX program (on many campuses) and most of the work on choice that the Feminist Majority does (also on college campuses) is run entirely by young women, as is Choice USA and the Pro-Choice Public Education Project. "Face it, younger women are the ones that are having abortions," says Amy Richards, 32, who administered an abortion fund through the Third Wave Foundation until just this past year. "And they are coming to abortion politics through personal experience—just as it was thirty years ago."

Real men and women raised with *Roe* have complex responses to abortion, as they do with many once black-and-white issues that 1970s feminists tackled three decades ago. Prior to *Roe*, an estimated 200,000 to 1.2 million illegal abortions were performed each year, according to the Center for Reproductive Law and Policy. About 10,000 women in the United States died annually from complications from illegal abortions.

Roe unquestionably liberated my generation of women to enjoy freer lives than our mothers did. For those of us who never knew a time when abortion wasn't safe and legal, we have the privilege of having complicated feelings about abortion. "I consider myself antiabortion but prochoice," says Mark Andersen, a 43-year-old author and activist in Washington, DC. A devoted Catholic vegan who doesn't even eat honey "for fear of causing problems for the bees," Andersen nonetheless votes for prochoice, Democratic candidates. "I think that the left has the pro-life platform overall, because it is concerned with the most vulnerable. Rick Santorum, for instance, isn't a pro-life candidate as a whole—just when it comes to the preborn."

Andersen's view is progress, in a way, as is writer Elizabeth Wurtzel's when she says that her abortion was a sad and nasty experience from start to finish. After all, if we have to put a fresh and smiling face on everything we do—even if the procedure is constantly under attack by the right—then we haven't come far from the days of the Stepford Wives. Wurtzel and Anderson want *better* choices for women, not fewer. Still, such complexity poses a challenge to the prochoice movement when it is accompanied by greater tolerance for abortion restrictions. Several surveys, notably the UCLA study of incoming freshmen, have reported a decline in the proportion of those who support abortion rights.

The left isn't always the firmest ally of reproductive freedom, either. In a 1989 cover story for *Ms.* magazine, just before *Webster v. Reproductive Health Services* almost overturned *Roe* and ushered in the state's right to restrict abortions, Gloria Steinem insisted that we look at choice as a human right, not a "'single issue' to be bargained away." Sadly, some on the left have cast abortion as a kind of distraction, the inconvenient reason we are (fearfully, shortsightedly) tethered to otherwise compromised Democratic candidates.

Clearly, however, our big problem is the conservative Republican government and its veritable free pass to spawn confusingly named anti-choice laws—laws that will affect poor women, young women and women of color most harshly because they are the most vulnerable and because they are the ones getting abortions. Poor women—whether teens or adults—are the only group whose abortion rate is rising. Black women are overrepresented when it comes to abortion, with a rate nearly four times that of white women. Latinas and Asian/Pacific Islander women have an abortion rate about two and a half times that of white women. It's illustrative to walk into a clinic in New York—"almost all of our patients are women of color," says the director of counseling for Parkmed Eastern Women's Center. And they're poor.

If Republicans don't quake in their boots at the thought of feminists coming after them, they are vulnerable as racists. Dr. Frist may not have openly pined for the plantation days, but he is from Tennessee, a state with a relatively large African-American population that has 13.5 percent of its population in poverty—constituents he is supposed to represent.

But for abortion to be perceived as a race and class issue, not just a white women's issue, the choice movement needs to represent—or at least connect with—the women getting abortions, who are the natural activists. The voices of young women, women of color and especially poor women (often also young women of color) tend not to inform abortion politics. You rarely find many women of color in prochoice organizations, especially on the boards. Whether the group is as huge as Planned Parenthood or as small as the New York Abortion Access Fund, you can almost bank on the fact that white women run it and black women (and to a lesser degree Latinas) are the "beneficiaries." Some current strategies of the prochoice movement, from focusing on the clueless young straw woman to NARAL's recent name change (to NARAL Pro Choice America, a moniker designed to appeal to mainstream—white, middle-class—America), aren't speaking to the women getting abortions, either. "It goes all the way back to Jane Roe," says Matthea Marquart, 27, the president of NOW-NYC. "If she had been a higher-income woman, she would have gone to Mexico to get an abortion."

"We are the real experts," feminists declared back when abortion was illegal. They took the debate out of the hands of men (doctors, judges and legislators) and put it in their own. Thirty years later, the most powerful feminist line on choice can't be forgotten: Decisions governing abortion should be made by the women getting the abortions.

Wedding Bells and Welfare Bucks

ALANA KUMBIER

***HipMama.com*, 7.17.02**

Attention, Single Mamas: George W. Bush has a proposal for you: a marriage proposal. That's right, he wants you to get married. You're particularly encouraged to don a bridal veil if you're on welfare and/or parenting as part of an unmarried couple. If you act now, you might even be able toget hitched before Congress makes its decisions about Bush's plan to fund marriage initiative and abstinence-only education programs with welfare dollars. The Administration is proposing the allocation of $400 million for marriage initiatives ($300 million at the federal level, with an additional $100 million dollar bonus for states that get the most women married or have 'successful' marriage initiatives), and $135 million for abstinence education, to be drawn from welfare funds.

These marriage initiatives are part of Bush's proposal for the reauthorization of the nation's welfare laws. In late February, Bush unveiled his welfare plan during a speech at a Catholic church in Southeast Washington. In his speech, Bush stated that the welfare policy should focus on the creation and maintenance of stable families, announcing that his "administration will give unprecedented support to strengthening marriage." As *Washington Post* staff writer Amy Goldstein reported, the White House plans to require states to include "explicit descriptions of their family-formation and healthy-marriage efforts" in the welfare plans they submit to the federal government. The House passed Bush's welfare legislation (HR 4737) in May, and the Senate is working on its welfare reform bill now, with hopes to have its work finished in July.

The proposal for welfare reauthorization put forth by the Bush Administration builds upon the "success" of the 1996 reforms. Bush's proposal calls for tougher work standards, which would require welfare recipients to work 40 hours per week (supposedly, in 1996, states had the option of allowing 20 hours of work and 10 hours of flexible activities, and states chose to enforce 30 hours of work instead, allowing two of those days to be used for narrowly-defined education and training activities), allocating $400 million for marriage promotion campaigns, and spending $135 million on abstinence education. Increased spending for childcare (for mothers and fathers who have to work those 40 hours), or for training or education for welfare recipients, aren't part of this proposal.

WHAT'S HAPPENING WITH WELFARE NOW

In order to better understand Bush's proposals for welfare reauthorization, as well as their potential effects, it's a good idea to revisit the 1996 reforms that created the current welfare systems in place across the U.S. Congress passed the Personal Responsibility and Work Opportunity Reconciliation Act (PRWOA) in 1996. This new law replaced existing welfare programs with Temporary Assistance for Needy Families (TANF), which was enacted with the stipulation that Congress would have to reauthorize TANF by the end of September 2002. The TANF law defined primary objectives for welfare reform as "promoting job preparation, work, and marriage; preventing and reducing the incidence of out-of-wedlock pregnancies; and encouraging the formation and maintenance of two-parent families." In this formulation, states were able to define who constituted a family, and what types of assistance different family units might receive (note that the language of the law does not require that parents be married, only that they share parenting responsibilities in the home).

Immigrants (even those with children who are U.S. citizens) are ineligible for any assistance, regardless of their familial status.

The TANF reforms set a five-year lifetime limit for welfare recipients (such that if an individual or family has received five years' worth of benefits, they will be ineligible for future assistance), and increased work requirements, while simultaneously creating stricter definitions of countable "work" activities. Under TANF, single parents must work 30 hours per week, and parents in two-parent families must work 35 hours per week (though in many states, like Montana, two-parent families have to work up to 60 hours a week to qualify for assistance) to be eligible for welfare assistance. Parents cannot receive TANF funds while pursuing further education or training, unless this training is part of a vocational education program or is specifically applicable to the recipient's job, and is supplemental to 20 hours of other work activity. Recipients cannot count parenting/childcare, literacy education, ESL courses or college study as work activities. While TANF does provide some childcare benefits, and may waive work activities requirements for parents who cannot find adequate childcare, recipients are often not informed about these benefits.

The TANF legislation's efforts to reduce out-of-wedlock births materialized in the form of annual $100 million "illegitimacy bonuses" to the five states that had achieved the greatest reduction in the number of out-of-wedlock births. These efforts were supplemented by federally funded "abstinence-only" education programs, for which $250 million was allocated.

According to some poverty rights and feminist activists, TANF's effects have been detrimental to welfare recipients, and their status as a foundation for similar legislation is highly problematic. In response to TANF's flexibility on family formation initiatives, 23 states have instituted "family cap" policies for welfare recipients, denying welfare assistance to children born to parents already on welfare, or placing tougher work requirements on mothers who exceed the family cap. NOW-LDEF notes that non-marital births have not decreased as a result of these initiatives. In at least one state (New Jersey), the reduction in out-of-wedlock births was concurrent with an increase in abortions.

We don't yet know the results of "abstinence-only" education, but as the NOW-LDEF site observes that the "education, mentoring, and counseling programs funded under the law must adhere to a specific set of eight tenets, such as 'sex outside of marriage is likely to be psychologically and physically harmful'," while not providing important information about taking measures to prevent sexually transmitted diseases and unwanted pregnancies.

Even with TANF funding, families on welfare often don't receive enough assistance to make ends meet, or to avoid serious hardship.

Though they may be working 30 to 40 hours a week, recipients still may not rise above the poverty level, if their jobs pay less than a living wage. Without the education or training necessary to prepare for better employment, parents may find themselves without viable options for advancement once their benefits run out.

STATE MARRIAGE INITIATIVES

As a result of the Personal Responsibility and Work Opportunity Reconciliation Act's emphasis on the formation and maintenance of two-parent families, several states have begun to experiment with different initiatives linking marriage initiatives with welfare funds. In West Virginia, TANF funds have been allocated to add a $100 bonus to families' monthly benefits if the parents on welfare marry each other. Oklahoma is working on a $10 million Marriage Initiative plan that includes public education campaigns, youth outreach and education, the integration of pro-marriage counseling in social service programs, and a specific religious initiative encouraging religious leaders to encourage their church and synagogue members to undergo pre-marital counseling. The Michigan Family Independence Agency, partially financed with welfare funds, was established to provide marital and family counseling and anger management courses to interested individuals. Utah has allocated a portion of its TANF surplus for a marriage education campaign that will be developed over a two-year period, and the state legislature raised the minimum age for marriage from 14 to 16 years old.

Arizona has been particularly gung-ho in its marriage initiatives. According to the NOW-LDEF, the state has allocated $1 million for marriage skills classes offered by community-based organizations, and it has established a Marriage and Communication Skills Commission, whose projects include the creation and distribution of a "healthy marriage" handbook to all couples applying for a marriage license, and funding vouchers for low income couples attending marriage-skills classes. The Arizona legislature also passed a Covenant Marriage law in 1998, "under which couples promise to stay married for life and renounce their legal right to a no-fault divorce."

FIGHTING FOR ALTERNATIVES THAT EMPOWER SINGLE MOTHERS

The very real possibility of building further ties between marriage initiatives and welfare money has been a call to action for a number of welfare advocates and activists, for feminists, for civil rights leaders, and for those in support of individual citizens' privacy and right to choice regarding marriage and family planning. These activists and advocates are working to raise awareness about flaws in current and proposed welfare policy, and to warn Americans about the threats such policies pose to families on welfare, as well as to the public at large.

In a recent interview, Dorian Solot, co-founder of the Alternatives to Marriage Project, an nonprofit advocacy organization that works to promote "equality and fairness for unmarried people, including people who choose not to marry, cannot marry, or live together before marriage," identified several flaws in the logic of state and federal marriage promotion initiatives. "The first problem is there's no evidence that promoting marriage will help anyone get out of poverty," Solot said. "If we agree that the purpose of welfare is to help people escape poverty, then we have no reason to believe that marriage is going to help us achieve that goal. The second problem is that there's an assumption that anyone who wants to can get married, and so of course there are gay and lesbian people who can't marry, heterosexual people who can't marry because they're not in a relationship, because their partner is abusive and not marrying is a really wise decision. Perhaps the third problem is the belief that if women marry, the guy they're marrying is going to be the guy on 'Who Wants to Marry a Millionaire'—when the reality is that the men that most poor women marry are poor men, and don't have the resources to get their families what they need and to get on their feet financially.

"There's a certain body of research about the positive effects of marriage, and that's what a lot of these policy arguments are based on," she noted. "But we don't know anything about whether marriages that are produced or coerced by government agencies have those same effects—in fact, there may be good reason to suspect they don't have the same positive effects, because maybe we need to be trusting people to make that very private decision themselves."

Solot acknowledges that it's difficult for many politicians and public figures to openly oppose these marriage promotion proposals. "Everyone loves marriage—there isn't really anyone who'll say 'I'm against marriage,' which makes it hard to criticize these proposals and means that all politicians need to be behind them, politically. But the reality is they don't even begin to address the realities of peoples' lives, particularly poor peoples'.

"I think that most of the people who are opposing or critiquing the marriage promotion proposals think marriage is great and don't have any problem with the idea that we should help build strong families and strong marriages, but do have problems with spending money to do that."

For Kate Kahan, Executive Director of Working for Equality and Economic Liberation (WEEL), a grassroots organization that started in response to welfare reform, fighting marriage promotion campaigns at the state and federal level has been both personally and politically important. Kahan, a single mother with a nine-year-old son, was on welfare and going to college when the 1996 welfare reforms happened. "I experienced that big transition of welfare reform personally, and barely finished college," she said in a recent interview. "I bring a strong feminist element and approach to this [work], and one of the big issues that everyone in this organization has had is this direct attack on women's private lives by trying to control who they marry and whether or not their children are illegitimate through welfare policy."

Kahan and her colleagues made an important discovery early on in their poverty-rights work, that they could build power through coalition-building with similar groups in the region (WEEL is based in Montana). "One of the things that's significant about what we've done is we've figured out pretty quickly that we are totally divided along state lines," Kahan said. "All of our welfare programs are different, and even if our folks are experiencing the same circumstances, all of our policies are so different. We figured out that what we needed to do was work across state lines and build our power, and so we started a regional network of seven western states working on welfare issues.

"People in the progressive community were shocked we were able to figure that out; it was pretty soon after welfare reform. We immediately identified the reauthorization of the welfare reform bill as something we needed to be involved in, and because we had the experience from the ground—our members, some of us staff members, had been there directly. That element was missing in '96 in the debates, and is an absolute necessity for the 2002 debates."

Through a particularly serendipitous turn of political events, Kahan's home state was thrust into the welfare-reform spotlight. "Montana has key congressional delegation for the welfare reform issue," she said. "Montana Senator Max Baucus is chair of the powerful Senate Finance Committee, the committee which holds jurisdiction over welfare. Essentially, Senator Baucus will be responsible for creating the welfare bill that will go to the President. Given this situation, WEEL and allies on the state level began an assertive education campaign focused on Montana's experience with welfare reform. This education work has led WEEL and their allies into the national spotlight due to its level of success in educating Senator Baucus on which welfare policies make sense for people on poverty. Senator Baucus has publicly denounced government involvement in whether or not low-income families should be married, thanks to WEEL's efforts."

"I see this as an issue of choice, hands down," Kahan continued. "We can relate this to issues we've seen in the past where restrictive policies have begun with low-income women, but didn't stop there. For example, the Hyde Amendment that restricted money going into any sort of abortion services for low-income women has resulted in tremendously scary debates about whether or not you should be able to get birth control if you're on Medicaid. Or, there are the sterilization efforts on the reservations—those are all direct, concerted attacks on low-income women, and they end up domino-effecting to affect all other women. I see this as the exact same thing—when restrictive policies start with low-income women, they don't stop there."

Aside from the potential future ramifications these marriage-welfare policies may have for low-income women and the public at large, feminists and welfare advocates are concerned with the effects these policies have on women and children who are facing domestic violence situations, for whom barriers to getting a divorce can be deadly.

"We do advocacy work at WEEL, so we help people navigate their way through the very complicated welfare systems we have now," Kahan said. "One of the main reasons that people call here for advocacy, over 50 percent of the time, is domestic violence, and they're in a situation where they can't get on assistance. I see this marriage promotion piece as being another barrier for women leaving, because if you go into a welfare office and you see a poster with a nuclear family saying 'You want more welfare benefits, talk to your caseworker,' or you have your case worker saying 'No, you should really go to this marriage counselor before you leave,' it's going to be deadly. That's one of my main concerns.

"I have personal experience with having been a young mother. I had little to no job experience when I went to apply for welfare, and I had $7 too much in my bank account, so I got turned away. I ended up not being able to get a job, and I got married to the father of my child. Two years later, I left a very violent home. Marriage wasn't the solution to my poverty or my son's poverty. If I hadn't left that home, I would have died, and that's reflected in so many of the women's lives that we work with."

Kahan realizes that the struggle to raise awareness about these marriage promotion campaigns, and about the importance of questioning and critiquing the Bush administration's proposals is a rhetorical one. Effecting specific material changes to improve the lives of families on welfare means going beyond simple, individual "solutions" like marriage. It also means making these issues relevant to the population at large.

Kahan and other welfare and civil rights advocates are ready to make specific arguments to populations who might not consider themselves implicated in welfare reform or marriage promotion. In Kahan, and WEEL's, case, these arguments come in the handy form of an activists' handbook that Kahan has produced to inspire and inform people who want to fight conservative welfare reform plans.

"Different people will relate to this issue from different angles," Kahan said. "There's the choice angle; this really starts to get at reproductive freedom. The privacy issues, we've all seen these when addressing healthcare and women's healthcare. There's also a lot of racist policy—this is really geared towards getting African American women to marry and get off welfare. There's a wage gap argument: these proposals totally ignore the fact that women don't make as much money as men. There's a discrimination argument: this clearly discriminates against gay and lesbian folks.

"I think it's racist and sexist policy specifically veiled in family values rhetoric," Kahan added. "We've seen this strategy before, many times. The Bush proposal for welfare offers over-simplified, band-aid solutions to the complex issues surrounding poverty in our country. Framing such superficial proposals in family values rhetoric completely avoids addressing the very real issue of poverty. So far, the democrats haven't figured out how to get out of the familiar corner such rhetoric has backed them into. It seems pretty obvious to me that capturing the debate back to one that addresses poverty and the needs of America's poor is imperative and not that difficult. After all, Bush isn't talking about poverty reduction in any way, shape or form."

Even some Republicans may find themselves siding with folks like Kahan and Solot. "It's so contradictory to the spiel you usually get from Republicans, that the government shouldn't be involved in people's private lives," Kahan said.

STRENGTHENING FAMILIES

It's important to note that most people who are opposed to policies that link marriage to welfare are not anti-family. Kahan and Solot agree that there are reasonable, constructive ways to help families on welfare. Both women stress the importance of creating and supporting policies that would allow mothers and fathers to care for their children materially and emotionally. WEEL's "Family Strengthening" proposal calls for an end to discrimination against unmarried, two-parent families, funding for at-home care programs that would allow low-income parents to choose to stay home with their children, increased funding for high-quality childcare, working to ensure that child support dollars are received by families, and protecting families in domestic violence situations as well as helping them through crisis.

"Parents need to be able to take care of their kids in a real way that makes sense," Kahan emphasizes at the end of our interview. "They need to get the money that's owed to them through child support, and we need to create more opportunities to help struggling families get out of poverty."

"If your criteria are children's well-being," Solot observed, "the programs that helped children the most were the ones that raised their parents' incomes, whether that was through helping them get jobs, or jobs that paid living wages, or less direct ways like ensuring they had transportation to get to work, or child care. When you add up families' total assets and incomes, the families who have more have their children doing better. Those kinds of programs are a lot more complicated, and nowhere near as appealing as just saying 'Oh, get married.'"

Altared States: Women on Welfare Talk About Marriage

CHISUN LEE AND SHARON LERNER

The Village Voice, 5.1.02

The Bush administration has presented marriage as the solution to poor women's problems. Would that it were so simple. Here, five women who could be targeted by the initiative talk about the complicated realities of their lives. Each has tried to be half of a stable, sanctioned union, but has wound up raising children in poverty and largely on her own.

SHENIA RUDOLPH

After Shenia Rudolph got divorced, she was very careful about who she let into her home. "I don't believe in having men coming in and out of the house," says Rudolph, who was sexually abused as a child and was living with her three children at the time. "I don't trust men around my kids." She managed to find a man who would live by her ground rules, taking a relationship slowly and not spending the night at her house. Their romance went on like this for ten years, with the couple planning to get married after Rudolph's oldest daughter was out of high school—and then Rudolph got pregnant. After she told her beau the news, he gave her some of his own: He was already married—and had been for about half of their decade-long relationship. Though she says her boyfriend wanted to continue seeing her, Rudolph ended the affair. As for the government's nudge toward the altar, Rudolph says, "What do they want me to do? Do they want him to be a bigamist?"

Now living in a one-bedroom, fifth-story walk-up with five kids (her most recent pregnancy turned out to be twins), Rudolph could use as much financial help as she can get. She reached her five-year welfare benefits limit in November, and though the babies' father pays $800 a month in child support through the state, she says she rarely receives that amount. Rudolph insists the next man in her life will have to contribute financially—"You can't afford to have men in your life who don't have nothing," she says.

Beyond that, the only reason worthy of getting involved once again, she says, is true love. "Some people stay in relationships 'cause they think it's good for the kids—and that's not good. Or for the security. I'm like, 'Get a dog, if you want security. Get an alarm system.' I'd rather be alone for the rest of my life, happy, than being with someone but feeling lonely when I'm with him." —Sharon Lerner

SONIA MORALES

"Two weeks before Thanksgiving, he decided he wanted to be free and single," says Sonia Morales, recalling her husband's departure two years ago. "You don't hold no one down. I said, 'If that's what you want to do, go ahead.'"

After ten years, they parted "on good terms," she thought. "Then he changed his beeper number," cutting off contact with her and her two children, she says. "To this day, I still don't know where he is." The *Voice* was unable to locate him.

Depression and smaller welfare checks made it impossible for her to make ends meet. She and her two children lost their apartment, bunked with a string of friends, and eventually landed in the city's shelter system. "It's going to be hard for me to get out of the shelter," she says. "The computer says I'm married," and the income from her phantom husband could disqualify her for public housing.

She fumes at the suggestion that marriage provides security for women. "Here I am, married to a man, and I can't even catch up with him! This is a husband. This is marriage. I'm homeless because I'm married." —Chisun Lee

ISABEL MENDEZ*

Isabel Mendez apologizes for her shaky state. She has just gotten off the phone with her ex-husband, with whom she has three children. "It was really hard for me to call him up and ask him for money," she says, but the less than $400 a month she receives in cash assistance and unemployment doesn't always last, even with the government paying the family's $312 rent. "He told me what nerve I have calling him and asking him for things."

The put-down is nothing compared to the physical abuse Mendez, 38, goes on to describe. In a history of assaults that included being kicked in the stomach when she was pregnant, the breaking point came one summer night six years ago when, she says, her husband raped her. "I called the cops. They said they couldn't do anything because I was married to him."

The sanctity of marriage was an excuse she had made to herself many times. "I'm Catholic, I stayed in there for religious reasons. I tried to get him to work it out. It got even worse."

Since the divorce, she has had to clear trash and dead rats from Long Island highways to keep her public assistance and cleaned welfare centers late at night for extra cash. But no amount of hardship would drive her back to her abuser, she says. "I wish we were never married. I want to be on my own, living my own life, even if it's hard. I just wish I had a good job, so I could support my kids and not bother with my ex anymore." —C.L.

TONYA WESTBROOK

"I met her in Prospect Park, two summers ago," says Tonya Westbrook, 27, mother of four. "I was there with a few friends, at a poetry reading, and we kept looking at each other. My friends dared me to go up and recite some of my work. Afterwards, she came over and congratulated me and said she liked what I had to say. We exchanged numbers."

Westbrook's partner Tawana has since become "like a second mother" to her children, the oldest of whom is 12. After troubled relationships with two men, each of whom fathered two of her children, "I decided to come out with it," she says. Being with a woman "was something that was in me for a while, but I never wanted to face it."

Raised Catholic, she left home when she was 15. "I was with this guy who took care of me. I was dependent on him for money." Money is still her chief problem; three months ago, she reached the five-year lifetime welfare limit Congress imposed in 1996. While her application to the state's supplemental program slumps through the system, the family receives reduced aid—$85 cash every two weeks, $225 a month in food stamps—and is facing eviction.

She hopes graduating from college next year will free her from poverty. She's resisted living with Tawana, a retail salesperson, because "I have a lot of baggage. I'm still on public assistance, I don't want to drop that on her. I want to be able to give back to her what she gives to me." By that she doesn't mean cash.

"She accepts me for who I am, with all my faults and everything. She's more than a partner, she's a best friend," says Westbrook. "We have our ups and downs, but I would like it to be forever."

Her life should be a lesson in love for the president, she says. "He assumes a woman being with a man is the American dream, but love comes in many forms. If you're willing to put up money for me to marry a man, why don't you let me marry the love of my life?" —C.L.

JULIA JACKSON*

Julia Jackson met her husband-to-be when she was 14, got pregnant at 15, and married at 16. "I thought I was in love," she remembers. "I thought I'd have a big house with a picket fence." Instead, when her husband was drafted to fight in Vietnam, Jackson ended up homeless. "They didn't have a shelter system back then, and I was roaming in the streets. I had my stuff in shopping bags and a baby in my arms."

After her husband returned from the war, the first few years of her marriage were relatively happy; he had steady work, first with a package delivery service and later as a city police officer. But, gradually, her husband became violent and started using drugs. "I was walking around beat up, with bruises, black eyes." She left him—several times. It was "like a revolving door," she says. "But I'd go back. How much can you drift in the street with six kids with you?"

Jackson finally left her husband and landed in a shelter when she was pregnant with their seventh child. Today, 33 years after her wedding, she is still married, though she hasn't seen her husband in years. She hopes to get a divorce when she saves enough money to pay for one, though she doesn't think she'll get married again.

"Marriage has to be a 50-50, understanding love relationship," she says. "It's supposed to be like on that show *7th Heaven*, where people can work together. I don't think I'll ever have that." —S.L.

**Names and identifying details have been changed.*

My Late-Term Abortion

GRETCHEN VOSS

***The Boston Globe,* 1.25.04**

Editor's Note: Thirty-one, in good health, Gretchen Voss, a freelance writer was told in the third month of her pregnancy that her baby would certainly be paralyzed and incontinent, most likely brain damaged. "Though the baby might live, it was not a life that we would choose for our child, a child that we already loved," she wrote. She and her husband, David, decided to terminate the pregnancy.

On November 5, 2003, George W. Bush signed the first federal ban on any abortion procedure in the 30 years since *Roe v. Wade*, and the first ban of a surgical technique in the history of this country.

"I'm pleased that all of you have joined us as the Partial-Birth Abortion Ban Act of 2003 becomes the law of the land," Bush said. After singling out 11 political supporters of the bill—all of them men—the president whipped the 400-strong, antiabortion crowd into a frenzy. "For years a terrible form of violence has been directed against children who are inches from birth, while the law looked the other way," he said to cheers and whoops and hollers.

The signing ceremony staged by the White House was part evangelical tent revival, part good ol' boy pep rally, ending with the audience muttering "Amen." The president stoked the crowd's moral indignation with emotional platitudes like "affirming a basic standard of humanity" and "compassion and the power of conscience" and "defending the life of the innocent."

But on that Wednesday afternoon, President Bush never addressed what, exactly, the ramifications of the bill would be. His administration portrayed it as a bill aimed solely at stopping a "gruesome and barbaric" procedure used by healthy mothers to kill healthy babies. That portrayal served to spark a national, emotional knee-jerk reaction, which precluded any understanding of the practical outcome of the legislation. But it was those very real practicalities that immediately prompted three lawsuits and got three federal courts to prevent the bill from actually becoming law, starting a fight that will probably drag on for years.

At the heart of the debate is a term that legislators concocted. They created a nonexistent procedure—partial-birth abortion—and then banned it. They then gave it such a purposely vague definition that, according to abortion providers as well as the Supreme Court, which ruled a similar law in Nebraska unconstitutional, it could apply to all abortions after the first trimester.

Though some proponents of the bill say that they merely want to ban a specific medical procedure—properly called intact dilation and extraction, which accounts for fewer than one-fifth of 1 percent of all abortions in this country, according to a 2000 survey by the Alan Guttmacher Institute—they never specifically called it that. Instead, the bill is written in such a way that the much more common procedure—dilation and evacuation, which accounts for 96 percent of second-trimester abortions, including my own—would also be banned.

Supporters of the ban have argued that this procedure is used on babies that are "inches from life." But in the bill, there is no mention of fetal viability (the point at which a fetus could live independently of its mother for a sustained period of time). Nor is there any mention of gestational age. Thus, the ban would cover terminations at any point during pregnancy. (In fact, *Roe v. Wade* already protects the rights of a fetus after the point of viability, which occurs sometime after the 24th week of gestation, in the third trimester of pregnancy. Massachusetts bans all abortions at and beyond the 24th week, except to protect the life or health of the mother. Indeed, according to the Massachusetts Department of Public Health, in 2001 there were only 24 abortions after the 24th week, out of a total of 26,293 abortions.) By not mentioning viability, critics say, this ban would overturn *Roe v. Wade*, which clearly states that women have the right to abortion before fetal viability.

So what does it all really mean? It means that all abortions after the first trimester could be outlawed. No matter if the fetus has severe birth defects, including those incompatible with life (many of which cannot be detected until well into the second trimester). No matter if the mother would be forced to have, for example, a kidney transplant or a hysterectomy if she continued with the pregnancy. (Legislators did not provide a health exception for the woman, arguing that it would provide too big a loophole.)

In the aftermath of the signing of the bill, its supporters spoke about having outlawed a medical procedure and protecting the nation's children. "We have just outlawed a procedure that is barbaric, that is brutal, that is offensive to our moral sensibilities," said Bill Frist, the Senate majority leader. Its opponents bemoaned an unconstitutional attack on legal rights. "This ban is yet another instance of the federal government inappropriately interfering in the private lives of Americans, dangerously undermining . . . the very foundation of a woman's right to privacy," said Gregory T. Nojeim, an associate director and chief legislative counsel for the American Civil Liberties Union.

But lost in the political slugfest have been the very real experiences of women—and their families—who face this heartbreaking decision every day.

I don't know what was worse, those three days leading up to the procedure (I have never called it an abortion) or every day since...

Walking around with a belly full of broken dreams, it felt like what I would imagine drowning feels like—flailing and suffocating and desperate. Semiconscious. Surrounded by our family, I found myself tortured by our decision, asking over and over, are we doing the right thing? That was the hardest part. Even though I finally understood that pregnancy wasn't a Gerber commercial, that bringing forth life was intimately wrapped up in death—what with miscarriage and stillbirth—this was actually a choice. Everyone said, of course it's the right thing to do—even my Catholic father and my Republican father-in-law, neither of whom was ever "pro-choice." Because suddenly, for them, it wasn't about religious doctrine or political platforms. It was personal—their son, their daughter, their grandchild. It was flesh and blood, as opposed to abstract ideology, and that changed everything.

I was surprised to find out that I would no longer be in the care of my obstetrician, the woman who had been my doctor throughout my pregnancy. It turned out that she dealt only with healthy pregnancies. Now that mine had gone horribly wrong, she set up an appointment for me with someone else, the only person who was willing to take care of me now. I felt like an outcast.

As we drove to his private office in Brookline that Monday, April 7, 2003, I couldn't shake the feeling that we were going to meet my executioner. I had never met this doctor, but I did look him up online. With thick, mad-scientistlike glasses, he looked scary. In person, though, he reminded me in both looks and manner of Dr. Larch in *The Cider House Rules*. He had the kindest, saddest eyes I had ever seen, and he sat with us for at least an hour, speaking to us with a heartfelt compassion and understanding that I had never encountered from any doctor before. His own eyes teared as Dave and I cried.

He explained the procedure to us, at least the parts we needed to understand. Unlike a simple first-trimester abortion, which can be completed in one quick office visit, a second-trimester termination is much more complicated, a two-day minimum process. He started it that day by inserting four laminaria sticks made of dried seaweed into my cervix. It was excruciating, and he apologized over and over as I cried out in pain. When I left the examining room, my mom and my husband were shocked—I was shaking and ghostly white. The pain lasted throughout the night as the sticks collected my body's fluids and expanded, dilating my cervix just like the beginning stages of labor.

The next morning, Dave and my mother took me to the hospital in Boston. I was petrified. I had never had any sort of surgery, and I fought the anesthesia—clinging to the final moments of being pregnant—as I lay in that stark white room. As I started to drift off, my doctor held one of my hands, and an older, female nurse held my other, whispering in my ear, "You're going to be OK, I've been here before, lean on your husband." It was my last memory. When I woke up, it was all over.

Dave had to return to work the next day. He didn't want to leave me, and he certainly didn't want to return to the furtive stares of his co-workers, all of whom knew that we had "lost the baby." I really don't know how he did it. My mother stayed with me at home for the next week, trying to glue my shattered pieces back together with grilled cheese sandwiches and chicken noodle soup. I had no control over my emotions. I felt like a freak in a world full of capable women having babies, and I couldn't stop whimpering: Why did my body betray me?

For months, I hid from the world, avoiding social outings and weddings. I just couldn't bear well-meaning friends saying, "I'm so sorry." So I quarantined myself, and would try to go about my day—but then, bam, heartbreak would come screaming out of the shadows, blindsiding me and leaving me crumpled on the floor of our house. It wasn't that I was questioning our decision. I knew we did it out of love, out of all the feeling in the world. But I still hated it. *Hated* it.

I wrote my doctor a long thank-you note on my good, wedding stationery. I thanked him for his compassion and his kindness. I wrote that it must be hard, what he does, but that I hoped he found consolation in the fact that he was helping vulnerable women in their most vulnerable of times. He keeps my note, along with all the others he's received, in a large bundle. And he keeps that bundle right next to his stack of hate mail. They are about the same size.

Because of the lawsuits, the Partial-Birth Abortion Ban Act of 2003 cannot be enforced, though it could be years before the abortion debate winds its way through the system and heads back to the Supreme Court. By that time, the composition of the court could be entirely different. "We are looking for a permanent restraining order," says Petra Langer, the director of public relations and government affairs for the Planned Parenthood League of Massachusetts. "Who knows what the long-term situation will be? If George Bush is reelected, all bets are off, unfortunately."

But even the short-term situation is bleak. The doctor who performed my termination has stopped doing the procedure, worried that he might get caught up in a lawsuit. He is not a lawyer or a politician, and he doesn't know what this law means for him right now. "I may go to jail for two years," he tells me. "They can suspend my medical license. It would cost me a fortune to have a lawyer to defend me."

The doctor who performed my termination talks about the women he has helped through the years—the pregnant woman who was diagnosed with metastic melanoma and needed immediate chemotherapy, the woman who was carrying conjoined twins that had only one set of lungs and one heart, the woman whose baby had a three-chambered heart and would never live. Now, he is turning these women away. "Now, today, I can say no, but what is she going to do?" he says sadly. "What is she going to do?"

In November 2003, Gretchen Voss, again pregnant, was told that the fetus she was carrying was perfectly healthy.

Sex, Lies, and Abstinence

JENNIFER BLOCK

***Conscience*, 4.25.03**

Last December, at the London offices of the sexual and reproductive rights organization International Family Health, employees found a festive musical email in their inboxes. Entitled "The 12 STDs of Christmas," the four-part harmony sing-along began: "On the first day of Christmas my true love gave to me/a bug that made it hard to pee." Stick figures danced at the bottom of the screen, displaying symptoms of each sexually transmitted infection. By the sixth day of Christmas, true love had brought with it "pubic lice, gonorrhea (five golden rings!), genital herpes, syphilis, chlamydia, and the possibility of HIV." Suffice it to say, the state of affairs had not improved by day 12.

"Don't play the sex lottery. Use a condom," was the message following the song, "Worried you've picked up something? Visit www.playingsafely.co.uk."

Who had cooked up this comic little e-card? None other than the UK's National Health Service. Well done, thought activists of their own government.

Meanwhile, across the pond, the US government's strategy for disease prevention was hardly in tune with the philosophy that has taken root around the world—and so masterfully expressed by the Brits: Give people accurate, comprehensive information and services, and they are more likely to stay healthy. Instead of finding similarly clever ways to disseminate such information to the American public, the Bush administration was actively trying to censor it.

The most blatant attack was the severe gutting of the Centers for Disease Control and Prevention's (CDC) fact sheet on condoms, which had disappeared from the website in July 2001 and been replaced, with significant battle scars in December 2002. Pre-Bush, the fact sheet had encouraged consistent condom use, advice supported by vast bodies of scientific research that show condoms to be 98–100 percent effective in preventing pregnancy and sexually transmitted infections, including HIV. "The primary reason that condoms sometimes fail," read the original fact sheet, "is incorrect or inconsistent use, not failure of the condoms itself." Following that statement was user-friendly guidance on proper use.

Now, according to the once nonpartisan CDC, abstinence is the "surest way to avoid transmission of sexually transmitted diseases." Along with the condom "how to," the CDC removed the "Programs that Work" section, which summarized several large studies of teenagers that found no increase or hastening of sexual activity among those who were taught about condoms.

Revising the CDC website is just one of the many ways the Bush administration has sought to distort and suppress scientific inquiry, not to mention sound public health policy, that contradicts its so-called family values.

"We've been monitoring a deeply unsettling trend where public health science is being supplanted by politics and ideology," says James Wagoner, president of Advocates for Youth, a proponent of comprehensive sexuality education. The Bush administration has stacked scientific advisory panels with ideologues who have scant credentials and conflicts of interest; flooded schools with medically inaccurate "abstinence-only" programs; punished HIV/AIDS prevention groups with audits; and gagged overseas healthcare workers who receive US funds, repeatedly exemplifying its willingness to let ideology trump the very pillars of democracy it claims to be defending.

This agenda is so ruthless that members of several domestic sexual and reproductive rights and health organizations speak of a pervasive "climate of fear" created by the Bush administration; a climate in which entities on various levels, from non-governmental HIV/AIDS prevention groups to high schools and even epidemiologists at the CDC, are being pressured to toe the party line.

"It's really remarkable," says Mariann Wang, an attorney at the American Civil Liberties Union. "They're really doing everything in their power, on every front, to keep people's mouths shut. And that goes from the top research scientists down to basic health care workers on the ground."

IGNORANCE UNTIL MARRIAGE

In middle and high schools across the country, teachers are being directed to adhere to the Federal Definition of Abstinence-Only Education, which requires that a program teach, among other things, that "a mutually faithful monogamous relationship in the context of marriage is the expected standard of human sexual activity" and that any other sexual activity "is likely to have harmful psychological and physical effects." By law, teachers cannot "promote or endorse" condoms or show adolescents how to use them, nor can they recognize any relationship outside of heterosexual marriage. Rebecca Schleifer, an HIV/AIDS researcher at Human Rights Watch, led a study of abstinence-only programs in Texas and calls them nothing less than "censorship."

A pamphlet distributed by the McLennan County (Texas) Collaborative Abstinence Project and obtained by Human Rights Watch cautions that "condoms have a 17 percent failure rate; that's 1 in 6." Another piece of McLennan literature reports that a "meticulous review of condom effectiveness" found that they "appear to reduce the risk of heterosexual transmission of HIV infection by only 69 percent" and that condoms break or slip as much as 25.5 percent of the time.

"We don't talk about contraception or condoms," a master teacher in Laredo, Texas, told Schleifer, "because that would be crossing the line that the state or federal guidelines have set. We don't mention the word 'condoms' at all." A curriculum director in Bell County expressed similar fear of losing federal funding: "We don't discuss condom use, except to say that condoms don't work." Schleifer found that when a sexually active student confronted a teacher, the response was often, "Well, that's something you did in the past; now you can renew your virginity."

"We call this programming," says Adrienne Verilli of the Sexuality Information and Education Council of the US (SIECUS), "Not only are they censoring information from young people, teachers feel that their jobs are in jeopardy if they say anything besides 'you should stop having sex.'"

Another facet of the McLennan program is television commercials. One shows a dad telling his son to use condoms followed by a voiceover warning, "Condoms will not protect people from many sexually transmitted diseases, and you could be spreading lies to your children." Schleifer spoke to counselors and teachers who heard from teens, including one who was an active intravenous drug user, who said they no longer bothered using condoms because they'd heard on TV they didn't work.

A total of $117 million will go toward abstinence-only programs like McLennan's in 2003, funding that every state but California has accepted, though 38 states—not Texas—still mandate that public schools also teach about HIV and other STDs.

PREVENTION UNDER FIRE

Abstinence-only as disease prevention doesn't stop in high school. All CDC-funded HIV/AIDS prevention spending is currently under review, and comprehensive programs are screeching in their tracks. For instance, an Advocates for Youth parent-child education curriculum, two years in the works for the CDC, was abruptly terminated last summer. "They gave no reason," says James Wagoner, who later heard a Department of Health and Human Services (HHS) spokesman tell National Public Radio that the project's videos were too graphic. "Young people used the correct terminology for male and female anatomy," he says. "It's absurd, what is the president going to do? Issue an executive order that henceforth every man, woman and child should refer to the penis as a dingaling?"

Advocates for Youth wasn't the only organization to feel the heat; Planned Parenthood and SIECUS were also fielding threats of audits—probably because all three launched the "No New Money" campaign (www.nonewmoney.org) which opposes the taxpayer cash flow toward abstinence-only programs. Sixteen HIV/AIDS prevention groups also came under scrutiny in what activists called a witch-hunt after some of them had signed onto a flyer protesting Tommy Thompson's speech at the XIV International Conference on AIDS in Barcelona in July 2002.

Even before Barcelona, however, the Stop AIDS project in San Francisco went through back-to-back federal audits after Mark Souder, a Republican representative from Indiana, accused the group of "promoting sex" and demanded an investigation.

"We spent the better part of 14 months responding to a series of federal inquiries," says Shana Krochmal of Stop AIDS, which not only took hundreds of staff hours, but a psychological toll as well. "This is a staff working with a community that continues to have a lot of reason to think that the government doesn't particularly care whether they live or die," says Krochmal. And as per a recent memo from HHS, Stop AIDS and other prevention groups must now post disclaimers on their website that warn the content "may not be appropriate for all audiences."

"Front line prevention providers are having to divert some of their energy into rearguard action against harassment by the federal public health apparatus," says Mark McLaurin, associate director for prevention policy at Gay Men's Health Crisis in New York. "And the truth of the matter is that the federal public health apparatus and prevention providers ought to be natural allies. We share the same goals. It doesn't make sense, if the CDC and this administration want to reach its stated goal of halving new infections by 2005."

There's new evidence that these tactics are spilling overseas as well to any foreign organization receiving USAID. A January 9, 2003, cable to local fund managers (based all over the world) regarding AIDS prevention emphasizes abstinence and directs that, "All operating units should review their own websites and any websites fully or partially funded by USAID to ensure the appropriateness of the material."

PRESIDENTIAL ADVISORY

Even the scientific community—a group that usually hovers above the political fray—began shoring up its own defenses as it came to light last fall that the Department of Health and Human Services was purging scientific advisory committees of scientists whose research might undermine the Bush administration's political goals, and replacing them with thinly credentialed ideologues, who, for instance, agree with raising permissible levels of lead in drinking water and oppose workplace ergonomic standards.

The Presidential Advisory Council on HIV/AIDS is another major battleground. Its co-chair, Tom Coburn, has accused the director of the CDC of "lying" about condom safety and asked that he be fired. These actions prompted scathing editorials in prestigious journals and sharp statements from groups like the American Public Health Association. According to the Federal Advisory Committee Act of 1972, committees must be "fairly balanced" and "not inappropriately influenced by the appointing authority." Donald Kennedy, editor of *Science,* referenced this law in rebuking the administration: "It would be a good idea for HHS Secretary Tommy Thompson and the White House Personnel Office to read the law, and then follow it."

Scientists were also incensed by the manipulation of the National Cancer Institute, which was prompted to revise its stance on a rumored link between abortion and breast cancer (a rumor that traces back to anti-choice groups). While the original web fact sheet maintained that there was no scientific evidence that abortion increases a woman's risk of breast cancer, the revised version called the available research "inconclusive." It took a weekend-long conference, convened in February 2003 with taxpayer dollars, to confirm, again, that there is no compelling evidence to support the anti-choice claims.

"There is a drive for ideology to be the guiding force in all sorts of programs," says Louise Melling, director of the American Civil Liberties Union Reproductive Freedom Project. "You see the government using its resources to prohibit dissemination of certain information and in some cases information that's needed to protect people's lives. You sort of want to pull out 1984."

GAGGED FROM DAY ONE

Bush's censorious activities seem to be gaining momentum, but the strategy was evident on his very first day in office, when he reinstated the "global gag rule" (or Mexico City Policy), which literally gags any foreign recipient of US family planning funds from so much as uttering the word "abortion," even where it is legal and even if they use their own funds to do so. The Center for Reproductive Rights (formerly the Center for Reproductive Law and Policy) is suing the Bush administration for violating the first amendment rights of its American attorneys working overseas and calls the policy "government sanctioned censorship—plain and simple."

"The gag rule is the most overt, blatant example of disregard for freedom of inquiry and scientific freedom," says Catholics for a Free Choice president Frances Kissling. "It is highly violative of common medical ethics." For example, a diabetic woman for whom a pregnancy could be life threatening would not be entitled to receive appropriate medical advice to abort. And on the macro level, the gag rule is "censorious and violative of national sovereignty," Kissling points out, because it actually prohibits health care workers from actively participating in the political process—they can't lobby, attend a rally, go on a march or sign a petition relating to abortion rights. "Here's an administration that wants to spread democracy around the world," says Kissling, "and they want to prevent people from participating in policy?"

"There's a very conservative element in the Department of Health and Human Services that is behind this whole movement," says Barbara Crane of Ipas, an international abortion rights group that turned down $2 million in US funds to protest the gag rule. "What we're seeing on the international side and coming on the domestic front is a tightening vice grip on programs, activities and speech that are involved in reproductive health in any way."

Bush tried to tighten that grip even more with his Emergency Plan for

AIDS Relief, a surprise announcement during his State of the Union speech that promised $15 billion in funds over the next five years. It took little time for activists to figure out that the package was a triumph of "Arthur Andersen-style accounting," as Africa Action director Salih Booker told the *Nation,* and by mid-February it looked like it was really just an excuse to extend the gag rule to HIV/AIDS money. At press time there was a bipartisan effort in Congress against that move, but its ultimate fate remained unclear.

Activists see the "family planning wars" as threatening 20 years of increasingly "client-centered," culturally sensitive care, effective public health policy, and tremendous gains in women's sexual and reproductive rights. And the cumulative effect is government-sponsored fear, intimidation, repression and regression. Shana Krochmal at Stop AIDS argues "We're back to fighting for the very basic ability to talk honestly and openly with people about their lives." Says James Wagoner: "It is unconscionable to promote ignorance in the age of AIDS, and yet that is what's happening."

Bush's War on the Condom: U.N. Report Documents the Failures to Curb AIDS

DOUG IRELAND

***LA Weekly,* 12.6.02**

The United Nations' latest report on AIDS, issued last week, underscores how the Bush administration's war on the condom has blocked HIV-prevention efforts around the world. A key finding: Nearly half of all new cases of HIV infection are women. But in May, at the U.N.'s Special Session on Children, Bush formed an unholy alliance with Iraq and Iran—you remember, two-thirds of the "axis of evil"—to successfully eliminate from the official declaration any references to the right of the world's children to "reproductive health services and education," including condoms for HIV prevention.

In sub-Saharan Africa, where teenage girls are treated as chattel and forced into sexual submission to older men—either by economic necessity or cultural tradition—the U.N. report notes that about 2 million of about 4.2 million new HIV infections are among females. Yet Bush threatened countries with trade and aid reprisals if they didn't toe the no-condoms, abstinence-only, anti-abortion line in the vote to weaken the U.N.'s commitment to providing life-saving information to those young women.

But that's only the tip of the iceberg. Countries like Cambodia have complained in public that U.S. policies preventing American foreign-aid dollars from being used to purchase, distribute and educate about condoms have crippled their HIV-prevention programs.

And, here at home, Bush—under the direction of political commissar Karl Rove—has been systematically placing HIV-prevention efforts into the hands of the Christian right—which is pushing the censorious line that abstinence before heterosexual marriage is the only permissible form of HIV-prevention education—and putting condom opponents in charge of AIDS education.

For example, Rove engineered the appointment of Oklahoma's Tom Coburn as co-chair of the Presidential Advisory Council on HIV and AIDS (PACHA). A former congressman and Baptist deacon, condom critic Coburn—a board member of the far-right Family Research Council—was considered the AIDS community's Enemy Number One in his years in the House. He earned this dishonor because this notorious homophobe, after having called safer sex a "lie," tried to have the head of the Centers for Disease Control (CDC) fired for advocating condom use to prevent AIDS; wrote unsuccessful legislation to replace anonymous HIV testing with mandatory reporting of the names of the HIV-infected (which AIDS educators say drives people away from being tested for the virus and forces the problem underground); and spurred intimidating investigations of nonprofit AIDS agencies.

For the position of PACHA's executive director, Rove picked Patricia Funderburk Ware, a former actress who has made a career out of promoting abstinence until marriage as the only acceptable guideline for sexual conduct. As the education head of Americans for a Sound AIDS Policy, a group funded by the Christian right, Ware not only lobbied against any efforts that promoted education and protection over abstinence but also against including HIV and AIDS in the Americans With Disabilities Act and its protections against discrimination. Moreover, Bush's appointees to the advisory council included no scientists and not a single person with HIV, while at the same time he stacked it with campaign contributors and Christian-right condom opponents—including Joe McIlhaney Jr., director of the Texas-based Medical Institute for Sexual Health, which provides condom-debunking information to abstinence educators across the country. McIlhaney, who was Bush's AIDS-prevention guru when Dubya was governor.

At the Department of Health and Human Services (HHS), Rove recruited conservative Claude Allen, a former top aide to Jesse Helms, to keep an eye on Secretary Tommy Thompson (who has an exaggerated reputation as a "moderate"). As Secretary of Health and Human Resources for right-wing Virginia Governor Jim Gilmore, Allen bent public-health priorities to the religious right's agenda and led a state-sponsored anti-safe-sex crusade he cooked up with the abstinence-only Institute for Youth Development, whose mission is to teach children to fear rather than understand sex. Allen says of condom use: "It's like telling your child, 'Don't use the car,' but then leaving the keys in the Lamborghini and saying, 'But if you do, buckle up.'" As deputy health secretary, Allen has been placed in charge of a censorious audit of AIDS groups designed to crack down on science-based safe-sex education.

Not only has Allen made explicit sex ed aimed at gay men his favorite target (despite soaring infection rates among under-25 gay males), but when Thompson was criticized by vociferous protests against Bush's AIDS betrayals during the secretary's speech at the international AIDS conference in Barcelona earlier this year, influential Indiana Representative Mark Souder—an evangelical Christian who says all gay sex is "immoral," and who chairs the House's oversight subcommittee on HHS—sparked a witch-hunt against a dozen respected AIDS service organizations (including San Francisco's Stop AIDS Project) because some of their members participated in the demonstration. Now being conducted by Allen, the HHS witch-hunting audit is designed to intimidate all of the 3,500 local AIDS service groups, which are dependent on federal funding for their existence, into staying silent on Bush's disastrous AIDS policies.

In October, a dozen congressmen led by L.A.'s Henry Waxman denounced the Bush administration's removal of medical information on condoms and sex from government Web sites, including those of the CDC and HHS. And Human Rights Watch recently issued a damning report on how Bush's pushing of abstinence-only has undermined prevention education about AIDS and other STDs.

While flat-lining domestic AIDS funding for the Ryan White Care Act and the AIDS Drug Assistance Program (which provides anti-AIDS drugs to the poor)—both of which are now facing crisis shortfalls in their budgets—Bush has added tens of millions to his 2003 budget for abstinence-only education, now up to $135 million. Rove's evil genius: The money is used as political patronage for religious-sponsored abstinence programs, particularly in the black and Latino communities—where new AIDS infections are soaring, and where churches are being enrolled to support Bush's 2004 re-election. (A coalition of 50 organizations—including the American Jewish Congress Commission for Women's Equality, chapters of Planned Parenthood, a United Church of

Christ ministry, the Unitarians and the National Abortion and Reproductive Rights Action League—has initiated a campaign to have Congress stop funding abstinence-only programs. Its Web site—*www.nonewmoney.org* —gives you a simple, clickable way to e-mail your Congress members.)

So, by politicizing AIDS education and prevention both globally and domestically, the Bush administration, in its macabre dance, is helping to push the numbers of new AIDS infections upward. Future generations will judge this for what it is: stomach-turning criminal negligence.

"Tell Me Everything": Teens Talk Back About Abstinence Education

MARY JO McCONAHAY

***Pacific News Service,* 7.23.03**

As abstinence-only sex education spreads to more schools nationwide, a "crew mom"—that's a soccer mom for kids who row—listens closely to teen-age car-seat chatter on sex, God and independence.

As a crew mom, I spend a lot of time listening to teenage girls in the car, and I can tell you the issue of abstinence-only sex education is not a big hit with the youngsters I transport.

They don't even have the programs in their own schools, but they're connected electronically to every corner of the country, and as teenagers of course, they have opinions on everything. They don't talk as we travel to or from the lake on days of pre-dawn practices—sleepy beforehand and cramming afterward on the way to school—but their chatter on afternoon practice days is constant.

"Maybe the abstinence part is a good idea," came a 15-year-old voice from the back seat one day. A smart kid, she rattled off the rate of increase of certain sexually transmitted diseases as other voices said "Yeah," or made other wise, assenting sounds. "I just don't want to be told it's about me and God."

Abstinence-only sex education is spreading through public schools much faster today than the older "comprehensive" kind because it is the only sex education being newly funded by federal dollars. Both types teach that abstinence is the only certain way to avoid pregnancy and an array of sexually transmitted diseases, from herpes to HIV/AIDS. But abstinence-only until (heterosexual) marriage programs, attached to 1996 welfare reform legislation by conservative Republicans, purposefully do not mention safer sex or contraceptives, forbidding not only arguably pertinent information, but ignoring the significant number of teenage kids who are sexually active. Theory: more information leads to more sex. And in these program materials, homosexual kids may as well not exist. Abstinence clubs for older kids at public, private and religious schools often are run by faith-based groups, and abstaining from sex is presented as good morality. President Bush has promised to fund the programs with at least $135 million a year; no increase for traditional sexuality education programs is in the works.

What is curious to me is that a couple of the girls who don't want their sex education to be about "me and God" are also vigorous in their religious faith. "Well it's supposed to be about education, right?" said one of them, not quite adding the implied, "Duh . . ."

For adults, abstinence-only programs are an issue at the nexus of sex, religion and politics. The programs unfold in a day when new legislation means taxpayer dollars may go freely and openly to faith-based groups, including those which discriminate in hiring on the basis of religion. They take place in a public school system whose chief, Education Secretary Ron Paige, recently had to scramble to insist he respects the separation of church and state, after telling the Baptist Press he would prefer, "all things being equal," to have a child in a school that teaches values "associated with the Christian communities."

The programs were championed early by then-governor Bush in Texas, the state that recently approved a law requiring doctors to warn women abortion could lead to breast cancer—a connection that doesn't exist, according to federal scientists and the American Cancer Society. And high school abstinence clubs nationwide openly, proudly groom their best and brightest to campaign against legal abortion.

But there are all kinds of teenagers in the country, and for most the issue is personal and immediate. An on-campus abstinence club supported by federal funds may be a godsend for girls pressured into having sex—often with older men—and for youngsters who are not virgins who want to change their lives, stay focused on school, and have the approval of peers who feel the same way. Sex education that emphasizes abstinence until marriage may give confidence and encouragement to adolescent boys and girls who hold those same beliefs, but feel pressured, too. However, if the salvation comes in a package that includes disrespect for homosexuals, teaches that only one set of values is morally correct for all, or that information leads to perdition, you're going to have trouble with members of one crew team I know.

"What gets me is they don't want to talk about certain things," I heard one girl venture. She is not usually the most talkative, has to struggle to keep up her times on the rowing machines but gives her all on the water. Her voice carried the kind of inevitable skepticism and rebellion that rule teenage years, that spell ultimate problems for any program that underestimates the savvy and integrity of kids. "I don't like it when people don't tell me everything—I want to know everything, then let me figure things out."

Why We Need Same-Sex Marriage

SEAN CAHILL, PH.D., DIRECTOR, POLICY INSTITUTE OF THE NATIONAL GAY AND LESBIAN TASK FORCE

Testimony to the United States Senate Judiciary Committee, 9.4.03

Editor's note: Since this testimony was presented, new legal ground has been broken in the area of gay marriage. The Massachusetts Supreme Judicial Court, in a dramatic 4–3 decision in February 2004, found no "constitutionally adequate reason" to deny marriage to same-sex couples, clearing the way for the nation's first legally sanctioned gay marriages. Pressing for similar change in California, the mayor of San Francisco ordered his county clerk to begin issuing same-sex marriage licenses, and some 4,000 lesbian and gay couples were wed at City Hall—before the state Supreme Court stopped the clerk's action in March 2004, pending a full legal review.

But no review has been deemed necessary in the Bush camp, where opposition to gay marriage is a given, especially in light of the president's religious convictions. While First Lady Laura Bush declared gay marriage to be a "very, very shocking issue" for some, the president took the more extreme step of calling for an amendment to the U.S. constitution explicitly banning gay marriage. For women, who have often been oppressed in traditional patriarchal marriages, Bush's call to preserve "the meaning of marriage" may have a chilling ring.

In May I attended the wedding mass of my friends Brendan Fay and Tom Moulton in Brooklyn, NY, officiated by two brave priests, one Catholic and the other Episcopal. Tom's mother and Brendan's sisters visiting from his native Ireland walked them down the aisle. Tom is a pediatric oncologist in the Bronx, Brendan a long-time human rights activist. They met seven years ago through the gay Catholic group Dignity, and own a small home in Queens. In July, Brendan and Tom went to Toronto and got legally married. Brendan just renewed his green card for a year. If the federal government would recognize their marriage, they would have peace of mind knowing that they would be able to stay in the U.S., and not have to leave Tom's native country to stay together. Binational gay couples occasionally have to move to a third country to stay together, as did Charles Zhang and Wayne Griffin, natives of China and New Hampshire, respectively. Fourteen countries, including South Africa and Israel, recognize same-sex couples for the purposes of immigration. The U.S. does not.[1]

Already hundreds of same-sex couples have gotten married since Ontario's highest court legalized gay marriage in June, and Canada's premier introduced legislation to legalize marriage throughout the country. British Columbia quickly followed suit, and Massachusetts' highest court will rule soon on the issue.

In reaction to these developments and the U.S. Supreme Court's landmark ruling striking down laws criminalizing homosexuality in *Lawrence v. Texas*, anti-gay activists are pushing the Federal Marriage Amendment to the U.S Constitution that would ban state or federal recognition of the marriages of same-sex couples, and would prevent courts from mandating equal benefits for gay couples at the level of state policy, as Vermont's highest court did in 1999. This comes seven years after Congress passed the Defense of Marriage Act banning federal recognition of same-sex marriages, and told states they were free to not recognize them as well.

HOW NONRECOGNITION HURTS GAY FAMILIES

The nonrecognition of same-sex marriages means gay couples do not have basic elements of family security. For example:

Lisa Stewart of South Carolina has terminal cancer. She worries what will happen to her 5-year-old daughter Emily if she dies. Will her ten-year partner Lynn be able to maintain custody in a state that is considering an anti-gay adoption ban? Being able to marry would ease Lisa and Lynn's minds, and protect the integrity of their family. How could anyone construe Lisa and Lynn's desire to maintain their family's security as a threat to other families?

Bill Randolph lost his partner of 26 years when the World Trade Center was attacked on September 11, 2001, but is not eligible for Social Security survivor benefits—benefits that would automatically be given to the surviving spouse in a heterosexual marriage.

Jeanne Newland left her job in Rochester N.Y. to go with her life partner, Natasha Doty, to Virginia where Doty had accepted a new job. Newland expected to find a job in short order, but after six months of trying unsuccessfully to find work, she applied for unemployment benefits—

benefits that would have been granted automatically if she had been married to her partner. New York state denied her claim, stating that following her partner was not a "good cause" to leave a job. This situation "just . . . didn't seem fair" to Newland.[2]

Bill Flanigan was prevented from visiting his life partner, Robert Daniel, when Daniel was dying in a Baltimore hospital in October 2000. Hospital personnel refused to acknowledge that Flanigan and Daniel were family. "Bill and Bobby were soulmates and one of the best couples I've known," said Grace Daniel, Robert's mother. When someone is dying, hospitals should be bringing families together rather than keeping them apart.[4]

The proposed Constitutional amendment wouldn't just ban civil marriage for same-sex couples; it would also prohibit conferring "marital status or the legal incidents thereof" on same-sex couples based on an interpretation of the federal constitution, state constitutions, or state or federal law. This could jeopardize hard-won domestic partner health benefits and registries, offered in nearly a dozen states and hundreds of municipalities, as well as by thousands of private employers. Civil unions, which afford most of the obligations, responsibilities and recognitions of marriage to Vermont gay couples at the level of state policy, could also be jeopardized. The proposed Federal Marriage Amendment would only embolden those who regularly legally challenge partner recognition and could deter state and local governments from offering domestic partner health insurance to their employees or registries for resident gay couples. States should be able to decide for themselves whether or not to offer domestic partnership, civil unions or civil marriage to same-sex couples.

THE PARTICULAR NEEDS OF LESBIAN AND GAY FAMILIES WITH CHILDREN

Some anti-gay activists claim that marriage is about procreation, that gay and lesbian couples don't have children, and therefore that they should be denied the right to marry. In fact, parenting is widespread among same-sex couples. According to the 2000 Census, same-sex partnered households were reported in 99.3 percent of all U.S. counties, and represented every ethnic, racial, income and adult age group.[3] While 72.4 percent of heads of household in reporting gay and lesbian couples were non-Hispanic white, 10.5 percent were black, 11.9 percent were Hispanic, 2.5 percent were Asian/Pacific Islander, 0.8 percent were American Indian, and 1.8 percent were multiracial.[4] This nearly corresponds to the ethnic makeup of the overall U.S. population.

Many same-sex couples are raising children. Thirty-four percent of lesbian couples and 22 percent of gay male couples[5] reporting on the 2000 Census have at least one child under 18 years of age living in their home.[6]

Many more are parents of children who do not live with them, or are "empty nesters." The 2000 Black Pride Survey, undertaken by the Policy Institute of the National Gay and Lesbian Task Force in collaboration with 10 Black Gay Pride organizations and five African American researchers, queried nearly 2,700 black gay, lesbian, bisexual and transgender people in nine cities. It found that almost 40 percent of black lesbians and bisexual women, 15 percent of black gay or bisexual men, and 15 percent of black transgender people reported having children. Twenty-five percent of black lesbians and 4 percent of black gay men reported that those children lived with them.[7]

While Americans are still split on the issue of same-sex marriage, an overwhelming majority does support equal access to the specific obligations, responsibilities and recognitions of marriage, all of which are threatened by the Federal Marriage Amendment. For example, most people feel that gays and lesbians should be entitled to inheritance rights (73 percent) and Social Security survivor benefits (68 percent). The U.S. public supports "legally sanctioned partnerships and unions" for gay couples by a plurality of 47 to 42 percent, according to one 2001 poll.[8] The public is evenly divided on civil unions, with 49 percent supportive and 49 percent opposed.[9] According to a 2001 poll, nearly 40 percent of the public supports the freedom of same-sex couples to marry.[10] Moreover, public support for equal marriage rights is growing rapidly: polls conducted in the last several months, for example, show that majorities in Massachusetts (50–44 percent), New Hampshire (54–42 percent) and New Jersey (55–41 percent) support same-sex marriage.[11] Similarly, 58 percent of college freshmen support the freedom to marry for same-sex couples, according to a 2001–2002 survey.[12]

We are hopeful that, with time and public education, a majority of Americans will understand and support equal treatment of same-sex couple families. However, the rights of members of a stigmatized minority should not be determined by the prejudices of the majority. James Madison warned that majority rule, unchecked, can lapse into majority tyranny.[13] Our system of representative government, separation of powers, checks and balances, and the Bill of Rights was designed to prevent against majority tyranny over unpopular minority groups.[14] We urge Congress to reject the Federal Marriage Amendment, which would enshrine discrimination in our country's most sacred founding document.

The U.S. Supreme Court just ruled that the state cannot single out gay people for harassment and discriminatory treatment. Justice Kennedy, writing for the majority in *Lawrence v. Texas*, spoke of "respect" for gay couples and warned that "the state cannot demean their existence . . . " These are important, basic principles of fairness.

The U.S. Constitution has traditionally been amended to clarify or expand rights, not to single out a group of people to deny them the protections of the Constitution and the Bill of Rights. This anti-gay marriage amendment would set a disturbing precedent and is not in the best tradition of American justice.

REAL PEOPLE, REAL FAMILIES

Marriage rights for gay couples are no longer an abstract hypothetical. Hundreds of gay and lesbian couples have married in Canada, and they are *married*. The American people have a choice in how they are going to treat these hopeful newlyweds. They can treat them with respect, dignity and fairness, or they can discriminate against them. We trust that most Americans will do the right thing. We know that many Americans are wrestling with this issue, and ask them to approach it with an open mind. We urge Congress to reject the Federal Marriage Amendment, which represents the divisive politics of the past, and to reject this political attack on gay and lesbian families.

NOTES

1. Cahill, S., Ellen, M., and Tobias, S. (2002). *Family Policy: Issues Affecting Gay, Lesbian, Bisexual and Transgender Families*. New York: Policy Institute of the National Gay and Lesbian Task Force. 54–56.
2. Rostow, Ann. (2002, Jan. 24). "Lesbian Sues State for Unemployment Benefits." *Gay.com / PlanetOut.com Network*. Available at http://www.gay.com/news/article.html?2002/01/24/2.
3. Bradford, J., Barrett, K., and Honnold, J., A. (2002). *The 2000 Census and Same-Sex Households: A User's Guide*. New York: National Gay and Lesbian Task Force Policy Institute. Available at http://www.ngltf.org/ pi/census.htm.
4. These data were gathered using Table PCT22 of the U.S. Census' American Factfinder, available at http://factfinder.census.gov. For information on how to access these data through the U.S. Census, see Bradford, J., Barrett, K., and Honnold, J., A. (2002). *The 2000 Census and Same-Sex Households: A User's Guide*. New York: National Gay and Lesbian Task Force Policy Institute. Available at http://www.ngltf.org/pi/ census.htm.
5. Some individuals in these couples would not identify as gay or lesbian, but by some other term for homosexual. Others would identify as bisexual. Still others would not want to be categorized. But the critical point is that these individuals are in an amorous, long-term, committed, partnered same-sex relationship widely viewed as a "gay or lesbian" relationship.
6. U.S. Census Bureau (2003). *Married-Couple and Unmarried-Partner Households: 2000*. http://www.census.gov/prod/2003pubs/censr-5.pdf
7. Battle, J., Cohen, C., Warren, D., Fergerson, G. and Audam, S. (2002). *Say It Loud: I'm Black and I'm Proud; Black Pride Survey 2000*. New York: National Gay and Lesbian Task Force Policy Institute. p. 14.
8. Kaiser (Henry J.) Family Foundation (2001). *Inside-OUT: A Report on the Experiences of Lesbians, Gays and Bisexuals in America and the Public's Views on Issues and*

Policies Related to Sexual Orientation. Cambridge: Author. Available at http://www.kff.org/content/2001/3193/LGBSurveyReport.pdf.; Rohter, L. (2000, June 10).

9. Newport, Frank (2003, May 15). "Six out of 10 Americans Say Homosexual Relations Should Be Recognized as Legal; But Americans are evenly divided on issue of legal civil unions between homosexuals giving them the legal rights of married couples." Gallup News Service.

10. Kaiser Family Foundation (2001).

11. Phillips, Frank (2003, April 8). "Support for gay marriage; Mass. poll finds half in favor." *Boston Globe*; Associated Press (2003, May 23). "Poll: New Hampshire residents favoring law for same-sex marriages"; Zogby International Poll, July 15–19, 2003.

12. "2001-2 Freshmen Survey: Their Opinions, Activities, and Goals." (2002, February 1.) *The Chronicle of Higher Education*. p. A37. Available at http://chronicle.com/free/v48/i21/opinions.htm.

13. Madison, J. (1987). Federalist 10. *The Federalist Papers.* New York: Penguin Classics.

14. Madison. Federalist 51.

WORLD

Globalization and Poverty: Economic Globalization Has Become a War Against Nature and the Poor

VANDANA SHIVA

Resurgence, **Issue 202, 9.10.00**

Who feeds the world? My answer is very different from that given by most people.

It is women and small farmers working with biodiversity who are the primary food providers in the Third World and, contrary to the dominant assumption, their biodiversity-based small farm systems are more productive than industrial monocultures.

The rich diversity and sustainable systems of food production have been destroyed in the name of increasing food production. However, with the destruction of diversity, rich sources of nutrition disappear. When measured in terms of nutrition per acre, and from the perspective of biodiversity, the so-called high yields of industrial agriculture do not imply more production of food and nutrition.

Yield usually refers to production per unit area of a single crop. Output refers to the total production of diverse crops and products. Planting only one crop in the entire field as a monoculture will, of course, increase its individual yield. Planting multiple crops in a mixture will have low yields of individual crops, but will have high total output of food. Yields have been defined in such a way as to make the food production on small farms, by small farmers, disappear.

This hides the production by millions of women farmers in the Third World—farmers like those in my native Himalaya who fought against logging in the Chipko movement, who in their terraced fields grow Jhangora (barnyard millet), Marsha (amaranth), Tur (pigeon pea), Urad (black gram), Gahat (horse gram), soy bean (glycine max), Bhat (glycine soya), Rayans (rice bean), Swanta (cow pea), Koda (finger millet). From this perspective, biodiversity-based productivity is higher than monoculture productivity. I call this blindness to the high productivity of diversity a "Monoculture of the Mind", which creates monocultures in our fields.

In Java, small farmers cultivate 607 species in their home gardens.

In sub-Saharan Africa, women cultivate as many as 120 different plants in the spaces left alongside the cash crops, and this is the main source of household food security.

Research done by FAO (the U.N.'s Food and Agriculture Organization) has shown that small biodiverse farms can produce thousands of times more food than large, industrial monocultures.

And diversity is the best strategy for preventing drought and desertification.

What the world needs to feed a growing population sustainably is biodiversity intensification, not chemical intensification or genetic engineering. While women and small peasants feed the world through biodiversity, we are repeatedly told that without genetic engineering and globalization of agriculture the world will starve. In spite of all empirical evidence showing that genetic engineering does not produce more food and in fact often leads to a yield decline, it is constantly promoted as the only alternative available for feeding the hungry.

That is why I ask: Who feeds the world?

This deliberate blindness to diversity, the blindness to nature's production, production by women, production by Third World farmers, allows destruction and appropriation to be projected as creation.

Take the case of the much-flaunted "golden rice" or genetically engineered vitamin A rice as a cure for blindness. It is assumed that without genetic engineering we cannot remove vitamin A deficiency. However, nature gives us abundant and diverse sources of vitamin A. If rice were not polished, rice itself would provide vitamin A. If herbicides were not sprayed on our wheat fields, we would have bathua, amaranth, mustard leaves as delicious and nutritious greens.

Women in Bengal use more than 150 plants as greens. But the myth of creation presents biotechnologists as the creators of vitamin A, negating nature's diverse gifts and women's knowledge of how to use this diversity to feed their children and families.

The most efficient means of rendering the destruction of nature, local economies and small autonomous producers is by rendering their production invisible.

Women who produce for their families and communities are treated as "non-productive" and "economically inactive." And women themselves are devalued, because for many women in the rural and indigenous communities their work co-operates with nature's processes, and is often contradictory to dominant market-driven "development" and trade policies, and because work that satisfies needs and ensures sustenance is devalued in general. Everywhere, food production is becoming a negative economy, with farmers spending more buying costly inputs for industrial production than the price they receive for their produce. The consequence is rising debts and epidemics of suicides in both rich and poor countries, such as the recent farmers' suicides in Punjab and Andhra Pradesh.

Economic globalization is leading to a concentration of the seed industry, the increased use of pesticides, and, finally, increased debt. Capital-intensive, corporate-controlled agriculture is being spread into regions where peasants are poor but, until now, have been self-sufficient in food. In the regions where industrial agriculture has been introduced through globalization, higher costs are making it virtually impossible for small farmers to survive.

The globalization of non-sustainable industrial agriculture is evaporating the incomes of Third World farmers through a combination of devaluation of currencies, increase in costs of production and a collapse in commodity prices.

Farmers everywhere are being paid a fraction of what they received for the same commodity a decade ago. In the US, wheat prices dropped from $5.75 to $2.43, soya bean prices dropped from $8.40 to $4.29, and corn prices dropped from $4.43 to $1.72 a bushel. In India, from 1999 to 2000, prices for coffee dropped from Rs.60 to Rs.18 per kg and prices of oilseeds declined by more than 30 percent.

The Canadian National Farmers' Union put it like this in a report to the senate this year:

> While the farmers growing cereal grains—wheat, oats, corn—earn negative returns and are pushed close to bankruptcy, the companies that make breakfast cereals reap huge profits. In 1998, cereal companies Kellogg's, Quaker Oats and General Mills enjoyed return on equity rates of 56%, 165% and 222% respectively. While a bushel of corn sold for less than $4, a bushel of corn flakes sold for $133. In 1998, the cereal companies were 186 to 740 times more profitable than the farms. Maybe farmers are making too little because others are taking too much.

And a World Bank report has admitted that "behind the polarization of domestic consumer prices and world prices is the presence of large trading companies in international commodity markets."

While farmers earn less, consumers, especially in poor countries, pay more. In India, food prices have doubled between 1999 and 2000, and consumption of food grains has dropped by 12 percent in rural areas, increasing the food deprivation of those already malnourished, pushing up mortality rates. Increased economic growth through global commerce is based on pseudo surpluses. More food is being traded while the poor are consuming less. When growth increases poverty, when real production becomes a negative economy, and speculators are defined as "wealth creators," something has gone wrong with the concepts and categories of wealth and wealth creation.

Women—as I have said—are the primary food producers and food processors in the world. However, their work in production and processing has now become invisible.

According to the McKinsey corporation, "American food giants recognize that Indian agro-business has lots of room to grow, especially in food processing. India processes a minuscule 1 percent of the food it grows compared with 70 percent for the US, Brazil and Philippines." It is not that we Indians eat our food raw. Global consultants fail to see the 99 percent of food processing done by women at household level, or by small cottage industry, because it is not controlled by global agribusiness. Ninety-nine percent of India's agroprocessing has been intentionally kept at the household level. Now, under the pressure of globalization, things are changing. Pseudo hygiene laws that shut down the food economy based on small-scale local processing under community control are part of the arsenal of global agribusiness for establishing market monopolies through force and coercion, not competition.

In August 1998, small-scale local processing of edible oil was banned in India through a "packaging order" which made sale of open oil illegal and required all oil to be packed in plastic or aluminum. This shut down tiny "ghanis" or cold-pressed mills. It destroyed the market for our diverse oilseeds—mustard, linseed, sesame, groundnut and coconut.

The take-over of the edible oil industry has affected 10 million livelihoods. The take-over of "atta," or flour, by packaged branded flour will cost 100 million livelihoods. These millions are being pushed into new poverty.

The forced use of packaging will increase the environmental burden of millions of tons of plastic and aluminum. The globalization of the food system is destroying the diversity of local food cultures and local food economies. A global monoculture is being forced on people by defining everything that is fresh, local and handmade as a health hazard. These are not recipes for feeding the world, but for stealing livelihoods from the poor to create markets for the powerful.

Recently, because of a World Trade Organization (WTO) ruling, India was forced to remove restrictions on all imports. Among the unrestricted imports are carcasses and animal waste parts that create a threat to our culture and introduce public health hazards such as mad cow disease.

The US Center for Disease and Prevention (CDS) in Atlanta has calculated that nearly 81 million cases of food-borne illnesses occur in the US every year. Deaths from food poisoning have more than quadrupled due to deregulation, rising from 2,000 in 1984 to 9,000 in 1994. Most of these infections are caused by factory-farmed meat. Now the giant meat industry of the US wants to dump contaminated meat produced through violent and cruel methods on India.

The waste of the rich is being dumped on the poor. The wealth of the poor is being violently appropriated through new and clever means like patents on biodiversity and indigenous knowledge.

Patents and intellectual property rights are supposed to be granted for novel inventions. But patents are being claimed for rice varieties such as the basmati for which the Doon Valley—where I was born— is famous, or pesticides derived from the neem which our mothers and grandmothers have been using. Rice Tec, a US-based company, has been granted Patent No. 5,663,484 for basmati rice lines and grains. Basmati, neem, pepper, bitter gourd, turmeric . . . every aspect of the innovation embodied in our indigenous food and medicinal systems is now being pirated and patented. The knowledge of the poor is being converted into the property of global corporations, creating a situation where the poor will have to pay for the seeds and medicines they have evolved and have used to meet their needs for nutrition and health care.

Such false claims to creation are now the global norm, with the Trade Related Intellectual Property Rights Agreement of the WTO forcing countries to introduce regimes that allow patenting of life forms and indigenous knowledge.

Instead of recognizing that commercial interests build on nature and on the contribution of other cultures, global law has enshrined the patriarchal myth of creation to create new property rights to life forms just as colonialism used the myth of discovery as the basis of the take-over of the land of others as colonies.

Humans do not create life when they manipulate it. Rice Tec's claim that it has made "an instant invention of a novel rice line" denies the creativity of nature, the self-organizational capacity of life forms, and the prior innovation of Third World communities.

When patents are granted for seeds and plants, as in the case of basmati, theft is defined as creation, and saving and sharing seed is defined as theft of intellectual property. Corporations which have broad patents on crops such as cotton, soya bean and mustard are suing farmers for seed-saving and hiring detective agencies to find out if farmers have saved seed or shared it with neighbours.

The recent announcement that Monsanto is giving away the rice genome for free is misleading: Monsanto has not made a commitment to stop patenting rice varieties or other crops.

Sharing and exchange, the basis of our humanity and our ecological survival, have been redefined as a crime. This makes us all poor. Nature has given us abundance. Women's indigenous knowledge of biodiversity, agriculture and nutrition has built on that abundance to create more from less, to create growth through sharing. The poor are pushed into deeper poverty by being made to pay for what were their resources and knowledge. Even the rich are poorer because their profits are based on theft and on the use of coercion and violence. This is not wealth creation but plunder.

Sustainability requires the protection of all species and all people and the recognition that diverse species and diverse people play an essential role in maintaining ecosystems and ecological processes. Pollinators are critical to the fertilization and generation of plants. Biodiversity in fields provides vegetables, fodder, medicine and protection to the soil from water and wind erosion.

As humans travel further down the road to non-sustainability, they become intolerant of other species and blind to their vital role in our survival.

We need urgently to bring the planet and people back into the picture. The world can be fed only by feeding all beings that make the world. In giving food to other beings and species we maintain conditions for our own food security. In feeding the earthworms we feed ourselves. In feeding cows, we feed the soil, and in providing food for the soil, we provide food for humans. This world-view of abundance is based on sharing and on a deep awareness of humans as members of the earth family. This awareness that in impoverishing other beings, we impoverish ourselves and in nourishing other beings, we nourish ourselves is the basis of sustainability.

The sustainability challenge for the new millennium is whether global economic man can move out of the world-view based on fear and scarcity, monocultures and monopolies, appropriation and dispossession and shift to a view based on abundance and sharing, diversity and decentralization, and respect and dignity for all beings.

Sustainability demands that we move out of the economic trap that is leaving no space for other species and most humans. Economic globalization has become a war against nature and the poor. But the rules of globalization are not god-given. They can be changed. We must bring this war to an end.

Since the 1999 protests in Seattle against the WTO, a frequently used phrase has been the need for a rule-based system. Globalization is the rule of commerce and it has elevated Wall Street to be the only source of value, and as a result things that should have high worth—nature, culture, the future—are being devalued and destroyed. The rules of globalization are undermining the rules of justice and sustainability, of compassion and sharing. We have to move from market totalitarianism to an earth democracy.

We can survive as a species only if we live by the rules of the biosphere. The biosphere has enough for everyone's needs if the global economy respects the limits set by sustainability and justice.

As Gandhi reminded us, "The Earth has enough for everyone's needs, but not for some people's greed."

Kitchen Table Politics: An Interview with Rhonda Perry

LAURA FLANDERS

1.16.04

Editor's note: Rhonda Perry is program director of the Missouri Rural Crisis Center, a grassroots organization of 5,500 farm and rural families struggling to confront the powerful global agribusiness interests that threaten the social, economic, and environmental fabric of rural America.

WHAT DOES US AGRICULTURAL POLICY AT THE MOMENT MEAN FOR WOMEN?

The impacts on women of both US agricultural policy and trade policy are obviously in some ways different in the US and in developing countries. The effects of agricultural policy in the US are such that you increasingly see women being compelled to take off-farm jobs, working multiple jobs even as they continue to work on the farm. This is a significant change, and it creates an incredible degree of stress: women go from being engaged landowners and decision-makers to being paid employees for somebody else.

HOW ARE WOMEN TREATED IN THE BIG AGRICULTURE COMPANIES?

Whether they accept work in the big agriculture companies or whether they go to work for Casey's convenience store in their town, or Wal-Mart, or a number of other relatively low-paying jobs, the changes they typically face are twofold. One, it's much-needed money, so you would think that this would be a good change. But secondly, to go from being a business-owner and a decision-maker to somebody who simply works for a paycheck at a very low level is a substantial setback. Women tend to take off-farm jobs in a farm crisis because they are typically the first to see that the ship is going down and that they may have to physically do something about it. And it tends to create some real tension in families: the man ends up running what was originally a joint farm partnership, and the woman has to hold down these multiple off-farm jobs. On the whole, it hasn't been positive for families or for women.

SO, WHEN PEOPLE DO NOT TAKE OFF-FARM JOBS, BUT THEIR FARM OR PRODUCT BECOMES INTEGRATED INTO A BIGGER, AGRIBUSINESS OPERATION, IS THERE AN EFFECT ON WOMEN IN THOSE SITUATIONS? OR DOES THAT NOT HAPPEN VERY OFTEN?

I think there are effects on women, although typically it doesn't happen a lot. Obviously it has happened in industries like poultry, and if you look at the leadership of organizations which represent those types of producers, like Contract Poultry Growers, they tend to be women—again, taking a leadership role when things get bad, saying "we've got to take a stand."

Generally I think these trade policies are not good for women, two-fold. One general reason is that women obviously have to deal with the basic systemic discrimination of getting paid less money no matter what industry they're in, and it also seems that the more powerless you are, the further you are away from being a beneficiary of these policies. So women in that respect generally are not going to be the beneficiaries.

Then there are some real similarities and differences between the impacts on women in the US and women in developing countries. In the US, as I said, women tend to take off-farm jobs that are non-union and minimum wage, at multinational corporations like Wal-Mart. In developing countries, in places like Africa, women are doing by far the majority of farm work for domestic agriculture. Whenever we have these trade agreements and people in these countries start producing for an export market rather than for a domestic market, the farm work on these export market crops is much more labor intensive. And so in these countries, as in the US, you once again see women who were previously running domestic farming operations for the domestic economy—making the decisions and doing the planting—now serving as basic farm-workers for an export market crop. So in both worlds these policies have lead to real setbacks in terms of women's roles in agriculture.

ON THE OTHER SIDE OF IT, IN TERMS OF THE WEALTHY, ARE THERE ANY WOMEN IN THE LEADERSHIP OF ANY OF THE HUGE AGRIBUSINESS COMPANIES, WHO ARE AMONG THE PEOPLE WHO HAVE BENEFITTED FROM ALL THIS?

Good question! I think women tend to play key roles in organizations and agencies which act as the political arm of these big corporations, helping them to get the very policies that they want. But while I'm sure there are *some* women who are major beneficiaries of these trade policies, because they're among the leadership of large agribusiness corporations, I can't say I know of any right now!

In the communities where you work, what kinds of changes are you seeing, looking back over the last three or four years, in the kinds of choices women have about the food that they eat, the work that they do and how their families are structured?

There have been some real changes in the last few years. A fairly dramatic change has been in the massive consolidation of supermarkets in low-income rural communities, resulting in an erosion of food choices. You now see farmers in many of those communities with only one place to sell their produce. Consumers in those areas are likewise left with just one supermarket to go to, with no competition, and much less access to healthy, good quality, affordable food. These are also areas that are not primary targets of niche marketing or local food, and so you have this large arena right out there in the heartland, whose economic base is agriculture, family farmers and food production, who are left with the dregs of the food market! And so this has really been a significant change. Even though people say "Consolidation has been going on for a long time," for most towns this has not meant, until now, that there is only one grocery store.

Finally, on the up-side, in terms of the organic and niche marketing that you mentioned, are women getting a piece of that pie, or is it a fairly elite, male-dominated arena?

It's both. I think there are two aspects to the niche marketing effort. Firstly, there's the "I just want more for me" niche marketing—and in some ways it's still a great thing, because it's providing better quality, locally or organically raised foods. However these efforts tend to be coming from people who just want to sell their produce to people who have a lot of money, and so they do not address the structure at all. And quite frankly, they tend to be men, not because they're bad or evil-hearted, but because in many cases they're moving into this kind of marketing simply because they can't make a living otherwise. The women have off-farm jobs already, so they're not the ones doing the direct marketing. But on the flip-side, in the same local food arena, there is a growing sense of the importance of community food security, and the niche-marketing efforts that are being driven by this understanding are somewhat different. They tend to recognize not only the need for a niche market, but also the need to bolster the whole community's access to affordable, good-quality, locally raised food. And it is women farmers who are primarily leading many of these efforts. In that respect, things are really looking better than they have in a long time.

I've always been extremely frustrated with organic, local niche marketing efforts that show an insensitivity or disregard for justice. The attitude is so often: "We just want to be a bunch of mini-capitalists, we just want to get ahead!" We've been saying for years, that's not going to get you very far, because anything that you can do and get paid a lot of money for, some corporation or so called "co-operative" can co-opt. We have to constantly differentiate ourselves, and maybe the way to do that is based on community and collective organization, as opposed to individual marketplace power—because none of us in these communities will ever have very much of that.

THANK YOU, RHONDA!

Global Sex Rules: The Price of Silence

MICHELE KORT

Ms., 8.03

They say the aim is to prevent abortions worldwide. But the impact of U.S. policy has produced something quite different in reality. Opportunistic, ideological and driven with a ferocity that is the hallmark of political extremism, a group of U.S. politicians is imposing health care standards on millions of women, rules that defy both common sense and fundamental notions of freedom. By silencing international family-planning providers, cutting off U.S. funds for the United Nations Fund for Population Activities (UNFPA) and hiring anti-choice ideologues to make women's health decisions, these politicians have put lives at risk. The case is clear: Women have died as a result.

Dr. Solomon Orero winces at the thought.

That's why he risks his distinguished career—and subjects himself to a possible 14-year prison term—in order to provide safe abortions in Kenya, where abortion is illegal.

"When I was in medical school," says the ob-gyn, "I saw so many women dying [from botched, unsafe abortions]. Some were my relatives, some were students: women in the prime of their lives. Occasionally they just died in my hands. I promised myself I would try to turn the tables."

Dr. Orero, a man who radiates compassion, is a hero to many women in his country. Although women with means can obtain illegal hygienic abortions in this African nation, poor women rely on crude methods: They ingest dubious concoctions or allow anything from bicycle spokes to sticks to be inserted in their uteruses. Orero has had to retrieve such things from his patients' bodies. He's had to reconstruct a woman's abdomen severely damaged by a botched abortion. And he's had to create a permanent colostomy for an 18-year-old after her untrained abortionist mistook her anus for her vagina.

"When a woman has an unwanted pregnancy, she'll go to any lengths [to end it]," he explains, with a mixture of anger and sadness. In Kenya, most women seeking abortions have already given birth to several children and simply can't afford another. In fact, too many pregnancies too closely spaced threaten the health and survival of both mothers and children. Also, for unwed women, pregnancy is stigmatized—they get thrown out of school, thrown out of their homes. Not surprisingly, for women as well as men in the developing world and Eastern Europe, birth control is either unaffordable or in short supply. One can't simply walk into a 7–11 and buy condoms. In addition, women don't often have a voice in sexual matters.

"Women are dying because we don't care enough for their lives," insists Orero. Furthermore, when a poor woman dies in a country such as Kenya, the children she leaves behind without her care and financial support may die as well. Considering that the average birth rate in Kenya is nearly five children per woman, one mother's death looms as a disproportionately large loss.

Orero is particularly concerned these days because of the Bush administration's escalating global war against reproductive rights. In his second day in office, the president fired the first salvo by reinstating the Mexico City Policy, more commonly known as the global gag rule. Established during the Reagan administration, it prohibits non-governmental organizations (NGOs) that receive U.S. Agency for International Development (USAID) monies to even mention abortion to clients (with some exceptions)—*even* if the NGOs aren't using U.S. funds for abortion services or advocacy. That's one step beyond the 1973 Helms Amendment, which outlawed U.S. funding for abortions overseas. The gag rule prevents family-planning clinics from steering clients toward safe abortion providers. But not only that, it stifles advocacy of abortion law reform in countries where the procedure remains illegal. In other words, while the United States loudly celebrates "democratic ideals," the First Amendment can't get a passport to travel.

USAID has been the key supporter of foreign family-planning clinics for the past half-century, currently supplying $446 million annually. So most insidiously, the gag rule on USAID has a chilling effect not just on overseas abortion rights but on all women's reproductive-health services. Sign the gag, lose your ability to provide integrated health care. Don't sign the gag, lose your financial ability to do so. Besides, as the American

College of Obstetricians and Gynecologists puts it, the restrictions "violate basic medical ethics by jeopardizing a health care provider's ability to recommend appropriate medical care."

MAKING WOMEN SUFFER

During the Reagan and first Bush administrations, international family-planning providers learned creative ways around the gag rule. Among other strategies, doctors waited "downstream" for women to induce abortions, then would treat them. When Bill Clinton took office he immediately removed the gag, providing a more "comfortable" environment for women's health services, according to Orero. "But now the rule is back with specific clauses," he says. "It's tougher."

Clinics that don't sign the gag rule often have to cut staff severely or close their doors. After they refused to be gagged, the Family Planning Association of Kenya cut its outreach program in half, shut three clinics and raised fees at other clinics. Marie Stopes International (MSI), a British NGO that offers reproductive-health services in 38 countries, had to cut 80 jobs in Kenya, close two clinics and scale back its rural outreach program.

"The gag rule has let Kenya down," MSI's Kenya Program Director Cyprian Awiti told the Fredericksburg, Va., *Free Lance-Star*: "The gag rule has made women suffer. The gag rule has made more women die, because they can't access safe family planning."

Of course, U.S. policies aren't affecting just Kenya and sub-Saharan Africa. In Nepal, for example, several family-planning clinics funded by UNFPA have closed, and the country's Family Planning Association has laid off more than 80 staff members. Yet the renewal of the gag rule comes at a time when the country has liberalized its very restrictive abortion laws. Now if a pregnant woman's life is at stake—a decision made by her doctor—she can legally get an abortion. That's a far cry from the early 1990s when dozens of Nepalese women were imprisoned after having had abortions. In one case, a 14-year-old girl was given a 14-year jail term for abortion and infanticide after undergoing an abortion procedure at seven months and then delivering a stillborn. The reason for her desperate abortion attempt: She'd been raped by her stepbrother.

"The closure of these family-planning clinics means that more women's lives are at risk," says Nepalese-born Pradeepta Upadhyay, an activist for South Asian women's health who championed the 14-year-old's case (she served four years). "Even though the [legalization] bill has been passed, the same affordable health care won't be there."

And she emphasizes, "Any policy made in America has a huge effect on the lives of women and men in developing countries."

"What makes this so tragic is that in our country, where we talk about getting contraceptives, condoms and abortion information as *rights*, it's impossible to understand a woman who has no *access* to services," says Amy Coen, president of Population Acton International (PAI) in Washington, D.C. "Pregnancy [elsewhere] can mean life or death, or can have severe physical complications."

In Latin America, despite being illegal, abortions tend to be safer than in sub-Saharan Africa. Still, the gag rule will force clinic closures simply because providers find it unconscionable to comply, causing them to lose U.S. funding for other services. The irony is hard to miss: The Bush administration ostensibly wants to stop abortions, yet its policies limit contraception—which could lower the number of abortions. A misguided political policy, in other words, is in fact producing *more* abortions. It's not surprising that the U.S. government's new advisors on international family planning include people who, like former Vatican envoy John Klink, consider many contraceptive devices and medications to be "abortifacients."

STIFLING THE U.N.

In its zeal to limit a woman's right to the full range of reproductive choices, the Bush administration hasn't stopped with a global gag.

In July 2002, Bush used the Kemp-Kasten Amendment—which prohibits U.S. funds from supporting organizations engaged in coercive reproductive-health practices—to withhold $34 million in already appropriated funds for UNFPA. The rationale? Despite findings to the contrary from three international monitoring teams, including a State Department group, the president agreed with allegations that UNFPA supports coercive abortions in China. That country's population-limiting policies have been used since the mid-1980s as a red herring to hamstring international aid for contraception.

This time, Bush pointed as evidence to a report from a small right-wing group called Population Research International (PRI), a spin-off of the anti-family-planning Human Life International. PRI, directed by Steven Mosher, has been championed by such vehemently anti-choice Republican members of Congress as Henry Hyde of Illinois and Chris Smith of New Jersey.

In fact, UNFPA funds neither voluntary nor coerced abortions. Its mission, in more than 140 countries, is to work with governments and NGOs to provide contraceptives, HIV/AIDS prevention, pregnancy care and education to combat violence against women. It supports such "controversial" health care as Pap smears, mammograms, prenatal checkups, Apgar health tests for newborns, vasectomies and aspirin for 13-year-old girls suffering from cramps. According to UNFPA, the monies the United States has withheld—12.5 percent of its annual budget—would have helped *prevent* 800,000 abortions, along with 2 million unwanted pregnancies, 60,000 cases of serious maternal injury and illness and, most ominously, 4,700 maternal and 77,000 infant deaths.

The UNFPA defunding so angered a retired French teacher in California and an attorney in New Mexico that they came up with the idea of raising the money themselves—by creating the remarkable 34 Million Friends campaign.

SIDETRACKING CAIRO, GAGGING AIDS?

In 1994, the U.N. Population and Development Conference in Cairo produced a landmark consensus linking family planning and economic development to reproductive rights and women's empowerment. Its recommended actions sound like a feminist blueprint: *yes* to gender equity, education and family planning; *no* to female genital mutilation and other violence against women. Conferees also set a goal that by the year 2015 there would be universal access to reproductive-health services. Now as the 10th anniversary of Cairo approaches (and in characteristic rebuke of the international community), Bush wants to undermine that plan of international action.

After making noise that the United States might withdraw from the Cairo agreement, the Bush administration sent an anti-abortion and anti-family planning delegation to the fifth Asian and Pacific Population Conference in Bangkok last December. Instead of focusing on how to further implement Cairo's recommendations, the U.S. delegates nitpicked over terms in the agreement. *Reproductive health* and *reproductive rights* were seen as code for *abortion*, and *consistent condom use* (suggested as a strategy for adolescent HIV/AIDS prevention) was deemed unacceptable since the mere mention of condoms might invite promiscuity. Forcing a vote on its objections, the United States lost 32–1 and 31–1, finding itself in the position of isolated minority rather than world leader.

The U.S. delegation's bias against nearly all forms of contraception led to at least one jaw-dropping moment in Bangkok. U.S. advisor Elaine Jones of the State Department lectured international experts on the efficacy of "natural" family planning, enthusing about the method *she* used: cervical-mucus monitoring.

International health providers now worry that the Bush administration has other gags waiting in the wings. A key concern is the promised $15 billion in U.S. aid for HIV/AIDS care in the 12 African and two Caribbean countries hardest hit by the disease. Although the administration has said it will distribute these funds to groups that also provide abortion services, it insists that those services be physically and financially separated—which is often unrealistic in places where health care is already so limited. For all intents and purposes, such a policy *is* a gag rule, which had previously not applied to AIDS funding.

TODAY THE WORLD, TOMORROW THE USA?

If the Bush administration can get away with gag rules overseas, what will stop them from trying it here? Bangkok notwithstanding, the administration has been almost unimpeded in its drive to weaken support for abortion and family planning internationally.

"It appears that this administration tests things abroad first, and that's what we're worried about," says Amy Coen of PAI. "It's very, very hard for women in the United States to feel the lack of rights so many women in the world live with: They don't get educated. They sometimes don't get as much food as the boys do. They have no property rights. They can't choose when to use contraceptives. The decisions the U.S. government makes are not widely reported, and they're in areas that are very technical and complicated, so programs are being eliminated and no one knows about this."

Consider what the federal, state and local governments have been up to lately:

- The Northern Kentucky public health board only narrowly defeated (by one vote) a proposal to *decline* $170,000 in annual Title X money for family-planning services on the grounds that birth control pills and IUDs cause abortions.
- Bush has been nominating and renominating anti-choice judges to key federal posts, such as Priscilla Owen, 5th U.S. Circuit Court of Appeals.
- The federal government signed on to the anti-abortion scare tactic of linking breast cancer to abortions by removing from the National Center Institute website a strongly worded fact sheet showing "no association" between the two and replacing it with a more ambivalent declaration.
- State legislatures have been flooded with anti-choice measures—in 2001 there were 398 in 49 states and the District of Columbia, according to the Ms. Foundation for Women. They include bills banning all or most abortions: setting burdensome "TRAP" (Targeted Regulations Against Abortion Providers) requirements on abortion providers; classifying fetuses as unborn children; creating state "Choose Life" or "Respect Life" license plates (with fees earmarked for "crisis pregnancy centers" that steer women away from legal abortions); setting up mandatory waiting periods for abortions ("come back in 24 hours") and parental notification/consent requirements for minors. "It's a chipping away, because we're not paying attention," says Coen.
- Gag rules may be harder to institute in the United States because of constitutional questions, but that doesn't mean the anti-choice forces won't be trying.

FIGHTING BACK

Despite the pressure from the Bush administration and Bush-emboldened anti-choice activists, equally impassioned pro-choice activists and legislators continue their efforts.

In March, Congressional Democrats Carolyn Maloney and Joseph Crowley of New York and Barbara Lee of California introduced the United Nations Population Fund Funding Act of 2003. HR 1196 would authorize the United States to appropriate $50 million for UNFPA in 2004 and $84 million in 2005—thus making up for the money withheld in 2003. To avoid a repeat of the China gambit, the law would withhold only "country-specific" funds if China failed to certify that it wasn't using coercive family-planning measures. In other words, the Bush administration would have to come up with a brand-new excuse to hold back all the UNFPA money next year.

In addition to the expected Democratic support, the House bill found its first co-sponsor in Iowa Republican Jim Leach. Also, James Greenwood (R-Pa.) has strongly criticized the gag rule and went to Kenya last year to see its ill effects first hand.

"Unfortunately, our party has been co-opted by so-called religious or neo-conservatives," Greenwood told a reporter. "They have persuaded themselves that if they cut funding to agencies that provide or counsel on abortions, somehow that will actually reduce abortions."

Before the Reagan administration, family planning was a popular Republican cause as well as a familiar Democratic one. George W. Bush's grandfather, Prescott Bush, was a staunch supporter of Planned Parenthood. George H. W. Bush supported a woman's right to choose—until Ronald Reagan asked him to change his position in order to become his vice-presidential running mate.

GETTING AROUND THE GAG

On the ground, foreign practitioners keep looking for creative ways to bypass the gag rule and the funding cuts. Dr. Solomon Orero travels around Kenya as part of the Kisumu Medical and Educational Trust, teaching health-care workers how to clean up botched abortions He performs abortions himself, too, because he's figured out a way around Kenya's anti-abortion law: He insists that abortions are aimed "at the preservation of the woman's life," which the law does allow.

The irony is that Kenya has been moving towards legalizing abortion, with Health Minister Charity Ngilu calling for the country to provide women with reproductive choice. But Orero points out that legal abortion is only a starting point if a nation lacks funding to supply and staff clinics. When Zambia liberalized its abortion law, for example, women in the country still had very limited access to services. Says Orero, "We want to put services in place *now* for when the law is eventually liberalized."

As the Cairo plan pointed out, reproductive rights are key to women's well-being. Says PAI's Coen, "The number of children you have profoundly affects the quality of your life. You can support and have a good life with three children but not with 10. And when you have hope in your own life, you can provide hope to your children."

Perhaps that is the most bitter aspect to this particular Bush administration polemic, its cynical strategy, so hostile to hope, so seemingly determined to put a domestic electoral agenda ahead of fundamental health issues.

Strange Bedfellows: Conservative Christians and the Bush Administration Are Aggressively Pushing a Controversial "Pro-Family" Agenda on the International Stage—And They're Teaming Up with Islamic Theocracies to Do It

STEVE BENEN

***Church and State*, Vol. 55, no. 8, 9.1.02**

Sudan, an Islamic theocracy in Northeast Africa, is classified by the U.S. State Department as a "state sponsor of terrorism." The Sudanese earned this status, reserved for only a handful of American adversaries, after providing sanctuary to Osama bin Laden, who operated a network of terrorists from that country from 1993 to 1996 while backing Sudan's theocratic military dictatorship.

Sudan has also drawn the ire of the international community for permitting widespread slavery and repeated human rights abuses. A year ago, the U.S. Commission on International Religious Freedom described the nation as "the world's most violent abuser of the right to freedom of religion and belief."

Nevertheless, at the United Nations, Sudan and the United States have repeatedly been on the same page lately. The U.S. has joined with Sudan—and a host of other Islamic countries—to undercut the international consensus on issues ranging from children's health to women's rights and global family planning.

Since his inauguration, President George W. Bush has adopted a firm stance on the U.S. relationship with countries around the globe. In an approach some have labeled the "Bush Doctrine," the president has made clear that in a post-Sept. 11 world, "you're either with us, or you're against us."

Since the terrorist attacks of that fall, the U.S. has had little trouble differentiating between our friends and foes in the global effort to prevent terrorism. Countries like England, Canada and France have offered reliable support for our military and diplomatic efforts in Afghanistan and elsewhere. In contrast, several countries, including Sudan, Syria, Libya, Iran and Iraq—the latter two composing part of what Bush calls an "axis of evil"—maintain strained relations with the United States for their suspected part in aiding terrorism.

On a growing number of international policy issues, however, the roles are entirely reversed. Under pressure from the Religious Right and its cohorts, the Bush administration has made allies of our enemies and adversaries of our friends.

This new international dynamic is part of a concerted strategy. Most of the Religious Right's international goals—undermining children's and women's rights while limiting access to abortion and family planning—are now formally being adopted by the White House, which is promoting these objectives at international forums.

Since Bush became president, many have recognized the Religious Right's high-profile role as "insiders" in Washington's official government corridors. What is less well known is the Religious Right's success in translating its White House access into international policy at venues such as the United Nations. By collaborating with the Bush administration and Islamic and Catholic allies, the Religious Right has turned its U.S. "culture war" into an international battle that impacts families around the world.

The shift in focus to foreign policy concerns came about as Christian conservatives realized that some of their key issues were being debated in other countries, and with an ideological ally in the Oval Office, they could exert influence to help shape the debate to their liking. "The American electorate was split right down the middle on these cultural wars, and nobody was going to win them," Richard Cizik, Washington director of the National Association of Evangelicals, told the *New York Times*. Explaining a shift in emphasis to international policies, Cizik said conservative Christians' work overseas is "going gangbusters."

Political pragmatism also leads domestic religious strategists to work with countries and leaders they might otherwise abhor.

"We look at [Islamic theocracies] as allies, not necessarily as friends," Austin Ruse, president of the Catholic Family and Human Rights Institute, told the *Washington Post*. "We have realized that without countries like Sudan, abortion would have been recognized as a universal human right in a U.N. document."

The most startling difference between domestic fights over social issues and international debates is the opposition the Religious Right and its government allies face in this country.

In the United States, when the Bush administration works in concert with the Religious Right on legislative proposals, an organized opposition—including progressive politicians, nonprofit organizations and an inquisitive media—exists to criticize the efforts. White House officials and right-wing religious leaders realize that an aggressive agenda that reflects a rigid religious ideology will face stiff resistance.

At the United Nations and on the international stage, the dynamics are far different. The United States is the world's strongest superpower. Its influence is unparalleled. When the Bush administration unites with fundamentalist Islamic theocracies and the Vatican at the U.N. under a shared religiously grounded worldview, as is becoming increasingly common, the result is an alliance that can dictate the outcome of several policy debates.

That influence was on full display in May when the Bush administration sent a delegation to a United Nations meeting on the rights of children. Countries gathered to expand on earlier work and create a new document, titled "A World Fit for Children." Tommy Thompson, secretary of the U.S. Department of Health and Human Services, led America's delegation. While America's traditional allies in Europe were advocating greater health and educational benefits and increased safety for children, the U.S. delegation instigated a polarizing debate over sex education and reproductive rights.

Debate grew fairly intense. Towards the end of the gathering, America's representatives threatened to pull out of the conference altogether unless the language on reproductive health services was changed. Realizing the difficulties in acting alone, America's delegation sought and received assistance from the Vatican's representatives at the U.N., as well as delegations from many fundamentalist Islamic countries, including Syria, Libya and Pakistan, who agreed with the approach favored by the Americans.

Other countries begrudgingly went along, and the word "services" was removed from the final document. The U.N. member nations, therefore, ultimately endorsed young people's access to reproductive health, but not any methods or mechanisms to get it. The move was hailed by the Family Research Council, which called the change a "huge pro-family, pro-life victory."

The U.S., the Vatican and Muslim countries also worked together to promote proposals to instruct children on the benefits of abstinence for all young women.

Critics noted several practical problems with the approach. "How can we talk about a plan of action for children that doesn't deal with sex education and information?" asked Brazilian negotiator Fernando Coimbra. "To face the challenges posed by HIV/AIDS and early pregnancy, we have to keep our children informed. To wait until they're over 18 is too late."

The U.S. delegation flatly rejected these arguments. To understand why, one need look no further than whom the Bush administration selected to represent America at the conference. Among those "helping" Secretary Thompson at the U.N. were employees of several Religious Right powerhouses. The Family Research Council's (FRC) William Saunders and Concerned Women for America's (CWA) Janice Crouse were on hand, as was Paul Bonicelli, a dean at Patrick Henry College, a Christian private school in Virginia created by Religious Right activist Michael Farris to cater to students from fundamentalist Christian home schools.

Bolstering the relationship between the Bush administration and the Vatican, John Klink, who has done negotiating work at the U.N. on behalf of numerous Holy See delegations, was asked to join Thompson and the Religious Right staffers at the children's summit. Klink is widely recognized for promoting the Vatican's anti-abortion positions, including opposition to giving the "morning after" pill to rape victims in refugee camps and all use of birth control.

Wendy Wright, senior policy director for CWA, told the *Village Voice* that America had to promote abstinence at the meeting because it "is just a plain healthier way to live." She added that her group opposed U.N. resolutions extending too many rights to children because it could lead to minors suing their parents and a general disruption of the "natural order."

"When we go outside the order set by God," Wright explained, "it's harmful to us."

Throughout the conference, America's proposals reflected a right-wing ideology, while ideas from our traditional allies were met with hostility from the U.S. delegation.

"The U.S. position on health issues and international instruments has been so combative and isolationist we've ended up alienating traditional friends, especially Europeans," a former U.S. senior official, speaking anonymously, told the *Los Angeles Times.*

Undermining U.N. efforts to improve children's health is not the only project the Religious Right considers an important international priority. Like their new politically expedient allies in the Middle East, Christian conservative activists are bent on undermining U.N. treaties on women's rights, as well.

Over 20 years ago, for example, the Convention to Eliminate All Forms of Discrimination Against Women (CEDAW) was endorsed by the U.N. Since then, 169 countries, including every industrial power in the world, has ratified it—except the United States. That leaves America in the same category as Afghanistan, Iran and Saudi Arabia. (President Jimmy Carter signed CEDAW in 1980, but the U.S. Senate never ratified it.)

On Capitol Hill, lawmakers began work this year on changing that. Several U.S. senators, led by Barbara Boxer (D-Calif.) and Joseph Biden (D-Del.), began laying the groundwork for a vote on CEDAW.

Initially, President Bush and the State Department offered support for the proposal. In a letter to the Senate Foreign Relations Committee in February, the White House listed CEDAW among a group of treaties that the "administration believes are generally desirable and should be approved."

The Convention endorses the principle of legal gender equality, recognition of a woman's right to work and gender equity in education. CEDAW does not address gay rights, abortion or international law superceding national sovereignty, but that hasn't stopped the Religious Right from using distortions and demagoguery to discredit the proposal.

Concerned Women for America, for example, labeled CEDAW "the Equal Rights Amendment on steroids," and claimed that those who promote it are "radical feminists." FRC President Ken Connor said that if the U.S. ratified CEDAW, this year's celebration of Mother's Day "will be our last." The Catholic Family and Human Rights Institute's Ruse, who closely monitors the U.N., described the Convention as "just about the most dangerous treaty that the U.S. government has ever considered ratifying."

Thomas Jacobson, Focus on the Family's United Nations manager, took the hyperbole one step further. He claimed CEDAW "seems to pit wives against husbands, girls against fathers, and to attempt to remove [women] from under any male authority."

Some supporters of CEDAW believe fundamentalist opposition to women's rights is a natural outgrowth of a Religious Right worldview.

"Where women have opportunities, they tend to balance tradition with modernity, and form a bulwark against fundamentalism," Shazia Rafia, a spokesperson for Parliamentarians for Global Action, told the *Daily Texan*. "That's why the first thing fundamentalists do is undermine women's freedoms."

The collective lobbying efforts are paying off for the Religious. Right. As the conservative attacks on CEDAW grew more intense, White House support evaporated. Attorney General John Ashcroft announced in May that the Justice Department was launching a new "review" of the treaty, which many believe may spell its demise.

International observers, meanwhile, have expressed disappointment with the Bush administration's tendency to join with Islamic theocracies on issues such as women's rights.

"This alliance shows the depths of perversity of the [U.S.] position,"

Adrienne Germaine, president of the International Women's Health Coalition, told the *Washington Post*. "On the one hand we're presumably blaming these countries for unspeakable acts of terrorism, and at the same time we are allying ourselves with them in the oppression of women."

While Bush's reversal on the U.N.'s treaty on women's rights raised eyebrows, the most glaring example of the Bush administration yielding to Religious Right pressure on international affairs is the president's contradictory actions on global family planning.

For his 2002 federal budget, President Bush appropriated $25 million for the United Nations Fund for Population Activities (UNFPA). Since its inception in 1969, the Fund has won widespread recognition for its work in improving the lives of women in developing countries. When the Bush administration announced its intention to further America's support for the program, few considered the move controversial.

Congress complied with the administration's request and allocated $34 million for the fund. The vote in the House was 357–66, while Senate support was unanimous.

Once Religious Right groups learned of the appropriation, however, they began putting pressure on the administration to reverse itself. Organizations such as the Family Research Council, Concerned Women for America and an anti-abortion group called Population Research Institute made unsubstantiated claims that the Population Fund spent money on forced abortions and sterilization in China. The claims have since been thoroughly debunked. The Population Fund's work in China is limited to 32 counties, all of which follow voluntary family planning programs. British officials sent a team of officials to China that concluded earlier this year that the U.N. program was actually helping steer China away from draconian policies.

In May, the Bush administration's own investigators found "no evidence that UNFPA has knowingly supported or participated in the management of a program of coercive abortion or involuntary sterilization in the [People's Republic of China]" and recommended release of the $34 million appropriation.

Instead of using the information as justification for its original position, the Bush White House suppressed the report, literally hiding it from public view for two months. In June, the White House announced that it was placing a "hold" on U.S. subsidies for UNFPA.

Lawmakers on the other end of Pennsylvania Avenue were displeased. Over 120 members of Congress cosigned a letter to the president, arguing that they considered the agreement on UNFPA to be binding. Bush said he disagreed and refused to release the funds he had asked for. When Congress announced it would take up legislation that would force release of the money for the Fund, Bush said he would veto the bill.

Even members of Bush's own party expressed frustration that the administration's policy actually promotes the very activities it claims to detest.

The bipartisan attempts to convince the White House were in vain. On July 22, Bush announced it had officially been decided to cut off all U.S. funding for UNFPA.

Critics say Bush's flip-flop on UNFPA has dramatic negative consequences on families around the world. Thanks to the reversal, they charge, fewer women will receive pre-natal care in developing countries, fewer doctors will be trained to deal with pregnancy complications, fewer HIV prevention programs will be able to operate and less medical equipment will be made available to expectant mothers in the Third World. All told, the U.N. estimates that by withholding once promised funds, Bush's new anti-UNFPA policy will result in 2 million unwanted pregnancies, 4,800 maternal deaths, 77,000 more deaths among children under the age of 5 and almost 1 million abortions.

Thoraya Obaid, executive director of UNFPA, said plainly, "Women and children will die because of this decision."

Bush's tendency to yield to Religious Right pressure on foreign policy issues seems unlikely to change anytime soon. In fact, Christian conservatives, conscious of their powerful political role, are becoming increasingly organized in order to more effectively lobby on international issues.

In October 2001, President Bush welcomed delegates of a "World Congress of Families" to the Washington, D.C., gathering with a letter noting that he has "committed my administration to work hard to help parents and encourage the formation and maintenance of loving families."

Attending the gathering were participants from several of the nation's most prominent conservative and Religious Right organizations, including the Family Research Council, the Heritage Foundation and Concerned Women for America.

Alongside the Christian conservatives was a representative from the Organization of the Islamic Conference (OIC), which includes 53 officially or predominantly Muslim nations, among them repressive regimes such as Iran, Iraq, Libya, Saudi Arabia and Sudan.

Mokhtar Lamani, a Moroccan diplomat who represents the OIC at the United Nations, told the *Washington Post* that a common approach to family issues unites the groups.

"The main issue that brings us all together is defending the family values, the natural family," Lamani said. "The Republican administration is so clear in defending the family values."

In the meantime, countries that have historically looked to America to represent steps forward for the rights of women, children and diverse families are now seeing an unwelcome change.

Wanda Nowicka with the Federation for Women and Family Planning in Warsaw, told the *Village Voice* that she sees America's shift to the right as a sign of things getting worse for families around the world.

"We used to be able to say, 'Look at those progressive countries like the U.S.,'" Nowicka said. "But now I'm afraid . . . progress is headed in a different direction."

The Unequal AIDS Burden

NOELEEN HEYZER, EXECUTIVE DIRECTOR, UNIFEM

***The Christian Science Monitor*, 7.18.02**

When a member of my staff asked a woman in rural Zimbabwe how many buckets of water it took each day to care for an AIDS patient, she answered simply: "Twenty-four."

But the task is far from simple, underscoring the extent of the HIV/AIDS epidemic's impact on women's lives. Twenty-four buckets means 24 trips to the well. Most of those carrying buckets are women, who have borne the brunt of caring for the growing numbers of people living with AIDS in Africa, where the epidemic has hit hardest.

According to UNAIDS, which released new statistics to coincide with the International AIDS Conference in Barcelona last week, more than 37 million adults are living with HIV/AIDS worldwide. Women now make up 49.8 percent of those infected, and in sub-Saharan Africa, 58 percent of the adults living with HIV/AIDS are women. More than two-thirds of newly infected 15- to 19-year-olds in sub-Saharan Africa are female. Increasingly sought after by older men—often in the belief that sex with a virgin can cure AIDS—young women are least able to say no to unsafe sex.

What UNAIDS's new figures and the "24 buckets" story show is that women are fundamentally more affected by the epidemic than men.

That women are more socially, culturally, and biologically vulnerable than men is a reality that arises directly out of the nature of global inequalities between the sexes. On the one hand, millions of women do not have the power or the wherewithal to say "No!" to unwanted or unprotected sex. At the same time, women—often sick themselves—are continuing to care for the sick, an extension of their daily responsibilities within the home.

Collecting water and caring for patients requires that whole families be mobilized. It means food security is threatened when mothers and daughters tend the sick rather than the garden or a paying job. Too often young girls are withdrawn from school—the one place they might learn how to protect themselves—in order to help their mothers and grandmothers.

Throughout the AIDS-stricken regions of the world, wide age gaps exist in communities that once thrived on intergenerational bonds. Families now often consist of the very old or the very young, with older women caring for orphaned grandchildren. Typically, female caregivers have no access to sanitary gloves, disinfectant, or information to protect themselves. In Zimbabwe women use empty plastic sugar bags to cover their hands. For those seeking medical care, drugs that are taken for granted in the industrialized world are simply not available or affordable for the majority of people living with AIDS.

Meanwhile, healthy girls and women trying to live "normal" lives in the midst of the epidemic have little if any means to protect themselves against infection. Research on HIV-killing microbicides is slow, and the female condom—the only, if not quite satisfactory, barrier method available to women—is too expensive or not available.

Governments that could aggressively respond to the disease with drugs, technical support, and funding are not doing so. At the same time, the coffers of the Global Fund for AIDS, Tuberculosis & Malaria remain at a fraction of the financial goals needed to improve the lives of the infected and those caring for them. This includes improvements in services the industrialized world takes for granted—things as basic as running water that requires only a twist of a knob, which would enable AIDS patients to live with dignity in clean bedclothes and linens.

If we are to tame and reverse the AIDS epidemic, we need to protect women's human rights and put an end to laws that violate them.

WAGES AND WELL-BEING

. . . and the Poor Get Poorer

KIM PHILLIPS-FEIN

***The Nation,* 8.4.03**

A year ago, Loretta Gruytch decided to go back to work.

The 71-year-old resident of Lebanon, Oregon, had suffered from high blood pressure for some time. But her medications cost $600 a month, and she and her husband (who also has health problems) live on Social Security. "You make a choice between paying rent and utilities and getting medication, and you have to have a place to live."

She'd held jobs in retail and as a mail carrier. She didn't think she could handle a forty-hour job, but she thought that twenty or twenty-five hours would be enough to pay for her prescriptions.

But she had put it off too long. While she was at a job interview at a local deli, she had a brain aneurysm and a stroke, and had to be rushed to the hospital. Her doctor helped her to enroll in Oregon's healthcare plan. For the past year, Gruytch has been able to get her medicine. But today, mired in budget crisis, Oregon is cutting back on health coverage. As a result, Gruytch may lose her prescription coverage altogether. She says, "I don't know what I will do if they take my medicine away."

On the other side of the country, 43-year-old Brooklyn resident Maria Jones has also slipped through the cracks of the social safety net, forced to choose between her daughter's education and her own health.

Jones came to the United States from Puerto Rico at the age of 18. She married young and had three children, but divorced her soldier husband after the marriage turned violent (they went through rounds of counseling first). When her children were young, she worked in a dentist's office. More recently, she was a childcare worker, making and selling crocheted and knitted goods on the side.

Two years ago Jones had a massive heart attack, leaving her face partially paralyzed for months. After her illness, she could not work, nor could she complete the work requirements she needed to get welfare. She began to fall behind on rent. Her youngest daughter—"my miracle baby"—was in her first year at Hunter College at the time, and living with her mother. Jones asked her daughter to apply for welfare. "I was always taught that families stick together, no matter what," says Jones. When a caseworker told her daughter that she would need to leave school and enroll in the Work Experience Program (WEP, the city's "workfare" program) to get benefits, she dropped out of school.

After she recovered somewhat, Jones told her daughter to go back to college. "She gave me one semester of her life. I was not going to let her give up her dreams to get welfare," she says. Now, she subsists on a disability check of $570 a month. Her rent is $680. "Unless I hit the lotto, I don't know what I am going to do."

In the Bush Administration's ideological war on the welfare state, Gruytch and Jones are collateral damage. Unlike with Clinton, who sought to end welfare "as we know it," the Bush agenda explicitly targets noncash benefits, like healthcare and education, which currently are available to poor and working poor people. Some of the changes the Administration seeks are subtle switches in rules—demanding additional paperwork for the earned-income tax credit, for example, or extra documentation for poor children to receive school lunch. Others replace federal entitlements with block grants to states.

Taken together, the proposed changes will make it more difficult for people to get healthcare, housing assistance, early childhood education and other minimal social benefits. They will fall especially painfully on the working poor. While President Clinton's 1996 welfare reform law rescinded the federal entitlement to cash assistance, the Bush proposals seek to end the social minimum wage.

One common thread of the Bush Administration's proposals is that they aim to turn federal entitlement programs into block grants. The idea of block-granting these programs, which began with Reagan's attacks on poverty programs and expanded with Clinton-era welfare reform, may sound like a technical change interesting only to policy wonks. But in reality, it is a way of quietly defunding social programs, slowly ending health coverage and rent supports for people who have them now. Just as the language of states' rights during the Jim Crow era was a way to disguise the demands of white segregationists, the language of block grants is a way of deflecting attention from the social costs of cutting back the welfare state.

The scariest proposals involve Medicaid. Right now, the program—which provides health coverage for about 48 million people—is administered by the states but jointly funded by the federal government and the states. Every dollar that a state spends on Medicaid is matched by some money from the federal government. In January, Health and Human Services Secretary Tommy Thompson proposed turning the program into block grants. If such a proposal became law, the federal government would give a fixed, capped amount to each state every year. Since there would be no built-in mechanism to increase federal spending should states' costs rise, this would be likely to erode funding in the long run. In addition, there would be no incentive to expand services (federal matching funds would be eliminated). Joan Alker, a senior research fellow at Georgetown University who focuses on healthcare, says, "If more people came on the rolls, if there was a new technology or drug, if there was an epidemic, states would be left holding the bag."

Under block grants, states might also get greater "flexibility" to determine benefit packages. They might even have the option to deliver services selectively for certain populations—to one part of the state, but not another. Currently, the Medicaid program is divided into two parts—"mandatory" recipients and "optional" recipients, and "mandatory" services and "optional" services. Mandatory recipients include pregnant women and children under 6 up to 133 percent of the poverty line, children under 19 below the poverty line, some low-income parents, children in foster care and elderly and disabled people on Supplemental Security Income (SSI). Mandatory services include hospital services, doctor's visits, nursing-home care, immunizations and lab services.

But a quarter of Medicaid recipients and the majority of elderly recipients are optional beneficiaries, meaning that the federal government does not require states to cover them. These include elderly and disabled people with incomes above the SSI limit (74 percent of poverty), working parents above mandatory income levels, pregnant women above 133 percent of poverty, and low-income children above the poverty line. Many services provided by Medicaid are optional as well—including prescription drugs (for anyone but children), home healthcare, vision and dental care. In a budget crisis, these would be the first ones to go if the federal government isn't funding them. Indeed, states have already started to cut "optional" populations off Medicaid. The people whose healthcare is threatened are marginal and poor. According to a report by Cindy Mann of Georgetown's Institute for Health Care Research and Policy, in 1998 the optional benefit population included 4.2 million children, 3.7 million working parents, 2.3 million elderly people and 1.5 million people with disabilities. Medicaid also covers a high proportion of nursing-home expenses. Denise Soffel, health policy analyst at New York's Community Service Society, says, "People aren't thinking about Granny in the nursing home using Medicaid dollars."

The Bush Administration's hopes for rapid Medicaid reform were stymied when members of the National Governors Association were unable to agree on a proposal endorsing block grants. But Congressional Republicans are still saying they will mark up a Medicaid reform proposal this year, and the Administration has not given up. "If they don't get it done this year, they will come back to it next year," says Melanie Nathanson of the Center on Budget and Policy Priorities (CBPP).

Other poverty programs, such as public housing, are also on the chopping block. The Bush Administration is contemplating a radical restructuring of the federal rent voucher program, under which low-income people pay one-third of their rent and the federal government makes up the rest. The voucher program is overwhelmingly used by working poor families, people with disabilities and elderly people, and helps several million people stave off homelessness each year. In New York City alone, about 100,000 people use housing vouchers, and there is a waiting list of 150,000.

In fact, thanks to the recession, the use of rent vouchers is rising across the country. But the Bush Administration is planning cutbacks that would leave 184,000 vouchers currently in use across the country without adequate funding to cover them. At the same time, the Administration envisions turning the entire rent voucher program into state-administered block grants. Legislation to accomplish this has been introduced in both houses of Congress. Despite volatile rental housing markets, the block grants would cap funding for vouchers. Vic Bach, housing expert at the Community Service Society, says, "Over time, the vouchers will be devalued and will cease to be an effective way of obtaining affordable housing." The program will be renamed Housing Assistance to Needy Families, an allusion to Temporary Assistance to Needy Families (TANF), the name of the program created by the 1996 welfare reform law. Conservatives such as Howard Husock of the Manhattan Institute dream of the day when there will be time limits and work requirements for public housing, and Michael Liu, an assistant secretary at Housing and Urban Development, has said that the Administration will not prohibit states from setting time limits for public housing. Counties in southern Delaware and Charlotte, North Carolina, are already experimenting with public-housing time limits. Another Bush housing proposal is a $50 monthly charge for families in public housing with little or no income. But some housing authorities have already tried minimum rents and given up—in one case, according to the CBPP, after tenants were found selling their blood to pay the rent.

Many liberals hoped that Clinton's welfare reform would mean an expansion of assistance for working-poor families—more generous daycare or health benefits, for example. But the Bush Administration is building on the most punitive aspects of the 1996 welfare law, seeking to expand work requirements while tightening access to education and training. Meanwhile, many people who left welfare for jobs during the 1990s boom have lost them as the economy has soured.

For example, 39-year-old Brooklyn resident Rosario Rodriguez left welfare a year ago when she landed a $6.50-an-hour job making maternity garments at a small Brooklyn factory. She liked the job, she says, even though she worked in a dirty, unheated room, lost her health benefits as she exceeded Medicaid's income limit ("it was a factory job, it had no healthcare") and got only a half-hour lunch break. But after six months, she was laid off as business slowed down.

Now she spends her days at the "job center," New York's euphemistic name for welfare offices, where there aren't any jobs to be found. She says, "My caseworker told me he would pray for me." Rodriguez suspects that she won't be able to find paid work, and will instead have to go into the city's Work Experience Program. Meanwhile, her daughter, a high school student, just had her first baby. Rodriguez would like to help out and stay home with her grandchild, but she fears this would result in a loss of benefits.

It's easy to overlook the connections between Bush's sweeping vision and the program changes of the Clinton years. But when it comes to TANF and to poverty, the two Presidents are very similar—in that both have emphasized work, regardless of its quality, and regardless of whether or not it is stable, pays a living wage or provides health coverage. The marketplace, not the government, is supposed to soothe poverty, even when all the evidence shows that it does not.

Against great odds, low-income activists struggle to fend off these attacks on the remnants of the welfare state. For example, Community Voices Heard, a group representing poor women in upper Manhattan, organizes around economic issues. It has not been an easy time, and activists are deeply frustrated. "A lot of people on WEP got jobs," said longtime activist Stephen Bradley at an organizing meeting on a rainy mid-May evening—jobs that they've now lost. "They got off welfare, but now they are back on welfare." Politicians, he says, are unresponsive: "We go and we plead our case, but they don't listen." Congressman Charles Rangel, who represents Harlem, has never consented to an in-person meeting with them. Harlem native Lloyd Anderson says, "People need to be able to pay their bills and take care of their children."

Through organizing and lobbying, people have made some advances. This past spring, Community Voices Heard and other community groups won passage of a City Council law that permitted people in WEP to attend college for part of their work requirement—though Mayor Bloomberg promptly vetoed the law. Healthcare for poor people in New York State was threatened with cutbacks, but these were averted when the state raised taxes on upper-income people to maintain Medicaid spending for the poor. And a successful action was held May 14, when about 100 activists thronged the lobby of Club for Growth, an elite Beltway fundraising organization that funnels money to conservative Republicans and pressed for the Bush tax-cut plan. Holding photographs of firehouses that are closing and schools in disrepair, they chanted, "Where's the jobs? Where's the jobs?"

Almost all the forces of the rich and powerful are stacked against them.

Right now, Bradley says, "People are desperate. We are like a lost society." His words ring true. As Loretta Gruytch faces life without the medication she needs, and Rosario Rodriguez prays for work, it is hard not to feel as though our whole society has somehow gotten lost. Yet at the same time, despite the array of forces against them, the dedication and courage of these activists in Harlem offer hope for the future. When Lloyd Anderson says, "It's getting ready to get hot," one can only hope that he is right.

Working Women's Lives and the "W Effect": An Interview with Ellen Bravo

PHOEBE ST. JOHN

1.7.04

Editor's note: Ellen Bravo is director of 9to5, National Association of Working Women. Founded in 1973, this grassroots organization works to gain economic justice for women.

HOW LONG HAVE YOU BEEN AT 9TO5, AND HOW LONG HAVE YOU BEEN INVOLVED IN THE WOMEN'S MOVEMENT?

Twenty-one and a half years at 9to5, and I've been involved in the women's movement since '68. It's a long time!

YOUR EXPECTATIONS OF THE BUSH ADMINISTRATION WERE PRETTY LOW...

I would say that's accurate!

WHAT DID YOU FEAR MOST, VIS-À-VIS WOMEN'S RIGHTS IN THE WORKPLACE?

I had a lot of fear for the areas that we focus on at 9to5. In terms of balancing work and family responsibilities, I was afraid he would do exactly what he's done, which is to try to limit the effect of the Family Medical Leave Act. And welfare: I knew that he would worsen what was already a bad situation with Temporary Assistance for Needy Families (TANF). I also worried about what he would do to the Equal Employment Opportunity Commission (EEOC), and that he would undermine the Women's Bureau. It has been worse than I imagined. I didn't have any idea he would be as bold with the EEOC as he's been.

Can you explain what he's trying to do to the EEOC?

The EEOC oversees antidiscrimination law. He's trying to privatize and dismantle it. They're "consolidating" offices, which means closing offices, downsizing offices. And they're setting up a National Call Center of contract employees—this is the privatization part—to manage intake. It's a disaster. They're saying it's a "pilot" project, but it's a two-year, nationwide pilot project! Work that requires a huge amount of training and experience, collaboration and collegiality, is being separated out into this lower paid, non federal employee system.

Why should women be worried about this?

Because so many women experience gender and race discrimination, and have to go through this government agency. It will make it much harder for them get justice in response to their complaints.

Looking back, what are the most important changes for working women that have come out of this administration? How much change has come out of the White House itself, do you think?

Here are a couple of White House-led initiatives. Clinton, just before he left office, issued a regulation allowing states to choose to use surplus unemployment funds to help provide wage replacement, for a period of time, for parents of newborns. Bush overturned it. Took it back.

Then there are the overtime regulations, which were issued by the Department of Labor and pushed through. Both houses of Congress said that the DoL couldn't do this, but they went through with it anyway. The Department of Labor would not have done this without either Bush's prodding or backing. These regulations are going to adversely affect lots of women, both women who will now be exempt from overtime and who will therefore have to work longer hours with no extra pay, and also women who count on overtime pay and who will lose the work to the people who don't have to be paid overtime.

How does the Bush team market something like that?

Oh, they're helping low-wage workers, didn't you know? It's what we call sleight of hand, the magician's trick. They say, "Look, over here! We're going to raise the minimum salary threshold and give more workers overtime protection!," hoping that while our eye is on that we won't notice the rabbit being taken out of the hat, which is the eight and a half million workers who are going to lose overtime protection altogether, because they'll be reclassified. And as for raising the minimum salary threshold, they spelled out to employers the ways to get around this. It's just outrageous.

What goes hand in hand with this is a bill that we helped defeat, called the Family Time Flexibility Act. I think the bill's defeat is interesting in that it shows that even among the Republicans there are still people who don't want to be labeled as anti-working family. The bill said that employers could have their employees "choose" to be compensated for overtime in time instead of pay.

So what was really at stake here?

The bill would have made it cheaper for employers to work people overtime. The granting of the comp time would be up to the employer, so there's no guarantee that you would get it when you want it. They could just give it to you when there's downtime, instead of laying you off. So it would save them money all round. People who "choose" overtime pay instead of comp time would be less likely to get assigned the overtime. And there's no guarantee against bankruptcy, that the employees would get the money for comp time they never enjoyed.

Bush made a big deal of appointing a woman, Elaine Chao, to head the Department of Labor. Is it an advance for women to have a woman Labor Secretary?

Gender helps only if the person acts in the interests of the majority of women. This Labor Secretary has acted on behalf of the rich and powerful, and not in the interests of the majority of women, so—no. In fact in some ways it hurts, because Bush can point to Elaine Chao and to Condoleezza Rice and say, hey, I have these powerful women on my team. But the powerful women are carrying out the agenda of a very malevolent male.

One of the first things Bush did upon coming into office was to repeal the workplace safety rules signed into law (at the last minute) by Bill Clinton. From what they heard in the media, many Americans think workplace injuries are pretty minor inconveniences that cost businesses a lot to prevent. What's the reality?

They're not inconveniences, they're injuries that can be lifelong and crippling. I know people who literally can't pick up a baby, can't sleep in the same bed with their mate because it's too painful if the sheet gets moved—because of the pain in their wrists from carpal tunnel. On the other hand, injuries like these are avoidable, and today's ergonomic standards are a reasonable means to prevent them.

When 9to5 and many other groups first started talking about office health and safety issues, we were laughed at. People said, "How can you use the words 'danger' and 'office' in the same breath?" Well, then, of course, many reporters started getting carpal tunnel syndrome, and they became very interested in the story. And now we see computers being sold with the line, "It's ergonomically designed." So the language and the acknowledgement of the need for attention to this we won a long time ago, but the fact is that if the need for these standards is real, we need public policy to guarantee them. This is an administration that above all else listens to Big Business, who obviously, in turn, doesn't want to spend the money, even though smart employers know it's good for the bottom line to prevent injury. But as we all know from the Enron debacle, running a company and caring about the interests of that company are not necessarily synonymous.

IS THERE STILL A GLASS CEILING? IS DISCRIMINATION TO BLAME, OR ARE WOMEN JUST MAKING DIFFERENT CHOICES THAN MEN?

It's much easier to think that this is about the choices women make rather than about institutional problems. Not only is there a glass ceiling, our view is that the solution isn't just to shatter that glass ceiling but to redesign the building. There's a problem in the way success is defined. If a woman has to be like a man, if she has to sacrifice a life and family so she can meet, move or travel at a moment's notice in order to advance, then that's a problem. Also, for women really to be equal, men have to share in childcare and household work, and they never will if they continue to get punished for it at work—so that, too, is a big problem in the design of the building.

I think it's interesting that since 9/11, many more people are conscious of the value of time with their families, and yet the recession, the war, and this administration's priorities have all made it much harder for families.

IN THE WAKE OF 9/11, THE AIRLINE INDUSTRY GOT HELP FROM GOVERNMENT—WHAT WAS DONE FOR AIRLINE EMPLOYEES WHO WERE LAID OFF?

Nothing, and many of those employees were women. I think the lopsidedness of the aid was very clear, that it went to help the owners and managers and not the people who lost their jobs. The money wasn't tied in any way to ensuring employment.

POST 9/11, THE BUSH ADMINISTRATION ESTABLISHED A DEPARTMENT OF HOMELAND SECURITY, AND IN THE PROCESS MANY CIVIL SERVANTS LOST THEIR

RIGHT TO ORGANIZE AND BELONG TO A UNION. THE BUSH TEAM ARGUED THIS WAS NECESSARY FOR "NATIONAL SECURITY"? WAS IT? WHAT'S REALLY GOING ON HERE?

Our view is that national security, antidiscrimination, these things are best served by people who are well trained and adequately compensated and who have safe-guards against mistreatment themselves—so, no. What we're really seeing here is an agenda of privatization. It's the priority of making business rule while undermining worker rights, unions, and worker protections. Those things come with federal employment, so privatization means fewer protections and more profits.

IN 2002, THE BUSH ADMINISTRATION INVOKED THE 1947 TAFT HARTLEY ACT TO FORCE LOCKED-OUT LONGSHORE WORKERS BACK TO WORK IN CALIFORNIA. IS THE RIGHT TO STRIKE IN DANGER AND IS IT A WOMEN'S ISSUE?

I think there has been some interesting activity among unions. The grocery workers strike, the organizing by home healthcare workers: these are all inspiring actions for working women, but they're really endangered by an administration that sympathizes with the employers who are trying to break the strikes. I think most working people see that sometimes the government can be your back-up, but that this government doesn't have your back, and in fact is out to stab you in the back.

HOW ARE WE DOING ADVANCING TOWARDS EQUAL PAY FOR WOMEN? THE DOL STATISTICS SHOW THAT THE WAGE GAP BETWEEN MEN AND WOMEN IS CLOSING UP—IS THAT A SIGN OF PROGRESS?

No. For one, as I mentioned earlier, they abolished the Pay Equity initiative, which was a real setback. And two, much of the gain for women, in terms of the gap, has come because of losses for men, and especially men of color—because of the losses of many manufacturing jobs. This is never what we had in mind. We want fairness for everybody, so for us it's not a moment of glory when men's pay is doing worse.

There have been gains for women, and women have fought hard for those gains, and we should appreciate them, but when you look at women as a whole there's a huge number who earn poverty wages.

CAN YOU TELL US ABOUT BUSH'S PROPOSAL FOR TEMPORARY ASSISTANCE FOR NEEDY FAMILIES?

Bush's proposal for TANF is to increase the number of hours women spend in unpaid work—he calls them "work requirements"—and to not increase at all the amount of money allowed for childcare. This is the opposite of what's needed. What's needed is more attention to getting women trained for decent jobs and getting them out of poverty. They need much more investment, not just in childcare but in flexibility for family care; people get sanctioned all the time because they stay home with a sick child.

And Bush's solution to poverty is marriage promotion and millions of dollars for that! It's this illusion, once again, that if women are poor it's their own fault—they could have just married, if only they weren't so loose and dissolute. Women-blaming has grown a lot under this administration. We have a view of poor women as lazy and bad role models, bad mothers, even though in fact most of them do work. They cycle in and out of employment and welfare because of their children's needs and the lack of institutional supports. Maybe a job was jeopardizing their child, or they lost it because their kid got sick and they had to stay home.

HOW MUCH DO YOU THINK A SECOND BUSH ADMINISTRATION WOULD BE ABLE TO ACHIEVE?

You mean, how much harm? Because that's really how I view it, and frankly I think at this point it's about lives. We shouldn't overlook the war: Iraq is a women's issue, and a workers' issue. There are so many women who are affected, many of them as combatants who signed up thinking it would be one way to get an education or make some extra money for their families, and had no clue that they would wind up in a place like Iraq, without adequate training.

And then there are the women family members. More and more military families are expressing their dismay with this war and how it has dragged on, and how the claims of "mission accomplished" were completely overinflated. It's been heartbreaking for a lot of people. And it became pretty clear that it wasn't an accident, the US "going it alone" in Iraq. If you mess it up, you get to clean it up, and it's US businesses that are very much cleaning up, in the reconstruction process.

MINIMUM WAGES, OVERTIME RULES, WORKPLACE SAFETY, THE RIGHT TO ORGANIZE AND BE INFORMED ABOUT ONE'S RIGHTS: SOME SAY THE BUSH ADMINISTRATION IS OUT TO REPEAL THE KEY LABOR LEGISLATION OF THE 20TH CENTURY. IN SO FAR AS WOMEN TEND TO BE THE LEAST PROTECTED WORKERS IN THE WORKPLACE ALREADY, DO THE POLICIES OF THIS ADMINISTRATION HAVE A DISPROPORTIONATE EFFECT ON WOMEN?

Yes, absolutely. Women are disproportionately found among non-union workers, low-wage, temp and part-time workers, so they are disproportionately among the most vulnerable classes of workers. Women also suffer gender discrimination, and women of color have the double jeopardy of race discrimination. Older women workers again face an additional burden of age discrimination. So when the government openly scales back the fight against discrimination and undermines basic worker protection laws, it's a very grim picture for working women.

IF YOU WERE LABOR SECRETARY TODAY, WHAT WOULD BE YOUR PRIORITIES?

My priorities would include labor law reform and helping workers organize. There are some really interesting labor law proposals, but it should be the Department of Labor leading that battle, instead of leading the opposition to it. Also the minimum wage: raising the wage floor, ensuring self-sufficiency standards, basic minimum needs budgets, and so forth. I would also seek to strengthen policies that would help people manage their family responsibilities.

When Karen Nussbaum was at the Labor Department there was a large study done on Family Medical Leave: clearinghouses were set up, awards were given, and a lot of attention was focused on identifying and replicating best practices—figuring out how to promote better public policy. That's what should be going on.

WE'RE CALLING IT THE W EFFECT—WHEN BUSH SAYS ONE THING AND DOES ANOTHER IN THE AREA OF WOMEN'S RIGHTS. HOW WOULD YOU CHARACTERIZE THE W EFFECT IN REGARDS TO LABOR POLICY AND WOMEN?

The efforts to privatize the EEOC and the changes in overtime are two different ways in which Bush says one thing and does another. They use language like "streamlining" when what we see is steamrolling—the steamrolling of worker rights. Language like "helping working families," when in fact they are taking away protections. And with the EEOC they tried to hide what they were doing until we forced it out in the open: they tried to sneak 5 million dollars in the war funding bill to help pay the cost of closing dozens of EEOC offices, without any discussion at all. We caught them and they finally modified their language, but not their plans—calling it "consolidation" instead of closure.

DOES THE RHETORIC WORK, DO YOU THINK? IF SO, WHY? WOULD YOU PUT ANY BLAME ON THE MEDIA?

I think the actions in Congress on the Family Time Flexibility Act show that it doesn't necessarily work. They're also getting a lot of heat right now for the language in the overtime regulations telling employers how to get around the minimum salary threshhold. But the point is, they are the power, and they can do it anyway—that's the problem.

The media does play a role. We've been desperately trying to get the media to cover the EEOC because no one knows that it's happening! And I think if they did, there would be a lot more pressure on Congress, and Congress would put a lot more pressure on the Department of Labor. That being said, Congress already did put pressure on them and said "you can't make these changes without reporting to us"—and they're doing it anyway! They're just flaunting their power!

TELL US VERY BRIEFLY ABOUT 9TO5.

9to5 just celebrated its thirtieth anniversary. It started in '73, and it's a national grassroots organization whose mission is to strengthen the ability of low-wage women to win economic justice. Most of our members are in nonmanagement low-wage jobs, and our priority campaign right now is winning family-flexible policies for low-wage women. We also do a lot of work around TANF, temp workers, part-time workers, discrimination and sexual harassment.

THANK YOU, ELLEN!

Wal-Mart Values

LIZA FEATHERSTONE

***The Nation,* 12.16.02**

Unlike so many horrible things, Wal-Mart can't be blamed on George W. Bush. The Arkansas-based company prospered under native son Clinton. Wal-Mart founder, the late Sam Walton, and his wife, Helen, were close friends with the Clintons, and for several years Hillary Clinton, whose corporate law firm represented Wal-Mart, served on the company's board of directors. And of course, Bill Clinton's "welfare reform," provided Wal-Mart with a ready workforce of women who had no choice but to accept the company's poverty wages, and discriminatory policies.

Still, Bush has most certainly been good for Wal-Mart. Retailers like to make campaign contributions to Republicans, partly because Republicans tend to oppose raising the minimum wage. But even compared to other large retail companies,

Wal-Mart's political contributions lean significantly to the right, and with good reason. Democratic appointments to the National Labor Relations Board (NLRB) are more sympathetic to workers and to unions, and Wal-Mart is a virulently anti-union company. Not a single Wal-Mart store in the United States has ever been successfully organized, and NLRB judges have repeatedly fined the company for violating workers' organizing rights. Wal-Mart workers have even been fired for trying to organize unions.

But it isn't just about laws and NLRB appointments. A right-wing president like George W. Bush creates a climate in which rogue employers like Wal-Mart feel they can operate with impunity, whether by busting unions, or by tolerating a sexist atmosphere in their stores. Under Bush, workers, especially women, have less cultural and political power, as business interests and the Christian right run amok.

The good news is that under Bush--more than under Clinton—Wal-Mart has been getting a lot of criticism. Headlines in major newspapers have asked questions like "Is Wal-Mart Bad for America?" The public has expressed increasing concern about the fact that most of Wal-Mart's goods are made in China, by women who have no organizing rights and work in sweatshop conditions. Closer to home, women are suing the company for sex discrimination, in what is potentially the largest civil rights class action in history. —Liza Featherstone

Wal-Mart is an unadorned eyesore surrounded by a parking lot, even its logo aggressively devoid of flourish. Proving that looks don't matter, however, the retail giant has a way with women: Four out of ten American women visit one of Wal-Mart's stores weekly. They like the low prices, convenience and overall ease of the shopping experience. Even snobbish elites are discovering its delights: A few months ago, *New York Times* fashion writer Cathy Horyn revealed, to the astonishment of fellow urban fashionistas, that much of her wardrobe comes from Wal-Mart ("Marc Jacobs?" "No, it's Wal-Mart"). Retail consultant Wendy Liebmann ecstatically dubs Wal-Mart the "benchmark by which American women rate all shopping."

Would that $15 runway knockoffs were Wal-Mart's primary contribution to women's lives. But Wal-Mart is not only America's favorite shopping destination; it's also the nation's largest private employer. The majority of Wal-Mart's "associates" (the company's treacly euphemism for employees) are women. Their average wage is $7.50 an hour, out of which they must pay for their own health insurance, which is so costly that only two in five workers buy it.

Yet Wal-Mart is not only a horrifyingly stingy employer: Many workers say it is also a sexist one. From the Third World factories in which its cheap products are made, to the floor of your local Wal-Mart, where they're displayed and sold, it is women who bear the brunt of the company's relentless cost-cutting. Ellen Rosen, a resident scholar in Brandeis University's Women's Studies Research Program, recently observed that around the world, Wal-Mart's business practices "may be leading to a new kind of globally sanctioned gender discrimination."

Gretchen Adams worked for Wal-Mart for ten years, in five different states. As a co-manager, she opened twenty-seven "Supercenters" (gargantuan, twenty-four-hour grocery/general merchandise hybrids). "There were so many inequities," she sighs with amazement, reflecting on her time at Wal-Mart. She saw men with little to no relevant experience earning starting salaries of $3,500 a year more than her own. "I had the title but not the pay," she says. "They take us for idiots."

Adams is now a witness in *Dukes v. Wal-Mart*, in which seven California women—current and former Wal-Mart employees—are charging the company with systematic sex discrimination in promotions, assignments, training and pay. Betty Dukes, for whom the suit is named, is a 52-year-old African American woman who still works at Wal-Mart. First hired by the company in 1994 as a part-time cashier in Pittsburg, California, she was an eager employee with a sincere admiration for founder Sam Walton's "visionary spirit." A year later, with excellent performance reviews, she was given a merit pay raise and a full-time job. Two years later, after being promoted to the position of customer service manager, she began encountering harsh discrimination from her superiors; she says she was denied the training she needed in order to advance further, while that same training was given to male employees. She was also denied the opportunity to work in "male" departments like hardware, and was made to sell baby clothes instead. "I can mix a can of paint," she told reporters just after filing the suit. "I want the chance to do it."

When Dukes complained about the discrimination, managers got back at her by writing her up for minor offenses like returning late from breaks, offenses routinely committed by her white and male co-workers, who were never punished, she says. When she kept complaining, she was denied a promotion and finally demoted back to her cashier job. She went to the Wal-Mart district office to complain, but the company did nothing. Being demoted was not just humiliating: It deprived Dukes of other promotions, and her cashier job offered fewer hours and a lower hourly wage. When she was once again eligible for promotion, four new management positions, none of which had even been posted, were filled by men.

Along with more than seventy witnesses, the other named plaintiffs in *Dukes v. Wal-Mart* tell similar stories:

- In August 1997, Patricia Surgeson, then a single mother of two, began working evenings as a part-time cashier in a Wal-Mart tire and lube department while attending community college. Within two weeks, while she was stocking shelves, she says, a male co-worker began grabbing and propositioning her. He was allowed to remain in his job, while she was transferred to the health and beauty aids department. Over the next four years, Surgeson held more responsible jobs at Wal-Mart, but these promotions weren't accompanied by raises. Many of her male co-workers were paid better than she was, she charges, even though they had less responsibility and were newer to the company.

- Hired to work in the returns department in the Livermore, California, store in fall 1998, Cleo Page, who had already worked in two other Wal-Mart stores, was quickly promoted to a customer service manager position. Interviewing a little over a year later for a promotion, she charges, she was told that it was a man's world, and that men controlled management positions at Wal-Mart. She was repeatedly passed over for promotions, which were given to male employees, and to white women. (Page, who is African American, also has a race discrimination claim against Wal-Mart, as does Betty Dukes, but these charges are not part of the class-action suit.) At one point, her store manager discouraged her from applying for the sporting-goods department manager position, she says, because "customers would feel comfortable" buying sporting goods from a man. She heard male co-workers complain that "women were taking over" the store, and she heard them ask each other if they knew other men who would be interested in working at Wal-Mart.
- Christine Kwapnoski, who is still employed in a Concord, California, Sam's Club (a division of Wal-Mart), has worked for the company since 1986. She charges that management positions were never posted, though when she heard one was opening up she'd tell supervisors she was interested. Still, the jobs were given to men less qualified than herself, whom she then had to train. A store manager suggested that she "needed to blow the cobwebs off" her makeup and "doll up." She says she saw men getting paid at higher rates than she was, and getting raises more often; in one instance, Kwapnoski, a divorced mother of two, questioned a male co-worker's raise, and was told he had a family to support.
- After thirty years of retail experience, Deborah Gunter began working at a Riverside, California, Wal-Mart in 1996 as a photo lab clerk. She says she applied for management positions and was passed over for less experienced men. She requested further training and never got it. When she was transferred to the Tire Lube Express department, she did the work of a support manager but never got the title or the pay.

Her supervisor sexually harassed her, and when she complained, her hours were reduced, she says. After she trained a man to fill the support manager job, he got the title and salary, and her hours were reduced. When she complained about her reduced hours and requested a meeting with the district manager to protest the discriminatory treatment, she was fired.

- And on and on. Women make up 72 percent of Wal-Mart's sales work force but only 33 percent of its managers. A study conducted for the Dukes plaintiffs by economist Marc Bendick found such discrepancies to be far less pronounced among Wal-Mart's competitors, which could boast of more than 50 percent female management. Even more striking, comparing Wal-Mart stores to competitors in the same location, Bendick's study found little geographic variation in these ratios, and little change over time. In fact, the percentage of women among Wal-Mart's 1999 management lagged behind that of its competitors in 1975. (Wal-Mart spokesman Bill Wertz says it's "too soon" to say how the company will defend itself against these charges.)

Depending on the outcome of a class-certification hearing next July before a San Francisco federal judge, *Dukes v. Wal-Mart* could be the largest civil rights class-action suit in history, affecting more than 700,000 women. [A decision is still pending. —ed.] Though a California judge ruled recently that the case must be limited to California plaintiffs, discovery is nationwide, as is the proposed class. If the plaintiffs have their way, any woman employed by the company from 1999 on would win damages. But even more important, says Brad Seligman, Betty Dukes's lawyer, "The idea is to change Wal-Mart. We will not have done our job unless we transform the personnel system at Wal-Mart and make sure there are additional opportunities for women."

Dukes is the culmination of a long history of individual sex-discrimination suits—including sexual harassment and pregnancy discrimination—against Wal-Mart, going back at least to 1981. Courts have often, though of course not always, ruled for the plaintiffs in these cases; in several sexual-harassment suits juries have awarded employees millions of dollars in punitive damages. Wal-Mart recently settled an EEOC sexual-harassment suit on behalf of a group of Wal-Mart employees in Mobile, Alabama, and several women unconnected to *Dukes* have discrimination suits under way.

Some of the lawsuits against Wal-Mart reflect common grievances cited by working women, inequities hardly unique to Wal-Mart, but that women's advocates rightly find particularly outrageous in the world's largest corporation. For example, a suit filed in Georgia by Lisa Smith Mauldin, a Wal-Mart customer service manager and a 22-year-old divorced mother of two, charges the company with sex discrimination because its health plan does not cover prescription contraceptives (it does cover other prescription drugs, but as the complaint spells out in painstaking legalese, only women get pregnant). Mauldin works thirty-two hours a week and makes $12.14 an hour, so the $30 monthly cost of the Pill is a significant burden for her (and certainly a prohibitive one for many fellow employees, who earn significantly lower wages). In September Mauldin's suit was certified as a class action, demanding reimbursement for all female Wal-Mart employees who have been paying for birth control out of pocket since March 2001, and demanding that Wal-Mart's insurance cover FDA-approved prescription contraceptives in the future.

Wal-Mart is also criticized for indifference to the workers, mostly young women, who make the products sold in its stores. While most major-clothing stores traffic in sweated labor, Wal-Mart's record on this issue is unusually bad. Much of the clothing sold at Wal-Mart is made in China, where workers have no freedom of association. Unlike many companies, Wal-Mart has adamantly refused to tell labor rights advocates where its factories are, rejecting even the pretense of transparency. Last year, Wal-Mart was removed from the Domini 400 Social Index, an influential socially responsible investment fund, for its failure to make sufficient efforts to uphold labor rights and for its "unresponsiveness to calls for change." Other than Nike, Wal-Mart is the only company that has been booted from the fund for this reason.

Last June, citing all of the above issues, the National Organization for Women named Wal-Mart its fifth "Merchant of Shame" and launched a public education campaign against the retailer. "It's part of our emphasis on economic justice. We don't think Wal-Mart is a woman-friendly workplace," says Olga Vives, NOW's vice president for action. NOW has asked Wal-Mart for a meeting to discuss its complaints, but since the company has not responded, Vives says, "we are getting their attention in other ways." On September 28, 600 NOW chapters demonstrated at Wal-Mart stores across the country, from Tallahassee to Salt Lake City.

NOW has been cooperating closely with the United Food and Commercial Workers, who have been trying for several years to organize Wal-Mart workers, an effort ruthlessly resisted by the company. Gretchen Adams, who quit Wal-Mart in December 2001, now works as an organizer with the UFCW. She's angry, not only about the way she was treated, but also about the plight of the hourly workers she supervised. "They were not paid enough to live on. There were a whole lot of single mothers," she says. "They would come in crying because they had hard decisions: whether to take their child to the doctor or pay their rent." Many hourly workers were on public assistance because their pay was so low, she recalls.

Not a single Wal-Mart store is unionized yet, but there's substantial evidence that many of the problems suffered by Wal-Mart's female employees would be alleviated by a union. A study on women in the retail food industry, published in February by the Institute for Women's Policy Research and funded by the UFCW, found that women workers in unions faced smaller gender and racial wage gaps, and earned 31 percent higher wages than women who were not in unions. In addition, the study showed that two-thirds of women in unionized retail jobs had health insurance, while only one-third of their nonunion counterparts did. Such advantages were even more dramatic for part-time workers, who are even more likely to be women.

At a November 18 press conference in Washington, D.C., to announce a UFCW-initiated National Day of Action on November 21—rallies were held in more than 100 cities and towns, supported by a broad coalition of religious, environmental, student and labor groups—NOW president Kim Gandy said Wal-Mart should know that "continuing their greedy, abusive ways will cost them the business of thinking consumers." This seems unlikely, though it's probably important to make the threat. In any case, the UFCW is not calling for a nationwide Wal-Mart boycott. "We are calling for a boycott in Las Vegas," says Doug Dority, president of the UFCW. In Las Vegas, where a vigorous organizing campaign is under way, Wal-Mart has committed numerous violations of the right to organize. Las Vegas is also the most heavily unionized city in the United States. Elsewhere, however, the UFCW is not ready to take that step. "It's hard to boycott and organize at the same time," says Dority. "Because Wal-Mart uses that against you: 'Hey, the union is trying to take away your job.'"

Still, it makes sense for activists to appeal to the possible solidarity between Wal-Mart's female customers and its female work force. UFCW vice president Susan Phillips said in a recent speech, "As women, we have tremendous power. We control both sides of the cash register. We are the cashiers on one side and we are the customers on the other side. If we join hands across the cash register, we can change the economic future for women in America." Far from telling consumers not to shop at the "Big Box," on the November 21 Day of Action many UFCW locals dramatized consumer power through "shop-ins," urging protesters to go into the store, buy something while wearing a T-shirt with the UFCW's phone number on it, and tell employees they supported their right to join a union. In Seekonk, Massachusetts, a UFCW local even gave each November 21 protester a $20 bill to spend at Wal-Mart, donating the purchases to a nearby women's shelter.

In fact, Wal-Mart customers and workers have much in common: They are increasingly likely to be anybody in America. The working poor are even more likely than other Americans to shop at Wal-Mart, not necessarily because they find it a shopper's paradise—though of course some do—but because they need the discounts, or live in a remote area with few other options. (Many Wal-Mart workers say they began working at their local Wal-Mart because they shopped there; when they needed a job, they filled out its application because Wal-Mart was already such a familiar part of their lives.) Through shoppers and "associates" alike, Wal-Mart is making billions from female poverty.

In addition to court mandates and worker organizing, changing Wal-Mart is going to take massive pressure from many constituencies; union locals will need an approach to coalition-building that is highly community-specific, yet networked nationwide, similar to that used by the progressive labor organization Jobs With Justice. The range of groups that turned out on November 21 was promising, and they have vowed to stay committed to a "People's Campaign for Justice at Wal-Mart."

Asked how long it will take to unionize Wal-Mart, Gretchen Adams, who is 56, answers without hesitation: "The rest of my life." But she's determined. As a manager opening a new store in Las Vegas, Adams says, "I was not allowed to hire any experienced help, because they might be union." Now, she deadpans, "I'm trying to get Wal-Mart the help it needs."

Why Privatizing Government Services Would Hurt Women Workers

ANNETTE BERNHARDT, LAURA DRESSER, AND CATHERINE HILL

***Institute for Women's Policy Research*, 10.00**

This Research In Brief summarizes key findings of the IWPR report *Why Privatizing Government Services Would Hurt Women Workers* by Annette Bernhardt and Laura Dresser. Using data from the 1998 Current Population Survey, Bernhardt and Dresser document job growth in the public and private sectors and examine the quality of jobs in terms of wages and benefits. Overall, this research finds that the public sector offers considerably better wages and benefits for women workers than does the private sector. For African American and Hispanic women, and for women who do not have a college education, the difference between public and private sector employment is especially pronounced. To a large extent, higher wages and better access to health and pension coverage in the public sector can be attributed to higher rates of union coverage.

JOB GROWTH IN THE PUBLIC AND PRIVATE SECTORS

The quality of jobs in the public and private sectors has become increasingly important over the past two decades as employment in the public sector has grown much more slowly than employment in the private sector. In 1979, 16 percent of men held public sector jobs while in 1998, only 13 percent did. For women, the number employed in the public sector dropped from 20 percent of the female work force in 1979 to 18 percent in 1998.

- Employment in the public sector declined for both women and men between 1979 and 1998, with especially pronounced declines for African American and Hispanic workers. Nevertheless, in 1998 almost one in five women held a public job (18 percent), a higher rate than among men (13 percent). This was especially true for African American women (22 percent).

Overall, public sector employment declined for both women and men during this period with a somewhat sharper decline among men.

PUBLIC SECTOR EMPLOYEES HAVE HIGHER WAGES AND BETTER ACCESS TO HEALTH AND PENSION BENEFITS

Focusing on the most current year for which data is available, 1998, IWPR finds that the median earnings in the public sector are higher than in the private sector for most categories of workers.

- Median wages for women without a college degree are 15 percent higher in the public sector. For women with a college degree, wages in the public sector are 7 percent higher than in the private sector.
- Among women, 72 percent of public workers participate in a pension plan and 69 percent have employer-provided health insurance. By contrast, in the private sector less than half have either benefit, and in the case of Hispanic women, less than a third do.

Thus, privatization is likely to erode the wages and benefits of women workers, especially for African American and Hispanic women and those with less formal education.

EXPLAINING WHY WAGES IN THE PUBLIC SECTOR ARE HIGHER THAN IN THE PRIVATE SECTOR

While wage ratios shown above are useful descriptions of employment conditions, they can also be misleading in that they do not account for differences in the public and private sector workforces. For example, workers in the public sector tend to be older (and hence could be expected to have higher earnings). Bernhardt and Dresser use a statistical regression analysis to distinguish components of the wage differential that can be attributed to the public/private sector distinction. Overall, controlling for race, region and work experience, women in the public sector are still more likely to have higher wages and better access to health and pension benefits than their counterparts in the private sector. While non-college educated men also benefit from somewhat higher wages and benefits in the pubic sector, particularly African American and Hispanic men, the effect is more pronounced for women workers. For example, women without a college degree earn wages in the public sector that are 5 to 6 percent above the earnings of their private sector counterparts.

However, once union membership and occupation variables were included, the differences in public sector and private sector wages largely disappeared. In other words, for women who have the same occupation, union status, education, work experience and race, the public sector does not, on average, pay better than the private sector. Unionization emerges as a central factor in understanding why the public sector pays better than the private sector.

GENDER EQUITY IN THE PUBLIC AND PRIVATE SECTORS

While women are paid better in the public sector in an absolute sense, the gap between men and women's wages remains. Comparison of the gender gap in public and private sector employment yields mixed results depending on race and educational background.

- The gender gap is smaller in the public sector, especially for women of color. But this overall result is driven largely by education. Only women with college degrees see greater pay equity in the public sector. For less educated women, gender inequality is as great in the public sector as in the private.

Overall, however, while there is clearly a gender bias in both sectors, women's wages are closer to men's wages in the public sector than in the private sector.

Another important indicator of equal opportunity is access to professional and managerial jobs. While the public sector is generally regarded as providing better access to professional and managerial occupations for women, Bernhardt and Dresser find that, if teachers are separated from other professional and managerial occupations, the public sector does not appear to provide greater opportunity for women.

- With the exception of teachers, women are no more likely to hold managerial, technical, or other professional jobs in the public sector than in the private sector (26.8 percent and 25.3 percent, respectively).

Because women in the public sector have more education than women in the private sector, we would expect them to be well represented in managerial and professional positions. That educational wealth has not translated into greater numbers of managerial jobs for women (while it has for men) indicates the continued presence of occupational barriers. Bernhardt and Dresser find that the public sector does not, in general, offer exceptional opportunities for women to hold managerial and professional positions (although other research by IWPR suggests that the public sector does offer better opportunities for women of color than the private sector).

RISKS OF PRIVATIZATION

The final part of Bernhardt and Dresser's research focuses on occupations, such as health care and child care workers, janitors, food preparation employees, and clerical and administrative staff, considered to be "at risk" for privatization. They find that women working in these "at risk" occupations have less education with close to half holding a high school degree or less.

- For women without college degrees, occupations "at risk" for privatization constitute 63.9 percent of their public sector jobs.
- Even though "at risk" occupations are not generally considered exceptional job opportunities, these jobs do pay better in the public sector than in the private sector.

Because the wage differential in the public and private sectors is largest for women without a college education, these women have the most to lose under privatization.

In sum, from a policy standpoint, there is good reason to be concerned about the continuing call for leaner government and the contracting out of as many public services as possible. On average, public sector jobs pay better and are more likely to include pension and health benefits. When government services are privatized, women—especially women of color and women who do not have a college education—could see significant declines in how much they earn and in their access to health and pension coverage. This does not mean that the public sector is a cure-all for inequality: glass ceilings and the gender gap in pay and benefits persist and in both the public and in the private sectors. But the bottom line is that privatization, and the de-unionization that frequently accompanies it, are likely to prove detrimental to the economic welfare of women workers.

Social Security Is a Women's Issue

ANNETTE FUENTES

***The Progressive,* Vol. 64, no. 1, 30, 11.1.00**

Gloria Willich was only forty-three when her husband died in 1966. They had three kids and a house in Browns Mills, New Jersey, with a $ 0 monthly mortgage. "He always worried that we might lose the house if anything happened to him," Willich says.

Willich wasn't working then. The future looked rocky until she visited the Social Security office. She found that she and her two youngest children were each entitled to survivor benefits. Although she decided to go back to work and to give up her benefit, she collected Social Security for her children. "I would have lost my house if I hadn't gotten the benefits for my kids," she says.

If Social Security back then had been the privatized system now being touted by conservatives, Gloria Willich's story might have a different ending. A variety of proposals to remake Social Security have cropped up, but they all boil down to this: divert a portion of the Social Security payroll tax into individual accounts invested in the stock market.

Opponents calculate that privatization would put all future Social Security beneficiaries at risk of diminished payments. But for women, who comprise 60 percent of all beneficiaries, the privatization scheme would be disastrous.

"Younger women should be very concerned about this," says Deborah Briceland-Betts, executive director of the Older Women's League. "It's not a generational debate. It's a gender debate."

Social Security is a pay-as-you-go system in which today's workers are paying the benefits of current recipients. But the benefits reach more than just retirees. One third of the total forty-eight million recipients are widows, widowers, or disabled people. Seven million recipients are the spouses and children of deceased workers. For 25 percent of older women living alone, Social Security is their only source of income. And without that monthly check, half of all women older than sixty-five would be poor.

The first problem posed by privatization is the assumption that the stock market will continue its upward spiral and deliver higher returns for retirees than would the current Social Security system, says economist Catherine Hill, study director of the Social Security Project for the Institute for Women's Policy Research in Washington, D.C. A proposal floated by the libertarian Cato Institute projects a 6.2 percent return for personal investment accounts, while other proposals claim returns as high as 7 percent.

"A lot of economists say the stock market is already inflated," says Hill. "Women have less money, earn less than men, and need to take fewer risks." Under privatization, women would have smaller investment accounts because they earn less. They would also get smaller yields and be more vulnerable to market fluctuations. And the new administrative costs—up to $50 per person per year by some estimates—would represent a bigger chunk of their accounts.

The Institute for Women's Policy Research compared benefits for a low-income single woman under a privatized system to current payments and found that investment accounts come up short. Using a realistic 4 percent rate of return on investment accounts, a woman earning $12,000 a year over thirty-five years ends up getting no more than 70 percent of the guaranteed Social Security benefit she is now entitled to. Social Security as structured may not be perfect, but it's a progressive system, replacing a greater percentage of earnings for low-income workers than for those with high incomes.

Many women leave the workforce to raise children or to care for elderly parents, so their own record of earnings is often low. But the system provides spousal benefits to women whose husbands had higher lifetime earnings, even if the marriage lasted just ten years. It's another component of Social Security that would be lost or diluted under a revamped system.

Privatization also threatens the disability and life insurance components of Social Security that women like Gloria Willich depend on. Women are 98 percent of the spouses or survivors receiving those benefits. But under the Cato proposal, for example, they would have to purchase such coverage from private insurers, which would be costly and less extensive than Social Security's benefits. People with preexisting conditions might be denied coverage altogether.

Despite all the changes in women's workforce participation in the last three decades, millions of women will still depend on Social Security to keep afloat. Women who work full-time earn just 75 percent of men's income, and they'll live longer than men, making them more dependent on monthly benefits. According to the Institute for Women's Policy Research, poverty among older women will be just as high twenty years from now.

"Women think it's a problem for the past generation and that 'I'll be OK because I work,'" says Hill. "But we're seeing a big increase in divorced and never-married women. So female poverty will be just as prominent but for different reasons." With so much at stake, working women should be sending a "hands-off Social Security" message to Washington, but they're not. "We haven't found that women are opposed to the stock market idea," says Hill. "They're not as immediately cynical about Wall Street as I'd like them to be."

Focus groups and polling on the issue have shown that people like the privatization idea in theory—until they learn more about how benefits could shrink, Hill says. And with the economy still going strong, privatization appears to be a smart, even prudent investment for retirement.

"Why are we even arguing about America's greatest social success? It's the boom of the stock market," says Briceland-Betts. "If the market took a dive, you'd have a totally different attitude."

But not all women have swallowed the privatization line. Gloria Willich has been an activist with the National Committee to Preserve Social Security and Medicare for three years. She covers central New Jersey, distributing literature and telling about the government program that helped keep her family together.

"I hear these young people say, 'Oh, those seniors, they're always asking for something,' "Willich says. "What we're fighting for now isn't for us. I don't want to see my children behind the eight ball. I'm fighting for my grandkids."

Women's Priorities Would Be Sacrificed to Pay for Bush Tax Cuts

***National Women's Law Center,* 3.11.02**

When President Bush proposed tax cuts two years ago, he said we could have it all and do it all: strengthen Social Security, improve education, provide a Medicare prescription drug benefit, set aside a reserve for emergencies, pay down the national debt—and have huge tax cuts.

Now it is clear we cannot. Due in large part to the $1.35 trillion Bush tax cuts of 2001,[1] the federal government is spending, not saving, the Social Security Trust Fund. It is about to run record-high deficits for "as far as the eye can see." And the Administration itself projects that, under its budget, the national debt will climb to more than $5 trillion within five years[2]—at the very same time the baby boomers begin retiring. And that is without counting the uncertain costs of war and its aftermath.

Nevertheless, instead of ensuring that critical national priorities can be met, President Bush has proposed several large *new tax cuts* at a cost of $1.9 trillion over the next decade—$2.7 trillion when all the tax cut-related costs are counted[3]—cuts that are overwhelmingly for the benefit of the wealthiest Americans. Next year alone, those with incomes of $1 million and up would receive an average tax cut of $90,000 just from President Bush's proposals to eliminate income taxes on stock dividends and speed up the effective dates of some of his previous tax cuts (the so-called "growth" package).[4] To put that into perspective, the millionaires' average tax *cut* is four times larger than the amount that single mothers with children—with a median income of about $22,000[5]—*earn* all year!

The President's proposals will do precious little to benefit women and their families. About half of all taxpayers would get a tax cut of less than $100; about one-third of all taxpayers, and one-half of single heads of household, would get nothing from the President's "growth" package.[6] Economic security is an issue of particular importance to older women, who are 77 percent more likely than older men to live in poverty.[7] Although President Bush claims that eliminating taxes on dividends would "help America's seniors make ends meet,"[8] very few older Americans (aged 65 or older) would get any help from a dividend tax cut. Less than one-quarter of older Americans,[9] and only about one-fifth of older women,[10] live in a family that receives *any* dividend income. Even fewer older women of color receive stock dividends: only six percent of the black and Hispanic elderly live in a family that receives dividend income.[11]

To the contrary, for the vast majority of women and their families, the President's tax and budget policies inflict only painful losses, both now and in the future. To make room for trillions of dollars of tax cuts for the best-off, the President's budget would shortchange top-priority programs today and drain the treasury of funds needed to secure a better future for women and their families. Here are just a few of the critical issues we could address by foregoing additional tax cuts for the wealthiest Americans:

- *Education*—Despite concerns regarding war, terrorism, and the economy, education remains the top priority concern for women.[12] For $304 billion, much less than half the cost of the President's $726 billion "growth" package, we could hire an additional 100,000 teachers to reduce class size, provide grants to repair 6,000 schools and assist with new school construction, and provide additional math and reading help for over nine million eligible low-income students.[13]

- *Homeland Security*—A recent poll found that women are far more personally concerned than men about the risk of terrorist attacks.[14] The President's budget cuts funds for "first responders" such as police and firefighters by nearly $3 billion, and hundreds of millions for airport security, port security, and border security.[15] For about $12 billion—or less than one-third of the cost of just *one* year of the President's $396 billion dividend tax cut—we could more adequately support state and local "first responders" in their efforts to prevent and respond to acts of terrorism for *three* years.[16]

- *Health Care*—Uninsured women are more likely than insured women to postpone needed care, skip important screening services, and be diagnosed at more advanced disease stages, and receive less therapeutic care,[17] and Latina and African American women are two to three times more likely to be uninsured than are white women.[18] For about the same cost as the President's $726 billion "growth" package, we could provide health insurance for the 33 million uninsured Americans with incomes below 300 percent of the federal poverty level ($26,580 for a single adult and $45,060 for a family of three).[19] Instead, the President proposes to radically restructure Medicaid and the Children's Heath Insurance Program in a way that will reduce access to health care for low-income women and their families.

- *Social Security*—Women have less in pensions and savings, and thus rely more on Social Security than men.[20] Women of color, in particular, count on Social Security in retirement; for over 80 percent of non-married elderly African American and Hispanic women, Social Security provides over half of their income in retirement, and for over half, it represents 90 percent or more of their retirement income.[21] Social Security faces a long-term shortfall and needs to be strengthened for the future. For the 75-year cost of the Bush tax cut agenda we could erase the *entire* 75-year, $3.7 trillion shortfall in Social Security *more than three times over*,[22] ensuring guaranteed, lifetime, inflation-adjusted benefits for the baby boomers and future generations. In addition, with the savings from freezing just the highest tax bracket where it is now—instead of accelerating the additional future cuts as the President wants—we could increase Social Security benefits for an estimated 5 million widows (and widowers).[23]

- *Medicare Prescription Drugs*—Prescription drugs play an integral role in health care, especially for older women who tend to live longer and have more chronic illnesses,[24] but Medicare doesn't cover them, and for many without other coverage the cost of needed drugs is prohibitively high. There are many proposals for adding a prescription drug benefit to Medicare and they vary in cost, but it is clear that $726 billion, the size of the President's "growth" package, would go a long way toward providing an adequate drug benefit to all seniors, *without* moving them into managed care plans to get it. [Note: The expansion of Medicare signed into law by President Bush in December 2003 provides prescription drug coverage. Some see the new plan as benefiting pharmaceutical companies more than seniors, however, because the government will pay top prices for drugs. —ed.]

- *Domestic Violence*—An estimated 1.5 million women are physically or sexually assaulted by their intimate partners every year, but emergency shelters are only able to provide residential services to about 300,000 women. For an additional $6 billion/year over current levels, which is just 15 percent of the cost of the $396 billion dividend tax proposal, we could shelter the thousands of women now turned away from shelters, and provide comprehensive services to help women escape violence, such as transitional housing, job training, services for children, legal advocacy, and community education and prevention.[25]

- *Children's Well-being*—For the amount of the President's $396 billion dividend tax cut, we could *both* provide Head Start for all unserved eligible preschool children in need of comprehensive services that prepare them for school and a productive future *and* provide health insurance to all of the 9.2 million kids who are still uninsured.[26] Instead, the President's budget estimates child care and after-school services for about 600,000 children,[27] narrows the scope of and dismantles Head Start, cuts several child nutrition programs, and weakens the Children's Health Insurance Program.
- *Unemployment Help and Job Training*—Over the past two years, the economy has lost more than 2 million jobs. The unemployment rate has increased by 50 percent overall, and by 74 percent for single mothers.[28] Despite this, the President has repeatedly refused to support extensions of unemployment assistance for all affected workers, and has proposed cutting job training programs for dislocated workers by $530 million below last year. For $10 billion, which is less than one-tenth of the $132 billion in savings yielded by freezing just the highest tax bracket where it is—instead of implementing the future, additional cuts scheduled for that top rate—we could guarantee all jobless workers at least 26 weeks of unemployment benefits, and expand eligibility for unemployment insurance to low-wage workers and part-time workers,[29] who are disproportionately women.
- *Social Services for Seniors*—Nearly three-fourths of all unpaid caregivers for older adults are women,[30] as are nearly four out of five of the elderly who live alone.[31] The President's 2004 budget freezes funding for Older Americans Act services that help the frail elderly stay independent, such as transportation, delivered meals, elder abuse prevention, personal care and chore services, with no adjustment for inflation or increased need. The *one-year* cost of the dividend tax cut alone (about $39 billion) would fund *all* Older Americans Act programs for millions of seniors, including a 10 percent per year increase, for 10 years.[32]

- *Child Support*—At the same time that President Bush proposes to cut taxes for the wealthiest Americans, the President also proposes to make up for some of that lost revenue by imposing new "user fees" on custodial parents, usually mothers, who are trying to collect court-ordered, unpaid child support. For $661 million,[33] less than one one-thousandth of the cost of the President's $726 billion "growth" package, we could avoid imposing what amounts to a new "child support tax" on cash-strapped parents struggling to support their children.
- *State Budget Crises*—States are facing their worst fiscal crises since World War II, and women and their families are paying a disproportionate price. Some states have cut back their school weeks to four days, raised tuition at state colleges and universities, cut child care help for working parents, and cut Medicaid eligibility, an important source of health coverage for low-income women and their children. Yet, the President's "growth" package provides no help at all for cash-strapped states. In fact, the President's new tax cuts would *cost* states $64 billion in additional lost revenue over the next 10 years, and that is on top of the lost revenues inflicted by the 2001 tax cuts.[34] State legislatures project states will have a $94 billion short-term shortfall: $26 billion shortfall in 2003 and at least $68 billion in 2004.[35] For less than the $104 billion cost of the President's proposal to accelerate the rate cuts in the top four tax brackets,[36] Congress could help states close their budge gaps.

President Bush's tax cuts shove aside programs important to women and their families in the short term. They will drain the treasury of the funds needed to protect and improve Social Security and Medicare—the real underpinnings of women's retirement security—over the long term. And they will burden future generations with a growing national debt. The Bush tax cuts must be paid for somehow, and it is clear that women and their families will be footing most of that bill.

Notes

1. One-third of the deterioration in the budget since 2000 has been caused by the Bush tax cuts enacted in the last two years, and that deterioration will grow larger every year. In fact, were it not for those tax cuts, the budget would be back in surplus in 2004 and for the rest of the decade. Richard Kogan, *Are Tax Cuts a Minor or Major Factor in the Return of Deficits?: What the CBO Data Show* (Center on Budget and Policy Priorities, February 12, 2003).

2. *See, Budget of the United States Government, Fiscal Year 2004,* Historical Tables, Table 7.1—Federal Debt at the End o f Year: 1940–2008, p. 117 (Feb. 3, 2003), available at http://www.whitehouse.gov/omb/budget/fy2004/pdf/hist.pdf.

3. The $2.7 trillion includes: $726 billion for the President's "economic growth" package; $624 billion to make the 2001 cuts permanent; $225 billion in other new tax cuts in the President's budget; an estimated $660 billion needed to fix the Alternative Minimum Tax, and increased interest on the debt of more $483 billion). John Spring, *Administration Tax Cut Proposals Would Cost $2.5 Trillion Through 2013* (Center on Budget & Policy Priorities, revised Feb. 10, 2003) available at http://www.cbpp.org/1-22-03bud.pdf.

4. Tax Policy Center, Revenue and Distribution Tables, Table 1.1, "Administration Stimulus Proposal: Distribution of Income Tax Change by AGI Class, 2003" (Revised Estimates: January 14, 2003) available at http://www.taxpolicycenter.org/commentary/admin_stimulus/section1/table1_1.pdf.

5. U.S. Census Bureau, "Presence of Related Children Under 18 Years Old—All Families by Total Money Income in 2001, Type of Family, Work Experience in 2001, Race and Hispanic Origin of Reference Person," Table FINC-03, detailed family income data from the Annual Demographic Supplement of the 2002 Current Population Survey, available at http://ferret.bls.census.gov/macro/032002/ faminc/new03_016.htm

6. Citizens for Tax Justice, "Bush 2003 Tax Plan a Big Fat Zero for a Third of Nation's Taxpayers" (Jan. 27, 2003), available at http://www.ctj.org/pdf/gwb0103.pdf.

7. In 2001 the poverty rate of older women was 12.4 percent, compared to 7.0 percent for older men. U.S. Census Bureau, *Poverty in the United States: 2001,* Table 1, available at http://ferret.bls.census.gov/macro/032002/pov/new01_001.htm

8. "The President's Jobs and Growth Plan: Helping American Families" (fact sheet on White House website), available at http://www.whitehouse.gov/infocus/economy/working_families.html

9. Social Security Administration, *Income of the Population 55 or Older: 2000*, Table 1.1, p. 3 (Feb. 2002).

10. NWLC calculation based on the March 2002 Current Population Survey.

11. Social Security Administration, *Income of the Population 55 or Older: 2000* Table 1.1 p. 11-12 (Feb. 2002).

12. *Demanding Quality Public Education in Tough Economic Times*, 2003 National Survey of Public Opinion, Extended Report, p. 9 (Public Education Network and Education Week, Feb. 2003), available at http://www.publiceducation.org/pdf/ 2003 ExtendedPollReport.pdf.

13. Information provided via email by Joel Packer, National Education Association, Feb. 7, 2003, on file with NWLC.

14. Lydia Saad, "Public Relieved about Terrorism as 'Orange' Alert Drags On," p. 2, Gallup News Service (Feb. 25, 2003), available at http://www.gallup.com/poll/releases/pr030225.asp.

15. Bill Ghent, "Senate Dems Fault Bush over Homeland Security Funds," *Government Executive Magazine* (Feb. 13, 2003). See also, Dana Milbank, "GOP Leader Challenges Bush Statements: House Republicans Sensitive to Criticism They Underfunded Homeland Security," *Washington Post*, p. A4 (Mar. 8, 2003).

16. S. 22, Justice Enhancement and Domestic Security Act of 2003, 108th Cong., 1st Sess. § 1106 (2003).

17. *See generally* Institute of Medicine Committee on the Consequences of Uninsurance, National Academy of Sciences, "Care Without Coverage: Too Little, Too Late" (2002).

18. One-third (33 percent) percent of Latina women and 19 percent of African American women are uninsured, compared to 13 percent of white women. Robert

Mills, *Health Insurance Coverage: 2001, Consumer Income*, Current Population Reports, #P60-220, Table 1, "People Without Health Insurance for the Entire Year by Selected Characteristics: 2000 and 2001" (September 2002), available at http://www.census/gov/prod/2002pubs/p60-220.pdf.

19. Information provided via email by Bill Vaughan, Families USA, Feb. 3, 2003, on file with NWLC.

20. *Women and Social Security Reform: What's at Stake*, p. 1 (National Women's Law Center, revised May 10, 2002), available at http://nwlc.org/pdf/WhatsAtStakeMay 20002 Revised.pdf.

21. *Women of Color and Social Security*, p. 1 (National Women's Law Center, Jan. 2003), available at http://www.nwlc.org/pdf/WomenofColorandSocialSecurityFactSheet2003.pdf.

22. Peter Orszag, Richard Kogan, & Robert Greenstein, *The Administration's Tax Cuts and the Long-Term Budget Outlook: The 75-year Cost of the Administration's Tax Cuts Is More than Three Times the Long-term Deficit in Social Security and Larger than the Long-term Deficits in Social Security and Medicare Combined* (Center on Budget and Policy Priorities, revised March 5, 2003), available at http://www.cbpp.org/3-5-03bud.htm.

23. See, Press Release from the Office of Rep. Xavier Becerra, "House Passes Legislation to Increase Social Security Benefits for Women: Ways and Means Member Says Bill Does Not Go Far Enough" (May 14, 2002), available at http://www.house.gov/becerra/pr020514.htm. *See also*, HR 4671, Social Security Widow's Benefit Guarantee Act of 2002 (107th Cong.).

24. Lisa Foley & Mary Jo Gibson, *Older Women's Access to Health Care: Potential Impact of Medicare Reform,* p. 5 (AARP Public Policy Institute, July 2000), available at http://research.aarp.org/health/2000_08_women.pdf.

25. Information provided via email by Juley Fulcher, National Coalition Against Domestic Violence, Feb. 7, 2003, on file with NWLC.

26. Children's Defense Fund, "Dividend Tax Cut Costly Enough to Pay for Children's Comprehensive Health Care and Head Start" (press release, Jan. 7, 2003), available at http://childrensdefense.org/release030107.php.

27. Children's Defense Fund, "White House Wages Budget War Against Poor Children" (pres release, Feb. 3, 2003), available at http://childrensdefense.org/release 030203.php.

28. NWLC calculations based on Bureau of Labor Statistics, Historical Data for the "A" Tables of the Employment Situation Release, "Table A-7, Selected unemployment indicators, seasonally adjusted," retrievable at http://www.bls.gov/ webapps/legacy/cpsatab7.htm.

29. "Help for the Unemployed in the House Democratic Economic Stimulus Proposal," House Budget Committee, Democratic Caucus (Jan. 6, 2003), available at http://www.house.gov/budget_democrats/analyses/econ_stimulus/unemployed.pdf.

30. National Alliance for Caregiving & AARP, *Family Caregiving in the U.S.: Findings from a National Survey*, p. 8 (June 1997), available at http://www.caregiving.org/finalreport.pdf.

31. U.S. Administration on Aging, "Older Women" factsheet, p. 2 (May, 2000), available at http://www.aoa.gov/May2000/FactSheets/OlderWomen.html.

32. Alliance for Retired Americans, *Bush Tax Plans Jeopardize Economic and Health Security of America's Seniors,* Issue Brief, p. 4 (Feb. 3, 2003), available at http://www.retiredamericans.org/pdf/Bush_IssueBrief_0203_2003.pdf.

33. U.S. Department of Health and Human Services, *FY 2004 Budget in Brief,* p. 82, available at http://www.hhs.gov/budget/04budget/fy2004bib.pdf.

34. Iris Lav, *President's Tax Proposals Would Reduce State Revenues By $64 Billion Over 10 Years,*

35. National Conference of State Legislatures, "Economic Recovery Requires State and Federal Cooperation, State Legislatures Say" (press release, Feb. 10, 2003) available at http://www.ncsl.org/programs/press/2003/pr030210.htm.

36. See, Urban-Brookings Tax Policy Center, "Table 13: Accelerate Income Tax Rate Cuts: Revenue Costs ($ billions), 2003-12," (Nov. 18, 2002) available at http://www.taxpolicycenter.org/commentary/speedup/table13.pdf.

Latina Girls' High School Drop-Out Rate Highest in U.S.

OLGA VIVES, WITH RESEARCH BY KRISTY McCRAY

***National NOW Times,* Fall 01**

The much publicized Education Reform Act, the first bill introduced in Congress by allies of George W. Bush, languishes in Congress without the votes necessary to become law, and the prospects for passing such legislation at this point seem slim.

"Leave no child behind," a phrase lifted by Bush from the Children's Defense Fund, rings hollow. His performance as Governor of Texas reveals the hypocrisy of his words: the state ranks among the highest in high school dropout rates. Thirteen percent of Hispanic students drop out of high school compared to 11 percent of African American and 6 percent of white students.

Latina girls leave high school at a much higher rate than any other group. This has added significance with the release of the 2000 census data which showed that Hispanics are virtually tied with African Americans as the largest minority group in the United States and at the current rate will be, by the year 2045, the largest people-of-color community in the U.S.

The reasons Latina girls leave high school before graduation are many. One major factor is pregnancy. A third of 9- to 15-year-old girls surveyed by the Academy of Educational Development cited pregnancy or marriage as the reason for dropping out of high school. The former governor of Texas did little to improve his state's teen pregnancy rate—in recent reports Texas ranked 46 of 50. And in 1997, Texas reported 52,728 births to girls ages 15–19; of those, 27,869 (52.8 percent of the total) were to Latina girls.

Other factors cited for the disproportionate high school drop-out rate of Latina girls are marriage, gender roles, stereotyping, family demands and economic status. Attitudes of teachers, a lack of proficiency in English, peer pressure, and a lack of role models are also contributing factors to this disturbing trend. Despite the alarming rate of drop-outs among Hispanic girls, there is no public outcry and little is being done to remedy this situation.

WHAT CAN FEMINISTS DO?

First, we must bring the light of day to an education system that disadvantages Latina girls. Reportedly Latina girls are often viewed by educators as submissive underachievers. This takes on added significance when reinforced by family at home. There are inadequate vocational programs for Latinas, sometimes none at all, and they suffer sexual harassment in the schools in greater numbers than other girls. As a result of this harassment, students often stay home, cut class, or don't contribute. They can't concentrate on school work and suffer lowered self-esteem and self-confidence.

Bilingual services are non-existent or poor at many schools and this leads to disillusionment. There is a pervasive negative attitude of school personnel toward non-English languages and the people who speak them. A critical factor in promoting Latina success is a school staff that believes that all students can succeed—valuing their languages and cultures, providing sound counseling, and involving parents.

Educational programs at all levels are key to reversing the trend. The future of Latina girls who drop out is bleak. Many enter the workforce at below-minimum wage jobs, enter into marriages that often result in domestic abuse, and/or stay at home to care for younger siblings while their mothers work outside of the home. Their world is one of few options, of increasing hardship and submission. We must insist on solutions at all levels of our society.

Latina girls need to know their options, and need the support of family, schools and peers in taking non-traditional career paths. Events in highs school or college campuses that feature successful Latinas in non-traditional fields can inspire Latina girls to think about their future and career options.

NOW members can lobby school boards for better curriculum and programs for Latina girls and special assistance/counseling programs aimed at reinforcing positive images. Feminists can take action to bring about real educational reforms to address these problems in our communities and to bring public education to a level of excellence for all children and young adults, helping them achieve individual goals. "Leave no child behind" must be more than hollow words; there is a real educational crisis in this country that is affecting children of color in disproportionate numbers. The political leaders who rubber-stamped the largest tax cut in history must be brought to account for its impact on the majority of the people of this country, those who bear the tax burden and receive the fewest services. It is an outrage that there are over 400,000 children living in poverty in the U.S., most in households headed by women, and particularly women of color. Tax dollars needed to address the disparities in our society have been given back to those that need them the least.

Erika Cerda, in a recent interview in the *Dallas Morning News,* gave as a reason for dropping out of high school that her "teachers were not explaining things very well." She "never fit in" at Sunset High School. "Kids were making fun of me," she said, because she was poor. We in NOW can make a difference in Erika's life by bringing about the social justice that eludes her.

Unconscionable Care: Is the Religious Right Compromising Your Health Care?

EMILY BASS

***Ms.*, 6.7.01**

Just six months after the Supreme Court decided *Roe v. Wade* in 1973, Congress enacted the Church Amendment. Largely unnoticed, the statute exempted individuals and institutions with religious and moral objections from performing abortions and sterilizations, even though they were receiving federal funds. By 1978, nearly every state had passed its own version of the amendment, in many cases expanding the scope of the exemptions.

To the extent that these laws protected individual rights, they seemed reasonable enough to most pro-choice advocates; after all, the abortion debate had been waged on the battlegrounds of conscience and the rights of women to make their own decisions. It seemed fair to take into account the personal choice of the providers being asked to perform abortions. In an era when private doctors were the norm, this rationale made sense.

But these laws also covered hospitals and clinics, and so pitted an abstract notion of institutional conscience against a woman's individual right to have an abortion. They also declared that in the shadowy realm of conscience, the basic medical principle of full disclosure did not apply to everyone—in most states with these laws, providers were not required to publicly post their "conscientious objections."

Fast-forward to the present; the Church Amendment and its state progeny have spawned a new generation of exemptions, and they go even further than the originals.

"Noncompliance clauses" (called "conscience clauses" by the religious right) began showing up in state legislatures in the early 1990s, not coincidentally at the same time that Bill Clinton's proposed health care reform bill was being debated. While they vary in specifics, the clauses allow religiously affiliated hospitals, employers, insurers, HMOs, or individual doctors to opt out, not only from performing abortions and sterilizations, but, in some cases, even from discussing abortions. They can also allow providers to refuse to offer, pay for, or talk about contraception. As with their predecessors, most of these clauses offer a veil of secrecy: providers are rarely required to inform anyone of their objections. By protecting a health care provider's right to refuse specific services, and giving this right precedence over a woman's right to make informed decisions about her health, noncompliance clauses create a parallel medical universe where professional obligations can be altered by personal beliefs.

Like other feminist struggles, this debate is, in part, a war of words. "Conscience clause" is a righteous, halo-wearing turn of phrase that puts a positive spin on legally sanctioned denial of standard health care; and that's the term you'll see used in the mainstream media. "What we need is to stress is whose conscience is going to be respected," says Frances Kissling, president of Catholics for a Free Choice. "Are we willing to respect the conscience of an institution above that of an individual?" Various organizations, including the ACLU, the ProChoice Resource Center, Planned Parenthood, NARAL, and Catholics for a Free Choice, are referring to them more accurately as noncompliance clauses, "religious loopholes," or "refusal clauses."

The clauses lay the groundwork for a range of chilling scenarios: a woman seeking an abortion leaves her doctor's office with a pamphlet on prenatal care, a handful of vitamins, and no referral to an abortion provider. A woman and her husband filling his-'n'-hers prescriptions for Viagra and Ortho Tri-Cyclen find that his are completely covered by insurance, while she has to fork over the entire cost of the Pill. A woman who has traveled a hundred miles to give birth to her sixth child in a rural hospital is refused the safe, simple procedure of having her tubes tied at the same time. And in a Catholic emergency room, a rape survivor is refused emergency contraception (EC)—if she knows to ask for it. If she doesn't, she will leave without learning that the option exists at all. Even if that survivor does get a referral, or a prescription for EC, she could then find that her local pharmacist refuses to fill it on the grounds of conscience. In each instance, the objector—doctor, insurer, HMO, hospital, or pharmacist—is favored over the woman.

AN INDEX OF PROGRESS?

Most noncompliance clauses are created by the conservative lobby and inserted into progressive state legislation. Just as Clinton's health care reform bill inspired such preemptive clauses in the early nineties, another push happened after Viagra was approved in 1998. For years, women's health advocates had been trying to introduce at the state level Equity in Prescription Insurance Coverage (EPICC) bills, which would require private insurers to pay for oral contraceptives. So when the FDA approved the miracle impotence drug—and many insurers quickly moved to cover the cost—women pointed out the hypocrisy and inherent sexism in covering Viagra and not the Pill. Their outcry helped put EPICC bills on the legislative agenda of nearly every state.

With the EPICC bills, however, came more noncompliance clauses. And with each new effort, the right-wing lobby extends its reach. Take the Women's Health and Wellness Act, which was being debated in New York at press time. The bill would require insurance companies to cover—and employers to pay for—contraceptives, as well as services like screening for cervical and breast cancer, and drugs for osteoporosis. But conservatives lobbied to exempt religious employers from insuring a range of birth control options—and got a boost from New York's Cardinal Edward Egan.

Pair the Church's political muscle with a tremendous increase in Catholic hospitals taking over secular institutions—there were approximately one hundred forty mergers between 1995 and 2000—and the result is frightening. In half of all religious hospital mergers from 1990 to 1998, reproductive health services were eliminated. The Catholic health care system is the largest nonprofit health care delivery system in the country, "serving" about 70 million patients each year. Many women are finding themselves in a situation where an entire network—hundreds of doctors—has opted out of offering comprehensive care, making it virtually impossible for them to switch to another doctor or clinic.

The fact is, most women are likely to be affected by noncompliance clauses, whether or not they use Catholic health services. Nearly every state in the U.S. has placed a health provider's right to refuse over your right to health services. "This is about quality access to health care for pluralistic communities where public resources are getting scarcer and scarcer," says Lourdes Rivera, an attorney with the National Health Law Program.

And while state legislatures accept ever-broader noncompliance clauses, the federal government is bending over backward to protect Catholic interests by accommodating Catholic HMOs competing for Medicaid and

Medicare contracts. The government has specified that they need not "cover, furnish, or pay for a particular counseling or referral service" that is objectionable to them on moral or religious grounds. Furthermore, if Bush's "faith-based" initiative moves forward, which would make it easier for religious organizations to receive federal funds, it could set up what one ACLU attorney refers to as "the über-conscience clause."

For affluent women who can switch plans or physicians or pay out of pocket, detouring around a noncompliance clause is inconvenient, but not necessarily life-threatening. But for low-income women, who may have to travel miles to get to their designated health care provider and wait for hours to be seen, getting the red light on a desired service can mean that there are no more options. "We're facing a world where privately insured women pay for the services they need, and low-income women are offered prayer," says Catherine Weiss, head of the ACLU Reproductive Freedom Project, which has held a series of workshops on noncompliance clauses.

NONCOMPLIANCE—NOW IN YOUR LOCAL DRUGSTORE

Almost immediately after the 1998 approval of the emergency contraceptives Preven and Plan B, pharmacists started refusing the fill prescriptions for these drugs—and codifying their right to do so in the regulations of state pharmacists associations. These codes are not law, but they do encourage individual pharmacists' acts of refusal. Groups like Pharmacists for Life International offer consulting and legal support if a pharmacist loses her or his job on the basis of a refusal.

For a woman trying to get the pills within 72 hours (a World Health Organization task force found that they're actually most effective in the first 12) any delay can be a problem. In rural areas, finding another pharmacist willing to dispense EC may be impossible. "It's the atypical woman who says, 'Excuse me, I am entitled to this and who are you going to send me to?'" says Nancy M. Yanofsky, president of the Pro-Choice Resource Center, which has launched a nationwide awareness campaign.

While pharmacists' regulations aren't binding, they do foster a climate in which women are intimidated and thwarted in efforts to access urgently needed health care services. And they are influencing lawmakers: in South Dakota, a noncompliance clause actually makes it legal for pharmacists to refuse to fill a prescription for EC. In response, Robert Tendler, a Connecticut pharmacist, has formed the national organization Pharmacists for Choice. "I do not have the right to impose my political, ethical, or moral views on anybody else," he has said. "When I put on the white coat and go behind the counter, my obligation is to the patient."

The current crisis is making women's health advocates take a hard look at how willing we've been to fight for our health rights. Some argue that concessions have been offered too quickly. Maryland, for example, was the first state to pass an EPICC bill. Women's advocates there, anticipating a fight, voluntarily inserted their own noncompliance clause, allowing religious organizations to opt out of covering contraceptives. "They didn't think much about it," says Caitlin Borgmann, state strategies coordinator for the ACLU Reproductive Freedom Project. "It seemed pretty innocuous."

Advocates in other states followed suit, and it took several episodes in which anti-choice legislators made eleventh-hour changes before progressives understood that introducing a clause of any kind is a hefty risk. "Advocates now realize they shouldn't have put in a clause to start off with," says Borgmann. "Once you've got it in there, you have nowhere to go."

A NEW POSITION

The solution, say Yanofsky and Weiss, is to reject all noncompliance clauses outright. Weiss points out that if you accept the premise that it is O.K. to provide exemptions based on religious beliefs, then a physician who is a Jehovah's Witness could refuse to provide blood transfusions. Of course, "the moral stance of certain religious groups receives more credence than others, and Jehovah's Witnesses clearly don't have as much clout as the Catholic Church," so they aren't allowed to impose their beliefs on their patients, she says.

"We haven't done what the civil rights movement did, which is to say, 'This is our line in the sand, don't you dare cross over it,'" says Yanofsky. "People are afraid if they say no to one thing, they won't get anything."

Equally important, say advocates, is the recognition that a medical standard-of-care, whether it is for reproductive health, HIV, or diabetes, is not open to editing or debate. "This is the only area in which we've created an exception to the general rule that physicians have to tell people about their options," says Jon Merz, a reproductive policy analyst at the University of Pennsylvania. Merz worries that a pregnant woman diagnosed with cancer in a hospital that does not perform abortions might be less likely to receive aggressive chemotherapy that could harm the fetus. When certain procedures are off limits, Merz asks, "What are the determinants of women's care?"

To get more women up in arms, the ProChoice Resource Center is sponsoring the Spotlight Campaign, a national series of conferences on noncompliance clauses that will bring lawyers, civic organizations, health care professionals, legislators, and reproductive rights advocates together. The ACLU Reproductive Freedom Project helps local groups oppose noncompliance clauses when they arise.

Since many states do not require health care providers to post their noncompliance status, the ProChoice Resource Center suggests that women ask health care providers and local hospitals what services they refuse to offer, and publicize this in editorials or with local community groups. "It's up to pro-choice women to find a channel for their outrage, and to ensure that there is full disclosure," says Yanofsky. "Bush and the anti-choice lobby are masters of flying under the radar."

WINNING HEARTS AND MINDS

Bush's Basket: Why the President Had to Show His Balls

RICHARD GOLDSTEIN

The Village Voice, 5.21.03

In the annals of infotainment, few moments match the sight of George Bush leaping from the cockpit of a fighter jet and striding across the deck of a carrier at sea. Top Gun: The Pseudo Event enchanted the public, horrified liberals, and galvanized the press. Suddenly media mavens noticed that Bush's handlers have elevated the photo-op to pure cinema. So what else is new?

Actually there *was* something novel about this occasion, but it passed utterly below the radar. Discretion prevented anyone from mentioning that Bush's outfit gave him a very vivid basket. This was the first a time a president literally showed his balls. Check it out—your subconscious already has.

This manly exhibition was no accident. The media team that timed Bush's appearance to catch just the right tone of sunlight must have chosen that uniform and had him try it on. I can't prove they gave him a sock job, but clearly they thought long and hard about the crotch shot. As students of the cinematic, they would know that the trick is to make the bulge seem natural, so it registers without raising an issue. Tight jeans (a staple of Bush's dress-down attire) can achieve this look, but nothing works like fighter-pilot drag, with its straps that frame and shape the groin. Most people presume this effect is merely functional. That frees the imagination to work, and work it does, in men and women alike.

Say what you will about the male body being objectified. We may expect a dude to display himself like an Abercrombie & Fitch model—but the president? Clearly Bush's handlers want to leave the impression that he's not just courageous and competent but hung. Why is this message important to send? That's a very salient question, if only because it's unlikely to be addressed.

Among modern presidents, Kennedy projected the studliest aura (though the sexual evidence was closely held at the time). Yet, in an era of body-hugging menswear, JFK wore loose-fitting suits. Clinton was perhaps the ultimate rogue in chief, but he shrank from showing his body—he wouldn't have dared. Cartoonists alluded to Clinton's libido by giving him a large bulbous nose, which became his emblem. Look at the face cartoonists have given Bush: The ears are outsized while the nose is modest. Big ears are not exactly phallic signifiers; if anything, they connote a state of permanent childhood, à la Mickey Mouse. In caricature Bush looks like a perplexed piker. There's a reason he once drew the ultimate Texas dis: "All hat and no beef." This sissifying contempt still lingers under the hoopla about Bush's prowess.

9/11 scared America into solidarity, but if people perceive the Republican agenda as an equal threat, their doubts about Dubya's manhood will resurface. They will notice his reliance on strong-willed advisers, his association with a patriarchal father, and even his diminutive size. Karl Rove's rangers must be aware of this possibility since they've crafted an image to counter Bush's macho problem. His public affect—the narrowed eyes, the locked-and-loaded look—is calculated to annul his liabilities, present and past. Imagine what the Republicans would make of a Democrat who was a cheerleader in prep school, who wrangled his way into Yale on family connections, and who weaseled out of active duty. Clinton was butch-baited for less.

Bush could easily have lived up to his home-state nickname, Shrub—and in the early hours of 9/11, he did. But rehabilitation is the master narrative of Bush's presidency. This party animal turned commander is Prince Hal to his own Falstaff.

Overcoming is a powerful American theme; hence the proliferation of log cabins and front porches in the iconography of presidents, even some who grew up in splendor. Bush may be a master of populist pretense, but he can't claim to be self-made. His saga rests on his quest to be a man. The real triumph of Bush's media team is not a matter of lighting and positioning but of creating a presidential persona that radiates steadfastness, plainspokenness, sexual continence, and righteous religiosity. These are the hallmarks of conservative macho.

But something about Bush's image seems as artificially enhanced as his crotch. His need to flaunt it can be read as a response to anxiety. If you have to show your balls, maybe it's because you can't take them for granted. That isn't just Bush's problem. If macho seems so tragicomically x-treme these days, it's because many men think masculinity could actually disappear.

All men must cope with the complications of feminism. I would argue that the demand for sexual equality is a major reason for the global rise of fundamentalism. Bush owes his fortune to this movement in America, but his appeal goes far beyond the Christian right. He represents a model that invites female initiative and counsel but not control. This is the Dred Scott compromise of our time, and it's evident in Bush's administration as well as in his marriage to an intelligent woman who knows how to stay three steps behind her husband. But Bush also embodies the primal uncertainty many men feel in the face of sexual change. This angst, which threatens to pop up like a sour belch, solidifies his bond with threatened men. They identify with his struggle to carry off the feat of macho, and many women empathize with that effort. A lot of people root for Bush to make it as a man, and they're happy to see his big basket (even if it does suggest a male version of the push-up bra).

If America remains preoccupied with terrorism, the sexual politics I'm describing will affect the 2004 election only obliquely. But if voters focus on other things, the macho issue could be as crucial as it was in 2000, when Al Gore was wussified. Rove's rangers have already begun bashing the Democratic candidate most likely to make Bush look like all cake and no beef: John Kerry.

First they questioned his patriotism, then they accused him of looking French, and now they're landing on his wife, casting her as a hyper-Hillary. Teresa Heinz Kerry's outspokenness, her devotion to her dead former husband, her current prenup, and her vow to maim any man who steps out on her are all being used to portray her as a ball-breaking bitch and John Kerry as her emasculated victim. So powerful is this harridan image that it actually allows the Bushies to bash Teresa for her wealth. If she doesn't finance Kerry's campaign, she's dissing him; if she does, he's a kept man.

Kerry isn't the front-runner [he became the front-runner in early '04 —ed.], yet the White House has singled him out for sexual calumny. To understand this fixation, you have to consider Kerry's stature (he towers over Bush), his war record, and his sloe-eyed Kennedy aura. In another era, these would be clear signals of masculinity. Today, you have to flash your stash, and Kerry's patrician style doesn't lend itself to that. But he does have those tales from 'Nam, and in a one-on-one he could expose the angst under Bush's aggression. If the economy tanks while Iraq seethes, we just might have a real contest.

Fasten your crotch straps. With luck, we're in for a bumpy ride.

Veiled Intentions: The U.S. Media's Hug and Run Affair with Afghan Women

MARIA RAHA

Bitch, Spring 03

To my dismay, the movie theater closest to my apartment relentlessly offered the most pitiful of Hollywood's already pitiful fare—that is, until September 11, 2001, after which *Kandahar,* a story of an exiled woman's return to Afghanistan, popped up on the dusty marquee. As the usual supply of teen schlock came and went, *Kandahar* hung steadfastly on for months—proof that the plight of Afghan women was becoming a distinctly mainstream concern.

The road of post-9/11 pop culture and news media is littered with as many nods to Afghan women as a typical Bush speech is with references to "the evildoers." To wit: As reported in *USA Today* in February 2002, the website for the Revolutionary Association of the Women of Afghanistan received such heavy traffic after a mention on *Oprah* that it crashed. As of this writing, a total of seven books on Afghan women have been released by major publishers since September 2001. Just weeks before the United States invaded Afghanistan, CNN re-ran *Beneath the Veil*, a documentary on the topic. Meanwhile, the word "burqa" became ubiquitous: It showed up on the American Dialect Society's 2001 Words of the Year list, and the editors of the *American Heritage College Dictionary* rushed to include it in their latest edition. Even the *New York Post* jumped on the burqa bandwagon (albeit in a completely bizarre way), using the word to describe the shroud with which Michael Jackson covers his children.

Finally, it seemed, the U.S. was paying attention to what many feminists had known since the Taliban took control of Afghanistan in 1996: The fundamentalist regime was committing countless human rights abuses every day. Before 9/11, campaigns by the Feminist Majority Foundation and others to call attention to the obstacles faced by Afghan women, to raise funds for Afghan women to be educated in refugee and underground schools, and to pressure the U.S. government to increase aid went largely ignored. Politicians in both parties paid lip service to Afghan women's plight, but this recognition didn't lead to any significant action. Even with support from Hillary Clinton and Mavis Leno, wife of Jay, efforts to raise international awareness heralded little mainstream attention.

Once Al Qaeda emerged as the force behind the 9/11 atrocities, however, the Bush administration started sounding rather, well, feminist in its stance toward the Taliban. But Bush, hardly renowned for championing the rights of women in America, let alone those in the Third World, was not demanding liberation for the women of Afghanistan out of principle or even compassion. If Afghan women were to gain freedom, it would not be because our government deemed their lives important, but because their oppression was justification for the U.S. bombing of their country.

While George rallied the troops with sweeping generalizations about good and evil, Laura was brought in, most likely to make his sudden concern for women's rights seem a bit less faux. In November 2001, she stepped out of her usual smiling, placid place just behind her husband's shoulder to deliver the weekly radio address usually given by her husband, on the topic of Afghan women. In her address, she claimed that "the brutal oppression of women is a central goal of the terrorists" and that "the fight against terrorism is also a fight for the rights and dignity of women." (Once could also apply such sentiments to violent protesters outside abortion clinics, but the religious right is not the particular face of terrorism with which either Bush is concerned.) In a May 2002 speech to the Organization for Economic Co-operation and Development, she declared: "Prosperity cannot follow peace without educated women and children. . . . When women are educated, people's lives improve in significant other ways as well," While her phrases ring with feminist tones, Mrs. Bush's words seem to have little to do with a sincere desire to improve conditions for women in Afghanistan. In the typically illogical black-and-white terms of propaganda, supporting the welfare of the world's women means supporting the war on terrorism—and, more insidious, supporting the war on terrorism means supporting the world's women, with no further action required.

As rhetoric in support of Third World women flourished, aid programs for those same women remained in constant jeopardy. In November 2001, the State Department issued its "Report on the Taliban's War Against Women," a large portion of which was devoted to the need for improved healthcare. But last summer, in direct opposition to the report's recommendations, Bush withheld $34 million in funding from the United Nations Population Fund, which provides global aid for women's reproductive healthcare. Supporting the fund does more to help the world's women than supporting the war on terrorism, but neither the Bush administration nor the mainstream media seem to see the contradiction in Bush's policy.

To position women's rights as a rallying point for war paints politicians and the public at large into a corner—particularly those of us who have long fought for the welfare of women. It's a calculated exploitation of leftist concerns in order to suppress dissenting thought. If supporting the war on terrorism means ensuring the freedom of some of the world's most oppressed women, by all means, we should support the war.

Furthermore, it's unclear in all this rhetoric exactly what "freedom" signifies for Afghanistan. If the mainstream press is to be believed, freedom in post-Taliban Afghanistan is merely about the right to look as one chooses, to shave one's beard or shed one's burqa. When the *New York Times* reported the start of entrance exams at Kabul University on December 23, 2001, journalist John F. Burns described the event as "a day for earrings and makeup and handbags and other casual flauntings. . . . In the hallways, the burqa . . . was now a fashion statement, tossed backward from the candidates' heads as if to say, 'Take a hike, Mr. Mullah.'" Granted, these changes in dress are certainly symbols of greater freedoms gained. However, the reportorial fixation on such victories assumes that what women desire most is the right to freely decorate ourselves, and trivializes the more complex and important issues Afghanistan faces, such as employment and widespread illiteracy, not to mention conservative backlash in the form of physical violence. Intentionally or not, the media reinforced Bush's uniformed rhetoric with an instant "happy ending"—one the public can interpret as success for both the U.S. and for Afghanistan, and one the administration can use to garner support for the next military action.

As the United States turns its attention from war in Afghanistan to war in Iraq, the struggle of Afghan women has faded from Bush's speeches (even as he recently allotted $3.5 billion in aid) and from the mainstream media (aside from the occasional feel-good piece celebrating such milestones as the first granting of driver's licenses to Afghan women). As they throw back their veils—which have come to encapsulate their oppression—Afghan women step into a new invisibility. In a media culture where silence equals nonexistence, the disappearance of Afghan women from the political stage defines the problem as "fixed" in the eyes of the public.

Against a backdrop of aggressive antifeminist and imperialist actions, administrative efforts in both warfare and healthcare prove that behind an utterly transparent "feminist" veil, we're still dealing with the same old cowboys.

The Thong vs. the Veil

CEDRIC MUHAMMAD

***Blackelectorate.com*, 11.26.01**

The sudden discussion and expressed concern for Afghanistan's female population is striking. To us it seems to have that same hollow and disingenuous feel as the campaign to stop slavery in the Sudan and the effort to keep Elian in America, away from his father. We also are picking up that same whiff of moral equivalency violations that are so prominently associated with the Elian and Sudan discussions. We thought of this over the weekend as we pondered the condition of women all over the world, including those in the United States of America. We thought of this as we watched the latest music videos on MTV and BET which featured the most scantily clad White, Black and Latino women to be found anywhere on the earth. We wondered at the end of the day, of the two groups of women most prominently featured on American TV these days, who gains more respect for their intellect and spirit—the Afghan woman who is so totally veiled that you can't even see her eyes or the Black woman in the R&B and Hip-Hop video who dances while wearing a bikini and thong? Is less more?

It was interesting to see women lament over the plight of Afghanistan's women, women who now want the U.S. government to ensure that the rights of women are protected in the newly constituted Afghanistan. But we couldn't help but remember that it was over 100 years before women obtained the right to vote in the newly constituted United States of America. Paradoxical.

Over the weekend while watching C-SPAN we caught an Imam from Oakland who powerfully made the argument that there are more women serving in Iran's parliament then there are women serving in the U.S. Congress. He also made a point that it has been the United States government that has supported some of the most repressive regimes, including the Taliban, in terms of woman's rights. The U.S., he indicated, has a very selective memory when it comes to defending women's rights.

It all made us think of a recent conversation we had with a brilliant Black woman where we made the point that many Muslim nations have already had female leaders—Presidents and Prime Ministers—while the United States has never had one. We also agreed that we were confident that a woman would not become president of the United States before we passed from this earth.

For all of the talk of the mistreatment of Afghan women, we wonder if more women are raped in Afghanistan than are raped here. We wonder, in proportion to the population of course, if there are more prostitutes there than there are here. We wonder where more women are victims of domestic abuse—in Afghanistan or in the United States of America? Accounting for the various language differences, we wonder where more women are referred to as "bitches" and "whores," in America or in Afghanistan? And where are women greater victims of sexual harassment? And is it not a fact that in the United States of America, the bastion of freedom, that women get paid less for doing the same work as their male counterparts? And is it not White *women*, not even Blacks, who are the greatest beneficiaries of affirmative action programs in the United States of America?

And for all of the talk of how women are mistreated in Islam and in Afghanistan, we don't totally disagree, but we ask the question: How many White or Black Christian women preach in the pulpit on Sunday? How many churches in this country still prevent women from being ordained or have never, in their history in America, had a female pastor?

That same Imam from Oakland that we referred to also made a sharp point over the different ways in which Catholic nuns, who are almost completely veiled, are perceived as opposed to Muslim women who are veiled. We wonder, will there be a parallel movement among those so concerned about the veiling of Arab, African and Afghan women, in Islam, to "liberate" the White Catholic nuns who are not only totally covered, save their faces, but who are not allowed to marry men? We must ask those people in America styled as fighting for the freedom of Afghan women if this mandatory dress code and prohibition on marriage for nuns qualifies as oppression.

We think this discussion on women's freedom, regardless to the motives of those most vocal in raising it, serves a great purpose and may raise some interesting facts and contradictions that many in the West, particularly in the United States, may not be thinking of at the present time.

On Rescuing Private Lynch and Forgetting Rachel Corrie

NAOMI KLEIN

***The Guardian,* 5.22.03**

Jessica Lynch and Rachel Corrie could have passed for sisters. Two all-American blondes, two destinies forever changed in a Middle East war zone. Private Jessica Lynch, the soldier, was born in Palestine, West Virginia. Rachel Corrie, the activist, died in Israeli-occupied Palestine.

Corrie was four years older than 19-year-old Lynch. Her body was crushed by an Israeli bulldozer in Gaza seven days before Lynch was taken into Iraqi custody on March 23. Before she went to Iraq, Lynch organised a pen-pal programme with a local kindergarten. Before Corrie left for Gaza, she organised a pen-pal programme between kids in her hometown of Olympia, Washington, and children in Rafah.

Lynch went to Iraq as a soldier loyal to her government. Corrie went to Gaza to oppose the actions of her government. As a US citizen, she believed she had a special responsibility to defend Palestinians against US-built weapons, purchased with US aid to Israel. In letters home, she described how fresh water was being diverted from Gaza to Israeli settlements, how death was more normal than life. "This is what we pay for here," she wrote.

Unlike Lynch, Corrie did not go to Gaza to engage in combat: she went to try to thwart it. Along with her fellow members of the International Solidarity Movement (ISM), she believed that the Israeli military's incursions could be slowed by the presence of highly visible "internationals." The killing of Palestinian civilians may have become commonplace, the thinking went, but Israel doesn't want the diplomatic or media scandals that would come if it killed a US student.

In a way, Corrie was harnessing the very thing that she disliked most about her country: the belief that American lives are worth more than any others—and trying to use it to save a few Palestinian homes from demolition.

Believing her fluorescent orange jacket would serve as armour, Corrie stood in front of bulldozers, slept beside wells and escorted children to school. If suicide bombers turn their bodies into weapons of death, Corrie turned hers into the opposite—a weapon of life, a "human shield."

When that Israeli bulldozer driver looked at Corrie's orange jacket and pressed the accelerator, her strategy failed. It turns out that the lives of some US citizens—even beautiful, young, white women—are valued more than others. And nothing demonstrates this more starkly than the opposing responses to Rachel Corrie and Private Jessica Lynch.

When the Pentagon announced Lynch's successful rescue, she became a hero, complete with "America Loves Jessica" fridge magnets, stickers, T-shirts, mugs, country songs and an NBC made-for-TV movie. According to White House spokesman Ari Fleischer, President George Bush was "full of joy for Jessica Lynch". Her rescue, we were told, was a testament to a core American value: as West Virginia senator Jay Rockefeller said to the Senate: "We take care of our people."

Do they? Corrie's death, which made the papers for two days and then virtually disappeared, has met with almost total official silence, despite the fact that eyewitnesses claim it was a deliberate act. President Bush has said nothing about a US citizen killed by a US-made bulldozer bought with US tax dollars. A US congressional resolution demanding an independent inquiry has been buried in committee, leaving the Israeli military's investigation—which cleared itself of any wrongdoing—as the only official investigation.

The ISM says that this non-response has sent a clear, and dangerous, signal. According to Olivia Jackson, a 25-year-old British citizen in Rafah: "After Rachel was killed, [the Israeli military] waited for the response from the American government and the response was pathetic. They know they can get away with it, and it has encouraged them to keep on going."

First there was Brian Avery, a 24-year-old US citizen shot in the face on April 5. Then Tom Hurndall, a British ISM activist shot in the head and left brain dead on April 11. Next was James Miller, the British cameraman shot dead while wearing a vest that said "TV". In all of these cases, eyewitnesses say the shooters were Israeli soldiers.

There is something else that Jessica Lynch and Rachel Corrie have in common: both of their stories have been distorted by the military for its own purposes. According to the official story, Lynch was captured in a bloody gun battle, mistreated by sadistic Iraqi doctors, then rescued in another storm of bullets by heroic Navy Seals. In the past weeks, another version has emerged. The doctors who treated Lynch found no evidence of battle wounds, and donated their own blood to save her life. Most embarrassing of all, witnesses have told the BBC that those daring Navy Seals already knew there were no Iraqi fighters left in the area when they stormed the hospital.

But while Lynch's story has been distorted to make its protagonists appear more heroic, Corrie's story has been posthumously twisted to make her, and her fellow ISM activists, appear sinister.

For months, the Israeli military had been looking for an excuse to get rid of the ISM "troublemakers". It found it in Asif Mohammed Hanif and Omar Khan Sharif, the two British suicide bombers. It turns out that they had attended a memorial service for Corrie in Rafah, a fact the Israeli military has seized on to link the ISM to terrorism. Members of ISM point out that the event was open to the public, and that they knew nothing of the British visitors' intentions.

In the past two weeks, half a dozen ISM activists have been arrested, several deported, and the organisation's offices raided. The crackdown is spreading to all "internationals," meaning there are fewer people in the occupied territories to either witness the abuses or assist the victims. On Monday, the UN special coordinator for the Middle East peace process told the security council that dozens of UN aid workers had been prevented from getting in and out of Gaza, calling it a violation of "Israel's international humanitarian law obligations".

On June 5 there will be a international day of action for Palestinian rights. One of the demands is for the UN to send a monitoring force into the occupied territories. Until that happens, many are determined to continue Corrie's work. More than 40 students at her former college, Evergreen State, Olympia, have signed up to go to Gaza with the ISM this summer.

So who is a hero? During the attack on Iraq, some of Corrie's friends emailed her picture to MSNBC asking that it be included on the station's "wall of heroes", along with Jessica Lynch. The network didn't comply, but Corrie is being honoured in other ways. Her family has received more than 10,000 letters of support, communities across the country have organised memorial services, and children from the occupied territories are being named Rachel. It's not a made-for-TV kind of tribute, but maybe that's for the best.

Celebrating the Many Roles of Women

LT. BRENDA BERKMAN, FDNY

The National Women's Law Center Award Dinner, 11.14.01

Thank you for honoring me tonight. By honoring me, you are honoring all the women rescue and recovery workers who have been doing their patriotic duty at Ground Zero and the Pentagon, in the armed forces and all over this country.

Who are these women? *Where* are the women rescue and recovery workers in the frenzy of media coverage of every little detail of Ground Zero that has occurred since September 11? We have all seen the stories about the rescue dogs and the "brothers" who are riding bikes across the country in memory of the firefighters killed at the World Trade Center. We have had the *New York Times* opine about the return of the "manly man"—referring to male firefighters as the new cultural icons. We immediately had columns by right-wing pundits arguing that the lack of media coverage of women rescue workers was "proof" that women could not and should not be firefighters. Many of these stories have been reported, written or produced by women.

I am here to tell you that the reality is that women *were* and *are* at Ground Zero. They have been there since the first minutes of the attack. Half of the women in the New York City Fire Department—and there are only 25 women out of 11,500 firefighters—put themselves in harm's way that first day and for many days thereafter. Fortunately, none were killed.

There were also countless women EMTs, New York City police officers, Port Authority police officers and other emergency workers who responded immediately. Three uniformed women lost their lives that day: Port Authority Captain Kathy Mazza, NYPD officer Moira Smith, and EMT Yamel Merino, who was working for a private ambulance service. Many more women were injured trying to save others—women who literally had to have pieces of the buildings removed from their bodies, women who suffered broken bones and other injuries requiring hospitalization.

Within hours of the first plane, Ground Zero was flooded with other women emergency workers and volunteers. Women by the dozens came from all over the country as part of search-and-rescue and other firefighter teams. Women nurses and doctors, women construction workers, women chaplains, military women, Red Cross women—women volunteering in every capacity, every minute of those first days and weeks.

Women continue to work at Ground Zero today. Women and men have worked together as one, desperately searching for any sign of life.

The *reality* is that women have contributed to the aftermath of the World Trade Center attack in every imaginable way. But the face the media has put on the rescue and recovery efforts in New York City is almost exclusively that of men. Where are the pictures or stories of Captain Kathy Mazza shooting out the glass in the lobby of one of the towers to allow hundreds of people to flee the building more quickly? Or of police officer Moira Smith helping people escape the towers, and last be seen going back into the building to help a trapped asthmatic person? Or of EMT Yamel Merino tending to an injured person when she herself was struck by the falling building? Or of the countless women working on the pile of debris to recover anyone who may have survived, or the remains of the thousands of people who were in the building or on the airplanes?

One of the hardest things for the women firefighters to bear has been their total invisibility at the hundreds of funerals for their fallen comrades—men we worked with for many years—our friends, our "brothers." At almost every funeral we attend, the mayor, the cardinal, the fire commissioner and almost every eulogist—except of course when we ourselves are the eulogists—talk exclusively about the *men* and the *brothers* our coworkers worked with. The other day, as I attended another funeral for one of my friends in St. Patrick's Cathedral, the cardinal asked the *men* who are the "bravest" to rise—totally ignoring the dozens of women firefighters and police officers in attendance from all over the country.

The word "fireman" has totally eclipsed the gender-neutral and accurate civil service term "firefighter." Not quite as often, but still too frequently, the same has happened as "policeman" returns, to the exclusion of "police officer."

Why has this happened? The reality is that women are on the front lines domestically and abroad in the war against terrorism, and we need to do more to acknowledge that fact. After our past wars, the contributions of our mothers and grandmothers in the war efforts were ignored. During World War II, Japanese Americans were "disappeared" into camps. It has only been recently that the historical amnesia about these events has been corrected. Those mistakes should have taught us that it is important to recognize the patriotism of *all* our citizens.

The struggle against terrorism and to preserve our way of life will be a long one. We will need to show our children and the world just exactly what it is that we are fighting for. This struggle is not to preserve buildings. It is a struggle to preserve freedoms and diversity, including the rights of women to participate in every aspect of our civic duties.

We *all* must make it our fight to raise the profile of women in this struggle: not just to give credit where credit is due, but also to ensure that American women are not made invisible in the way the women of Afghanistan have been forced into invisibility by the Taliban. The United States as a society is better than that. I would ask all of you to do everything you can to show your children that:

Women are firefighters;
Women are patriotic;
Women are heroes.

We should do no less for the women who put themselves on the line, not just on 9/11 but every day—especially those who gave their lives to protect our freedoms.

Unsung Heroes

LAURA FLANDERS

***The San Francisco Chronicle,* 10.23.01**

Anthrax scares have thrust the United States into new consciousness, we're told. Suddenly, regular Americans are fearing for their lives not only when they fly, or travel or rise high in an elevator. We're worrying at home, at the office, wherever we open the mail.

Last Wednesday on ABC's *20/20,* Barbara Walters invited the mayor of Belfast to share his experience. We're speaking to someone who is familiar with what we're going through, Walters said. But Belfast has no experience of assault by anthrax. Cincinnati has.

Early last week, I received the following account from Debi Jackson, director of Cincinnati Women's Services:

"Feb. 18, 1999, will be forever etched in my memory," Jackson writes. "I came to my clinic, Cincinnati Women's Services, on that morning expressly to counsel a patient who was unable to talk to me at any other time. I had a few minutes free before I was leaving to enjoy the rest of my day off. I chose to take that time to open the mail . . .

"The last piece that I opened was a business-size manila-colored envelope with a return address label from a medical instrument company with which I was unfamiliar. When I opened the envelope and saw the paper smudged with a brown powdery substance with a crudely drawn skull and cross-bones, I felt a shiver run down my spine.

"Above the skull was typed 'anthrax' and below was typed 'have a nice death.' I asked one of my staff to close the door to my office so no one but me would be exposed."

You don't have to go to Northern Ireland to find people familiar with daily terror. Abortion providers have lived with it for decades.

Last week, 90 Planned Parenthood clinics in 13 states received anthrax threats, and many papers quipped that women's clinics were the most prepared to handle suspicious packages, the least rattled, the most informed. When it comes to looking for experts, however, major media have gone elsewhere.

The National Abortion Federation (NAF, the professional association of abortion providers in the United States and Canada) released a press statement October 15. "This type of threat is unfortunately not new to abortion providers," the federation's director, Vicki Saporta, said. "Those who are opposed to a woman's right to choose have not hesitated to resort to bio-terrorist threats and attacks to advance their personal agenda."

In response to anthrax threats received at more than 80 clinics from late 1998 to 2000, NAF developed a brochure, "Anthrax: Bio-terrorism Against Reproductive Health Care Clinics." The manual has been distributed to abortion providers around the country, as well as to law enforcement officials, including the ATF and FBI.

A smart U.S. attorney general would commission a special print run of those brochures for national distribution—and pay NAF a grateful sum for having such useful materials to hand. Caring broadcasters would interview Saporta. A friendly American who, with others, has figured out how to protect her constituency from anthrax would be a more reassuring figure to see on national TV than the mayor of a far-off town associated in the U.S. mind (sadly) only with 30 years of unending terrorism and war.

What about our anti-choice U.S. attorney general would make him loath to distribute the NAF's materials to a frightened nation, or even to tell the people that such safety manuals exist? What is about our national media that make them reluctant to cast women's rights defenders as anti-terror heroes on par with "HazMat" teams and firefighters?

In 1999, Debi Jackson in Cincinnati was the first person in the city's history to receive an anthrax threat. Her office was shut down for two days, after which she and her staff returned to work.

Want to see model Americans who refuse to let terror stop them? Who maintain their beliefs, their values, and keep on doing what they know is right no matter what? Meet Debi Jackson and the staff of Cincinnati Women's Services. Meet Vicki Saporta and the North American organizations that comprise the NAF.

The Truth About Women and the Recession

ASHLEY NELSON

AlterNet, 7.29.03

The current economic downturn is hitting women about as hard as men, though like many pressing social issues today you wouldn't know it by looking at mainstream culture.

Instead we read about women like Molly. Her husband, Tom Pyles, was one of three laid-off male executives profiled in a recent article, "Commute to Nowhere," in the *New York Times Magazine*. Once fat and happy as a self-identified "spoiled banker's wife," the recession came as a complete shock to Molly. She didn't sleep for weeks after finding out how much her husband lost in the stock market. "[She'd] never had any reason to examine the portfolio in the past," the author explains. Now Molly, who is Chinese, but emigrated from London, is contemplating working. "I never thought I'd have to work in America," she laments.

Jennie Wetterman was also living the American dream only a few years ago when her husband was making big bucks during the Internet boom. "The summer of 2001, I was at the pool everyday," she recently told *Newsweek* in an article covering, in large part, "the quiet, often painful transformation that takes place when Dad comes home with a severance package." "I went scuba diving, sky diving—I must have read 30 books that summer." When her husband was laid off, she was forced to take a job at Old Navy. "I don't want to be in this situation two years down the road," she says flatly. "I'll have to put my foot down."

From these portraits, it is easy to forget that 60 percent of women work outside the home, or that nationwide they have been neck and neck with men in the unemployment lines. Currently, unemployment is at 6.1 percent for men and 5.2 percent for women, and for much of this year that gap has been even smaller. In February and March, only .3 percentage points separated men from women. Nevertheless, it is difficult to find a voice today that even acknowledges how the tough economy has directly affected women. Instead these days—when people like Dick Cheney are deemed worthiest of tax cuts—it seems all the sympathy we can muster is for white, formerly well-paid men.

The *Newsweek* piece, for instance, falsely states that women are weathering the recession better than their male counterparts—"especially white-collar men who've been victimized by corporate downsizings." The *Times* article too downplays the effect the recession has had on women. While it acknowledges that women are being hit almost as hard as men, it focuses exclusively on the latter, flippantly dismissing women by saying that joblessness for men "entails surrendering an idea of who they are." Women in similar situations? Well, they "simply adapt and find some job." Just this month, *People* magazine perpetuated this same myth by profiling the struggles of two white, laid-off men.

Some analysts researching women and employment take issue with these portraits. "The idea that women don't mind being unemployed is a gross overgeneralization," counters Joan Williams, professor of law and director of the Program on Gender, Work and Family at American University Law School. "While middle-class masculine identity is very closely entwined with having a job," she adds, "it is the purest of sexism to say that being unemployed is fine for women." In fact, "women have very different relationships to employment. Some can take it or leave it, but for others their sense of identity is just as intertwined with employment as men's. . . . Being laid off can crush them."

But from profiles like those in the *New York Times Magazine* and *Newsweek* one would think the only effect the recession has had on women is that it has drastically affected their vacation schedules. "I love traveling, and I don't do that anymore," complains Molly. Don't even mention clothes shopping.

In reality, compared to previous downturns, this recession has been much harder on women. According to a study done by economists Heather Boushey and Robert Cherry, while the ratio of white men who have been unemployed for six months or longer has remained steady compared to the last recession (18.5 percent in 1992 vs. 18.6 percent in 2003), for women long-term unemployment has increased by 3 percent—from 15.2 percent in 1992 to 18.2 percent in 2003. "That's a huge increase," says Boushey, who works at the Center for Economic and Policy Research in Washington.

Likewise, white women have seen their employment rates fall far more than they did during the early 1990s. Between 1990–1992, they saw their employment rates fall by only .2 percent. During this current downturn, from 2000 to 2003, that rate has increased seven times to 1.4 percent. The rate for white men is about the same now as it was during the previous downturn.

African Americans have been hit even harder. The current unemployment rate is 11.3 percent and 9.7 percent for black men and women respectively. For white men, it is 5.4 percent. And according to the Economic Policy Institute (EPI), low-income single mothers have seen their jobless rate rise faster than the overall rate between 2000 and 2002, averaging 12.3 percent last year. Needless to say, the articles cited focus overwhelmingly on white families.

Of course, that women are being hit as hard as men by this recession is due in part to their increased financial attachment to the workplace. In this sense, they have merely "caught up" with men, who have traditionally fared much worse in recessions. Considering this, one might assume they would garner at least as much sympathy as men, if not necessarily more. But this has not been the case.

Not only are women's economic struggles ignored, in many cases womeny are cast as bitter wives determined to make life difficult for their already demoralized husbands. Molly's husband, Tom, spends his nights at "networking" meetings (10 sessions for $600) with the fellows. "At least you get emotional support. You can't get that at home . . . [There] you get attitude, 'Why don't you have a job yet?'"

Jeff Einstein, another laid-off male exec profiled in the *New York Times Magazine,* couldn't agree more. A few weeks after being fired, his wife, Mara, told him "to be a man . . . to do what I had to do to support my family." In her defense, all Mara can say is, "A lot of people were telling me that if their husband wasn't working for this long they'd throw him out of the house."

Ignoring the difficulties unemployed women are facing, these profiles emit a nostalgia for the days when men were men, and women were wives. Laurie and Jonathan Earp may be smiling in their *Newsweek* photo-op, but don't be fooled. "By marrying a lawyer, I thought he'd be able to bring in the money," says Laurie, who "reluctantly [became] the breadwinner" after her husband was laid off. "This is not the life I wanted." In a similar situation, Sean Zebrowskis still has some hope. "I'm still looking for a job. When I get it, Sherie can go back to sleeping in."

While the article purports to reveal a new breed of stay-at-home dad, it focuses overwhelmingly on the difficulties such role reversals can cause, particularly if a father is forced into the position by a layoff. A full page is given to Laura Doyle, author of *The Surrendered Wife,* to spout off about how such swapping is simply unnatural—even if it is brought on by a layoff. "Wives who are happy to be the sole earners are as rare as supermodels . . . Women want their husbands to cherish, adore and protect them, just as they did during courtship."

At a time when gruff masculinity is in—when enemies are smoked out of their holes and the President models Top Gun gear—the idea that men should be at the controls, in politics and at home, is as prevalent as ever. Since 9/11, two key female figures in the Bush administration, Karen Hughes and Mary Matalin, have stepped down citing family concerns. For the past few months, Condi Rice seems to be vacationing in an undisclosed location. And, as *Time* magazine recently reported, even the Eminem-stomping Lynne Cheney has agreed to back off, dropping a controversial new book project on academia to write a children's book entitled *America: A Primer.* It's a relief "not to have to have an opinion about everything," she told the magazine.

Popular culture too has been in step with this neo-traditional trend. I guess a reality show just isn't a reality show if it does not rely on the assumption that in relationships women really just want the money. Erin ditched Rob for the $1 million on *For Love or Money.* Jill on *Married by America* just couldn't overlook the fact that Kevin had no job prospects. And *Mr. Personality* saw fit to hide not only the male contestant's faces, but their occupations as well, all so single gal Hayley could make an honest decision.

Given that these cultural markers are so out of step with working women's realities, it is no surprise that public policy is as well. While men and women both face an uncertain economic future, women have fewer safety nets to count on. In a study released in March 2003, the National Employment Law Project and the Program on Gender, Work and Family reported that men are more likely than women to receive unemployment insurance benefits in 41 states. Forty-three states, for instance, do not pay unemployment benefits to part-time workers, the majority of whom are women. "They can be ineligible for unemployment benefits unless they are willing to switch to full-time, which a lot of them can't because they just don't have the child care," Williams said. Federal welfare reforms, which limit lifetime benefits to five years, also put an added burden on low-income women.

Women's increased attachment to the workplace is not the only reason they are being hit harder by this recession. Traditionally female fields—like the service industries and retail—were flattened by 9/11. Since then, services have barely grown at all. And vacancies in retail trade, reports EPI, fell by over 20 percent last year. Since taking office, the Bush administration has seen to it that nearly every aspect of women's lives is rolled back. With Title IX under attack, young girls may never know what it feels like to be a Mia Hamm. In one out of three high schools, teenagers are refused information on birth control and abortion. And Jessica Lynch, comatose on a stretcher, has become the poster girl for women in the military.

Now, with the male breadwinner model back, seemingly by popular demand, and the Bush administration doing little to set the record straight, women may see the economic gains they made during the last decade reversed too. When that happens, conservative politicians and media outlets will continue to have a field day, but you can bet that the majority of women—who either enjoy work or simply need the money—won't be merely lounging around by the poolside avoiding portfolios.

Queers Without Money: They Are Everywhere, but We Refuse to See Them

AMBER HOLLIBAUGH

The Village Voice, 6.20.01

> *I mean, homosexuals have high incomes, they have high levels of education; they're owners of major credit cards. There was a survey done. So you're not talking about poor people, homeless people living under a bridge. —Reverend Lou Sheldon, conservative Christian leader*

I lived the first year of my life in a converted chicken coop in back of my grandmother's trailer. The coop was hardly tall enough for my 6'4" father and 5'8" mother to stand up in. My dad, a carpenter, tore out the chickens' egg-laying ledges and rebuilt the tiny inside space to fit a bed, table, two chairs, a basin they used as a sink (there was no running water), a shelf with a hot plate for cooking, and a small dresser. They used the hose outside to wash with, and ran extension cords in from my grandmother's trailer for light and heat. My bed, a dresser drawer, sat on top of the table during the day. At night it was placed next to where they slept.

I was sick the entire first year of my life. So was my mother, recovering from a nasty C-section and a series of ensuing medical crises. By the time she and I were discharged, three months later, whatever money my parents had managed to save was used up, and they were deeply in debt. They had been poor before my birth, and poor all of their lives growing up, but this was the sinker.

After my first year, we moved from the chicken coop into a trailer. My father worked three jobs simultaneously, rarely sleeping. My mother took whatever work she could find: mending, washing, and ironing other people's clothes. But we never really recovered. We were impoverished. Growing up, I was always poor. I am also a lesbian.

This, then, is my queer identity: I am a high-femme, mixed-race, white-trash lesbian. And even after all these years of living in a middle-class gay community, I often feel left outside when people speak about their backgrounds, their families. And if you listen to the current telling of "our" queer tale, people like me would seem an anomaly. Because, we are told—and we tell ourselves—queerness can't be poor.

Yet this seeming anomaly is the tip of the proverbial iceberg. It represents hundreds of thousands of us who come from poor backgrounds, or are living them still—and are very, very queer.

That would seem obvious when you combine the proportion of the population reputed to be queer (between 4 and 10 percent) with the 37 million poor people in America. Yet the early surveys done on gay and lesbian economic status in this country told a different tale: that queers had more disposable income than straights, lived more luxurious lives, and were all DINKs (Dual Income No Kids). "My book begins as a critique of those early surveys, which were done largely to serve the interests of gay and lesbian publications and a few marketing companies," says economist M.V. Lee Badgett in her new book, *Money, Myths, and Change: The Economic Lives of Lesbians and Gay Men.* "Those surveys are deeply flawed."

Badgett notes that "opposition to gay people is often based on the perception that queers are better-off than everybody else; that we're really asking for 'special rights'—and that breeds resentment." Badgett's research shows something else. It constitutes the first true picture of queer economic reality. Among other things, Badgett found that:

- Gays, lesbians, and bisexuals do not earn more than heterosexuals, or live in more affluent households.
- Gay men earn 13 to 32 percent less than similarly qualified straight men (depending on the study).
- Though lesbians and bisexual women have incomes comparable to straight women—earning 21 percent less than men—lesbian couples earn significantly less than heterosexual ones.

But . . . try finding representations of poor or working-class gay people on *Will & Grace.* See how hard you have to search for media images of queers who are part of the vast working poor in this country. Find the homeless transgendered folks. Find stories of gay immigrants, lesbian moms working three jobs, bisexual truckers falling asleep from too many hours on the road, gay men in the unemployment line. Try finding an image of queer people who are balancing on the edge—or have fallen off.

The myth of our wealth goes deep, so deep that even other gay people seem to believe it. We have tried to protect ourselves from the hard truths of our economic diversity by perpetuating the illusion of material wealth, within the confines of male/female whiteness. This is a critical aspect of how we present ourselves in this country at this point in time. We treat the poverty that exists among us—as well as the differences of class—as a dirty secret to be hidden, denied, repelled. We treat economic struggle as something that functions outside the pull of queer desires, removed from our queerly lived lives.

As Badgett notes, by celebrating the myth of queer affluence, we have "drawn attention to exactly the kind of picture that Lou Sheldon is drawing of gay and lesbian people." There is a richer—and ultimately more sympathetic—queer reality: "We are everywhere—but we're all different."

Why is it so hard to acknowledge this? Why is poverty treated as a queer secret? And why does it produce a particular kind of homosexual shame? Bear with me. Imagine what you've never allowed yourself to see before.

When I directed the Lesbian AIDS Project at Gay Men's Health Crisis, stories of the hundreds of HIV-positive lesbians who were a part of that project literally came roaring out of those women's mouths. These were lesbians who had almost never participated in queer politics or visited any of New York City's queer institutions. On those rare occasions when they had tried, they quickly departed, unseen and unwelcomed.

Andrew Spieldenner, a young gay organizer of color who has worked for years with men who have sex with men, has a name for this phenomenon. He calls it "a queer and invisible body count." It is made up of poor lesbians and gay men, queer people of color, the transgendered, people with HIV and AIDS and—always and in large numbers—the queer young and the queer elderly.

The Metropolitan Community Church, a largely gay denomination, reports that the demand for food at its New York pantry has doubled since the beginning of welfare reform in 1996. The Lesbian & Gay Community Services Center says that homeless people in their addiction programs have tripled since then. The Hetrick-Martin Institute, which serves "gay and questioning youth," estimates that 50 percent of homeless kids in New York City are queer.

"We are entering a time when the economy is going into a slump," says Joseph De Filippis, who coordinates the Queer Economic Justice Network. "This isn't going to be like the '90s, when it was easy for employers to give things like domestic-partner benefits. There are going to be more and more of us who are affected by joblessness and economic crisis. And the welfare reform law expires in 2002. It's our issue, damn it. It has always been our issue."

Ingrid Rivera, director of the Racial & Economic Justice Initiative of the National Gay and Lesbian Task Force, has lived this issue. "I was on welfare, I was homeless, I thought I'd be lucky if I finished high school. I am a woman of color, I am a mother, and I am queer. I've worked and lived in a poor world and I've worked in queer organizations that are primarily white. I've seen it from both perspectives, and there's a kind of disconnect. In the gay, mostly white world, race and economic justice isn't talked about as a queer issue. And because of that split, queerness becomes a white thing."

Poverty and outright destitution can happen to anyone—and the queerer you are, the fewer safety nets exist to hold you up or bounce you back from the abyss. Queerness intensifies poverty and compounds the difficulty of dealing with the social service system. The nightmares—even in this city, with its gay rights law—include:

- Being separated from your partner if you go into the shelter system. Straight couples can remain together by qualifying for the family system.
- Being mandated into homophobic treatment programs for drug or drinking problems and having the program decide to treat your queerness instead of your addiction. If you leave the program, you lose any right to benefits—including Medicaid.
- Being unable to apply as a family for public housing.
- Ending up a queer couple in the only old-age home you can afford and being separated when you try to share a room.

Barbara Cassis came from a wealthy Long Island family. But when he began to understand and acknowledge his transgendered nature, his parents kicked him out. He was homeless, young, and broke. "Thank God for drag queens," she says, looking back. "A drag queen found me crying in Times Square and took me home. She talked to me about what I was going through, let me stay with her in her apartment, taught me how to support myself, how to get clients as a prostitute or in the gay bars where I could work as I transitioned. But then she died of AIDS and I was homeless again."

The homeless shelters were the worst experience of all for Barbara as a trans woman. Often, it felt easier to just stay on the streets. If you're homeless, and you haven't transitioned—which costs a fortune—you're forced to go to a shelter based on birth gender. The risk of violence and danger is always high for everyone; the shelters are crowded, short of staff, and the staff that is there has no training in how to deal with trans or gay issues. So if you are a trans person, just taking a shower means that you're taking your life in your hands.

"It took me years to get on my feet," says Cassis, now an administrative assistant at the Positive Health Project, "to start dealing with being HIV-positive, and get the training and education I needed to find a decent job. It has also taken years for me to reconcile with my family, which I have. If it hadn't been for the kind of people the gay community often discounts and despises, I wouldn't be here today."

Like my mother said, the only difference between a poor drunk and a rich one is which drunk can hide it. The shame of being poor is an acutely public shame, difficult to hide. And *queer* homosexuality—the kind of queerness that makes gender differences and radical sexual desires crystal clear—this queerness triggers similar ruinous social perils.

We punish people in this country for being poor and we punish homosexuality. When both are combined, it does more than double the effect: It twists and deepens it, gives it sharper edges, and heightens our inability to duck and cover or slide through to a safer place. It forces you to live more permanently outside than either condition dictates.

The problem intensifies when you realize what queers are in the mind of America. We stand for the culture's obsession with the erotic. It is we who are portrayed as always doing it or trying to, we who quickly become the sexual criminals at the heart of any story. We are the ones who are dangerous; our sexuality is more explosive, more explicit, more demanding, more predatory.

And so it goes for poor people: part stereotype (read trailer trash or welfare queen), part object of blame for being too stupid not to have done better. The underlying assumption is that the only appropriate desires are those that rest comfortably atop plenty of money. The desires and needs afforded by wealth—and plenty of it, earned or not—are appropriate, acceptable, good. But messy desires? Desires that combine with class and color? Desires and needs that ricochet around the erotic? These needs are not acceptable. They are condemned.

No wonder the gay movement can't see the poverty in its midst. The one thing this culture longs for and seems to value in queer life is the image of wealth. It appears to be the only thing we do right. And it is the only piece of our queerness that we can use when our citizenship is at stake. We learned this at the beginning of the AIDS crisis, when we activated that wealth to do what the government wouldn't: We built institutions to care and protect and serve our own. It is a riveting example of how we have claimed our own and valued what the mainstream culture despised about our lives. We could do the same with queer poverty.

"If the community got involved in the issues of being queer and poor," says Jay Toole, a lesbian in the LGBT caucus of the Coalition for the Homeless, "it would be like the community saying, 'I'm here, and here's my hand. You can go further, I'm here.' "

Toole is finishing school now. She plans to work as a substance abuse counselor, to go back into the shelters and bring gay people into the community, "so that they don't have to be so alone as I was. Because when Ann Duggan [from the Coalition] brought me back down to the Lesbian & Gay Center from the shelter, it was finally like coming home."

Whatever Happened to the Gender Gap?

JENNIFER L. POZNER

***Women's Review of Books*, 2.5.02**

Let's call it "The Case of the Missing Gender Gap." Ever since September 11, corporate media have denied that men and women have significant differences of opinion on terrorism and war, despite contradictory evidence in polls conducted before and after we dropped our first bomb on Afghanistan. To solve this mystery we have to start at the beginning of George W. Bush's new world order—when, in the president's words, anyone who did not support America's "war on terrorism" would be judged to be in cahoots with "the evildoers."

Following the devastating attacks, major news networks subjected a shocked nation to video clips of the Twin Towers being struck by planes, exploding in flames and collapsing, often accompanied by "Oh my God!" audio, on repetitive-loop day and night. (Talk about a recipe for post-traumatic stress disorder.) These painful images sometimes appeared in split-screen while anxious anchors interviewed current and former White House and Pentagon officials, security experts and CIA spooks, who presented military retaliation and civil liberties rollbacks as necessary and inevitable. While such sources made up more than half the authorities appearing on NBC, ABC and CBS in the week following the attacks, experts from the international law community who could advocate legal, non-military responses to crimes against humanity were nowhere to be seen on these programs, according to a survey by the media watch group FAIR.

Feminists and progressives who dared give the question "Why do they hate us?" an answer more substantial than the ubiquitous "because we love freedom"—say, by noting that the Arab world has never forgotten Madeleine Albright's 1996 comment on CBS that half a million dead Iraqi children were "worth the price" of US sanctions—were quickly labeled traitors, or worse.

When Susan Sontag sinned in the *New Yorker*'s first post-9/11 issue by noting that US foreign policy might have contributed to the vicious anti-American sentiment behind the attacks, *Newsweek*'s Jonathan Alter blasted her in a scathing column titled "Blame America at Your Peril." It was "ironic," Alter hissed, that "the same people always urging us to not blame the victim in rape cases are now saying Uncle Sam wore a short skirt and asked for it."

And when a small but vocal peace movement called for the US to "prosecute the criminals" rather than bomb innocent Afghans, their dissent was either ignored or distorted by a derisive press—as when the *New York Times* reported a late September anti-war action in DC under the headline "Protesters in Washington Urge Peace With Terrorists."

Amid this "with us or against us" feeding frenzy, poll stories proliferated, with headlines like the *Washington Post*'s September 29 "Public Unyielding in War Against Terror; 9 in 10 Back Robust Military Response." The numbers seemed overwhelming: the "9 in 10" figure measured Bush's approval rating, while upwards of four-fifths of the public generally supported some sort of military action. According to the *Post*, Americans were "unswerving" in their support for war and unified in their "demand for a full-scale response."

But were they, really? Buried at the end of the 1,395-word story was the striking information that women "were significantly less likely to support a long and costly war" then were men, and their hesitant support might develop into "hardened opposition" over time. In fact, though 44 percent of women said they'd favor a broad military effort, "48 percent said they want a limited strike or no military action at all."

The gender gap appeared again in an October 5 CNN/*USA Today*/Gallup poll, which found that 64 percent of men thought the US "should mount a long-term war" and just 24 percent favored limiting retaliation to punishing the specific groups responsible for the attacks—but that women were "evenly divided—with 42 percent favoring each option." Though 88 percent of women and 90 percent of men support some military action, women reconsider in greater numbers as soon as conditional questions are asked, Gallup's analysis showed. For example, only 55 percent of women said they would support military action if a thousand American troops would be killed, whereas 76 percent of men would still support a lengthy war under these circumstances; women were also much less likely than men to support war if it would continue for several years, bring about an economic recession, or provoke further terrorist attacks at home.

When presented with only two possible post-9/11 alternatives—"drop some bombs" or "do nothing"—it's not surprising that majorities of the public would choose the former. What's alarming is that politicians, pundits and the press first roundly ignored the *Post* and Gallup data about women's more conditional approach to the "war on terrorism," then claimed the traditional gender gap familiar from the Persian Gulf and Kosovo crises had disintegrated with the Twin Towers.

Polls whose results seemed to confirm the media's image of a flag-waving, Rambo-embracing populace met with a much warmer reception. When an early November poll by the Council on Foreign Relations and the Pew Research Center for People & the Press found that women's support for increased military spending doubled from 24 to 47 percent after September 11, and that the same number of men and women (64 percent) now favor the creation of a missile defense shield, a front-page *Christian Science Monitor* story reported that "Women's voices are resonating across the country and doing away—for the first time in recent history—with the gender gap on many military issues." The article was headlined "In this war, American women shed role as 'doves'"—even though separate Gallup data, also from November and referenced in the same article, showed that women were more than twice as likely as men to be "doves." The Pew research was featured in outlets from leading dailies to tabloids (e.g., the *Daily News*), debate shows (e.g., *The McLaughlin Group*) and the conservative press (e.g., *Insight on the News*). the *Washington Post* crowed, "When it comes to attitudes toward the military, men are from Mars, and so are women," while a *Washington Times* op-ed praised "Missile Defense's Feminine Mystique."

While polls were covered selectively, news content about women and war was often opportunistic. Outlets seized on the restrictive burqa forced on Afghan women as a symbol of the Taliban's cruelty and a reason why they should be vanquished, and ran triumphant visuals of women removing their coverings upon the Taliban's ouster—yet only rarely devoted serious attention to the history of extreme violence and sexual assault committed against Afghan women by the US-endorsed Northern Alliance, or asked whether they might oppress or violate women once installed in the Afghan government. On the domestic front, the Bush administration was portrayed as a bastion of women's empowerment. Andrea Mitchell began a late November MSNBC segment this way: "In the war on terrorism, American women are playing a major role at almost every level, especially the top. It's a striking contrast with the way women have been treated in Afghanistan." Republican bigwigs like Condoleezza Rice, Karen Hughes and Mary Matalin are "not only making the strategy; their gender is part of the strategy, a weapon to attack the Taliban's treatment of Afghan women," Mitchell said. As a result, a Republican official told the *Washington Post* in early January, George W. Bush "has not only erased any question about legitimacy, he has also erased the gender gap."

Perhaps the gradations in women's support for or opposition to the war didn't make the news because focusing on simple, surface-level "do you or don't you?" questions requires less research and investigation—always premium in our profit-driven, time-is-money media climate—and provided sexier numbers. Certainly women's differing degrees of dissent might have seemed inconsequential to some of the country's most powerful—and pro-war—journalists. *Time* magazine's defense correspondent Mark Thompson confessed to warm fuzzies for tight-lipped military leader Donald Rumsfeld, telling the *Chicago Tribune* that "Although he has not told us very much, he has been like a father figure." With stars (and stripes) in his eyes, CBS's Dan Rather actually volunteered to suit up, telling *Entertainment Tonight* that if George Bush ever "needs me in uniform, tell me when and where—I'm there." ABC's Cokie Roberts unself-consciously admitted an almost blind faith in our boys at the Pentagon: "Look, I am, I will just confess to you, a total sucker for the guys who stand up with all the ribbons on and stuff," she told David Letterman. "And so, when they say stuff I tend to believe it." (This eager journalistic acceptance was surely music to the ears of the unnamed military official who told the *Washington Post*'s Howard Kurtz that lying would be an integral part of the Pentagon's press strategy.)

But to find the simplest reason why women's perspectives were missing or misrepresented by media, forget all this cerebral posturing. A college-style drinking game will do the trick. The rules are simple (and almost guaranteed not to get anyone drunk). Grab a few friends and the remote control, start flipping between network news broadcasts, pour a drink every time a female expert is interviewed about terrorism and war. I promise you, you'll end up parched—and peeved.

Take the Sunday morning talk shows on ABC, NBC, CBS, CNN and Fox, for example. According to a study released in December by the White House Project, a nonpartisan women's leadership group, women were a measly 11 percent of all guests on five of these influential, agenda-setting programs from January 1, 2000 to June 30, 2001. As if this wasn't dismal enough, that number fell to just 9 percent for six weeks after September 11. And women fared no better in print: in the month after the terrorist attacks, men wrote a whopping 92 percent of the 309 bylined op-eds published by the *New York Times*, the *Washington Post* and *USA Today,* according to a survey I conducted for FAIR.

To Nancy Nathan, executive producer of NBC's *Meet the Press,* the underrepresentation of women on programs like hers is irrelevant. "I don't think the female viewpoint is different from the generic, overall viewpoint," Nathan told me. There's no conspiracy to suppress women's voices, she said, it's just that men hold most power-positions in Washington, so they are the most sought-after guests. Women might have unique perspectives to add to health care or reproductive services discussions, she added, and with those sorts of stories the talk shows might be able to book people outside the male-dominated pool of officeholders. But programs like *Meet the Press* "are not having long discussions about issues that are not at the forefront of the agenda." The White House Project study's authors can "advocate more women on the air," Nathan said; "but the object here is to deliver the news, not to get women on the air."

Nathan's perspective perfectly echoes one of journalism's most entrenched conventions: news is what the powerful say and do, not what the public experiences. But Sunday morning talk shows move the public debate by framing certain topics as cutting-edge and others as unimportant—if they were to address reproductive rights or health care regularly, those issues would be at the forefront. Not to mention that women are invested in all issues, not just abortion and breast cancer; women are 90 percent of the world's sweatshop workers, for example, and are doing groundbreaking work in feminist economics—meaning that journalism and those who rely on it suffer when women are overlooked as sources for stories on globalization, labor and world finance.

The news-follows-power principle not only eschews diversity, but its self-perpetuating cycle prevents change. Social and political issues will continue to be filtered through a primarily white, male, corporate lens, thereby reinforcing their authority and sidelining women, people of color, labor and all marginalized groups and issues.

Washington Post columnist Judy Mann ended the year with this reflection:

". . . a society in which women are invisible in the media is one in which they are invisible, period . . . Women are a majority in the United States. By rights, in a democracy, we should occupy 50 percent of the slots on the op-ed pages of America's newspapers. We should occupy 50 percent of the top editorships in newspapers. We should be allowed to bring what interests us—as women and mothers and wives—to the table, and I don't mean token stories about child care. I mean taking apart the federal budget and seeing if it is benefiting families or the munitions millionaires. I mean looking at the enormous amount of money we've squandered on the "war on drugs" and asking the obvious question: Why are we building more prisons instead of rebuilding broken lives? I mean challenging the miserly foreign-aid budget and raising hell because we are not doing our share to educate women and girls in emerging countries. The Taliban could never have taken root in a society that educated and empowered females."

This is the type of insight Mann has offered the *Post* for 23 years; the column, published on December 28, was her last. Mann—the first journalist to use the term "gender gap" in the press —is retiring right at a moment when women's voices are being thoroughly drowned out on the op-ed pages and the public stage.

Mann's final headline read, "A Farewell Wish: That Women Will Be Heard." For that wish to become reality, we need to force the issue. Write the *Post* and encourage them to replace Mann with an analytically and politically savvy feminist writer. Pressure the Sunday talk shows to interview female experts, and to recognize that women's concerns focus on cutting-edge issues, but will only be seen as such if they are subject to healthy debate in prominent forums. Contact local news outlets when women are ignored, distorted, or covered in opportunistic ways. Conduct studies calling attention to the gender breakdown of particular outlets' bylines and sources, then hold press conferences, release reports and attempt to meet with editorial boards to discuss ways to improve. Organize around the concept that journalism has a responsibility to cover a variety of perspectives, not just those of people in power.

Media conglomerates are not magnanimous; they will not change their priorities without major incentives. In the 1930s, Eleanor Roosevelt would only speak to female reporters at her press conferences, forcing newspapers to employ women journalists. In the 1970s, newspapers and TV networks had to be sued before they'd stop discriminating against women in hiring and promotion; feminist columnist Anna Quindlen began her decade-long run on the *New York Times* op-ed page as a result of one of those class-actions, and proceeded to write about gender, race, class and sexuality issues as if they mattered.

It's time for us to reprioritize media as a top feminist issue. Today, Quindlen's spot at the *Times* is filled by Maureen Dowd, who's often as inclined to write about high-society balls as feminist concerns. Today, right-wing women like Ann Coulter, Kathleen Parker, Peggy Noonan, Mona Charen, Amy Holmes and Laura Ingraham maintain a high profile in the mainstream media, while progressive feminist writers like media critic Laura Flanders or journalist Barbara Ehrenreich are most often heard in the Left press. And today, NBC darling Katie Couric's astronomical new salary notwithstanding, women still have little power inside the media industry: according to various studies (cited in "Power Shortage for Media Women," *Extra!*, August, 2001), they are only 13 and 14 percent of radio and TV general managers, 20 percent of news executives in Fortune 1000 news companies, and 12 percent of corporate board members in media/entertainment companies.

We need to ask ourselves: What are we going to do about this, today?

WOMEN TAKE ACTION

Four 9/11 Moms Battle Bush

GAIL SHEEHY

***The New York Observer*, 8.25.03**

In mid-June, F.B.I. director Robert Mueller III and several senior agents in the bureau received a group of about 20 visitors in a briefing room of the J. Edgar Hoover Building in Washington, D.C. The director himself narrated a PowerPoint presentation that summarized the numbers of agents and leads and evidence he and his people had collected in the 18-month course of their ongoing investigation of Penttbom, the clever neologism the bureau had invented to reduce the sites of devastation on 9/11 to one word: *Pent* for Pentagon, *Pen* for Pennsylvania, *tt* for the Twin Towers and *bom* for the four planes that the government had been forewarned could be used as weapons—even bombs—but chose to ignore.

After the formal meeting, senior agents in the room faced a grilling by Kristen Breitweiser, a 9/11 widow whose cohorts are three other widowed moms from New Jersey.

"I don't understand, with all the warnings about the possibilities of Al Qaeda using planes as weapons, and the Phoenix Memo from one of your own agents warning that Osama bin Laden was sending operatives to this country for flight-school training, why didn't you check out flight schools before September 11?"

"Do you know how many flight schools there are in the U.S.? Thousands," a senior agent protested. "We couldn't have investigated them all and found these few guys."

"Wait, you just told me there were too many flight schools and that prohibited you from investigating them before 9/11," Kristen persisted. "How is it that a few hours after the attacks, the nation is brought to its knees, and miraculously F.B.I. agents showed up at Embry-Riddle flight school in Florida where some of the terrorists trained?"

"We got lucky," was the reply.

Kristen then asked the agent how the F.B.I. had known exactly which A.T.M. in Portland, Me., would yield a videotape of Mohammed Atta, the leader of the attacks. The agent got some facts confused, then changed his story. When Kristen wouldn't be pacified by evasive answers, the senior agent parried, "What are you getting at?"

"I think you had open investigations before September 11 on some of the people responsible for the terrorist attacks," she said.

"We did not," the agent said unequivocally.

A month later, on the morning of July 24, before the scathing

Congressional report on intelligence failures was released, Kristen and the three other moms from New Jersey with whom she'd been in league sat impassively at a briefing by staff director Eleanor Hill: In fact, they learned, the F.B.I. had open investigations on 14 individuals who had contact with the hijackers while they were in the United States. The flush of pride in their own research passed quickly. This was just another confirmation that the federal government continued to obscure the facts about its handling of suspected terrorists leading up to the September 11 attacks.

So afraid is the Bush administration of what could be revealed by inquiries into its failures to protect Americans from terrorist attack, it is unabashedly using Kremlin tactics to muzzle members of Congress and thwart the current federal commission investigating the failures of September 11. But there is at least one force that the administration cannot scare off or shut up. They call themselves "Just Four Moms from New Jersey," or simply "the girls."

Kristen and the three other housewives who also lost their husbands in the attack on the World Trade Center started out knowing virtually nothing about how their government worked. For the last 20 months they have clipped and Googled, rallied and lobbied, charmed and intimidated top officials all the way to the White House. In the process, they have made themselves arguably the most effective force in dancing around the obstacle course by which the administration continues to block a transparent investigation of what went wrong with the country's defenses on September 11 and what we should be doing about it.

They have no political clout, no money, no powerful husbands—no husbands at all since September 11—and they are up against a White House, an Attorney General, a Defense Secretary, a National Security Advisor and an F.B.I. director who have worked out an ingenious bait-and-switch game to thwart their efforts and those of any investigative body.

THE MOM CELL

The four moms—Kristen Breitweiser, Patty Casazza, Mindy Kleinberg and Lorie van Auken—use tactics more like those of a leaderless cell. They have learned how to deposit their assorted seven children with select grandmothers before dawn and rocket down the Garden State Parkway to Washington. They have become experts at changing out of pedal-pushers and into proper pantsuits while their S.U.V. is stopped in traffic, so they can hit the Capitol rotunda running. They have talked strategy with Senator John McCain and Senate Minority Leader Tom Daschle. They once caught Congressman Porter Goss hiding behind his office door to avoid them. And they maintain an open line of communication with the White House.

But after the razzle-dazzle of their every trip to D.C., the four moms dissolve on the hot seats of Kristen's S.U.V., balance take-out food containers on their laps and grow quiet. Each then retreats into a private chamber of longing for the men whose lifeless images they wear on tags around their necks.

After their first big rally, Patty's soft voice floated a wish that might have been in the minds of all four moms: "O.K., we did the rally, now can our husbands come home?" Last September, Kristen was singled out by the families of 9/11 to testify in the first televised public hearing before the Joint Intelligence Committee Inquiry (JICI) in Washington. She drew high praise from the leadership, made up of members from both the House and Senate. But the JICI, as the moms called it, was mandated to go out of business at the end of 2003, and their questions for the intelligence agencies were consistently blocked: The Justice Department has forbidden intelligence officials to be interviewed without "minders" among their bosses being present, a tactic clearly meant to intimidate witnesses. When the White House and the intelligence agencies held up the Congressional report month after month by demanding that much of it remain classified, the moms' rallying cry became "Free the JICI!"

They believed the only hope for getting at the truth would be with an independent federal commission with a mandate to build on the findings of the Congressional inquiry and broaden it to include testimony from all the other relevant agencies. Their fight finally overcame the directive by Vice President Dick Cheney to Congressman Goss to "keep negotiating" and, in January 2003, the National Commission on Terrorist Attacks Upon the United States—known as the 9/11 Commission—met for the first time. It is not only for their peace of mind that the four moms continue to fight to reveal the truth, but because they firmly believe that, nearly two years after the attacks, the country is no safer now than it was on September 11.

"O.K., there's the House and the Senate—which one has the most members?" Lorie laughed at herself. It was April 2002, seven months after she had lost her husband, Kenneth. "I must have slept through that civics class." Her friend Mindy couldn't help her; Mindy hadn't read the *New York Times* since she stopped commuting to Manhattan, where she'd worked as a C.P.A. until her husband, Alan, took over the family support. Both women's husbands had worked as securities traders for Cantor Fitzgerald until they were incinerated in the World Trade Center.

Mindy and Lorie had thought themselves exempt from politics, by virtue of the constant emergency of motherhood. Before September 11, Mindy could have been described as a stand-in for Samantha on *Sex and the City.* But these days she felt more like one of the *Golden Girls.* Lorie, who was 46 and beautiful when her husband, Kenneth van Auken, was murdered, has acquired a fierceness in her demeanor. The two mothers were driving home to East Brunswick after attending a support group for widows of 9/11. They had been fired up by a veteran survivor of a previous terrorist attack against Americans, Bob Monetti, president of Families of Pan Am 103/Lockerbie. "You can't sit back and let the government treat you like shit," he had challenged them. That very night they called up Patty Casazza, another Cantor Fitzgerald widow, in Colt's Neck. "We have to have a rally in Washington."

Patty, a sensitive woman who was struggling to find the right balance of prescriptions to fight off anxiety attacks, groaned, "Oh God, this is huge, and it's going to be painful." Patty said she would only go along if Kristen was up for it.

Kristen Breitweiser was only 30 years old when her husband, Ron, a vice president at Fiduciary Trust, called her one morning to say he was fine, not to worry. He had seen a huge fireball out his window, but it wasn't his building. She tuned into the *Today* show just in time to see the South Tower explode right where she knew he was sitting—on the 94th floor. For months thereafter, finding it impossible to sleep, Kristen went back to the nightly ritual of her married life: She took out her husband's toothbrush and slowly, lovingly squeezed the toothpaste onto it. Then she would sit down on the toilet and wait for him to come home.

THE INVESTIGATION

Kristen was somewhat better-informed than the others. The tall, blond former surfer girl had graduated from Seton Hall law school, practiced all of three days, hated it and elected to be a full-time mom. Her first line of defense against despair at the shattering of her life dreams was to revert to thinking like a lawyer.

Lorie was the network's designated researcher, since she had in her basement what looked like a NASA command module; her husband had been an amateur designer. Kristen had told her to focus on the timeline: Who knew what, when did they know it, and what did they do about it?

Once Lorie began surfing the Web, she couldn't stop. She found a video of President Bush's reaction on the morning of September 11. According to the official timeline provided by his press secretary, the President arrived at an elementary school in Sarasota, Fla., at 9 a.m. and was told in the hallway of the school that a plane had crashed into the World Trade Center. This was 14 minutes after the first attack. The President went into a private room and spoke by phone with his National Security Advisor, Condoleezza Rice, and glanced at a TV in the room. "That's some bad pilot," the President said. Bush then proceeded to a classroom, where he drew up a little stool to listen to second graders read. At 9:04 a.m., his chief of staff, Andrew Card, whispered in his ear that a second plane had struck the towers. "We are under attack," Mr. Card informed the President.

"Bush's sunny countenance went grim," said the White House account. "After Card's whisper, Bush looked distracted and somber but continued to listen to the second graders read and soon was smiling again. He joked that they read so well, they must be sixth graders."

Lorie checked the Web site of the Federal Aviation Authority. The F.A.A. and the Secret Service, which had an open phone connection, both knew at 8:20 a.m. that two planes had been hijacked in the New York area and had their transponders turned off. How could they have thought it was an accident when the first plane slammed into the first tower 26 minutes later? How could the President have dismissed this as merely an accident by a "bad pilot"? And how, after he had been specifically told by his chief of staff that "We are under attack," could the Commander in Chief continue sitting with second graders and make a joke? Lorie ran the video over and over.

"I couldn't stop watching the President sitting there, listening to second graders, while my husband was burning in a building," she said.

Mindy pieced together the actions of Secretary of Defense Donald Rumsfeld. He had been in his Washington office engaged in his "usual intelligence briefing." After being informed of the two attacks on the World Trade Center, he proceeded with his briefing until the third hijacked plane struck the Pentagon. Mindy relayed the information to Kristen:

"Can you believe this? Two planes hitting the Twin Towers in New York City did not rise to the level of Rumsfeld's leaving his office and going to the war room to check out just what the hell went wrong." Mindy sounded scared. "This is my President. This is my Secretary of Defense. You mean to tell me Rumsfeld had to get up from his desk and look out his window at the burning Pentagon before he knew anything was wrong? How can that be?"

"It can't be," said Kristen ominously. Their network being a continuous loop, Kristen immediately passed on the news to Lorie, who became even more agitated. Lorie checked out the North American Aerospace Defense Command, whose specific mission includes a response to any form of an air attack on America. It was created to provide a defense of critical command-and-control targets. At 8:40 a.m. on 9/11, the F.A.A. notified NORAD that Flight No. 11 had been hijacked. Three minutes later, the F.A.A. notified NORAD that Flight No. 175 was also hijacked. By 9:02 a.m., both planes had crashed into the World Trade Center, but there had been no action by NORAD. Both agencies also knew there were two other hijacked planes in the air that had been violently diverted from their flight pattern. All other air traffic had been ordered grounded. NORAD operates out of Andrews Air Force Base, which is within sight of the Pentagon. Why didn't NORAD scramble planes in time to intercept the two other hijacked jetliners headed for command-and-control centers in Washington? Lorie wanted to know. Where was the leadership?

"I can't look at these timelines anymore," Lorie confessed to Kristen. "When you pull it apart, it just doesn't reconcile with the official storyline." She hunched down in her husband's swivel chair and began to tremble, thinking, There's no way this could be. Somebody is not telling us the whole story.

THE COMMISSION

The 9/11 Commission wouldn't have happened without the four moms. At the end of its first open hearing, held last spring at the U.S. Customs House close to the construction pit of Ground Zero, former Democratic Congressman Tim Roemer said as much and praised them and other activist 9/11 families.

"At a time when many Americans don't even take the opportunity to cast a ballot, you folks went out and made the legislative system work," he said. Jamie Gorelick, former Deputy Attorney General of the United States, said at the same hearing, "I'm enormously impressed that laypeople with no powers of subpoena, with no access to insider information of any sort, could put together a very powerful set of questions and set of facts that are a road map for this commission. It is really quite striking. Now, what's your secret?"

Mindy, who had given a blistering testimony at that day's hearing, tossed her long corkscrew curls and replied in a voice more Tallulah than termagant, "Eighteen months of doing nothing but grieving and connecting the dots."

Eleanor Hill, the universally respected staff director of the JICI investigation, shares the moms' point of view. "One of our biggest concerns is our finding that there were people in this country assisting these hijackers," she said later in an interview with this writer. "Since the F.B.I. was in fact investigating all these people as part of their counterterroism effort, and they knew some of them had ties to Al Qaeda, then how good was their investigation if they didn't come across the hijackers?" President Bush, who was notified in the President's daily briefing on Aug. 6, 2001, that "a group of [Osama] bin Laden supporters was planning attacks in the United States with explosives," insisted after the Congressional report was made public: "My administration has transformed our government to pursue terrorists and prevent terrorist attacks."

Kristen, Mindy, Patty and Lorie are not impressed. "We were told that, prior to 9/11, the F.B.I. was only responsible for going in after the fact to solve a crime and prepare a criminal case," Kristen said. "Here we are, 22 months after the fact, the F.B.I. has received some 500,000 leads, they have thousands of people in custody, they're seeking the death penalty for one terrorist, [Zacarias] Moussaoui, but they still haven't solved the crime and they don't have any of the other people who supported the hijackers." Ms. Hill echoes their frustration. "Is this support network for Al Qaeda still in the United States? Are they still operating, planning the next attack?"

CIVIL DEFENSE

The hopes of the four moms that the current 9/11 Commission could broaden the inquiry beyond the intelligence agencies are beginning to fade. As they see it, the administration is using a streamlined version of the tactics they successfully employed to stall and suppress much of the startling information in the JICI report. The gaping hole of 28 pages concerning the Saudi royal family's financial support for the terrorists of 9/11 was only the tip of the 900-page iceberg.

"We can't get any information about the Port Authority's evacuation procedures or the response of the City of New York," complains Kristen. "We're always told we can't get answers or documents because the F.B.I. is holding them back as part of an ongoing investigation. But when Director Mueller invited us back for a follow-up meeting—on the very morning before that damning report was released—we were told the F.B.I. isn't pursuing any investigations based on the information we are blocked from getting. The only thing they are looking at is the hijackers. And they're all dead."

It's more than a clever Catch-22. Members of the 9/11 Commission are being denied access even to some of the testimony given to the JICI—on which at least two of its members sat!

This is a stonewalling job of far greater importance than Watergate. This concerns the refusal of the country's leadership to be held accountable for the failure to execute its most fundamental responsibility: to protect its citizens against foreign attack.

Critical information about two of the hijackers, Khalid al-Mihdhar and Nawaf al-Hazmi, lay dormant within the intelligence community for as long as 18 months, at the very time when plans for the September 11 attacks were being hatched. The JICI confirmed that these same two hijackers had numerous contacts with a longtime F.B.I. counterterrorism informant in California. As the four moms pointed out a year ago, their names were in the San Diego phone book. What's more, the F.B.I.'s Minneapolis field office had in custody in August 2001 one Zacarias Moussaoui, a French national who had enrolled in flight training in Minnesota and who F.B.I. agents suspected was involved in a hijacking plot. But nobody at the F.B.I. apparently connected the Moussaoui investigation with intelligence information on the immediacy of the threat level in the spring and summer of 2001, or the illegal entry of al-Mihdhar and al-Hazmi into the United States.

How have these lapses been corrected 24 months later? The F.B.I. is seeking the death penalty for Mr. Moussaoui, and uses the need to protect their case against him as the rationale for refusing to share any of the information they have obtained from him. In fact, when Director Mueller tried to use the same excuse to duck out of testifying before the Joint Committee, the federal judge in the Moussaoui trial dismissed his argument, and he and his agents were compelled to testify.

"At some point, you have to do a cost-benefit analysis," says Kristen. "Which is more important—one fried terrorist, or the safety of the nation?" Patty was even more blunt in their second meeting with the F.B.I. brass. "I don't give a rat's ass about Moussaoui," she said. "Why don't you throw him into Guantanamo and squeeze him for all he's worth, and get on with finding his cohorts?"

The four moms are demanding that the independent commission hold a completely transparent investigation, with open hearings and cross-examination. What it looks like they'll get is an incomplete and sanitized report, if it's released in time for the commission's deadline next May. Or perhaps another fight over declassification of the most potent revelations, which will serve to hold up the report until after the 2004 Presidential election. Some believe that this is the administration's end game.

Kristen sees the handwriting on the wall: "If we have an executive branch that holds sole discretion over what information is released to the public and what is hidden, the public will never get the full story of why there was an utter failure to protect them that day, and who should be held accountable."

Against the War but Married to It

KAREN HOUPPERT

***The Nation,* 11.10.03**

It is morning on March 20, 2003, the first day of the war against Iraq. And on this Army post in upstate New York, it is raining. Hard.

As Defense Secretary Donald Rumsfeld's early-morning radio address reminds waking Americans that there is sacrifice involved in patriotism, two dozen soldiers with forty-pound rucks on their back practice urban warfare techniques in a march across Fort Drum's main road. Machine guns in hand, the soldiers approach an intersection and pan the horizon. Two of them dart into the center of the street to stop traffic. Then, one by one, the mostly very young soldiers file past, their camouflaged uniforms caked with mud, their grim and grimy faces fractured by rivulets of rain. Three minivans with moms on the way to the commissary or the office or to drop the kids at school pause on one side of the intersection. Two soldiers in a Humvee pause on the other side. As traffic backs up, no one honks with irritation, as they might in New York City. The drivers sit patiently, respectfully, at the intersection, as if waiting for the passage of a funeral procession. They have seen this a hundred times.

Later that afternoon, in Clark Hall, Frederick Calladine, chief of casualty and mortuary affairs at Fort Drum, briefs a group of forty soldiers. These men and women have the dubious distinction of being the newly appointed "casualty notification officers" for their units. As such, they are getting the PowerPoint ABCs of military mortuary protocol. "Wear your dress uniform," Calladine reminds them, and remember that some wives want to kill the messenger. "Give them the news, then get the hell out of Dodge," he advises.

Meanwhile, outside the post's gates, on a narrow median of grass a few miles away in the center of Watertown, a small gaggle of six peace activists stands in the dusk, in the pouring rain, trying desperately to keep the requisite candles lit in this candlelight peace vigil. Two cardboard posters, the Magic Marker beginning to run, are taped to sticks that have been jabbed into the soft ground. Writ large: We Support Our Troops. Writ small: Bring Them Home!

On this first day of the war, the sole military wife at the peace vigil, Christiane Langer, is understandably emotional. Her soldier husband has not been deployed—yet—but she knows the possibility exists. She also knows she is on dangerous ground. For Langer, coming out against the war in this very conservative community, home of one of the country's largest Army bases, has meant wrestling with her conscience: Will it jeopardize her husband's career if she speaks out? Will she jeopardize her own values if she doesn't? Does silence equal complicity?

Growing up as a child in Germany, Langer was weaned on horror stories about World War II. "I grew up with knowledge about the Holocaust, and the message that I took away from that was, we have a responsibility to speak up when we see the government doing wrong," she says. She is sympathetic with her friends, the many, many military wives who she says are against the war in Iraq but are afraid to voice their opinions. Still, she made a conscious decision to make her opinion known.

Fast-forward six months, and Langer is less alone. Today, the murmurs of discontent among military families are growing louder.

Dozens of interviews with military families in the Fort Drum area and beyond show that there is a growing unease with Bush's Iraq policy. Some is direct. "This is just not a war I believe in," says Tammy Schmitt, wife of an Air Force officer who was stationed at Fort Drum. And some is oblique. "You have to support the troops, what are you going to do?" another Fort Drum military wife tells me, then goes on to voice indignation at Bush's after-the-fact plea for United Nations support and the troubling fact that no weapons of mass destruction have surfaced in postwar Iraq. "I'm surprised the CIA hasn't planted some. I'm like, please, just plant something and let me believe."

At the moment, opposition to the war among military families is mostly bubbling beneath the surface. Those with the loudest voices are parents. But parents of soldiers have a long tradition of speaking out to protect their kids; they are largely immune from the repercussions. (Uncle Sam isn't likely to blame GI Joe for the sins of his father—or his hippie mom.) What is new are the rumblings of discontent among wives, for whom the stakes are much higher. (And I say wives, rather than spouses, because every one of the male spouses I've encountered comes from inside the establishment, ex-soldiers themselves, and thus has a distinct perspective.)

While the numbers of those willing to go public with their critical views are small, the symbolism is powerful. After all, military families can personally attest to the waste of manpower, the unnecessarily harsh conditions soldiers endure and the inadequate compensation families receive. And they're an irresistible photo-op—typically patriotic in get-up with fatherless (temporarily, hopefully) kids in tow.

Candance Robison, a 28-year-old Texan with a 1-year-old son and 6-year-old daughter, recently organized a protest in Crawford, Texas, where President Bush was spending his vacation. Though she has "zero experience" as a political activist, Robison's learned fast. Since her husband, an engineer in the Army Reserve, was deployed to Iraq in February, she has written letters to the President, organized protests and most recently traveled to Washington to testify at a Congressional briefing. She tells me she addressed her remarks there to the Defense Secretary. "Donald Rumsfeld, get the spare room ready because me and the kids are coming to stay," Robison said, with her cocky Texas drawl. She explained that the Army pay was far less than what her husband had been making as a sales manager at his civilian job. Though his employer had been making up the difference since her husband's deployment, the company can't be expected to continue, now that the deployment has been extended a year. "'Hope you and the missis can put us up!' I told them."

From the beginning, Robison questioned the necessity of this war—"I needed more evidence that there were weapons of mass destruction before I was ready to accept that my husband might come home in a body bag"—but her husband was excited and eager to go. "He believed in what we were going over there to do," she says. "He felt that there were weapons of mass destruction and was very anxious to try and do what he had been training to do for twenty years." But that's changed: "'I would be here and be proud to do my job, but I'm not even sure what my mission is,' he says now."

While Robison's husband supports what she's doing, many in his stateside military community don't. "One of the wives who heads up the family support group read me this supposedly official memo over the phone," Robison said. "She said I am essentially aiding terrorism by speaking out. 'Well,' I said, 'That wouldn't be me, that would be our President—the one who is leaving our soldiers there as sitting ducks.' Then she said that I am never to speak out on behalf of the family support group or the US military. Well, I never have. Because I'm not a member of either one!" Robison is unusual among military wives in that she didn't grow up a military brat (as many have), she has never lived on an Army post and she currently lives an hour from the nearest military facility. But most wives live their lives deeply immersed in the military community. For them, the gap between holding certain political beliefs and speaking out publicly about these beliefs looms like a canyon. Crossing over it carries tremendous risk.

Just imagine: Your extended family and friends live hundreds of miles away, so your entire social support network consists of other military families. It extends from your neighbor, who picks up your kids after school because you're in a pinch, to your commander's wife, who makes a call because your parents need an extended pass to be on-post and help you care for your newborn, to a fellow spouse, who shares with you a glass of wine and a kvetch, to the chain of command, which provides information about your husband's safety and date of return. In this world, silence can equal self-preservation.

"The wives are afraid. In fact, everybody told me, 'Do not come here and talk to a journalist,'" Langer says, explaining that she had intended to bring along other antiwar wives to speak with me when we met for our second interview at Watertown's Salmon Run Mall. "I thought I would find some to talk to you because we are all of the same opinion about the war—and most of them I would consider quite outspoken...but they are too nervous." Langer says they had almost convinced her to cancel the interview. "Several told me stories about their husbands getting in trouble because of their wives being outspoken. 'If you find your name in the paper, your husband's career is ruined,' they said."

Whether this is true or not is almost irrelevant. As long as the fear of repercussion exists, vocal opposition will be stifled. Indeed, the rules regarding a soldier's political activism are so filled with legalistic minutiae—ranging from a straight-out ban on any partisan activism and on the use of "contemptuous words against officeholders," to specifying that "large" political signs may not be displayed on soldiers' cars, but standard bumper stickers may—as to make most of them afraid to exercise any of their free-speech rights. As one Fort Drum soldier quipped: "Ironically, we're out there defending all these rights that are then denied to us as soldiers."

Clearly, a soldier's wife who questions the necessity of American intervention in Iraq steps into a hornet's nest of military values. When husbands spend all day doing what they're told, even when they might think it's stupid, there is a way in which blind faith becomes virtuous. Following orders on the double may be practical in wartime, but it also seeps into almost all aspects of military work and life. Doubt is for the lazy and faint of heart; questioning equals complaining. Within that culture, military wives typically preface any criticism—or political analysis, for that matter—by pointing out that the President of the United States is their husband's boss. What they mean by this is that it's not nice to call their husband's boss a jackass. But what they also mean is that it's hard to accept the sacrifices the military requires of them without believing that it is for some greater good, that their husband missed the birth of their daughter because our national security was at stake. So they believe.

Sort of.

But doubt creeps in around the edges. "I understand the wives, and especially the soldiers, who feel they have no choice but to support the war because otherwise you go insane because you can't live with it, with that contradiction," says Langer. "You can't go into a war and say, I'm totally against it but I'm going to shoot somebody anyway. That doesn't work. And the wives are in the same shoes. In your mind..." Langer struggles to find the right words. "It is possible to train your mind to support something that maybe, in your true heart, that's not what you believe in. I see that in this community."

In these circumstances, counting on any organized opposition from inside the military might be unrealistic. But perhaps being a peace activist, by nature, requires some determined optimism. Nancy Lessin and Charley Richardson, co-founders of the antiwar group Military Families Speak Out (MFSO), became so persuaded that there were thousands of military families privately fuming about Iraq that they created an organization to represent them in November 2002.

Richardson and Lessin, veterans of the 1960s peace movement and parents of a soldier son who's been deployed to Iraq, were quick to recognize the unique power military families could bring to the larger antiwar effort. "We were very concerned about media coverage that tried to characterize the antiwar movement as those who supported the troops and those who didn't," says Lessin. With that in mind, she and Richardson, who were invited to speak at rallies and demos and even at Congressional briefings, tried to erase that distinction. For example: "We're glad to be here at the biggest pro-troop rally in the country," Lessin told half a million New Yorkers when she spoke at the February 15 antiwar rally there.

While MFSO's membership is still only about 1,000, Richardson says the group is attracting increasing interest. "When President Bush made his reckless 'bring 'em on' comment from the safety of his briefing room, surrounded by armed guards, military families were incensed," he says. Banding together with Veterans for Peace, MFSO began a "Bring Them Home Now" campaign, which has been flooded with thousands of e-mails. The letters prove revealing. One wife, who is a soldier herself and had been deployed to Iraq, now fumes about her husband, a reservist who remains there. "It sickens me every time I see news articles quoting dignitaries coming from [Iraq] saying, 'the soldiers are in good spirits,' 'morale is high,'" she wrote. "I'm here to tell you, it's all lies. Morale is at an all-time low. Soldiers are hating life there, so much so that some are taking their own lives rather than deal with the situation. It has become that drastic." In the short term, there is nothing she can do; in the long term she has plans: "As much as I love the military, when this enlistment is up, I'm running so fast for the civilian border, as is my husband. At this point, when it is time for re-election, I would vote for anyone whose last name wasn't Bush."

Interestingly, wives consistently place blame at the top of the military hierarchy. "I do not blame my husband's battalion commander," one wife writes. "I realize this does not come from him. I blame the Department of the Army and more importantly, I blame President Bush and his Administration."

What makes spouses a potentially more powerful ally for peace activists is that they hold more sway over their husbands' re-enlistment decisions—and that can be a mighty tool. It's certainly a vulnerable spot for the military. For example, in its 2003 statement to Congress the Air Force expresses concern about the fact that 77 percent of its enlisted force is eligible to re-enlist—or not!—in the next two years.

But teasing out the implications of military antiwar sentiment can be tricky. If military wives base their opposition to the war on the grounds that the troops have been there too long, and are overworked and constantly deployed, it can backfire—witness the ongoing debate about whether more troops will solve the Iraq crisis. (In September, Senator John McCain was on "Face the Nation" goading the President to send more troops to Iraq. He expanded from there: "We have to have a bigger Army. We have to have a bigger military and we have to go about understanding what's necessary in order to do that.")

Further, calls to "Bring Them Home Now" by a wide spectrum of groups do not necessarily indicate a broad consensus about the perils of US military aggression. While some who oppose the war do so on principle, others object because they worry that the personal price—the potential death of a loved one—is just too high.

Perhaps the most tireless activists have both reasons in mind, like Langer, who protested week after week on the Watertown square. "We think that our husbands—when they signed up for the service and also us, when we co-signed by marrying them—were well aware that the ultimate sacrifice might be their lives," she says. "But we want to be sure, as wives, that there is absolutely no doubt whatsoever that this sacrifice was necessary." When asked whether that means she is against this particular engagement or whether she identifies herself as a pacifist, Langer laughs. "I identify myself as a hypocrite," she says. "I'm a pacifist who married a soldier."

Arab Women Staying Alive

AHDAF SOUEIF

***The Guardian,* 3.13.03**

In Baghdad on any given day you might come across her. I will not tell you her name—but she is tall and slim with brushed silver hair. She dresses in black with black trainers and thick black socks. Her husband, now dead, was an Iraqi ambassador long ago. Now she sets out from her home every morning and walks. She walks though the streets looking and listening and asking questions. Her project is to memorize what is happening to the people and the daily life of her country. She's 88 and doesn't have much time.

None of us have much time.

Have you ever seen a patched book? Here it is: SJ's slim volume *The Poet.* SJ has a Ph.D. in Arabic literature from Baghdad University. The ancient piece of machinery coaxed into printing her book either dries up or floods. On pages where the damage is too bad SJ writes out the missing words by hand on a piece of paper and glues it in place. "War gives birth," she writes, "and mothers do the bringing up." She sells *The Poet* at 125 dinars a copy, hoping eventually to pay back the 3,000 dinars it costs to produce. Three thousand dinars equals $1.50.

Do you see these women represented in the western media? Arab women are generally portrayed as victimized, subservient. They sit next to silent, wide-eyed children in Iraqi hospitals, they stumble among the ruins of their homes in Jenin. Many in the west seem to think they need to be dragged out from under their veils and scolded into standing up for themselves. But as we all try to block, to temper, to survive the coming horror, it is crucial for sympathizers in the west to understand the truth. The women's movement started in Egypt, Palestine and Syria in the 1880s. By the 1960s women in many Arab countries had the vote, equal pay for equal work and maternity and childcare legislation that is still a dream in the west. Massive women's organizations worked to improve women's education and health care. Women (and men) campaigned for reforms in the personal laws and notched up several successes. But now all this is on hold.

I'm asked what Arab women are doing in these critical times. They are doing what they have to do: toughing it out, spreading themselves thin, doing their work, making ends meet, trying to protect their children and support their men, turning to their friends, their sisters and their mothers for solidarity and laughs. There was a quieter, more equable time when women's political action was born of choice, of a desire to change the world. Now, simply trying to hold on to our world is a political action.

F is an Egyptian architect. She has always been active in women's organizations. She did voluntary literacy work with poor urban women and her book on mothers and children was published by the UNDP. Her husband is one of the 14 anti-war activists detained recently in Cairo. When she took her two daughters, both engineering students, to visit him in Tora jail, they were astounded at the hundreds of women and children waiting to visit political detainees. Children were waiting to visit grandfathers in their 70s. F's husband (now released) is from the left but most long-term detainees are Islamists. The majority are unofficially detained. They have never been to court and there is no document that gives them prisoner status. They are not allowed to give power of attorney to anyone. Without documents, wives cannot draw their husbands' salaries, cannot travel, cannot marry off a daughter or even bury a child. Because of the conditions in the jail, the detainees' families have to provide them with food, clothes, books, cigarettes. The distance from the center of Cairo to Tora jail is 20 miles. Because the detainees have no official status there is no agreed system for visits. The women show up and hope that they and their provisions will be allowed in. If they are not they have to come back next day. F and her colleagues now find themselves campaigning at least for the proper application of the hated emergency laws under which Egyptians have labored since 1981.

The emergency laws proscribe demonstrations or unauthorized public gatherings. Six of the marches that have taken place in Cairo over the last two weeks have been women's marches called by women's NGOs. Unlike marches involving men they managed to reach both the American and Israeli embassies. Men who demonstrate get shot before they come anywhere near these, but the authorities are still wary of brutalizing women in public. It seems, though, that their patience may be wearing thin; a recent demo saw 150 women cornered by some 2,000 riot police. Last Saturday's demonstration in front of the Arab League headquarters linked Iraq and Palestine, for while the world's attention is on Iraq, Ariel Sharon's army shoots at ambulances and bulldozes houses down on top of pregnant women. Since November 2000, 51 Palestinian women have had to give birth at check points; 29 of their 51 babies died. And yet Palestinian women continue to have babies. Is that a political choice? At the center of most women's lives are the children. Soha, a nursing student, breaks down and cries in her home in Aida Camp when a rocket whizzes through her kitchen window at supper-time and out through the facing wall into the mercifully empty bedroom. Her mother tells her to buck up and not scare the children. It is sobering to note that the first Palestinian woman to make the political decision to become a human bomb was a nurse, caring daily for children injured or maimed by Israeli bullets. In between these two extremes, the giving and the giving up of life, hundreds of thousands of women go about their business as best they can.

Karma Abu Sharif, though 60 years younger than our Baghdadi friend, does not walk the streets of Ramallah. She sits at home and compiles the *Hearpalestine* newsletter and website, recording what she can of the daily demolitions, expropriations, arrests and killings. Keeping the children alive. Keeping culture alive. Preserving history and telling the story—these seem to be at the heart of our women's concerns right now.

The UN's Peter Hansen, writing in this paper last week of the terrible hunger in Gaza, says that "the Palestinian extended family and community network have saved the territories from ... absolute collapse". Women are the backbone of these families and networks and they are performing the same function in Iraq. Families who have, share with those who have not, through the agency of the churches and the mosques.

Last night IK told me that her mother, in Baghdad, has sold the Virgin's gold. An icon of the Virgin that has been in the family for more than 300 years. A neighbor in trouble—Christian, Jew or Muslim—would come and whisper a prayer, perhaps make a pledge. When the afflicted was healed, the traveller berthed, the child conceived, the neighbor would fulfil the pledge. Over the decades the Virgin was adorned with the most delicate filaments of gold. To her children's appalled protests that the gold was not hers to sell, their mother replied that the Virgin had no need of gold when there were people in the city who were starving. But what comes next? Where do you go after you've sold the Virgin's gold?

Women of the Promised Land

SILJA J. A. TALVI

LiP Magazine, **11.14.02**

"A climate of fear and an obsession with reprisal now grip our two peoples. We women refuse to be paralyzed or polarized by such fear." —Statement from The Jerusalem Center for Women and Bat Shalom, April 15, 2002

"We cannot afford to waste any more time, or any more lives. We need to think of a new approach. We as women want to bring a new understanding to the situation in the Middle East." —Palestinian feminist Maha Abu-Dayyeh Shamas, in a speech before the UN Security Council, May 7, 2002

"Where are you men of Ramallah?!"

Such were the cries of Palestinian women who took to the streets, en masse, in the nascent stages of the first Intifada.

Today, the televised battles between Jewish Israelis and Palestinians have largely been framed as an ongoing battle of angry men locked in a deadly and senseless spiral of armed conflict.

But in the beginning, it was women who were the first to take to the streets. All throughout the West Bank, they demonstrated loudly and non-violently for an end to the Israeli occupation of Palestinian territories.

Throughout the late 1980s and early 1990s, the members of Palestinian women's and neighborhood committees devoted their lives to building a comprehensive and concrete resistance movement—effectively carrying the Palestinian revolution to a point where the world sat up and was forced to take notice. By March 1988, in fact, there were an average of 115 women's marches in the Occupied Territories per week, many of them in protest over miscarriages suffered from tear gas, as well as in grief over the injuries and deaths of children, parents, friends, and husbands.

The demonstrations themselves thrust Palestinian women into a new role in their society, sparking debate over difficult gender issues including "honor killings," bride prices, spousal abuse, occupational status, and equal payment, as well as the physical safety of women who rejected the rules and constraints of Islamic shari'a dress, including the wearing of the hijab.

Yet then, as now, the televised images broadcast into homes across the world were of rock-throwing Palestinian boys and men, engaged in David and Goliath-styled skirmishes with the heavily armed young male soldiers of the Israeli Defense Forces (IDF).

Lesser known—and rarely reported on—has been the remarkable extent to which Palestinian and Israeli women have worked together and organized for a peaceful end to the 35-year occupation.

Away from the public spotlight, Palestinian and Israeli female dissidents and journalists have endured torture in Israeli prisons, while dedicated Orthodox Jewish women have objected loudly, on religious principles, to the Occupation. Feminist Jewish lesbians have joined the likes of the internationally-recognized Women in Black in organizing protests and vigils. Palestinian and Israeli women academics have written declarations, essays, articles and books about their opposition to the Israeli government's brutal occupation of the West Bank and Gaza, and have issued stinging criticisms of the Palestinian Authority's summary executions, jailings and squelching of dissenting viewpoints.

More so than any other Palestinian woman, the high-profile negotiating skills of the articulate and analytical Hanan Ashrawi defied gender lines and societal expectations. Replying to a 1992 question about how it felt to be the only woman in the Palestinian and Israeli negotiating teams, Ashrawi told a *Ms.* interviewer the following:

> "It is a tremendous responsibility, a great challenge. It is also a great victory for women in general, and in particular for Arab and Palestinian women. Because this didn't come out of a vacuum but as a result of a long history of women's struggle in the Occupied Territories, Palestine. I came buttressed by a clear feminist vision and agenda and a new definition of value . . . My role legitimizes women's struggles; I can speak out on behalf of all the women whose voices have not been heard. This is collective work, not tokenism."

PUSHED OUT OF THE SPOTLIGHT

In 2002, the feminist peace movement continues to try to advance a shared vision similar to Ashrawi's, but women's voices now barely register in the coverage of the Israeli-Palestinian conflict except in the roles of vitriolic settlers, terrorized mothers, shellshocked refugees, and bloodied, frantic shoppers rushing to get away from a suicide bombing.

"Those of us who remain committed to the joint work and have sustainable relationships are continuing to meet when possible, but the closures and curfews mean that scheduling is improvisational and crazy-making," explains Terry Greenblatt, the director of one of Israel's more prominent feminist peace organizations, Bat Shalom.

Bat Shalom and the Palestinian women's peace organization, The Jerusalem Center for Women, comprise what's known as The Jerusalem Link—a group that works together toward "a real peace—not merely a treaty of mutual deterrence, but a culture of peace and cooperation between our peoples."

Women's organizations like these have made a difference in keeping the prospect of peace and cooperation alive and visible in the face long odds. But, as Greenblatt explains, "We are [still] struggling against chauvinism, misogyny, stereotypes, and the fact that in Israel most of our political leaders are catapulted from distinguished army careers right into the Knesset."

Sexism is hardly unique to Israel, where women have worked hard to attain proportionate representation and leadership positions in the political system, in labor unions, and in the workplace. But misogyny in the Holy Land wears a particular face. Jewish and Arab Israeli feminists openly talk about problematic gender relations when the predominant construction of masculinity is that of a sabra (native-born) strong Jewish man, born out of the ashes of the Holocaust, and raised with the intertwined narratives of Arab anti-Semitism and anti-Arab Zionism.

A different reality looked possible for Israel from the early 1910s through the 1950s when the anarchistic kibbutzim—the largely self-sufficient communal farms and settlements that became the backbone of Israel's early agricultural success—promised the idea of a new, egalitarian future for Jewish men and women alike.

In the wake of the 1967 and 1973 Israeli-Arab wars, a markedly more militaristic, male-dominated Israeli identity began to emerge. The creation of the new, macho Israeli identity existed alongside other troubling developments: increasingly influential and right-wing ultra-Orthodox Jews and a growth in the number of fanatical settlers in the Occupied Territories. In this context, the prospects for Israeli women's true equality dimmed immeasurably.

Such losses, of course, have not taken away from the fact that Israeli women, Jewish and Arab alike, are still free to pursue nearly any occupation or lifestyle that they choose, and are among the most well-educated, politically-informed and independent women in the Middle East. Despite this, women's peace activism has not yet been accorded the legitimacy and import that it deserves.

Today, in the midst of the second (and more deadly) al-Aqsa Intifada, Palestinian women are no longer playing a central a role in organizing, whether in street demonstrations, campaigning, or the writing of the bayanat leaflet communiques which circulated widely among Palestinians in the first Intifada. In a *Jerusalem Post* inteview, Professor Eileen Kuttab, the director of the Women's Studies Institute at Bir Zeit University, explained that Palestinian women have struggled to find a constructive, nonviolent role in the latest uprising, which has created widespread hunger, poverty and suffering.

"Oslo came, and it didn't deliver for women," she told the *Post* in February 2002. "We weren't really included in the negotiations. When the political structures were established in the Palestinian Authority, women were not given the opportunity to become more involved."

Today, only five members of the Palestinian Legislative Council are women. Hanan Ashrawi herself moved on from Arafat's cabinet in 1998 to found the East Jerusalem-based Miftah (the Palestinian Initiative for the Promotion of Global Dialogue and Democracy). And earlier this year, Ashrawi agreed to become an information attaché for the Arab League, something which has been interpreted as a "defection" from a Palestinian establishment that did not seem to take kindly to her ardent support of women's and Palestinian civil rights—despite her pivotal and longstanding role in fighting for Palestinian independence.

In an address before the U.N. Security Council in May 2002, Palestinian feminist and Director of the Women's Center for Legal Aid and Counseling Maha Abu-Dayyeh Shamas explained the situation facing Palestinian women this way:

> "The Palestinian women's movement has succeeded in making inroads in addressing cultural values and attitudes particular to the Arab world that handicap the healthy development of girls and women. We Palestinian women were in the process of engaging ourselves in legislative development at the local as well as the international levels ... We were witnessing the development of a budding but vibrant young feminist movement, an essential sector for democratic development within the Palestinian society. However, the last so-called Israeli re-occupation of Palestinian-controlled areas has manifested itself in the systematic destruction of all that we have been able to achieve in the last ten years."

As it currently stands, the political future of these two peoples—Semitic cousins to one another in religious and ethnic heritage, cuisine and culture—has been left in the hands of the corrupt, male-dominated Palestinian Authority on one side, and the warmongering Sharon and his fractious Knesset on the other.

Upcoming Israeli elections may indeed help to bring down Sharon's scarred and violence-riddled term as prime minister, but they are hardly likely to bring about true gender parity—or a peaceful solution to the ever-deepening political crisis—as long as Israeli-styled military bravado remains the order of the day.

"Is it not preposterous that not a single Israeli woman, and only one Palestinian woman, have held leadership roles at a Middle East peace summit?" asks Gila Svirsky, who has been a key figure in both Women in Black and the Coalition of Women for Peace. "Instead, the negotiators have been men with portfolios of brutal crimes against each other—military men who have honed the art of war and who measure their success by the unconditional surrender of the other. Is it any wonder that we are still locked in combat?"

WOMEN'S PROPOSALS FOR PEACE

Suicide bombers, who could fairly be characterized as the most visible and barbaric consequence of a conflict gone mad, are openly criticized by Israeli and Palestinian feminists alike for their murderous actions. But for all of the Israeli government's demands for an end to such violence, peace activists insist that Israel will not see an end to the mounting death toll until it is willing to withdraw, unilaterally, from the Occupied Territories and dismantle Jewish settlements.

Toward that end, Israel's Coalition of Women for a Just Peace—consisting of nine different women's peace organizations—has made these five demands its platform:

1. The Occupation of the West Bank and the Gaza Strip must end.
2. The Occupation must end with a sovereign, independent and secure Palestinian state.
3. Jerusalem must be the capital for both Israel and Palestine.
4. Israel must acknowledge its responsibility for the refugees and negotiate a just solution.
5. There must be a shared cooperative destiny between Israel and Palestine which removes the enormous present economic disparity between Israelis and Palestinians.

"There is one future for us both," read an April 15, 2002 peace declaration by The Jerusalem Center and Bat Shalom. "We believe that women can develop an alternative voice promoting sound approaches and effective peace initiatives between our two nations and peoples."

And it is toward this overreaching goal that women's groups from Israel and Palestine have continued to devote themselves to the prospect of a peaceful and equitable solution to over thirty years of conflict.

Earlier this year, both Bat Shalom's Greenblatt and Abu-Dayyeh Shamas took precisely this message to the U.N. Security Council with the support of the U.S.-based feminist organization, Equality Now. The women asked member nations to recognize "the vital role of women in the resolution of the current conflict in the Middle East," and to create a means "through which women can contribute . . . to conflict resolution efforts."

Greenblatt, Abu-Dayyeh Shamas and other organizers have called for the implementation of Security Council Resolution 1325, particularly where Israeli and Palestinian women are concerned. SCR 1325, adopted in October 2000, affirms the importance of equal participation and the full involvement of women in all efforts toward the maintenance of peace.

"A process that should lead to a political solution . . . should not be left to the confines of the generals, and should be transparent to the relevant societies," said Abu-Sayyeh Shamas in her presentation to the Security Council.

"We have to address and understand each other's history with an open mind," she added. "If we leave it only to men we get Israeli generals and Palestinians who will not be defeated and there is no room to negotiate ... The participation of women in any future peace process is essential to maintain connection to the realities of the relevant societies and their yearnings for peace and security."

Thus far, the request has received an encouraging response. The next step, says Greenblatt, is to ask U.N. Secretary-General Kofi Annan to convene a special commission of women peace activists through the office of the U.N. Special Advisor on Gender Issues.

Such progress and cause for optimism notwithstanding, the Israeli-Palestinian conflict is "going to get much worse, and it is going to be bad for a very long time," admits Greenblatt. "The price of peace is going to be expensive and painful—for both sides."

Greenblatt adds that the impending war against Iraq has Israelis and Palestinians worried about another counter-attack on Israel, which not only poses danger for innocent civilians, but also gives the Israeli government further justification for land expropriations and crackdowns against Palestinians.

"As an Israeli woman," Greenblatt says, "I know that if war is the answer, we are still not asking the right question."

Women Are Opening Doors: Security Council Resolution 1325 in Afghanistan

FELICITY HILL AND MIKELE ABOITIZ

Women for Afghan Women, 10.02

After September 11, 2001, the world became aware of the suffering of women in Afghanistan. Women's nongovernmental organizations (NGOs) around the world had been trying to raise awareness for years, but only after September 11 did these women appear so prominently in the *New York Times*, the *Washington Post*, and on CNN and similar high-profile news media. Only then did women appear on the radar screen of international policy makers. International media attention focused on the Taliban's war on Afghan women, with less attention given to the need for women to be present at the peace table.

As the U.S.-led war in Afghanistan developed, women's organizations around the world saw an opportunity to turn a terrible situation into a positive outcome. It was not enough that the Taliban were pushed out of Afghanistan; it was not enough that the Unites States and the international community spoke about women's issues. It was time to let women speak for themselves and decide their future.

WILPF AND THE NGO WORKING GROUP ON WOMEN, PEACE, AND SECURITY

At the Women's International League for Peace and Freedom (WILPF),[1] the process of empowering women to find peace started a long time ago. WILPF is an old and well-established organization, dating back to 1915, when its founders and leaders outlined a new and compassionate concept of human security. That year some 1,300 women from Europe and North America gathered in The Hague, the Netherlands. These women originated both from countries at war with each other and from countries that were neutral. All came together in a congress of women to protest the killing and destruction wrought by the war raging in Europe. They envisioned a security that does not rest on military strength but rather lies in equitable and sustainable economic and social development.

These 1,300 women issued 20 resolutions; some were of immediate importance, while others aimed at reducing conflict and preventing war by establishing the foundation for a permanent peace among the world's nations. Neutral governments were called on to press warring nations to stop fighting and settle their differences by negotiations that would be held within the borders of neutral countries. Grievances and remedies would be voiced and met with impartiality.

This vision translates into an equal distribution of resources to meet the basic needs of all people and guarantees full and equal participation of men and women in all levels of society, including in its decision making. The women organized "envoys" to carry these resolutions to both neutral and belligerent states in Europe and to the president of the United States. Jane Addams, having been elected president of the congress and of the International Women's Committee (the beginning of WILPF), met with President Woodrow Wilson, who, according to government records, said that the congress's resolutions were by far the best formations for peace that had been put forward to date.[2] Again, according to the records, Wilson "borrowed" some of their ideas for his own peace proposals. In total, the congress had small delegations that visited fourteen countries during May and June of 1915. WILPF was founded as an international organization to work globally. Two of WILPF's original founders, Jane Addams and Emily Greene Balch, received the Nobel Peace Prize, in 1931 and 1946, respectively, for their peace efforts and international views and work.

Women's voices are needed not only at the negotiating tables but also in the larger political institutions that generate and dictate security policy. The utter failure of current conceptions of security, largely defined by men, suggests the need for new approaches by new people. The full and equal participation of women at all levels of national and international life would undoubtedly contribute to addressing the current human security vacuum. Women are still suffering disproportionately in situations of armed conflict, but as more women participate in decision making and negotiating peace and security issues, the hope is that armed conflict will no longer be a tolerable solution and that preparation for armed conflict will not be confused with security.

With this concept in mind, WILPF has organized rallies, lobbied politicians, and pushed members of the United Nations (UN) to find solutions to inequalities as a means of solving all armed conflicts. In 2001 WILPF joined Amnesty International, the Hague Appeal for Peace, International Alert, International Peace Research Association, and the Women's Commission for Refugee Women and Children, and created the NGO Working Group on Women and International Peace and Security. This working group seized a window of opportunity and pushed for a thematic debate in the United Nations Security Council after Ambassador Anwarul Karim Chowdhury of Bangladesh, president of the Security Council, made a ground-breaking statement on March 8, 2000, linking equality, development, peace, and the need for women's urgent involvement in these matters. The combination of contributions from the Namibian presidency of the Security Council, the NGO Working Group, the Division for the Advancement of Women (DAW), and the United Nations Development Fund for Women (UNIFEM) helped to identify and bring the experiences and expertise of civil society into the sacred and once-exclusive realm of the Security Council.

Besides creating a list of experts and NGOs that would speak to the issues in the Security Council, members of the working group lobbied and debated with every Security Council member. Furthermore, they compiled packets of relevant documents with summaries that they hand-delivered to all Security Council members and undertook media strategy to maximize attention on this issue. Synergy among NGOs, UN departments, and governments brought together the strengths of each segment and ensured success. Representatives of WILPF expressed hope and relief that issues so long ignored were at last being registered at the highest levels.

SECURITY COUNCIL RESOLUTION 1325

It was a profoundly moving and historic moment when women at last filled the public gallery of the Security Council on October 24, 2000, applauding and cheering. After fifty-five years of efforts on the part of the United Nations to end the scourge of war, women's perspectives on war and peace had finally been acknowledged in the Security Council. Women from Sierra Leone, Guatemala, Somalia, Tanzania, and international NGOs had spoken to members of the Security Council in an Arria Formula meeting[3] the previous day. Arria Formula meetings offer an opportunity for NGO experts to brief the ambassadors on specific topics. These meetings focused on the suffering of women in war, their undervalued and underutilized work to prevent conflict and build peace, and the leadership they demonstrate in rebuilding wartorn societies.

As a result, on October 31, 2000, Security Council members unanimously passed Resolution 1325, which calls for:

- The participation of women in decision-making and peace processes
- Gender perspectives and training in peacekeeping
- The protection of women
- Gender mainstreaming in UN reporting systems and programmatic implementation mechanisms.

Resolution 1325 provides a tool for women because it requires gender sensitivity in all UN missions including peacekeeping, women's equal participation at all negotiating tables, and the protection of women and girls during armed conflict. The last paragraph of this resolution notes that the Security Council "decides to remain actively seized of the matter." This resolution provides an important tool in shifting the UN system from words to action.

SC 1325 IN ACTION: AFGHANISTAN

On the surface, Resolution 1325 might seem like empty words that may never be implemented, but for women's groups involved in peace building in conflict zones worldwide, it is a historic statement with significant implications that can be quoted and used in related contexts. Moreover, as a Security Council resolution, it is binding international law that for the first time officially endorses the inclusion of civil society groups, notably women, in peace processes and in the implementation of peace agreements. Women finally have a tool they can use to become part of the planning for the future of their country. Afghan and non-Afghan women have used this resolution to demand that Mr. Lakhdar Brahimi, the secretary-general's special representative for Afghanistan, meet with five Afghan women immediately after he was appointed.

The United Nations strongly supported the inclusion of women at the Bonn meetings in December 2001. Because of the prioritization of this issue, a few women did participate in the Bonn negotiations. However, the presence of a mere three women as delegates and two as advisors is not enough. Women's involvement in these matters cannot be restricted to a small number of token individuals who are supposed to represent all women. Three people cannot represent so many others, especially when the population they represent is as disparate as Afghan women.

However, acknowledging that there is much room for improvement does not by any means diminish the importance and historic achievement of the participation of women at Bonn. Considering that women are usually absent at high decision-making levels and virtually invisible from negotiations on cease-fires, peace agreements, and postconflict reconstruction, women activists for peace did feel some sense of accomplishment in the participation of five women at the Bonn negotiations. Years of activism, raising awareness, and conferences organized by women in New York, Berlin, and all over the world played a major part in that achievement. We regard it as a turning point and an important benchmark along the road to full and equal participation for women in all aspects and at all levels of governance.

Women rarely participate in negotiating cease-fires and drafting treaties because they do not occupy leadership positions in governments or other armed groups. Women are not leading warring parties. Rather, women constitute the majority of those executed, enslaved, impoverished, and damaged. Ultimately, however, women must be involved in the peace process not only because they suffer disproportionately, or because they have previously been excluded, but because of their contribution to the world is invaluable.

If the importance of the resolution is recognized, it will have profound implications for change. It has the potential to be an effective tool in the hands of the United Nations, NGOs, and governments. In order to ensure collaboration and coordination, Secretary-General Kofi Annan established a task force on women, peace, and security, composed of representatives from fifteen UN entities. This task force is developing an action plan on the implementation of the resolution and will produce a comprehensive report on the role of the United Nations within the year.

UNIFEM also appointed two independent experts who will produce a report with recommendations to the United Nations, governments, and NGOs. The Office of the Coordination of Humanitarian Affairs (OCHA) launched its fund-raising appeal immediately after the resolution was passed to benefit women in conflict zones. The Department for Disarmament Affairs produced a series of briefing papers showing the connections between gender and the full range of disarmament issues, land mines, small arms, weapons of mass destruction, and the peace movement. These developments are only a few examples of the shifting climate within the United Nations.

A LOOK INTO THE FUTURE

Since the passage of this momentous Resolution, reports on UN peacekeeping operations, such as those on Afghanistan (S/2000/1106), the Democratic Republic of Congo (S/2001/128), Western Sahara (S/2001/148), and other countries, have included material on gender and the situation of women in their countries. The gender unit in East Timor is outstanding in the kinds of reports and information it has produced for the Department of Peace Keeping Operations and the Security Council. It has shown concretely that the efforts of the United Nations on gender, while difficult to establish at first, have enhanced the effectiveness and the sense of integrity of the United Nations in the field. The training that has taken place through the Gender Unit in East Timor will enable women to occupy key positions in the new government. The technical assistance and guidance given to the NGOs trying to navigate the sometimes intimidating UN system should not be underestimated.

Men still disproportionately dominate all of the formal governing bodies of peace and security. Let's face it—they have totally and utterly failed in their efforts. Wars continue to rage everywhere. The fragility of the most militarily powerful nation on earth is exposed. And the result of militarizing countries—arming, training, and paying thugs—turns out to be the formula for antisecurity.

To pressure their governments to take action, women's groups must be made aware of treaties and laws that have been agreed on by their governments to address gender concerns. Nongovernmental organizations can support and sustain women's efforts using the tools provided in Resolution 1325 by:

- Pressing governments to increase the numbers of senior women in the United Nations
- Contributing women's names to rosters for these positions
- Pressing for greater involvement of national and international negotiators in conflict zones and monitoring their actions
- Ensuring that local civil society groups are integrated into all levels and aspects of conflict prevention, resolution, and management
- Lobbying governments to contribute funds for gender training of peacekeepers
- Ensuring gender training in armies
- Monitoring and lobbying for increased civil society involvement in the design and implementation of humanitarian assistance programs in refugee camps
- Collecting gender-sensitive data and testimonies to provide greater accuracy and understanding of the needs of refugees and internally displaced persons
- Monitoring the implementation of Resolution 1325 at national and international levels
- Lobbying for greater consultation with UN agencies in follow-up processes and reports.

A WILPF project in the works will help women monitor progress and share news, campaigning tools, and contact details. Our new website (www.peacewomen.org) aims to pull together the efforts of women working for peace in conflict zones. We wish to make it impossible for the world, especially the United Nations, to ignore the peacebuilding work of women. We exist to support women in their efforts to attain peace and justice, abolish oppression, and to challenge colonialism, discrimination, aggression, occupation, and foreign domination.

One section of the site gathers a comprehensive database of women's organizations in every country to facilitate networking and resourcing.

Another section provides a collection of resources, including annotated bibliographies of books, articles, NGO reports, and tools for organizational building that feed critical thinking on sexism and militarism and enable women's groups to proceed in their work better informed. The third part translates the UN resolution into understandable language, focusing on war, peace, and security, and highlighting UN efforts that pertain particularly to women affected by war. The final section features campaigns and news of women who are working for peace and justice around the world.

The words of Security Council Resolution 1325 have translated into action and must continue to do so. The people who comprise the United Nations must ensure that women are included at every level of peace and security, from local communities to international criminal tribunals for countries coming out of conflict.

The doors were open just wide enough for women to squeeze into the peace negotiations in Afghanistan. They came with the knowledge that war is a gendered activity. Now, concerned women and men must use the words of Resolution 1325 to force the doors permanently open, to enter *all* rooms where peace agreements are negotiated and where peacekeeping operations are planned. Afghanistan must be the testing ground for the implementation of Resolution 1325.

NOTES

1. WILPF has offices in New York City and Geneva
2. Gertrude Bussey and Margaret Tims, *Pioneers for Peace, Women's International League for Peace and Freedom:* 1915–1917 (Oxford, U.K.: Alden Press, 1980), p. 21.
3. Informal, off-the-record exchanges between security council members and NGOs, often used to provide expert testimony on specific issues, particularly humanitarian concerns.

Shelf Life. Librarians: Liberals with Backbone

CHRISTOPHER HAYES

***The American Prospect*, 2.19.03**

When progressive provocateur Michael Moore was down and out, he found help from an unlikely source. After September 11, Moore's publisher, HarperCollins, told him that his new book, *Stupid White Men*, wouldn't be released unless he cut some controversial sections and rewrote others. When Moore balked, HarperCollins told him it would simply cancel the book. That December, a few days after he learned that his book was destined for early recycling, Moore went to speak to a meeting of the progressive group New Jersey Citizen Action. He told group members of his plight and read a few chapters from the doomed book. When members asked him what they could do, Moore told them that there were more important battles to fight.

Ann Sparanese, who was sitting in the audience, didn't see it that way. "Problem is, I am a librarian," says Sparanese, head of reference at the Englewood Library in New Jersey. "I was shocked . . . I think we're used to books being censored by the government for having either classified or embarrassing information in them, but this was actually being censored by a publisher who had already invested in printing the book . . . That really kind of stunned me."

When Sparanese got home from the meeting, she sent out an e-mail to several professional listservs, and HarperCollins soon found itself flooded with thousands of outraged phone calls. "We're getting hate mail from librarians!" screamed one exasperated publishing rep, according to Moore. Within weeks the book was released, and soon it was sitting atop the *New York Times* Best-Seller Lists.

The librarians had taken on a publishing giant—and won. Surprised? Don't be.

The sedate shushers of your childhood have stepped into the political arena, and they've emerged as one of the most vital and effective progressive forces in the country. Over the past several years, librarians, and their professional governing body, the American Library Association (ALA), have been behind some of the most significant civil-liberties battles in the country—from the fight over the Communications Decency Act (which the Supreme Court struck down as the result of a lawsuit brought by the ALA and the American Civil Liberties Union) to the controversy over the USA PATRIOT Act (which the ALA sharply criticized in a recent resolution) to the question of whether to strengthen copyright restrictions on digital media (which the ALA opposes).

It may be because of their buttoned-down image that librarians have such wells of political capital. Of all the common stereotypes of various professions—the sleazy lawyer, the absentminded professor, the kindly grocer—few are more potent than that of the mousy, officious librarian. That image is so ingrained that it's nearly impossible to think of librarians as agitators, radicals or troublemakers. But in these times of bipartisanship and muted dissent, that's exactly what they've become.

"We are one of the few voices out there who are saying to this administration, 'Wait a minute: You can't take information away from the public and not suffer the consequences,'" says Judith Krug, director of the ALA's Office of Intellectual Freedom (OIF). The role of librarians in a democracy—as stewards of information and facilitators of debate—makes them natural civil-liberties crusaders, Krug says. "Our professional responsibility is to bring people and information together," she adds. "Because if we don't have the information, we can't govern ourselves."

Krug has been the OIF's director since the office's inception in 1967, when the ALA created it to defend and protect the principles outlined in the association's Library Bill of Rights—which includes the provision that library "materials should not be excluded because of the origin, background, or views of those contributing to their creation" and also calls on librarians to "challenge censorship in fulfillment of their responsibility to provide information and enlightenment."

For much of the OIF's history, upholding these principles has meant defending the jobs of those unfortunate souls who had the temerity to keep *Tropic of Cancer* or *Are You There God? It's Me, Margaret* on their local shelves.

But that was before the digital revolution, the explosion of the Internet and the attendant changes in the library world. During the early 1990s, libraries were some of the first institutions to champion Internet access for all, and as online services grew at a rapid pace, libraries became the prime portals for those Americans who could not afford access from their homes. Then, in 1996, President Clinton signed into law the Communications Decency Act (CDA), which made it a crime for anyone to distribute "patently offensive" or "indecent" Internet material to minors. Because librarians facilitate Internet use for millions of minors, they realized that they were sitting squarely in the act's crosshairs. So they fought back.

The ALA, along with the ACLU, filed a lawsuit that challenged the act, arguing that its effect would be to limit Internet content to what was acceptable to minors. In 1997 the Supreme Court struck down the law by a 7-to-2 ruling, but the bill's proponents were unfazed. They crafted a second piece of legislation, the Child Online Protection Act (COPA), designed to avoid the constitutional pitfalls of the first bill. When the High Court remanded COPA back to an appeals court that had already struck it down, conservative legislators went after the victorious librarians with yet another piece of federal legislation, the Child Internet Protection Act (CIPA), which requires all libraries receiving federal money to install filtering software on their Internet terminals.

Filtering software is designed to screen offensive or pornographic material, but it routinely blocks a lot more than that. Medical information, for instance, often doesn't make it past the software, and one study found that it also barred users from viewing the Web sites for Super Bowl XXX, the former Beaver College (it has since changed its name to Arcadia University) in Pennsylvania and the office of former House Majority Leader Dick Armey (R-Texas), who, not surprisingly, supported the bill. Librarians have once again challenged the law on constitutional grounds, arguing that the filtering would amount to censorship for adults using the computers on which the software is installed. An appeals court has already declared the law unconstitutional, and arguments before the Supreme Court are set for March 5.

It was because of the prolonged battle over Internet censorship that librarians were gaining notoriety and political muscle just as civil liberties were about to suddenly and unexpectedly come under the knife. Some librarians argue that the USA PATRIOT Act—passed a month after September 11 with a single dissenting Senate vote from Sen. Russ Feingold (D-Wis.)—represents the largest encroachment on civil liberties since the days of J. Edgar Hoover. "This is the worst it's ever been," says Krug gravely. "I've been in this office for 38 years. It's like I get up in the morning and I go to turn on the radio and I'm like, 'Oh God, what's gonna greet me today?'"

One aspect of the law is particularly troubling to librarians. Section 215 lets federal agents issue search warrants for the borrowing records of library patrons under the 1978 Foreign Intelligence Surveillance Act (FISA), which established a secret court to approve search warrants against suspected spies. Previously cases fell within FISA jurisdiction only if foreign surveillance was the "primary purpose" of the investigation; now that threshold has been lowered to "a significant purpose." If a FISA warrant for, say, the borrowing records of a suspected terrorist is issued to a librarian, he or she has no choice but to turn over the relevant material—and then keep the whole thing to herself. (FISA comes with a built-in gag order.) It's possible that federal agents have been using their expanded powers to go through thousands of borrowing records since 9/11, and it's also possible that this power has yet to be exercised. But because the warrants are a secret, no one except the government can say for sure. (Though in an anonymous survey of 1,505 libraries conducted by the University of Illinois Library Research Center, 15 respondents said they were omitting information about run-ins with law enforcement because of legal restrictions.)

The ALA has joined the ACLU in filing a Freedom of Information Act lawsuit, demanding that the Department of Justice tell the public how many times Section 215 has been used. At its conference in January, the ALA passed a resolution strongly criticizing the act, and the group is currently considering possible legal and legislative avenues to challenge it.

Librarians aren't just taking on the government, either: They've also picked a fight with big business, challenging entertainment- and publishing-industry-backed changes to copyright law that would make it more difficult for libraries to distribute digital books and magazines. And they've started a program called Lawyers for Librarians that will train lawyers around the country on how best to defend librarians' civil liberties.

All of this activity has prompted the usual hand-wringing from the cultural right. Dr. Laura Schlessinger has crusaded against librarians, saying they want "to make sure your children have easy access to pornography, under the guise of free speech." In a *Los Angeles Times* article last November about the ALA's burgeoning political influence, Rep. Charles W. Pickering, Jr. (R-Miss.), one of CIPA's chief sponsors, expressed concern that librarians were promoting a "radical, extremist social agenda."

Opposition to the ALA's platform isn't just coming from the right-wing fringe. CDA, COPA, CIPA and the USA PATRIOT Act all passed with broad bipartisan support. With Republicans currently controlling all three branches of government, a populace scared out of its wits by daily terrorism warnings and an anemic Democratic opposition, Krug and the ALA realize that they have their work cut out for them. That's why they've hired Emily Sheketoff, a veteran Washington insider and lobbyist, to be the first non-librarian to run the group's Washington office. And it's also why the group has more than doubled its lobbying budget over the past four years, from $360,000 to $750,000.

But no matter how shrewd their lobbying efforts, librarians may soon find that entering the political fray on such hotly contested issues comes with substantial costs. As states face budget crises, many libraries are staring down massive cuts—even branch closings—and it's at times like these when it pays to have politicians in your corner. The ALA has made its share of enemies, and last year a federal bill that would have doubled library spending failed to make it to a floor vote.

Nevertheless, Krug, who will be attending Supreme Court arguments on CIPA in early March and is gearing up for another fight over the forthcoming PATRIOT Act II, remains uncowed. "We have the First Amendment to the United States Constitution behind us," she says, "and that is one hell of a bulwark to stand against." The politics of the moment may seem stacked against them, but, as HarperCollins found out, adversaries underestimate this new breed of librarian-progressives at their own peril.

Against Rosa's Odds: On the Road With a Welfare Warrior

CHISUN LEE

The Village Voice, 6.12.02

Wide awake on three hours of sleep, Rosa sends her teenagers off to school, boards a bus headed south, and watches Brooklyn streak away. She wears layers against the air-conditioning, but they are no insulation from anxiousness. She taps her thin fingers on the side of the seat and shivers.

On monitors jutting from the ceiling, a tape of a recent *West Wing* episode plays. President Bartlett denounces a Republican proposal to spend welfare money on promoting marriage for the poor—art imitating politics in the 107th Congress. The busload of real-life New York City welfare recipients cheers.

But Rosa can't get into it. "I gotta practice," she mutters, smoothing out a sheet of paper on her lap. With her lean, lanky limbs, gelled hair, and glossed lips, she could pass from not much of a distance for an adolescent. As jittery as a teen facing the SATs, she was up until 2 a.m. writing this speech. The prospect of making her public-speaking debut at a rally in the streets of Washington, D.C., had her tossing and turning and out of bed at five.

Having dropped out of high school, divorced an abuser, and raised three children on her own, Rosario Rodriguez well qualifies to speak on behalf of welfare recipients nationwide. There are some 1.5 million adults on welfare across the country, and about 55 percent never finished high school. Nearly all adults on welfare are women, most of them single mothers. Over half of them have, like Rosa, suffered domestic violence.

Moreover, Rosa has come up in the nation's harshest welfare system, the one that Rudolph Giuliani bragged purged recipient rolls by half. It is a model for George Bush and congressional conservatives in shaping federal welfare reform this year. They are seeking unprecedented increases in the amount of labor required to get assistance, and strict limits on school and job training. The Senate's slim Democratic majority is the last hope for those wanting to maintain the 1996 welfare law's already stringent rules, with perhaps more flexibility for education and child care. The Senate debate is set to begin mid-June, so Rosa and a few hundred of New York's poor headed to D.C. on May 21 to plead their case.

She may be a natural spokesperson, but Rosa has rarely felt qualified for anything. "From my marriage to losing jobs to being on welfare, I thought I was a failure," she says. The rally looms many hours away, but she can already envision disaster, her voice or her guts giving out. After all, defeat has snapped at her heels most of her 39 years.

Painfully shy, the young Rosa preferred solitaire to socializing. But Angel Jesus Rodriguez noticed her anyway. She got pregnant and with one semester to go dropped out of Brooklyn's John Jay High School in 1982 to get married and have a son named for his father. Soon after, Melissa and Andrew arrived, and Rosa's dream of having a family was complete.

But not long after they wed, her husband got angry and shook her, hard. "He said he was sorry, he would never do it again," she says. Rosa's mother, a devout Catholic from Puerto Rico who married at age 12, told her daughter that men would be men. "She said, 'Just keep quiet. Don't get him angry. Just do what you're supposed to do as a wife.'" Rosa convinced herself, "Everything's going to work out. He loves me." Then, she says, "he did it again."

Rosa bore the slaps and bruises as discreetly as she could, or, as son Angel, now 19, says, "She just used to take it." He recalls witnessing the abuse, like the time his father shoved her down a flight of stairs in their Brooklyn building. "He would get drunk and take it out on her," he says. . . .

In an unusually candid interview, obtained with Rosa's consent, Rodriguez denies that he shook her after their wedding or pushed her down the stairs. But he says, "Yes, I used to drink a lot. Come home drunk, and sometimes not too drunk. I used to argue with her a lot. Everybody curses at each other. . . ." Asked several times whether he had ever struck Rosa, he says, "I might have, but as far as I can recall, no. One time, I believe so. . . ."

Rosa says the family endured not only violence but also relentless poverty, and was on public assistance from the start. Her husband concedes he preferred drinking with friends over his sporadic work as a security guard. Rosa redeemed soda cans to buy diapers, and stretched meals with donations from relatives.

Photographs show Rosa over the years becoming a thin shadow of her former, full-faced self. Five-foot-three, she has at times dipped to 90 pounds. Her domestic troubles killed her appetite and caused ulcers, and a pack-a-day nicotine habit took firm hold. At her lowest, she says, she thought about suicide. "But when I went to open the bottle of pills, I was like, what am I doing?"

Frustration eventually overtook her fear. . . . Rosa kicked her husband out of the apartment for good, but he continued to have trouble taking no for an answer, according to several orders of protection issued by Brooklyn Family Court between 1995 and 2000. It took several years for Rosa to find a free divorce lawyer, but in 2000, a judge terminated the marriage, citing "Cruel and Inhuman Treatment."[. . .]

Without a high school diploma, Rosa possessed one skill she felt sure of, raising children. In 1994, she landed a job at a day care center, after volunteering persistently. Her family left welfare for the first time. But after a few years, she says, she was accused of poor performance and fired, and she lost the next job after questioning a parent's care of a sick child. She learned that fast-food wages would not cover the bills. By the middle of 1999, Rosa was broke, supporting three teenagers, and facing public assistance in Giuliani's New York.

Signs of want surrounded the family in their rent-regulated Park Slope one-bedroom, which had not been renovated or painted since the Rodriguezes moved in some 15 years earlier. Swarms of hundreds of cockroaches would well from cracks in the walls and stove, photographs show. There were two sets of metal bunk beds to hold four, and two gaunt tabbies to kill the rodents. Second-hand furniture weathered the years under thick coats of shiny black paint. Rosa cherished a single luxury: a half-dozen painted plates, her china.

An able-bodied adult without very young children, Rosa was scheduled by her welfare caseworker for maximum time in Work Experience Program (WEP)—35 hours a week for $153 in aid every two weeks. . . . She pleaded to be placed in a GED program, something she had previously been unable to do. Before a crowded center, her caseworker issued a loud—and illogical—refusal: "You've got no education, no skills, no nothing!" Despite the onlookers, Rosa cried.

Eventually she was placed two days a week in a city-contracted program advertised to deliver education and job training. Supervisors told her to arrive in a suit or be sanctioned—which would mean reduced benefits. Class time meant being supplied with the yellow pages and a telephone and being ordered to call around for job openings. Sometimes they gave her a crossword. The rest of the week, she wheeled a trash can along Third Avenue in Brooklyn, not far from where she lived, cleaning her neighbors' mess. "I wouldn't have minded if I got paid" a living wage, says Rosa, but the Department of Sanitation told her "you need a GED to pick up garbage for them."

One day Rosa was waiting to meet with her caseworker when somebody handed her a flier asking whether she was fed up and angry and inviting her to learn her rights. "Welfare makes you crazy. I was desperate. I was like, I gotta do something," she says.

And so she met the women of Families United for Racial and Economic Equality, or FUREE, a nonprofit community-based organization in Park Slope. "In the beginning, I was thinking, these people are nuts," Rosa recalls. They sat around shouting about dignity and social justice, and cracking jokes about politicians, and they were mothers on welfare.

Her first protest ever was at City Hall. Recipients gathered to denounce Giuliani's campaign to slash the welfare rolls while failing to provide meaningful training or sometimes food stamps. A giant puppet of Giuliani-as-Hitler bobbled in the breeze. "I couldn't believe all these people," says Rosa. "I was like, I don't want to get arrested."

She agreed to hand out fliers, but generally she tried to escape notice. "Rosa put herself down a lot," friend Isabel Rodriguez (no relation) recalls. "She said she's ugly, which is a lie. One time, somebody asked who she was. She said, 'I'm nobody.'" But, Rosa found, these women did not look for her failings—many faced similar challenges. She began to smile more often, though she couldn't quite shake the habit of shielding her grin with a hand.

Rosa and an advocate unraveled miles of red tape to get her into a respected GED program at Sunset Park Adult and Family Education Center. Her caseworker balked, but Rosa demanded a fair hearing—after learning she could—and won. She began commuting four days a week to a hushed, carpeted room in a large church, where she is neither divorcee nor aging dropout, but simply a student. When the semester ends this month, Rosa says, she will require perhaps another year of classes before she'll be able to pass the exam. Getting approval to continue, she predicts, will require more battles, ones she is not at all certain she will win.

And so as conservatives and liberals in Congress debate welfare reform—to raise or maintain current work requirements, to limit or expand educational opportunity—Rosa has much at stake. There are her education and future employability, her children's school supplies and clothing and possibly college. Since the government ties rent aid to welfare compliance, there is the roof over their heads. She wonders, "Are we going to survive any new work requirements?"

The FUREE women nominate Rosa to deliver a speech during a day of protest in D.C. with recipients from other cities. She is, they enthuse, the perfect example of poor women struggling to survive in the nation's harshest welfare system. In a burst of brazenness—or insanity, she begins to think—she agrees.

So Rosa swallows bubbles of terror on the bus ride down, running her eyes over the wrinkled page where she has carefully drafted her message. "My name is Rosario Rodriguez," it begins. "I am a welfare recipient."

With the others, Rosa wends through the Senate office building distributing letters opposing "make-work" increases and demanding more education and training. In front of Hillary Clinton's three-story townhouse, she totes a poster depicting a two-faced senator—Clinton's rightward lean on welfare is discouraging her liberal colleagues—at a protest that later garners headlines. . . .

Late in the afternoon, she arrives at the rally, on the corner of 16th and H. The anti-globalization event means to link world poverty to domestic welfare policy. The crowd numbers several hundred. The microphone volume is cranked high, and Rosa waits alone by the elevated stage through speech after speech, not knowing when she is up.

Her notes rattle in her cold fingers. A couple of friends approach to whisper encouragement, but Rosa barely nods in response. An eternal second later, it is her turn. The moderator blares, "Come on, show 'em what you're made of, girl!"

Rosa climbs onto the stage and steps to the mic. She reads from her paper, "My name is Rosario Rodriguez. I'm a welfare recipient. I've been a welfare recipient since 1999. I've complied with the program completely." Then she stumbles and loses her place. Silence stretches while she scans the page in her hand, seeming frantic. "I'm sorry, I'm really nervous," she finally says, her whisper exploding through the speakers.

The crowd responds with a warm roar. She looks startled. Familiar voices call out, "Go, Rosa!" And suddenly she's back. She begins again, this time loud and strong. She tosses aside the paper she's held all day, and the words just tumble out.

"I lost my job, and I had to go to welfare. It's hard out there, to depend on the damn system!" Rosa gets a round of amens and applause. "They tell you you have no skills and put you into WEP. There are hundreds of thousands of people out there who are treated badly and put into WEP. If you don't know what WEP is, it's when you pick up garbage from highways." She's crying now, her breathing ragged. But she's not scared, she's mad.

"I wish the politicians could walk in my shoes, so they could know how I really feel—walking around out there without the right shoes, without lunch, nine to five, every fucking day!" The crowd screams and stamps. Rosa inhales and belts: "We have to organize! We have to stop this! We have to beat the system!"

She exits to whistles and cheers, shaking all over. "Rosa, Rosita," a sister intones. Hands reach out and tousle her hair. Arms gather her into an embrace. A smile grows at the corners of her mouth. She nailed it.

Now the rule makers in suits will decide the rest.

Mighty in Pink

LIZA FEATHERSTONE

***The Nation,* 3.3.03**

"It's not easy to be warm and fashionable at the same time," smiled Nina Human of Atlanta, who, ensconced in a billowing pink scarf, was succeeding admirably. It was a sunless late afternoon in January, and Human was at the Women's Peace Vigil in front of the White House, protesting the Bush Administration's impending war on Iraq. Human has never protested anything before, but she has spent many sleepless nights worrying about this war. She learned about the vigil, organized by the Code Pink Women's Pre-emptive Strike for Peace, on the web. "I told my husband and my boss: 'I'm going,'" she said.

The name Code Pink is, of course, a clever spoof on the Bush Administration's color-coded terrorism alerts. The idea grew out of the observation of organizers—including Starhawk, Global Exchange's Medea Benjamin and Diane Wilson of Unreasonable Women—that women were leading much of the current antiwar organizing and that more women than men opposed the war on Iraq.

In October, women all over the country began wearing pink to protests, while Benjamin and her cohorts conceived the Women's Vigil, a constant, rolling presence in front of the White House. The vigil began November 17 and will conclude with a week of actions in the first week of March, ending on March 8, International Women's Day. Code Pink-inspired vigils are regularly held in Utah, Texas and elsewhere, and a group of women in Albany, New York, will keep a rolling fast and vigil until March 8. Code Pink is not an organization but a phenomenon: a sensibility reflecting feminist analysis and a campy playfulness, influenced in style and philosophy both by ACT UP and the antiglobalization movement.

Though everyone is moved by the seriousness of the issue—many participants feel that the survival of the planet is at stake—the actions have been high-spirited. In December a Code Pink posse disrupted a press conference held by Charlotte Beers, a public relations expert hired by the State Department to market the war on terrorism, especially in Islamic countries. In the middle of the event Code Pink activists unfurled a pink banner, which admonished, Charlotte, Stop Selling War. An action in New York City on Martin Luther King Day targeted Laura Bush, who was speaking at the Sheraton, holding signs urging her to Tell George Not to Go to War. Even when Code Pink actions are small, says Medea Benjamin, "we're dressed in pink, so it's hard to ignore us."

Code Pink is part of a rising tide of creative and memorable feminist antiwar activism. In early January a group of Point Reyes, California, women spelled out PEACE on a beach with their naked bodies, protesting Bush's "naked aggression." A few weeks later and many degrees colder, a group of New York women did the same. The Lysistrata Project, named for the Aristophanes character whose name means "she who disbands armies" (Lysistrata organized Athenian and Spartan women in a sex strike in order to get men to stop making war), is working to make the connections between peace and reproductive freedom. The Raging Grannies, a guerrilla theater group with origins in the Canadian antinuclear movement, have also been a vibrant presence. These activists are joined by established international groups like Women in Black and the Women's International League for Peace and Freedom.

Historically, women's resistance to militarism has taken many forms—and ideas about it have varied. In her 1938 treatise *Three Guineas*, Virginia Woolf argued that as a woman, she had no reason to be patriotic, as the state denied her equal property and citizenship rights. She wrote, "If you insist upon fighting to protect me, or 'our' country, let it be understood, soberly and rationally between us, that you are fighting...to procure benefits which I have not shared . . . in fact, as a woman, I have no country. As a woman I want no country. As a woman my country is the whole world."

Other feminists have suggested that whether because of biology or culture, women's traditional roles as caregivers—especially as mothers—lend us a more life-affirming worldview, one that frowns on war and violence. In this spirit, in 1961 a national organization called Women Strike for Peace organized 50,000 women nationwide to walk off their jobs and out of their kitchens, to demand that their elected representatives embrace a nuclear test ban. These women wanted to protect their children, but as historian Amy Swerdlow has pointed out, they also felt a motherly responsibility to the world. As one WSP participant put it: "No mother can accept lightly even the remote possibility of separation from the family which needs her. But mankind needs us too."

The otherwise admirable antinuclear activist Dr. Helen Caldicott has appealed to popular audiences with an even less subtle traditionalism. "As mothers we must make sure the world is safe for our babies," she once said in a speech. "I appeal especially to the women to do this work because we understand the genesis of life.... We have wombs, we have breasts, we have menstrual periods to remind us that we can produce life!"

No Code Pink participant that I interviewed discussed her womb or her period (for this I was grateful). But Nina Human, the protester from Atlanta, said she felt that "women need to get together because it's our sons and daughters they'll force to go over there." Besides, she added, "I think women are basically more peaceful people."

This sort of sentiment doesn't sit well with Jenny Brown, a Gainesville, Florida, activist who is a member of Redstockings (yes, this radical feminist group, founded in the 1960s, is still around). "Since when are women naturally peaceful?" asks Brown. "Harriet Tubman carried a gun when she ran the underground railroad." Brown is only 37, but her thinking comes out of a venerable tradition. In January 1968, radical feminists protested the Jeanette Rankin Brigade, an all-women peace formation. They held a funeral procession and buried traditional womanhood. As Brown explains, "They felt that appeals based on women's peaceful natures would only assure men that they were not a threat."

Particularly given the Bush Administration's ferocious attack on reproductive rights, now would be an especially bad time to reinforce traditional gender stereotypes or to exalt the cult of compulsory motherhood. The notion that women are biologically—or even culturally—destined to breed and to nurture could feed the forces of reaction. As radical feminists have long suggested, denying women's capacity for aggression—and militancy—also denies our power.

But asked about the emphasis on mothering, activists say it hasn't played a significant role in contemporary feminist antiwar organizing. "Some people like it," says Medea Benjamin. "But we really want to be inclusive. A lot of our friends don't have kids. We don't want it to sound corny, old or off-putting." Code Pink's mission statement emphatically rejects biological determinism:

> Women have been the guardians of life—not because we are better or purer or more innately nurturing than men, but because the men have busied themselves making war. Because of our responsibility to the next generation, because of our own love for our families and communities and this country that we are a part of, we understand the love of a mother in Iraq for her children, and the driving desire of that child for life.

Those standing in front of the White House had widely varying theories about why women should oppose war. Some pointed out that militarism is nourished, at least in part, by our ideas about masculinity. Gail Kielson, an activist who fights domestic violence in western Massachusetts, sees connections between the Bush Administration's bellicose, cowboy rhetoric and violence against women. Gesturing with some frustration toward the White House, she said she and others in her field have recently noticed "a curious, scary upsurge" in domestic violence: "There is a parallel between the President's attitude toward Iraq, and what men do in their homes."

The National Organization for Women has made a strong statement against war on Iraq, and has actively assisted the Women's Vigil from its Washington, DC, headquarters, which is just around the corner from the White House. NOW's statement does not mention women's peaceable natures, but focuses on practical objections to war with Iraq: Its massive cost would divert funds from education, healthcare and welfare, creating economic hardship, of which "women will bear the greatest burden."

NOW also points out, "A U.S. invasion of Iraq will likely...[endanger] the safety and rights of Iraqi women—who currently enjoy more rights and freedoms than women in other Gulf nations, such as Saudi Arabia."

Feminists were divided over the war in Afghanistan: Some applauded the overthrow of the Taliban, while others objected on anti-imperialist, nonviolent or practical grounds. Yet there is little controversy on Iraq. Bush has feebly attempted to use feminism to justify invasion, fantasizing that a "democratic" Iraq would show "that honest government, and respect for women, and the great Islamic tradition of learning can triumph in the Middle East and beyond." But feminists aren't buying it; few see reason to hope war will relieve the miserable condition of the Iraqi people, women included.

NOW's statement also makes the point that militarism often hurts women in unique ways, a point well understood by a group of Okinawan women at the White House vigil. Their protest group was founded in 1995, when a 12-year-old Okinawan girl was raped by US soldiers. The women had traveled to Washington to protest the impending war on Iraq, and spoke excitedly through a translator. Said Noriko Akahane, "Women don't want the military anywhere."

In addition to its political openness, one of the most convincing reasons for Code Pink's success is that it's fun. As Benjamin puts it, "Women like hanging out with other women." Indeed, the mood at the vigil, and at its nearby (tiny) administrative office, is buoyant. "Can't you feel the energy?" says Robin Metalitz, a student at George Washington University. Maddy Bassi, who is taking time off from school to work with Global Exchange, has been coordinating the Women's Vigil—as well as a women's delegation to Iraq. "A few nights ago, I thought, 'I miss men!' So I went to a bar," she laughs. "But then, I wished I hadn't. I wanted to be back here!"

While some feminist activists are organizing against the war by using their identity and cultural power as women, many women—and men—are simply organizing with a feminist analysis. New Yorkers Say No to War (NYSNTW) is a good example, says Chris Cuomo, a feminist philosopher now teaching at Cornell University and active in the group, founded just after September 11. Its first meeting, held at Eve Ensler's apartment, was a who's who, as Cuomo puts it, of "the New York cliterati," including Urvashi Vaid, Laura Flanders, Sarah Schulman and other notables. Not all members of the group are women, but from the beginning, women have been running the show.

Even though the words "women" and "feminism" don't appear in the group's name, a gender analysis has always been at the forefront: The organization has held teach-ins on women and militarism, and hosted speakers from the Revolutionary Association of the Women of Afghanistan. Many members of New Yorkers Say No to War come from the global justice movement, which has been deeply influenced by feminism, especially in its culture, which emphasizes consensus-building and communication.

Discussion in such groups is, for the most part, open and respectful. Like global justice activists, feminists have always tried to put political ideals into practice within their organizations, "creating another reality in a hostile context," as Cuomo puts it. "If peace isn't happening here," she asks, "how are we making it out there? There's an understanding that we're creating the new world here and now."

It is a measure of the success of this vision—and of feminism—that few feminists wish to exclude men from their organizations, and that so many male antiwar activists embrace feminist associations. The Women's Vigil welcomes men and has many male fans. As Medea Benjamin points out, "Men like to talk to women." Some local men come by every day. "They stand with us. It's nice because we're in control, and they're fetching things for us," explains Benjamin matter-of-factly. "Some men have baked us cakes."

Other men have been challenging militaristic masculinity on their own. At the Washington march on January 18, a group of tall, middle-aged men stood on the sidelines singing "We Are a Gentle, Angry People." A group of women singing that song—a classic of the "womyn's music" genre—might have seemed clichéd, dated, a bit wimpy. But in this rendition, the song sounded ironic and subversive, yet completely sincere: an optimistic glimpse of a different world. Just like Code Pink.

WHAT'S ON THE HORIZON

Whose Security?

CHARLOTTE BUNCH

The Nation, 10.23.02

When I talk with feminists from other countries, whether from Europe or the Third World, I am repeatedly asked: "Where are the voices of the U.S. women's movement against what the Bush Administration is doing globally, using the excuse of 9/11?" While I know that many U.S. feminists are concerned about these issues, it is clear that our voices are not being heard much—outside, or even inside, this country. The perception created by the Western media is that virtually all Americans support Bush's militaristic threats, his "you're with us or against us," evil-axis rhetoric, and his unilateralist positions against global treaties from the Kyoto Protocol on the environment to the newly created International Criminal Court. When I mention activities like the weekly Women in Black vigils against U.S. policy in the Middle East held in New York and other cities, or feminists working to change the composition of the U.S. Congress, where only Barbara Lee spoke out against the Bush madness immediately after 9/11, they are somewhat relieved.

Yet it is clear that feminists in the United States do not have much impact on U.S. foreign policy, which is military- and corporate-driven. Even though Bush used Afghan women's rights to drum up support for his war, this did not lead to a sustained commitment to Afghan women. It is puzzling to many outside this country how a women's movement that has had such profound influence on U.S. culture and daily life could have so little effect on, or seemingly even concern for, U.S. foreign policy and its impact on women worldwide. The consequences of this failure are disastrous for women in many countries, and they threaten the advances that the global women's movement made in the 1990s.

Current U.S. foreign policy makes it harder to build women's international solidarity in a number of ways. The widespread sympathy that the world offered Americans at the time of 9/11 has given way to anti-Americanism and rage at what the U.S. government is doing in the name of that event. On the day of the attacks, I was still in South Africa following the UN World Conference Against Racism held in Durban the week before. People expressed intense concern about what had happened, especially when they learned that I lived in New York. And this was in spite of the great frustration that most felt about the inexcusable disdain for other countries the Bush Administration had just exhibited during the world conference. But now, resentment and anger at the United States is the overriding sentiment in many other nations. Even some feminist colleagues elsewhere tell me that they are now asked how they can really work with Americans, given how little opposition to Bush's foreign policies they see happening here.

This resentment stems in part from the fact that 9/11 is not seen as a defining moment for the rest of the world—at least not in terms of what happened that day. In many places, people have long lived with terrorism, violence and death on a scale as great or greater than 9/11. So while they agree that this was a terrible and shocking event, they consider the U.S. obsession with it, including the assumption that it is the defining moment for everyone, to be self-indulgent and shortsighted.

Of course, September 11 has been a defining event within the United States. But how we understand it in a global context is important. First, we must recognize that our government's responses to it were not inevitable. This event could have taken the country in other directions, including toward greater empathy with what others have suffered, toward more concern for human security and the conditions that give rise to terrorism, and toward recognition of the importance of multilateral institutions in a globally linked world. But that would have required a very different national leadership. Instead, it has become the rationale for an escalation of the regressive Bush agenda domestically and internationally, including more unrestrained exercise of U.S. power and disregard for multilateralism. Other governments have also used the occasion to increase military spending and to erode support for human rights. In that sense, it has become a defining moment because of how it has been used. But the issues highlighted by 9/11 are not new and have been raised by many other events both before and after it.

Indeed, 9/11 has raised the profile of many of the issues feminists were already struggling with globally, such as:

- growing global and national economic inequities produced by globalization, structural adjustment, privatization, etc.;
- the rise of extremist expressions of religious and/or nationalist "fundamentalisms" that threaten progress on women's rights around the world (including in the United States) in the name of various religions and cultures;
- the escalation of racist and sexist violence and terrorism in daily life and the growth of sexual and economic exploitation and trafficking of women across the globe;
- an increase in militarism, wars, internal conflicts and terrorism, which are affecting or targeting civilians and involving more women and children in deadly ways.

Since 9/11 has been used to curtail human rights—including freedom of expression—in the name of "national security," it has added a greater sense of urgency to these concerns, but it has also made it more difficult to address them effectively from a feminist perspective.

HUMAN VS. NATIONAL SECURITY

The call to redefine security in terms of human and ecological needs instead of national sovereignty and borders was advancing pre-9/11 as an alternative to the state-centered concept of "national security," rooted in the military/security/defense domain and academically lodged in the field of international relations. For feminists this has meant raising questions about whose security "national security" defends, and addressing issues like the violence continuum that threatens women's security daily, during war as well as so-called peacetime.

The concept of human security had also advanced through the UN—first defined in the UN Development Program's 1994 Human Development Report and later taken up by Secretary General Kofi Annan in his Millennium Report in 2000, which spoke of security less as defending territory and more in terms of protecting people. But efforts to promote the concept of human security—which emerged out of discussions in which women are active, from the peace movement and the debate over development—were set back by 9/11, with the subsequent resurgence of the masculine warrior discourse. The media have been dominated by male "authority" figures, providing a rude reminder that when it comes to issues of terrorism, war, defense and national security, women, and especially feminists, are still not on the map.

Yet it is women who have been the major target of fundamentalist terrorism, from Algeria to the United States, over the past several decades. And it is mostly feminists who have led the critique of this growing global problem—focusing attention not only on Islamic fundamentalism but on Protestant fundamentalism in the United States, Catholic secret societies like Opus Dei in Latin America, Hindu right-wing fundamentalists in India, and so on.

The events of 9/11 should have generated attempts to address the very real threats to women's human rights posed by fundamentalism, terrorism and armed conflict in many guises. Instead, the occasion was used to demonize the Islamic Other and to justify further militarization of society and curtailment of civil liberties. Growing militarization, often with U.S. support and arms, has brought an increase in military spending in many other regions, from India and Pakistan to Israel, Colombia and the Philippines. Meanwhile, the Western donor countries' pledges to support economic development at the UN International Conference on Financing for Development in March

2002 fell far short of what would be needed to even begin to fulfill the millennium promises made in 2000 for advancing human security.

Thus, while human security is a promising concept, it is far from being embraced as a replacement for the national security paradigm to which governments remain attached and have made vast commitments.

SEPTEMBER 11 AND HUMAN RIGHTS

The excuse of 9/11 has been used not only to curtail human rights in the United States—which some here are challenging—but also around the world. The human rights system is in trouble when the U.S. government pulls out of global agreements like the ABM treaty, aggressively works to undermine new instruments like the International Criminal Court and says it is not bound by international commitments made by previous administrations, such as the Beijing Women's Conference Platform—parts of which its delegation renounced at the UN Commission on the Status of Women in March 2002. All international treaties and human rights conventions depend on the assumption that a country is bound by previous agreements and cannot simply jettison them with every change of administration. This erosion of respect for human rights also appears in the U.S. media, where some mainstream journalists have defended, as a necessary part of the war on terrorism, the Bush Administration's defiance of international norms regarding political prisoners, and even suggested that the (selective) use of torture may be justified. These are the kinds of arguments put forward by governments that torture and abuse rights and are contrary to the most accepted tenets of human rights.

Indeed, the erosion of the U.S. commitment to human rights helps legitimize the abuses of governments that have never fully accepted or claimed these standards. For while the U.S. government has often been hypocritical in its human rights policies, open disregard for international standards goes a step further and thus strengthens fundamentalist governments and forces that seek to deny human rights in general, and the rights of women in particular.

Ironically, even as public discourse demonizes Islamic fundamentalists, the unholy alliance of the Vatican, Islamic fundamentalists and right-wing U.S. forces is still working together when it comes to trying to defeat women's human rights. Feminists encountered this alliance in full force at the International Conference on Population and Development in Cairo (1994) and at the World Conference on Women at Beijing (1995), as well as during the five-year reviews of those events in 1999 and 2000. One need only look at the allies of the Bush Administration at the UN children's summit in May 2002—such as the Holy See, Sudan, Libya, Iraq and other gulf states—to understand that this alliance is still functioning globally. We need to closely track the connections among various antifeminist "fundamentalist" forces, not only at the UN but in other arenas as well, such as in the making of world health policies, or even in the passage of anti-women's rights national legislation in countries where outside forces have played a key role.

A high-profile example of how the Bush Administration is seeking to weaken the UN's role in protecting human rights was its effort to insure that the UN High Commissioner for Human Rights, Mary Robinson, would not get a second term. She was among the first to frame her response to 9/11 from the perspective of international law, by suggesting that these acts of terrorism be prosecuted internationally as crimes against humanity rather than used as a call to war, but she was quickly sidelined. Because of this, along with her efforts to make the World Conference Against Racism a success in spite of the U.S. contempt for it, the Bush Administration adamantly opposed her reappointment. This opposition dovetailed with that of a number of other governments unhappy with her attention to their human rights abuses. Robinson is only one of the UN officials the Bush Administration has targeted in its efforts to purge the institution of its critics and anyone else promoting policies not to its liking.

The Bush Administration's policies post-9/11 have provided cover for other governments, such as China, Pakistan, Russia and Egypt, to jettison even a rhetorical commitment to certain human rights in the name of fighting terrorism or providing for national security, or for some countries even in Europe it has been an opportunity simply to label issues like racism and violence against women as lower-priority concerns. This has a particular impact on women because it reverses the broadening of the human rights paradigm, which had begun to encompass issues like violence against women and to focus more on socioeconomic rights in the 1980s and 1990s.

Women's rights advocates are still seen as the new kids on the human rights block. Feminists only recently won the recognition of women's rights as human rights, and that is now jeopardized even before those rights have been fully accepted and mechanisms for their protection institutionalized. The need to articulate a feminist approach to global security that insures human rights and human security, and recognizes their interrelationship, is therefore more urgent than ever.

CHALLENGES AHEAD FOR GLOBAL FEMINISM

Women have transformed many aspects of life over the past forty years, and we all live differently because of it. Looking at the world in 2002, however, we have to ask what went wrong: Why have feminists not had a greater impact on global issues? How can we more effectively address current challenges like an increasingly militarized daily life, the rise in the political use of fundamentalism in every religion and region, and the widening economic gap between the haves and have-nots?

Often what American feminists must do to help women elsewhere is not to focus on their governments but to work to change ours so that U.S. policies and corporate forces based here stop harming women elsewhere. To do this, we need to engage in more serious discussion that crosses both the local/global and the activist/academic divides. If we look at women's movements over the past thirty to forty years, their strength has been in very rooted and diverse local bases of action as well as in the development of highly specific research and theory. There has also been rich global dialogue and networking among women across national lines over the past two decades. But in the United States these discourses rarely intersect.

Because the local/national/domestic and the global/international are mostly seen as separate spheres, we often have trouble determining what local actions will have the greatest impact globally. Thus, for example, there has been little interest here in using international human rights treaties like the Convention on the Elimination of All Forms of Discrimination Against Women (CEDAW), to advance domestic issues. There is a tendency not to see the international arena as adding anything to causes at home. But just as women's global networking and international solidarity have helped sustain feminist activists who are isolated in their home countries, U.S. feminists can benefit from the support of women elsewhere, which we will need if we are to challenge what is now openly defended as the American Empire.

Women's activism in the United States must be both local and global to succeed. We must grapple with the dynamic tension between the universality and specificity of our work. Only through such a process can feminists address not only the needs of each situation but also the larger global structures creating many of these conflicts. Then we can move toward an affirmative vision of peace with human rights and human security at its core, rather than continue to clean up after the endless succession of male-determined crises and conflicts. This is our challenge.

No Place for a Woman

LESLEY ABDELA

***The Times* (London), 4.29.03**

Just after the liberation of Basra, as I stared at my TV watching the British military commander appoint clerics to help run Iraq's second-largest city, I realized that there was something familiar about it all—echoes of Bosnia, Kosovo, Timor, Sierra Leone and Afghanistan. I was witnessing the latest rebirth of a nation in which women are being almost completely left out of the new power structures and discussions over the future of their society.

In 1958 Iraq had one of the first female government ministers in the region. It was one of the first countries in the Middle East to have a woman judge. There are many educated Iraqi women. They have a great deal to contribute to the peace-building and governance process. Women may seem invisible because they are not looting and fighting, but that is no reason to exclude them. Fifty-five percent of Iraqis are women. There are resourceful leaders among them who deserve to be recognized as such.

And it's not just the military who need to swap their night-vision goggles for gender spectacles; diplomats and politicians lack vision too. Yesterday Jay Garner, the retired U.S. Army general who heads the Pentagon's civil administration in Iraq, held the second meeting of what has been officially described as "representative groups from across Iraqi society." Garner says he wants to include fair representation of all ethnic and religious groups, but so far has made no mention of the largest group in Iraq—women.

He says the aim is for Iraqi people to decide procedures and structures for choosing an interim government to begin the rebirth of their nation. I do not know how many women took part in yesterday's meeting, but it is unlikely to be "broadly representative of the population." At the first post-Baathist meeting in Ur there were seventy-six men and four women.

Why is it that in the aftermath of dictatorship and conflict everyone talks about human rights and democracy, yet women find themselves having to fight hard for any voice at all? Hardly days after liberation from Saddam, Iraqi women fear they will end up living under a distorted legal system with a constitution denying them almost all their basic human rights.

On Saturday I was at a conference in Geneva hosted by the Centre for the Democratic Control of the Armed Forces, a Porsche-end of the market think tank funded by the Swiss Government. Twenty of us with international conflict experience were acting as an advisory board on women and war. Among us we had experience of conflicts in Africa, the Balkans, the Middle East, the Caucasus and Asia.

Dr. Krishna Ahooja-Patel, president of the Women's International League for Peace and Freedom, has spent twenty-five years working inside the UN system. She spoke of her frustration: "UN Resolution 1325 was passed in 2000, stating clearly that women must be included in all aspects of peacemaking and peace-building discussions. It didn't happen in Afghanistan and so far it doesn't look as though it is being implemented in Iraq. The question we should ask is 'Why?'"

I have been asking that question almost every waking minute of the past three weeks. With colleagues, I have been engaged in intensive lobbying alongside Iraqi women fighting for the right to have an equal place with men in discussions on the future of their country.

In 2000, Britain's UN Ambassador, Sir Jeremy Greenstock, championed and piloted Resolution 1325 through the Security Council. Its implementation has clearly not yet become embedded in the workings, nor the psyche, of post-conflict reconstruction in a way in which equal inclusion of women as peace builders automatically clicks into place. In post-conflict interim administrations, the U.S., UK and UN have a history of latching on to the first local people to come across their radar screens and entrenching them in power. These are almost without exception men, and usually the noisy ones more interested in swag and political muscle than in such effeminate and tedious concepts as universal human rights and democracy, though some swiftly learn to use Western-speak in their siren calls to coalition ears.

Last week, sitting in the BBC Radio 4 Woman's Hour studio, I took part in a discussion with Iraqi women. The presenter, Jenni Murray, stared at me. "Lesley, haven't we had this same conversation before, at the time of Kosovo, and at the time of Sierra Leone, and at the time of Timor, and the time of Afghanistan?" Yes, I agreed. I'm beginning to feel like a metronome.

In Kosovo (where I worked for the Organization for Security and Cooperation in Europe as deputy director for democratization), Igbal Rugova, leader of Motrat Qiriazi, an umbrella group of rural women's networks, told me: "The international community has marginalized us women in a way we never experienced before. We have never felt so marginalized as we feel now."

During the Kosovo crisis, Tony Blair said repeatedly that the NATO bombing of Serbia and Kosovo was for democracy and human rights. Apparently not for women. Within weeks of the Prime Minister's statement, the UN mission in Kosovo appointed a seventeen-member interim government and enabled the appointment of interim municipal governments. All seventeen in the interim government and most of the members of the interim municipalities were men—some of them known local "mafia" godfathers.

The senior male diplomats heading the UN and OSCE mission set a target for proportionality across the ethnic groups when deciding on interim government appointments. They justified ignoring proportionality for women saying it would be "alien to local culture and tradition." Didn't they know that women had been judges, lawyers, magistrates, academics, trade unionists, doctors, activists in civil society?

I had hoped that out of the manifest failures of Kosovo, a template would spring to ensure that in the aftermath of a conflict and war a nation's women were never again so excluded, derided, patronized and sidelined. But the following year in Sierra Leone the British authorities installed 150 "paramount chiefs," of whom 147 were men. Then in Afghanistan the international community entrenched warlords. It took a massive international lobby campaign, led in the UK by Joan Ruddock MP, to get even two Afghan women included at the post-Taliban Bonn conference. And so far Iraq looks like being just another cut and paste from the same old outworn, shabby text.

Aided by U.S. and UK officials, the Iraqi opposition met in London in mid-December. The Follow-up Co-ordinating Committee (FCC) formed at the end of the conference contained just three women out of the sixty-five members. Women have continued to be significantly marginalized in follow-up opposition gatherings. In Salahaddin in February, the conference's final statement made not a single reference to the future of women in Iraq, nor any reference to their rights or to gender equality.

Alarm bells are also ringing among those concerned for women's inheritance, property, land and shelter rights. Garner has said he will set up a Bosnia-Dayton style commission to arbitrate what is just and fair. He promises inclusivity for all ethnic groups, religions, cultures—but with no mention of women.

The human rights lawyer Margaret Owen, the founder of Widows for Peace and Reconstruction, has observed the failures of a similar process in the Balkans. She says: "The issue of land and property reclamation has particular implications for women, especially widows and the wives of the disappeared. Since the Dayton accords in Bosnia they have been unable to return to their villages because of violence and the threatening presence of those who supported their abusers."

In March, a Kurdish women's group founded by Dr. Nazand Begikhani, an expert reporter to several British legal bodies on women's human rights in the Middle East, sent an open letter to the UN Secretary-General, Kofi Annan, President George Bush and the European Union. It stated: "If there is to be any hope of securing for Iraq in the post-Saddam era a democratic federal system based on pluralism, justice and gender equality, women must be full participants in the process, not mere spectators."

Last week six activists traveled from Iraq to Washington to speak for Iraqi women. Two of them, Rend Rahim Francke and Zainab al-Suwaij, had gone to the April 15 meeting in Ur to take part in the first gathering of the FCC after the fall of the Baath regime. They and Iraqi women inside and outside Iraq were dismayed to discover that only four of the eighty delegates were women.

In an April 23 meeting at the State Department with the Secretary of State, Colin Powell, and the under-secretary of state for global affairs, Paula Dobriansky, Rend Rahim Francke, executive director of the Iraq Foundation, spoke of the challenge Iraqi women face in trying to gain political participation. Their message: Iraqi women constitute at least 55 percent of their country's population and they want a voice in its rebirth.

Above all, they want a secular constitution that does not discriminate against women. Dr. Shatha Beserani, an Iraqi doctor living in London, founded the Iraqi Women for Peace and Democracy Campaign in 2000. She estimates that despite the noisy Iran-funded religious movement, out of a population of 25 million as many as 75 percent would support a secular constitution. She says any new legal code should repeal Sharia and introduce a secular legal system that does not discriminate against women.

Dr. Beserani and other Iraqi women say that any new constitution for Iraq should be constructed from a gender-balanced team.

There is a precedent. The negotiating team which drew up the South African Constitution was 50 percent female. The former South African High Commissioner in London, Cheryl Carolus, believes this remarkable gender balance was fundamental to an outcome acceptable to twenty-six different political parties.

One thing must be made clear in any new world order: if universal human rights do not obtain precedence over so-called "custom and tradition," several billion women will be treated forever as pack animals. It is amazing how men do not view the introduction of computers and mobile phones as a break with custom and tradition, but the minute there is discussion of women's advance, men bond across cultures in defense of "local culture and tradition."

We should remind Iraqi men that Iraqi women shared the horrors of Saddam and the terrors of bombing and should be taking an equal place in shaping a peaceful, prosperous future.

And all should take inspiration from the clarion call enshrined in the magnificent South African Constitution: "United in diversity, based on democratic values, social justice and fundamental human rights; and every citizen equally protected by law."

Transnational Feminist Practices Against War

PAOLA BACCHETTA, TINA CAMPT, INDERPAL GREWAL, CAREN KAPLAN, MINOO MOALLEM, AND JENNIFER TERRY

10.01

As feminist theorists of transnational and postmodern cultural formations, we believe that it is crucial to seek non-violent solutions to conflicts at every level of society, from the global, regional, and national arenas to the ordinary locales of everyday life. We offer the following response to the events of September 11 and its aftermath:

First and foremost, we need to analyze the thoroughly gendered and racialized effects of nationalism, and to identify what kinds of inclusions and exclusions are being enacted in the name of patriotism. Recalling the histories of various nationalisms helps us to identify tacit assumptions about gender, race, nation, and class that once again play a central role in mobilization for war. We see that instead of a necessary historical, material, and geopolitical analysis of 9/11, the emerging nationalist discourses consist of misleading and highly sentimentalized narratives that, among other things, reinscribe compulsory heterosexuality and the rigidly dichotomized gender roles upon which it is based. A number of icons constitute the ideal types in the drama of nationalist domesticity that we see displayed in the mainstream media. These include the masculine citizen-soldier, the patriotic wife and mother, the breadwinning father who is head of household, and the properly reproductive family. We also observe how this drama is racialized. Most media representations in the US have focused exclusively on losses suffered by white, middle-class heterosexual families even though those who died or were injured include many people of different races, classes, sexualities, and religions and of at least 90 different nationalities. Thus, an analysis that elucidates the repressive effects of nationalist discourses is necessary for building a world that fosters peace as well as social and economic justice.

Second, a transnational feminist response views the impact of war and internal repression in a larger context of global histories of displacement, forced migrations, and expulsions. We oppose the U.S. and European sponsorship of regimes responsible for coerced displacements and we note how patterns of immigration, exile, and forced flight are closely linked to gender oppression and to the legacies of colonialism and structured economic dependency. Indeed, history shows us that women, as primary caretakers of families, suffer enormously under circumstances of colonization, civil unrest, and coerced migration. Taking this history into account, we critique solutions to the contemporary crisis that rely on a colonial, Manichean model whereby "advanced capitalist freedom and liberty" is venerated over "backward extremist Islamic barbarism." Furthermore, we draw upon insights from post-colonial studies and critical political economy to trace the dynamics of European and U.S. neo-colonialism during the Cold War and post-Cold War periods. Thus questions about the gendered distribution of wealth and resources are key to our analytical approach. Neo-liberal economic development schemes create problems that impact women in profound and devastating ways in both the "developing regions" as well as the "developed world." So while middle-class Euro-American women in the United States are held up as the most liberated on earth even while they are being encouraged to stand dutifully by their husbands, fathers, and children, women in developing regions of the world are depicted as abject, backward, and oppressed by their men. One of the important elements missing from this picture is the fact that many women in Afghanistan are starving and faced with violence and harm on a daily basis not only due to the Taliban regime but also due in large part to a long history of European colonialism and conflict in the region. The Bush administration's decision to drop bombs at one moment and, in the next, care packages of food that are in every way inadequate to the needs of the population offers a grim image of how pathetic this discourse of "civilization" and "rescue" is within the violence of war. We see here a token and uncaring response to a situation to which the United States has contributed for at least twenty years, a situation that is about gaining strategic influence in the region and about the extraction of natural resources, not the least of which is oil.

Third, we want to comment on the extent to which domestic civil repression is intrinsically linked to the violence of war. Thus the effects of the current conflict will be played out in the United States and its borderzones through the augmentation of border patrolling and policing, as well as in the use of military and defense technologies and other practices that will further subordinate communities (especially non-white groups) in the US. Such state violence has many gendered implications. These include the emergence of patriarchal/masculinst cultural nationalisms whereby women's perspectives are degraded or wholly excluded to create new version of cultural "traditions." And, for many immigrant women, other devastating effects of state repression include increased incidents of unreported domestic violence, public hostility, and social isolation. In practical terms, policing authorities charged with guaranteeing national security are likely to have little sympathy for the undocumented immigrant woman who is fleeing a violent intimate relationship, unless her assailant fits the profile of an "Islamic fundamentalist." Thus we need an analysis and strategy against the "domestication" of the violence of war that has emerged in these last few weeks and whose effects will be felt in disparate and dispersed ways.

Fourth, we call for an analysis of the stereotypes and tropes that are being mobilized in the current crisis. These tropes support, sustain, and are enabled by a modernist logic of warfare that seeks to consolidate the sovereign (and often unilateral) power of the First World nation-state. When President Bush proclaims that "terrorist" networks must be destroyed, we ask what this term means to people and how it is being used to legitimate a large-scale military offensive. The term is being used to demonize practices that go against US national interests and it permits a kind of "drag-net" effect at home and abroad which legitimates the suppression of dissent. We also want to inquire into constructions of "terrorism" that continue to target non-native or "foreign" opposition movements while cloaking its own practices of terror in euphemisms such as "foreign aid." Deconstructing the trope of "terrorism" must include a sustained critique of the immense resources spent by the US in training "counter-terrorists" and "anti-Communist" forces who then, under other historical circumstances, become enemies rather than allies, as in the now famous case of Osama bin Laden. We are concerned about the ways in which the "war against terrorism" can be used to silence and repress insurgent movements across the globe. We also emphasize how racism operates in the naming of "terrorism." When the "terrorists" are people of color, all other people of color are vulnerable to a scapegoating backlash. Yet when white supremacist Timothy McVeigh bombed the Murrah federal building in Oklahoma City, killing 168 men, women, and children, no one declared open season to hunt down white men, or even white militia members. The production of a new racial category, "anyone who looks like a Muslim" in which targets of racism include Muslims, Arabs, Sikhs, and any other people with olive or brown skin, exposes the arbitrary and politically constructed character of new and old racial categories in the United States. It also reveals the inadequacy of U.S. multiculturalism to resist the hegemonic relationship between being "white" and "American." Finally, the short memory of the media suppresses any mention of the Euro-American anti-capitalist and anti-imperialist "terrorist" groups of the 1970s and 1980s. A critical attention to the idioms of the present war mobilization compels us to deconstruct other politically loaded tropes, including security, liberty, freedom, truth, civil rights, Islamic fundamentalism, women under the Taliban, the flag, and "America."

Fifth, we recognize the gendered and ethnocentric history of sentimentality, grief, and melancholy that have been mobilized in the new war effort. We do not intend to disparage or dismiss the sadness and deep emotions raised by the events of 9/11 and its aftermath. But we do think it is important to point out that there has been a massive deployment of therapeutic discourses that ask people to understand the impact of the events of September 11 and their aftermath solely as "trauma." Such discourses leave other analytical, historical, and critical frameworks unexplored. Focusing only on the personal or narrowly defined psychological dimension of the attacks and the ensuing war obscures the complex nexus of history and geopolitics that has brought about these events. We are not suggesting that specific forms of therapy are not useful. But the culture industry of "trauma" leads to a mystification of history, politics and cultural critique. Furthermore, therapeutic discourse tends to reinforce individualist interpretations of globally significant events and it does so in an ethnocentric manner. Seeking relief through a psychotherapeutic apparatus may be a common practice among Euro-American upper- and middle-class people in the United States, but it should not be assumed to be universally appealing or an effective way to counter experiences of civil repression and war among people of other classes, ethnicities, and cultural backgrounds. Signs of the current trauma discourse's ethnocentricity come through in media depictions staged within the therapeutic framework that tend to afford great meaning, significance, and sympathy to those who lost friends and family members in the attacks on the World Trade Center and the Pentagon. By contrast, people who have lost loved ones as a consequence of US foreign policy elsewhere are not depicted as sufferers of trauma or injustice. In fact, they are seldom seen on camera at all. Similarly, makeshift centers in universities around the United States were set up in the immediate wake of 9/11 to help college students cope with the psychological effects of the attacks. They tended to assume that 9/11 marked the first time Americans experienced vulnerability, overlooking not only the recent events of the Oklahoma City federal building bombing, but moreover erasing the personal experiences of many immigrants and U.S. people of color for whom "America" has been a site of potential or realized violence for all of their lives.

Sixth, our transnational feminist response involves a detailed critical analysis of the role of the media especially in depictions that include colonial tropes and binary oppositions in which the Islam/Muslim/non-West is represented as "uncivilized" or "barbaric." We note the absence or co-optation of Muslim women as "victims" of violence or of "Islamic barbarism." We note as well the use of those groups of women seen as "white" or "western" both as "rescuers" of non-western women but also as evidence of the so-called "civilizing" efforts of Europe and North America. We see these discursive formations as a result not only of colonialism's discursive and knowledge-producing legacies, but also of the technologies and industrial practices that produce contemporary global media, and transnational financing of culture industries. We seek especially to analyze the participation of women in these industries as well as the co-optation of feminist approaches and interests in the attack on a broad range of Islamic cultural and religious institutions, not just "Islamicist/extremist" groups. Thus we point out as a caution that any counter or resistance media would need to have a firm grasp of these histories and repertoires of practice or risk reproducing them anew.

Seventh, we call for a deeper understanding of the nature of capitalism and globalization as it generates transnational movements of all kinds. Thus, we seek to counter oppressive transnational movements, both from the "West" as well as the "Non-West," with alternative movements that counter war and the continued production of global inequalities. We note in particular that religious and ethnic fundamentalisms have emerged across the world within which the repression of women and establishment of rigidly dichotomized gender roles are used both as a form of power and to establish a collectivity. Such fundamentalisms have been a cause of concern for feminist groups not only in the Islamic world but also in the United States. Feminist and other scholars have noted that these movements have become transnational, through the work of nation-state and non-governmental organizations, with dire consequences for all those who question rigid gender dichotomies. Since these movements are transnational, we question the notion of isolated and autonomous nation-states in the face of numerous examples of transnational and global practices and formations. The recent displays of national coherence and international solidarity (based on nineteenth- and twentieth-century constructions of international relations), cannot mask the strains and contradictions that give rise to the current crisis. Thus, we need an analysis of the numerous ways in which transnational networks and entities both limit and at the same time enable resistance and oppression. That is, the complex political terrain traversed by transnational networks as diverse as al-Qaida and the Red Cross must be understood as productive of new identities and practices as well as of new kinds of political repression. Transnational media has roots in pernicious corporate practices yet it also enables diverse and contradictory modes of information, entertainment, and communication. Feminist analysis of these complex and often contradictory transnational phenomena is called for.

In closing, we want to make it very clear that we oppose the U.S. and

British military mobilization and bombing that is underway in Afghanistan and that may very well expand further into the West, Central, and South Asian regions. We are responding to a crisis in which war, as described by the George W. Bush administration, will be a covert, diversified, and protracted process. At this moment we call for a resistance to nationalist terms and we argue against the further intensification of U.S. military intervention abroad. We refuse to utilize the binaries of civilization vs. barbarism, modernity vs. tradition, and West vs. East. We also call for an end to the racist scapegoating and "profiling" that accompanies the stepped up violations of civil liberties within the territorial boundaries of the United States. We urge feminists to refuse the call to war in the name of vanquishing a so-called "traditional patriarchal fundamentalism," since we understand that such fundamentalisms are supported by many nation-states. We are also aware of the failures of nation-states and the global economic powers such as the IMF and the World Bank to address the poverty and misery across the world and the role of such failures in the emergence of fundamentalisms everywhere. Nationalist and international mobilization for war cannot go forward in our name or under the sign of "concern for women." In fact, terror roams the world in many guises and is perpetrated under the sign of many different nations and agents. It is our contention that violence and terror are ubiquitous and need to be addressed through multiple strategies as much within the "domestic" politics of the US as elsewhere. It is only through developing new strategies and approaches based on some of these suggestions that we can bring an end to the violence of the current moment.

A Mystery of Misogyny

BARBARA EHRENREICH

***The Progressive,* 11.30.01**

A feminist can take some dim comfort from the fact that the Taliban's egregious misogyny is finally considered newsworthy. It certainly wasn't high on Washington's agenda in May, for example, when President Bush congratulated the ruling Taliban for banning opium production and handed them a check for $43 million—never mind that their regime accords women a status somewhat below that of livestock.

In the weeks after September 11, however, you could find escaped Afghan women on *Oprah* and longtime anti-Taliban activist Mavis Leno doing the cable talk shows. CNN has shown the documentary *Beneath the Veil*, and even Bush has seen fit to mention the Taliban's hostility to women—although their hospitality to Osama bin Laden is still seen as the far greater crime. Women's rights may play no part in U.S. foreign policy, but we should perhaps be grateful that they have at least been important enough to deploy in the media mobilization for war.

On the analytical front, though, the neglect of Taliban misogyny—and beyond that, Islamic fundamentalist misogyny in general—remains almost total. If the extreme segregation and oppression of women does not stem from the Koran, as non-fundamentalist Muslims insist, if it is, in fact, something new, then why should it have emerged when it did, toward the end of the twentieth century? Liberal and leftwing commentators have done a thorough job of explaining why the fundamentalists hate America, but no one has bothered to figure out why they hate women.

And "hate" is the operative verb here. Fundamentalists may claim that the sequestration and covering of women serves to "protect" the weaker, more rape-prone sex. But the protection argument hardly applies to the fundamentalist groups in Pakistan and Kashmir that specialize in throwing acid in the faces of unveiled women. There's a difference between "protection" and a protection racket.

The mystery of fundamentalist misogyny deepens when you consider that the anti-imperialist and anti-colonialist Third World movements of forty or fifty years ago were, for the most part, at least officially committed to women's rights. Women participated in Mao's Long March; they fought in the Algerian revolution and in the guerilla armies of Mozambique, Angola, and El Salvador. The ideologies of these movements were inclusive of women and open, theoretically anyway, to the idea of equality. Osama bin Laden is, of course, hardly a suitable heir to the Third World liberation movements of the mid-twentieth century, but he does purport to speak for the downtrodden and against Western capitalism and militarism. Except that his movement has nothing to offer the most downtrodden sex but the veil and a life lived largely indoors.

Of those commentators who do bother with the subject, most explain the misogyny as part of the fundamentalists' wholesale rejection of "modernity" or "the West." Hollywood culture is filled with images of strong or at least sexually assertive women, hence—the reasoning goes—the Islamic fundamentalist impulse is to respond by reducing women to chattel. The only trouble with this explanation is that the fundamentalists have been otherwise notably selective in their rejection of the "modern." The nineteen terrorists of September 11 studied aviation and communicated with each other by e-mail. Osama bin Laden and the Taliban favor Stingers and automatic weapons over scimitars. If you're going to accept Western technology, why throw out something else that has contributed to Western economic success—the participation of women in public life?

Perhaps—to venture a speculation—the answer lies in the ways that globalization has posed a particular threat to men. Western industry has displaced traditional crafts—female as well as male—and large-scale, multinational-controlled agriculture has downgraded the independent farmer to the status of hired hand. From West Africa to Southeast Asia, these trends have resulted in massive male displacement and, frequently, unemployment. At the same time, globalization has offered new opportunities for Third World women—in export-oriented manufacturing, where women are favored for their presumed "nimble fingers," and, more recently, as migrant domestics working in wealthy countries.

These are not, of course, opportunities for brilliant careers, but for extremely low-paid work under frequently abusive conditions. Still, the demand for female labor on the "global assembly line" and in the homes of the affluent has been enough to generate a kind of global gender revolution. While males have lost their traditional status as farmers and breadwinners, women have been entering the market economy and gaining the marginal independence conferred by even a paltry wage.

Add to the economic dislocations engendered by globalization the onslaught of Western cultural imagery, and you have the makings of what sociologist Arlie Hochschild has called a "global masculinity crisis." The man who can no longer make a living, who has to depend on his wife's earnings, can watch Hollywood sexpots on pirated videos and begin to think the world has been turned upside down. This is *Stiffed*—Susan Faludi's 1999 book on the decline of traditional manhood in America—gone global.

Or maybe the global assembly line has played only a minor role in generating Islamic fundamentalist misogyny. After all, the Taliban's home country, Afghanistan, has not been a popular site for multinational manufacturing plants. There, we might look for an explanation involving the exigencies—and mythologies—of war. Afghans have fought each other and the Soviets for much of the last twenty years, and, as Klaus Theweleit wrote in his brilliant 1989 book, *Male Fantasies*, long-term warriors have a tendency to see women as a corrupting and debilitating force. Hence, perhaps, the all-male madrassas in Pakistan, where boys as young as six are trained for jihad, far from the potentially softening influence of mothers and sisters. Or recall terrorist Mohamed Atta's specification, in his will, that no woman handle his corpse or approach his grave.

Then again, it could be a mistake to take Islamic fundamentalism out of the context of other fundamentalisms—Christian and Orthodox Jewish. All three aspire to restore women to the status they occupied—or are believed to have occupied—in certain ancient nomadic Middle Eastern tribes.

Religious fundamentalism in general has been explained as a backlash against the modern, capitalist world, and fundamentalism everywhere is no friend to the female sex. To comprehend the full nature of the threats we face since September 11, we need to figure out why. Assuming women matter, that is.

Gender Smarts: Will Sex Ever Make Us as Smart as Race When It Comes Time to Vote?

GLORIA STEINEM

AlterNet, 11.1.02

When the stock market took a plunge and my pension fund went down with it, I had the classic female fear of becoming a bag lady. But I also had another thought: If "it's the economy, stupid," then this disaster will have been worth every penny. Even people who don't care about the female half of the country, and who would be perfectly happy to bomb everything, will be mad as hell and looking for change.

I know this sounds contrary. There hasn't been much criticism of Bush & Company since terrorism caused the country to circle its wagons. Even before that, there was the idea that Bush and Gore were pretty much alike, so why bother?

I remember when that tactic was first created by Richard Nixon, who suppressed mainstream-to-progressive voter turnout by pretending to be like Jack Kennedy. Now, rightwing extremist candidates get away with charging "negative campaigning" if their opponents so much as report their voting records. As for the media, they seem hooked on the idea that objectivity requires being even-handedly negative, and so suppress interest in politics even more.

When combined with the physical difficulties of voting—which are greater here than in any other country—this smokescreen has allowed a smaller proportion of people to rule this nation than in any democracy in the world. Older, richer, whiter voters are far more likely to go to the polls to vote their interests than younger, poorer, voters of color are to vote their hopes. Indeed, 36 million women aren't registered at all, and 40 percent of those who *did* vote ended up supporting candidates who were opposed to women's majority views on issues as crucial to life as reproductive freedom, protection of air and water, and support for public education.

Still, there was a twelve-point gender gap that made the difference in hundreds of races, from school boards and the U.S. Senate to Bush's defeat in the popular vote. Clinton couldn't have won either of his races without this culturally female voting pattern that favors center-to-progressive issues. Nor could Gore have won any of the big electoral states if his greater support among white women hadn't compensated for his low level of support among white men—and then some.

Yet imagine what those results would have been—and what they could be on Tuesday—if white women were to vote with a little more of the self-respect and enlightened self-interest of, say, African American male voters, who chose Gore over Bush by 85 percent. Or better yet, African American female voters who, perhaps doubly educated by race and sex, rejected the rightwing platform by a nearly unanimous 94 percent.

The truth is that European American women remain the largest group in this country that votes for leaders who don't vote for us. Some of this is due to candidates who downplay their real positions, some to being surrounded by the belief that issues affecting the female half of the country can't be serious, some to media that fail report issues as they impact our daily lives, and some to other causes; for example, being born into families that normalize inequality, or depending on the income and approval of supremacist men.

But I will go to my grave believing that one day, sex will make us as self-respecting and smart in our political behavior, as devoted to our own longterm empowerment and enlightened self-interest, as does race. There will come a time when we take prejudice that affects only females as seriously as we do race, class and other biases that also affect males.

If even a tenth of the women now letting others decide their fate were to register and vote out of self-respect, many of the policy-based dangers and humiliations we read about everyday would diminish or end. For example:

- Women's reproductive systems make us the canaries in the mine of environmentally caused cancers that are the great majority of all cases, and are occurring in younger and younger women. Yet this Administration and its Congressional supporters have done everything in their power to weaken and end environmental protections, both national and international.

- A woman dies every minute in the world because of pregnancy-related causes. Many deaths are due directly to Bush's Global Gag Rule that threatens to deprive foreign entities of desperately needed U.S. aid if they provide, lobby for, or speak out about legal abortion—even with their own funds—a rule that could have been overturned in Congress by only four more votes. Bush Administration policy also opposes sex education, emergency contraception, and funds for international voluntary family planning, thus skyrocketing the number of dangerous and illegal abortions.

- In the United States, too, having children is the single greatest determinant of women's economic status, education and health, but we are only one Supreme Court appointment away from losing the Constitutional right to control our own reproductive lives. Globally, the greatest danger to the environment is population growth, and the surest way to curb this growth is to give women the power to do so, yet Bush and his allies in Congress push policies shared mainly by the Vatican and the Moslem Brotherhood.
- Women are the fastest growing part of the prison population; the most likely to be poor and supporting children; the most frequent victims of violence and sexual abuse; and the largest source of underpaid or unpaid labor, nationally and internationally. Yet the Bush Administration is not focusing on those ills, but is investigating Title IX, one of the few measures that has helped equalize women's opportunity in sports and education.

Any one of those—not to mention Bush's plan to bomb Saddam Hussein, thus giving him reason to use his sinister weapons—would be reason enough to vote this Tuesday, but I'll take a plummeting stock market if it has the same result. If there are even a few more members of Congress with the guts to say "No!" to Bush & Company, I will be one happy bag lady.

Building a Movement for Reproductive Self-Determination: An Interview with Dorothy Roberts

LAURA FLANDERS

1.17.04

Editor's note: Dorothy Roberts teaches at Northwestern University School of Law and is the author of *Killing the Black Body: Race, Reproduction, and the Meaning of Liberty* (1997). Her 1991 article "Punishing Drug Addicts Who Have Babies: Women of Color, Equality and the Right of Privacy," condemns the phenomenon of charging pregnant women who are overwhelmingly black and poor with criminal, prenatal drug use. As the Bush administration came to power, a key case in this area was decided by the Supreme Court. In *Ferguson v. City of Charleston,* the Court ruled that pregnant women cannot be subject to "warrantless, suspicionless searches simply because they are pregnant." At issue was a policy developed by the Medical University of South Carolina (MUSC), the local police department, and local prosecutors which permitted MUSC to conduct nonconsensual drug tests of pregnant women whom the MUSC staff suspected of drug use. Positive results could then be reported to police, who would threaten to arrest the women or charge them with drug and child abuse if they refused treatment. The March 2001 decision by the justices was a victory for low-income pregnant women who use public hospitals.

WHAT HAPPENED SINCE THE *FERGUSON* DECISION?

At the time the case was decided, the program, in which tests for crack cocaine were involuntarily performed on pregnant women, had already halted at the University of South Carolina hospital, and so nothing really came of the decision in a direct sense. In some ways things have gotten worse; prosecutions continue to be brought against women for substance abuse during pregnancy.

IS THIS ONLY A LOCAL PRACTICE?

My sense is that it's mostly at the local level, but it's connected to national policy in a couple of ways. The policy of punishing women who have a health problem is definitely connected to, and perpetuated by, the war on drugs—the general demonization and criminalization of people who use drugs.

I also think it's connected to the broad effort that's going on at the national level to identify the fetus as a living child, and to give the fetus more and more rights. The Bush Administration is clearly pushing for this, and it's being pushed at the local level as well. Certainly I think the prosecution of mothers for using drugs while pregnant is part of a bigger effort to make the fetus appear like a child, deserving all the rights of a child.

WHO IS MOSTLY PROSECUTED FOR PRENATAL DRUG USE?

Well, it continues to be poor, black women who smoke crack. There have been some cases involving white women, and other drugs and alcohol, but the majority of women who are either prosecuted or have their babies removed from them at the hospital are poor, black mothers. There have been a couple of fairly high-profile cases where mothers were charged with homicide because these mothers smoked crack during pregnancy and their babies were stillborn. In one case, Regina McKnight was sentenced to prison after a very brief jury deliberation, even though there was no evidence her crack actually caused the stillbirth. Just the coincidence of the two was enough to convince the jury she was guilty of homicide by child abuse. She's now serving a long prison sentence in South Carolina. There was an effort to bring her case before the U.S. Supreme Court and they denied the petition.

BUSH HAS CLAIMED THAT HIS AGENDA IS ONE OF COMPASSIONATE CONSERVATISM, THAT HE WANTS TO HELP PEOPLE WHO HAVE PROBLEMS WITH DRUGS OR POVERTY. HAVE WE SEEN AN INCREASE IN TREATMENT PROGRAMS FOR PEOPLE WHO ARE ON DRUGS, AND SPECIFICALLY FOR THE WOMEN YOU'VE JUST DESCRIBED AS THOSE MOST LIKELY TO GET CAUGHT UP IN PROSECUTIONS?

Generally there have been cuts in state budgets for programs like drug treatment. At the federal level, significant cuts in social services can surely be expected because of the budget deficit and the money drained by the war on terror and the war in Iraq.

SO, WITH RESPECT TO THE PUNITIVE TREATMENT OF DRUG-ADDICTED WOMEN, WHAT DO YOU THINK THE POLICY AGENDA IS HERE?

I would look at the prosecutions in conjunction with a whole slew of punitive policies, like welfare reform. The message of these policies is that poor children fare badly because of their mothers' behavior, and not because there aren't good jobs for these mothers and it's impossible for many single mothers to earn a living that can adequately support their children. Not because there are bad schools in their neighborhoods—no, it's the mother's fault!

SO, ON THE QUESTION OF REPRODUCTION, WHAT ARE SOME OF THE EFFECTS OF THIS CONTRADICTION—OPPOSING A WOMAN'S RIGHT TO CHOOSE AND THEN FAILING TO PROVIDE ADEQUATE ECONOMIC SUPPORT AFTER THE BIRTH?

This situation pressures poor women toward long-acting methods of birth control and in fact discourages them from having any children at all. It sounds very sinister, but I think that there are forces in this country that would prefer if poor women, especially poor women of color, black women and immigrant women, didn't have children, or had very few children. And certainly, there are social forces that don't want these women having children while on welfare, at so-called public expense.

More generally, blaming these women for problems they face in raising their children is a way of discouraging support for any kind of meaningful social change. It's a way of saying that the system we have is fine, it's these devious mothers that are not acting right, and if they would just get married, their children would be fine—we could end poverty that way. It's a way of convincing a majority of the public that they should accept policies that are grossly unjust.

HOW HAVE CONDITIONS FOR POOR WOMEN AND MOTHERS HAVE BEEN EXACERBATED IN THE LAST FEW YEARS? FOR INSTANCE, WHAT DO YOU MAKE OF LEGISLATION LIKE THE PROTECTION OF VICTIMS OF UNBORN VIOLENCE ACT?

Right. Things have happened on several fronts. The federal government extended Children's Health Insurance Program benefits to fetuses but not to pregnant women. The global gag rule was reinstated, affecting women in struggling societies around the world. And Bush's appointments for key offices clearly formed a big part of these efforts: appointees such as John Ashcroft and Tommy Thompson, and his judicial nominees like Judge Pickering.[1]

Then there are Bush's statements about stem cell research, defining embryos as people. Let's also not forget he made Wade Horn the head of welfare reform and family support in the Department of Health and Human Services. And he's just announced 1.8 billion dollars to promote marriage.

TALK TO ME ABOUT THAT. SOME OF HIS PROPOSALS HAVE BEEN CAST AS BEING AIMED AT HELPING VULNERABLE UNBORN VICTIMS OF VIOLENCE, OR UNBORN CHILDREN NEEDING HEALTH CARE—OR IN THIS CASE, POOR PEOPLE WHOSE MARRIAGES NEED HELP.

There's a way of characterizing all of those moves as helpful, and there are ways in which they do, or could, provide services to needy people. But the problem is that the help is provided in a way that furthers an agenda to restrict reproductive freedom and other family decisions for poor women. The basic premise of the marriage promotion scheme is, once again, that the reason why these mothers can't support their children adequately is because they're unmarried. Special benefits are offered on the condition that women conform to a social program that denies the structural, systemic reasons for poverty and inequality.

WHAT KIND OF REPRODUCTIVE HEALTH SERVICES DO YOU THINK COMMUNITIES REALLY NEED?

Communities need to have economic and practical access to a wide range of contraceptives, not just the most risky, long-term contraceptives, along with access to abortion services and counseling. But there also has to be a social context of reproductive health services that makes the use of these services truly non-coercive. I think it's very much tied to the issue of welfare reform; providing contraceptives within a society that punishes mothers for having children is wrongheaded. We need social conditions that give women real freedom to decide whether or not to have children, and if they decide to have children, to raise their children with the resources they need to do so.

Communities also need healthcare services that include diagnosis and treatment for reproductive tract diseases and illnesses. They need non-punitive drug treatment programs that are woman-centered: typical drug treatments are still based on a confrontational male model, rather than a holistic model. There are examples of drug treatment programs that can work, but they tend to be pilot programs that only serve a tiny portion of the women who need them.

SO, WE'VE HAD A REPRODUCTIVE RIGHTS MOVEMENT FOR A CENTURY, THAT AT LEAST IN NAME CLAIMS TO BE PRO-ACCESS AND PRO-FREE CHOICE, AND YET WE'RE STILL IN THIS MESS. WHY DO YOU THINK THE REPRODUCTIVE RIGHTS MOVEMENT IS SO WEAK, RELATIVELY SPEAKING—TOO WEAK TO STOP THE SETBACKS WE'RE SEEING NOW?

Part of the reason is that there have always been conflicting goals within the reproductive rights movement. From its very inception it veered away from what I see as its feminist beginnings, with Margaret Sanger's initial advocacy of birth control, toward a eugenic approach. Even Sanger, while she was still at the helm, allied with eugenicists. And so from the very beginning you had as a major component of the birth control movement the population control agenda, the use of birth control to keep socially frowned-upon groups from having children. This of course weakened the movement's radical and feminist potential, and also made large groups of people very suspicious. To this day there is a huge distrust of the birth control movement in the black community. And because it was dominated by elite white women for so long, and even more recently only included women of color in token positions, the birth control movement continues to suffer from a lack of cohesion. On the other hand, I do think there has been a significant advance in both the inclusion of women of color in the movement generally, and in the creation of organizations by women of color. These organizations are forming coalitions amongst each other, but also with predominantly white reproductive rights organizations.

HOW DOES THAT AFFECT THE AGENDA AND THE ORGANIZING?

It's creating a more progressive, exciting and broad ranging conception of what reproductive rights mean. Just very recently there's been a lot of activity in this area. For example, there's now an organization called Sister Song, which is a coalition of sexual and reproductive health organizations made up of women of color. In November 2003 they held a large conference, and it was very exciting, attended by hundreds of people. I think definitely the future of the reproductive rights movement must rely upon the very prominent involvement of organizations of women of color, groups that not only center on reproductive rights and sexual health, but also are more social justice oriented.

One illustration of the value of contributions from these new groups concerns the march that's scheduled to take place in April 2004, in Washington, D.C. That march was originally named the March for Choice and it was being organized by the typical, predominantly white organizations. There was a great deal of dissension on a number of fronts: Both women of color and feminists involved in welfare reform work wanted to make sure that women's work caring for children would be addressed in this march. As a result of all this conflict, the leaders have called in Loretta Ross, a black woman and long-time reproductive rights organizer, to help plan and promote the march. I know the National Black Women's Health Initiative, which I am involved in, was invited to be one of the main organizers, and I'm not sure we've decided what to do yet—but at least we were invited to participate.

YOU WERE ONLY NOW INVITED TO PARTICIPATE?

(Laughs) It was a couple of months ago. You see, there was a lot of concern about this march. But the name of it changed, to "March for Women's Lives"—the term "choice" was taken out because it has been associated with a one-dimensional focus on the right to choose abortion, overlooking the social context and a broader range of reproductive rights issues. So I do think the lead-up to this march shows how these new groups can influence the mainstream agenda within the reproductive rights movement, to some extent, opening it up and making it more inclusive and more progressive. In the last five years we've seen more and more of this.

WHAT DOES THE TERM "REPRODUCTIVE SELF-DETERMINATION" MEAN FOR YOU?

It means the ability and human right of individuals to make their own decisions about their reproductive health, and lives, without coercion either from governments or unjust social conditions.

DO YOU THINK WE'RE GETTING CLOSER TO REALIZING THAT RIGHT, IN SPITE OF ALL THE MISERABLE NEWS?

I do think that among feminists and progressives now, more people are aware of the importance of reproductive self-determination and what it involves. So there has been progress at this level, even as there's been a definite increase in the efforts to oppose reproductive rights. For example, there's a greater awareness now that when a woman with a crack problem is punished for having a baby, it's a reproductive rights issue. And the medical and public health communities, along with others in the legal community, have made strides toward changing punitive policy.

WE'VE BEEN TALKING A LOT ABOUT THE NARROW VISION OF THE WHITE-DOMINATED REPRODUCTIVE RIGHTS MOVEMENT. IN THE LAST FEW YEARS UNDER THE BUSH ADMINISTRATION WE'VE SEEN A REAL INCREASE IN SO-CALLED SECURITY MEASURES TARGETED AT THE IMMIGRANT POPULATION AND THE ARAB POPULATION. DO YOU HAVE A GRASP ON WHAT NEW THINGS WE NEED TO BE LEARNING, AS WE CONTINUE TO BROADEN OUR VISION OF REPRODUCTIVE SELF-DETERMINATION, WHEN WE HAVE THESE LARGE POPULATIONS WHO MAY NOT ONLY FEAR ASKING FOR HELP OR INFORMATION, BUT ALSO MAY NOT HAVE ORGANIZED GROUPS TO TURN TO?

Historically, immigrant groups have been one of the main targets of coercive reproductive policy. Even before the war on terror and the increase in surveillance of Arabs and Muslims in this country, there were efforts to deny citizenship to children of undocumented immigrants and to deny reproductive health services to undocumented, pregnant immigrant women. So immigrant women have been facing these kinds of restrictions on their reproductive decision-making for a long time, the public supporting these coercive policies out of concern that these immigrant women would bear children in this country who would automatically be entitled to citizenship. I can easily see this concern being extended to other groups being targeted in the war on terror. It's amazing to me how we've allowed such drastic infringements of people's basic rights, including the right to an attorney, and the right to learn charges and have a trial before you're put in prison for a long time! So I worry that this climate, in which the value of protections we have against government power are being rapidly diminished, could have lasting repercussions for other kinds of rights we enjoy, including reproductive rights.

THANK YOU!

NOTES

1.In January, 2004, on the eve of the Martin Luther King Jr. holiday, President Bush by-passed Congress to install Judge Charles Pickering to the Fifth Circuit Federal Court of Appeals. The executive appointment is valid for one year, until the next Congress convenes in January 2005. Pickering's appointment was opposed by civil rights groups and women's groups throughout the country because of his record of opposition to federal civil rights mandates, and was challenged by Democrats over his 1994 actions from the bench to reduce the sentence of a man convicted of burning a cross near the home of an interracial couple.

U.S. Feminism Lite: Claiming Independence, Asserting Personal Choice

KATHA POLLITT

Le Monde diplomatique, 7.03

The collective action that changed women's public and private lives in the United States is over: personal choice is now seen as the only true value.

The women's movement has transformed the United States in just over 30 years. Stroll through a park and you're likely to see a team of girls playing soccer. Drop in at a law or medical school and women occupy almost half the seats. Women own about one in four of small businesses, and have made inroads in such masculine preserves as bus driving, bartending, the clergy and military—12 percent of the armed forces are now female.

In private life the rules are rapidly changing: girls and women are more willing to ask men out, and with women's age at first marriage the latest ever, they come to marriage with a firmer sense of who they are; they now expect to work, to share domestic chores, and to have a full and equal partnership with their mates. In liberal communities practices that seemed bizarre a generation ago may be rare, but raise few eyebrows: lesbian co-parents, or educated single women with good jobs, who have babies through artificial insemination or adopt children.

So is American feminism, as its detractors claim, a finished project kept alive only by ideologues? Not so: the rosy picture above is only a part of the truth. Women are still paid less (24 percent on average), promoted less, and concentrated in poorly paid, stereotypically female jobs. Women working full-time still make only 76 cents for every $1 earned by men. Only in porn movies can women expect to earn higher salaries than men.

Men still overwhelmingly control U.S. social, political, legal and economic institutions and machinery. Rape, domestic violence and sexual harassment are huge problems. In four out of five marriages, the wife does most of the housework and childcare whether or not she also works full-time (and whether or not her husband considers himself egalitarian). The flip side of girls' achievement is the pressure on them from the media, fashion, boys, each other, to conform to a prematurely sexualized, impossible beauty ideal. In schools and colleges, anorexia, bulimia and other eating disorders are endemic.

Feminism has made the United States more equal, more just, more free, more diverse—more American. But it still has a long way to go. The sociologist Arlie Hochschild calls it a "stalled revolution"—in women's roles, hopes and expectations to which society has yet to adjust. Although most mothers, even of infants, are in the workforce, 45 percent of which is female, the typical worker is still seen as a man with a wife at home, thanks to whom he can be totally available to his employer.

The rules for pensions, social security and unemployment benefits disadvantage women, who are usually the ones to take time off to care for children or sick family. The social supports that ease poverty, childcare and the working mother's double day in European welfare states barely exist in the US: 41 million people lack health insurance; and welfare reform has forced poor single mothers into jobs that are often precarious and do not pay a living wage. Without a national system of daycare or pre-school, finding affordable childcare can be a nightmare even for prosperous parents. It took the women's movement more than twenty years to win passage of the Family and Medical Leave Act, which gives workers in large companies just twelve weeks' leave to care for newborns or sick relatives: since the leave is unpaid, few can afford to take it.

Caught between the old ways and the new, many Americans blame feminism for difficulties. Men no longer give their seats to pregnant women on the subway? Legal abortion has destroyed chivalry. Not married although you'd like to be? Feminism has made women too choosy and men too childish. Infertile? You should have listened to your biological clock instead of Gloria Steinem. The women's movement has never had a good press: every few years it has been declared dead. But demonizing feminists is now a preoccupation of ideologues across the political spectrum. On the right, misogynist radio hosts—"shock jocks"—rant against "feminazis", as if a woman who doesn't laugh at a sexist joke is about to invade Poland. Fundamentalist preachers such as televangelist Pat Robertson claim feminism "encourages women to leave their husbands, kill their children, practice witchcraft, destroy capitalism and become lesbians."

The American left, such as it is, is officially pro-feminism, but suspicious of the women's movement—too bourgeois, too white, too preoccupied with abortion rights. For communitarians, feminists threaten the family and the social cohesion married families supposedly produce, and, by focusing on paid labor and individual autonomy, introduce capitalist values into the home.

So much criticism is daunting. It is often said that young women reject feminism. Millions of women under thirty grew up with the idea of gender equality and take their rights for granted. But polls show that they are reluctant to call themselves feminists. "A few weeks ago," wrote Wendy Murphy, a professor at Harvard Law School, "I asked my students (all women) to raise their hands if they believe in social equality for women: they all raised their hands. Then I asked if they believe in economic equality for women: they all raised their hands. Then I asked if they believe in political equality for women: they all raised their hands. Finally, I asked for a show of hands from those who considered themselves to be feminists. Only two raised their hands, and one was a reluctant half-raise."[1] Asked why she avoided the word, a student said: "I just don't see myself as a bra-burning man-hater." Another felt she had been raised as her brother's equal, so had no problems. A third didn't want to limit her politics to gender: she called herself a humanist.

What will happen to them when they enter the legal profession, where 61 percent of firms have no women partners, seventy to eighty-hour weeks are normal and taking time off for children is the kiss of career death? When feminism becomes a matter of individual initiative—a bra-wearing humanist making her way in a man's world—how does a woman understand and overcome structural gender-based obstacles to equality? Does she join with other women, or blame herself?

The common European stereotype is that U.S. feminism is obsessed with political correctness and victimology. But PC is mostly a rightwing fabrication, a label that can be used to mock women who object to demeaning or hostile language or behavior. The U.S. media loves stories about excessive PC—the little boy suspended from school for kissing a little girl, the professor who removed a reproduction of Goya's *Naked Maja* from her classroom. The reality is usually more trivial and ambiguous than the reports: the little boy, who had a history of disruptive behavior and genuinely upset the girl, only sat out a party. The professor lost patience with male students who leered at the Maja instead of practicing their Spanish. Even if the teachers acted foolishly, why are these incidents worldwide news?

It is the same with victimology. The intent is to make those who are disadvantaged and injured ashamed to acknowledge their pain or demand redress: that would be whining, complaining, asking for special treatment. But many women are victimized—raped, beaten, disrespected or discriminated against. When a woman insists on prosecuting her rapist or abuser or harasser, isn't she refusing to be a victim? Are there feminists who will make extreme claims of victimization? For sure. But they are a very small strand in a broad, even contradictory movement. Since the 1960s American feminism has been fractious and diffuse, encompassing Marxist professors and freemarket stockbrokers; nuns and logicians; lipstick lesbians and Catholic mothers of six.

Feminism is strong in surprising places: among nurses, who have used feminist theory to redefine themselves as holistic healers and patient advocates. While liberal advocacy organizations like the National Organization for Women (NOW) and Feminist Majority focus on electoral politics, young women put out small counter-cultural magazines—"zines", start rock bands, and organize campus productions of *The Vagina Monologues*, Eve Ensler's hilarious play about women's sexuality, which is performed as a fundraiser at colleges around Valentine's Day.

A debate that seems to have exhausted itself is the pornography war of the 1980s and early 1990s. The brouhaha was immensely destructive to the movement, because it raised questions about sexuality and agency in non-negotiable terms; and it pitted two very American principles with deep historical roots against each other: freedom of speech versus Puritanism. When it came to the idea of women enjoying pornography, two important feminist principles were in conflict: the quest for pleasure without guilt versus humane values like intimacy, responsibility, non-violence, equality. Both sides cited studies supporting claims that pornography did or did not lead to actual violence against women. Intellectually the debate was exciting, but it left bitterness and had little to do with campaigns to protect real women from actual violence.

On the university campus today sex-positivity rules. It is fashionable among young feminists to go to strip clubs, and even work in them. While older feminists reluctantly defended President Bill Clinton from impeachment, young feminists defended what they saw as Monica Lewinsky's bold sexuality. The monolithic, moralistic feminism of the 1970s has given way to a multiplicity of feminisms—queer theory and social constructionism have thrown the idea of woman up in the air. Suggest that a man who's had a sex change isn't really a woman, and you may find yourself tagged as an old-fashioned essentialist.

Anti-feminists claim that feminism is a set menu, but it is more like a cafeteria, where each woman takes what she likes. Personal choice seems to be the only value: there are no politics, and no society—to suggest that a choice isn't really free is to insult a woman's ability to know what is best for herself. Having a facelift, which twenty years ago most feminists saw as a humiliating capitulation to sexist standards of beauty, today can be a present a woman gives herself: "I'm doing this for me." The academic focus on parody and performance can reduce feminism to an ironic wink: yes, I'm still in the kitchen, but my collection of 1950s refrigerator magnets means I'm not just a housewife. This is feminism lite.

These internal debates are nothing to the threat posed to progress by the ascendancy of George Bush, the Republican party and the Christian right. Thirty years of political and legal advances are at risk. Abortion rights, already threatened in many states, are the most obvious target: new limits are sure to pass at the federal level and in many states as well, and many new anti-abortion rightwing judges will likely rule against legal challenges to them. The Bush administration has allocated millions of dollars for abstinence-only sex education in schools, pro-marriage classes for poor single mothers, and religious-based social services whose aim is Christian conversion; Bush has packed federal panels and commissions with fundamentalists, social conservatives, anti- feminists and other opponents of women's rights. Wade Horn, a key figure in the father's rights movement, is in charge of family issues at the Department of Health and Human Services. Diana Furchgott-Roth, who argues that sex discrimination in employment does not exist, sits on his council of economic advisers. Dr. David Hagger, who opposes legal abortion, refuses to prescribe contraception to unmarried women and wrote a book suggesting bible reading as a treatment for premenstrual symptoms, sits on a medical panel overseeing contraception.

And those girls playing soccer in the park? The Bush administration is considering weakening legislation that requires schools to work toward equalizing athletic opportunities for the sexes. Bush-instigated challenges to affirmative action threaten the ability of businesswomen to obtain government contracts,[2] workers to enter non-traditional occupations, and students to attend non-traditional vocational programs, which are still highly sex-segregated. If these changes happen, will women—those who call themselves feminists and those who don't dare use the word—come together to defend their rights?

NOTES

1 Op/Ed in the *Boston Herald*, 15 April 2000.

2. Until now the U.S. administration had to make a certain number of contracts with companies headed by women.

War on Terror or War on Women? The View from Latin America

YIFAT SUSSKIND, ASSOC. DIRECTOR, MADRE

MADRE, 10.03

Most Americans judge George Bush's fixation on national security to be an appropriate response to the atrocities of September 11, 2001. But for millions of women in Latin America, the U.S. "war on terror" is a cynical euphemism for the Administration's unbridled greed, macho militarism, and callous disregard for the needs of the world's majority. In this article, women human rights activists from Nicaragua, Mexico and Colombia discuss how the "war on terror" impacts their communities and what they are doing to challenge U.S.-driven policies that rob them of their rights. In partnership with MADRE, an international women's human rights organization encompassing a network of women in ten countries, these women deliver a powerful message to their own governments and to the Bush Administration: there is no such thing as national security. For security to be genuine, it must be global. Moreover, "state security" must be grounded in human security, based on protection of women's human rights, including the rights to food, housing, health care, education and decent work.

STATE SECURITY V. FOOD SECURITY: HUNGER IN NICARAGUA

The day after the attacks on the United States, U.S. trade representative Robert Zoellick launched his "countering terror with trade" campaign, capitalizing on the attacks to reinfuse U.S. economic policy with a sense of mission not seen since the Cold War. Suddenly, free trade became an exercise in freedom itself. As Zoellick said, "Trade is about more than economic efficiency. It promotes the values that are at the heart of this protracted struggle" (*The Washington Post*, 10.3.01). Zoellick counseled that the way to avert "threats to our security" was by offering "economic hope" to poor nations (Ibid.). Like others in the Administration, Zoellick seemed untroubled by the fact that long before September 11, more than a billion people around the world were surviving on less than one dollar a day. After the attacks, however, Zoellick reasoned that since poverty is a "breeding ground" for terrorism, we must alleviate the plight of the world's poor by promoting trade and investment.

"How lucky for Bush that increasing corporate profits turns out to be the key to fighting terrorism," laughed Mirna Cunningham, an Indigenous leader and medical doctor from Nicaragua's North Atlantic Coast. Mirna underscored that Zoellick's argument embodies the main fallacy of neo-liberal economics: that guaranteeing huge profits for corporations somehow benefits poor people. "Here in Nicaragua, any child can tell you that the big lumber, mining and fishing companies have robbed poor people of their lands and livelihoods," said Mirna. Indeed, after more than a decade of U.S.-imposed economic policies in Nicaragua, corporations control over 40 percent of the country's natural resources.

"On the North Atlantic Coast, where I am from," said Mirna, "the rain forests on which local Peoples depend for food, water, medicines and which are source of our cultural and spiritual practices are being destroyed. When women go out to haul water, fish or gather plants, they are confronted with armed guards protecting land that is now corporate property. Women are responsible for making sure that our families have food, water and the healing plants they need. Without our lands, women cannot care for their families." In a region where a full 75 percent of the population already suffers from malnutrition, traditional diets are being undermined. Meanwhile, processed foods imported from the U.S., such as white bread and cola, are aggressively marketed. Women, who have less access to food in the first place because of gender discrimination, are especially threatened.

"We have already lost so much," said Mirna. "Yet Bush continues to pressure our government to sell off our forests and lagoons. Indigenous Peoples are fighting back. Last year, the people of Awas Tingni blocked the government's sale of their territory to the SOLCARSA lumber company. It was a landmark legal victory that we will build on to win further recognition of our collective rights as Indigenous Peoples. The Bush Administration insists that Nicaragua's government support its wars and respect its need for security. But Bush does not respect our need for security—for job security or food security, for example. "

Zoellick and the many CEOs in Bush's Cabinet present their dogma as plain truth rather than ideology. Like the Islamic fundamentalists targeted in the "war on terror," proponents of strict neo-liberalism espouse an absolute and literal interpretation of a theory and implement it without regard for context or room for critique. As Mirna said, "Bush has declared that market fundamentalism is the best defense against Islamic fundamentalism. But as Indigenous Peoples we are skeptical of missionaries bearing any kind of fundamentalism, whether religious, cultural, political or economic."

CORPORATE PROFIT AS NATIONAL SECURITY: FTAA & PLAN PUEBLA-PANAMA IN MEXICO

Topping the Bush Administration's economic agenda for the hemisphere are the Free Trade Area of the Americas (FTAA) and Plan Puebla-Panama.

The FTAA, which some activists have described as "NAFTA on crack," would turn all of Latin America (except Cuba) into one big free-trade zone, mainly for the benefit of U.S. corporations. Regulations on foreign investment would be minimal and governments would have to treat foreign investors the same as domestic businesses. Because multinational corporations can out-compete most local businesses, the policy undermines efforts to promote sustainable industry in poor countries. The FTAA would even allow corporations to sue governments for enforcing certain labor and environmental standards. After September 11, 2001 the Bush Administration stepped up pressure on Latin American governments to sign onto the FTAA, which the Administration sees as an economic arm of the "war on terror." In fact, Bush's National Security Strategy of September 2002 describes the FTAA as a component of US national security in the hemisphere.

Plan Puebla-Panama, a regional expression of the FTAA, would create an extensive free-trade zone, build a giant network of highways and railroads and develop the oil and electric industries from Mexico's Puebla state all the way to Panama. Some of Mexico's largest oil reserves are thought to lie beneath the lands of Indigenous communities in Chiapas, where a decade-long struggle for democratic rights is underlain by a contest for control over this valuable resource. "You can see which areas are believed to be richest in oil," explained Carolina*, a young Indigenous woman and social activist. "These are the places where the government has stationed the most troops since September 11. After the U.S. was attacked by men from Saudi Arabia, Bush decided that he could no longer rely on oil from the Middle East. He doubled U.S. military to Mexico and we saw a sharp rise the number of soldiers in Chiapas."

Carolina is a member of K'inal Antzetik, a local organization founded in 1991 as a women's weaving cooperative. "We now work in a variety of ways," said Carolina, "to advance the rights of Indigenous women within our communities and the rights of Indigenous communities in Chiapas. We offer women reproductive health care and counseling for survivors of military violence."

"Women suffer from the presence of soldiers, both government troops and the more brutal paramilitary forces," said Carolina. "Women live in fear that their families will be hurt, their houses burned down and their lands taken by the army to build military camps or roads. These threats cause tremendous psychological stress. We have seen more mental health problems among women in our community. When the army comes, it is no longer safe for women to be outside. Girls are raped and forced to become prostitutes for the soldiers. Others have been kidnapped by paramilitaries and held as slaves to cook, clean and provide sex for the men."

"We know that the FTAA and Plan Puebla-Panama will mean even more soldiers on our lands," said Carolina. "Bush says that oil is a matter of U.S. national security. Well, we Indigenous are used to being called threats to national security. We are working to develop alternatives to Bush's economic model, which sees us as expendable obstacles to increasing oil revenues. This year, we are training women to work as carpenters, to improve their productivity as farmers and to learn business skills. Our aim is to develop economic autonomy at the community level and improve women's ability to feed their families."

TEACHERS AS TERRORISTS: THE EROSION OF HUMAN RIGHTS IN COLOMBIA

Even before September 11, Colombia ranked as both the worst human rights offender in the hemisphere and the largest recipient of U.S. military aid. Now, Bush's "war on terror" has allowed the Colombian government to use U.S. military aid directly for operations against the leftist guerrillas that it has been battling for forty years. The new policy has fueled the armed conflict and given the government a green light to subordinate human rights and democratic process to its counter-terrorism operations.

"For the first time since the 1980s, the United States is undertaking a counterinsurgency effort in Latin America, giving weapons, training and money to a government that relies on paramilitary death squads," said Cecilia*, who works with a small women's organization in Bogotá. "Since Bush declared his 'war on terror,' civilian deaths have risen to almost twenty a day. That's nearly double the figures for 2000. Last year, another 400,000 people—mostly poor Indigenous and Afro-Colombians—were driven from their homes." To date, more than two million Colombians have been displaced. Most are women with children who are surviving in overcrowded, makeshift neighborhoods, where they have no source of income. "We organize social safety nets among displaced families; educate women about their rights and help them respond to the many forms of violence that permeate their lives," said Cecilia.

"The 'war on terror' has made our work more dangerous. Now the Colombian government thinks it has permission from the White House to treat critics as terrorists." Shortly after September 11, Bush pushed to revoke human rights conditions on military aid for its allies in the "war on terror." As a result, hard-won human rights protections in Colombia and elsewhere were unraveled. A new "anti-terrorism bill" granted the Colombian military sweeping powers, including the right to detain people as young as sixteen without a trial. The bill also allowed the government to declare a State of Emergency under which constitutional rights are suspended. "Last year," said Cecilia, "half of all those detained under counter-terrorism measures were social activists and human rights workers. Schoolteachers have become a major target of the death squads. Teachers are labeled as terrorists for allegedly influencing students the wrong way and more than one is killed every week."

"Security has become a code-word for justifying government violations of our basic rights. For most Colombians, the real cause of insecurity is the government itself: its social policies, which keep people poor and landless; and its alliance with the paramilitaries, which are responsible for most of the killings. But how can we hold our government accountable when the U.S. says that anything is allowed in the name of national security? How can we fight for the rights of political detainees when people in the Bush government defend the use of torture against their prisoners in Guantanamo Bay?"

REDEFINING SECURITY

In their struggles for a broad range of human rights, Mirna, Carolina, Cecilia and many other women throughout Latin America are creating a powerful alternative to the model of security enshrined in Bush's "war on terror." "We need to ask what security means for the world's majority, for poor women and their families," said Mirna. "What are the needs of women—we who are denied rights and resources, but given responsibility for the health care, day care, nutrition, housing, teaching and emotional well-being of the vast majority of the world's people? What do we need to keep ourselves and our families safe from poverty, preventable disease and violence? What needs to change for women to be part of decision-making in our families, communities and at all levels of government?" As women human rights activists throughout the hemisphere address these questions, we build a new definition of security, one that is rooted in human rights protections, state accountability and women's perspectives of the world's needs.

* Carolina and Cecilia are pseudonyms for protection from government or paramilitary violence.

CREDITS

Abdela, Lesley. "No Place for a Woman." *The Times* (London), copyright © 2003, by permission of the author.

Bacchetta, Paola, Tina Campt, Inderpal Grewal, Caren Kaplan, Minoo Moallem, and Jennifer Terry. "Transnational Feminist Practices Against War," copyright © 2001, by permission of the authors.

Bass, Emily. "Unconscionable Care: Is the Religious Right Compromising Your Health Care?" *Ms.*, copyright © 2001, by permission of *Ms.* magazine.

Baumgardner, Jennifer. "*Roe* in Rough Waters." *The Nation*, copyright © 2003, by permission of *The Nation*.

Benen, Steve. "Strange Bedfellows: Conservative Christians and the Bush Administration Are Aggressively Pushing a Controversial 'Pro-Family' Agenda on the International Stage—And They're Teaming Up with Islamic Theocracies to Do It." Reprinted by permission of *Church and State Magazine*, the monthly publication of American United for Separation of Church and State, copyright © 2002.

Berkman, Brenda, Lt. "Celebrating the Many Roles of Women," copyright © 2001, by permission of the author.

Berkowitz, Bill. "TeamBush to Abused Women: Fuhgedaboutit!" *WorkingForChange*, copyright © 2002, by permission of the author.

Bernhardt, Annette, Laura Dresser, and Catherine Hill, "Why Privatizing Government Services Would Hurt Women Workers," copyright © 2000, by permission of the Institute for Women's Policy Research.

Block, Jennifer. "Sex, Lies, and Abstinence" *Conscience*, copyright © 2003, by permission of the author.

Bunch, Charlotte. "Whose Security?" *The Nation*, copyright © 2002, by permission of *The Nation*.

Cahill, Sean, "Why We Need Same-Sex Marriage," copyright © 2003, by permission of the author.

Chideya, Farai. "Working-Class Women as War Heroes." *AlterNet*, copyright © 2003, by permission of AlterNet.

Easton, Nina J. "The Power and the Glory: Who Needs the Christian Coalition When

You've Got the White House? The Religious Right's Covert Crusade." *The American Prospect*, copyright © 2002, by permission of *The American Prospect*, all rights reserved.

Ehrenreich, Barbara. "A Mystery of Misogyny." *The Progressive*, copyright © 2001, by permission of *The Progressive*.

Elliston, Jon and Catherine Lutz. "Hidden Casualties: An Epidemic of Domestic Violence When Troops Return from War." *Southern Exposure*, copyright © 2003, by permission of the authors.

Enloe, Cynthia. "Sneak Attack: The Militarization of U.S. Culture." *Ms.*, copyright © 2001, by permission of *Ms.* magazine.

Featherstone, Liza. "Mighty in Pink." *The Nation*, copyright © 2003, and "Wal-Mart Values," *The Nation*, copyright © 2002, by permission of *The Nation*.

Flanders, Laura. "Unsung Heroes." *The San Francisco Chronicle*, copyright © 2001, by permission of the author

Flanders, Laura and Rhonda Perry, "Kitchen Table Politics: An Interview with Rhonda Perry," copyright © 2004 by Rhonda Perry and Laura Flanders.

Flanders, Laura and Dorothy Roberts, "Building a Movement for Reproductive Self-Determination: An Interview with Dorothy Roberts," copyright © 2004 by Dorothy Roberts and Laura Flanders .

Fuentes, Annette. "Social Security Is a Women's Issue." *The Progressive*, copyright © 2000, by permission of *The Progressive*.

Goldstein, Richard. "Bush's Basket: Why the President Had to Show His Balls." *The Village Voice*, copyright © 2003 Village Voice Media, Inc., by permission of *The Village Voice*.

Gonzales, Patrisia. "Upstanding Native Women." Universal Press Syndicate, copyright © 2003, by permission of the author.

Hayes, Christopher. "Shelf Life. Librarians: Liberals with Backbone." *The American Prospect*, copyright © 2003, by permission of *The American Prospect*, all rights reserved.

Heyzer, Noeleen. "The Unequal AIDS Burden." *The Christian Science Monitor*, copyright © 2002, by permission of *The Christian Science Monitor*.

Hill, Felicity and Mikele Aboitiz. "Women Are Opening Doors: Security Council Resolution 1325 in Afghanistan," from Sunita Mehta, ed., *Women for Afghan Women*, copyright © 2003, by permission of Palgrave Macmillan.

Hollibaugh, Amber. "Queers Without Money: They Are Everywhere, but We Refuse to See Them." *The Village Voice*, copyright © 2001, by permission of the author.

Houppert, Karen. "Against the War but Married to It." *The Nation*, copyright © 2003, by permission of Random House, Inc., and the author. This piece forms part of a book called *The Waiting Wives Club* forthcoming in March 2005 from Ballantine Books.

Ireland, Doug. "Bush's War on the Condom: U.N. Report Documents the Failures to Curb AIDS." *LA Weekly*, copyright © 2002, by permission of the author.

Klein, Naomi. "On Rescuing Private Lynch and Forgetting Rachel Corrie." *The Guardian*, copyright © 2003, by permission of the author.

Kort, Michele. "Global Sex Rules: The Price of Silence." *Ms.*, copyright © 2003, by permission of *Ms.* magazine.

Kumbier, Alana. "Wedding Bells and Welfare Bucks." *HipMama.com*, copyright © 2002, by permission of the author.

Lee, Chisun. "Against Rosa's Odds: On the Road With a Welfare Warrior." *The Village Voice*, copyright© 2002 by Village Voice Media, Inc., by permission of *The Village Voice*.

Lee, Chisun and Sharon Lerner. "Altared States: Women on Welfare Talk About Marriage." *The Village Voice*, copyright © 2002 by Village Voice Media, Inc., by permission of *The Village Voice* and Sharon Lerner.

McConahay, Mary Jo. "Tell Me Everything": Teens Talk Back About Abstinence Education. *Pacific News Service*, copyright © 2003, by permission of the author.

Morse, Russell. "Call Me American: A Young Man Contemplates Going to War." Pacific News Service, copyright © 2001, by permission of the author.

Muhammed, Cedric, "The Thong vs. the Veil" *Blackelectorate.com*, copyright © 2001, by permission of the author.

Murray, Bobbi. "Orphaned By the Drug War." *AlterNet*, copyright © 2002, by permission of AlterNet.

National Women's Law Center. "Women's Priorities Would Be Sacrificed to Pay for Bush Tax Cuts," copyright © 2002, by permission of the National Women's Law Center.

Nelson, Ashley. "The Truth About Women and the Recession." *AlterNet*, copyright © 2003, by permission of AlterNet.

Nelson, Jill. "A Mean-Spirited America: Today, I Fear My Own Government More Than I Do Terrorists." *MSNBC.com*, copyright © 2003, by permission of United Media.

Phillips-Fein, Kim. ". . . and the Poor Get Poorer." *The Nation*, copyright © 2003, by permission of *The Nation*.

Pollitt, Katha. "U.S. Feminism Lite: Claiming Independence, Asserting Personal Choice." *Le Monde diplomatique*, copyright © 2003, by permission of *Le Monde diplomatique*.

Pozner, Jennifer L. "Whatever Happened to the Gender Gap?" *Women's Review of Books*, copyright © 2002, by permission of the author.

Raha, Maria, "Veiled Intentions: The U.S. Media's Hug and Run Affair with Afghan Women," *Bitch*, copyright © 2003, by permission of the author.

Riverbend. "Baghdad Burning: Girl Blog from Iraq." www.riverbendblog.blogspot.com, copyright © 2003, by permission of the author.

Rogova, Igo. "A Cautionary Tale from Kosovar Women to Women in Post-War Iraq." *Kosova Women's Network Newsletter*, copyright © 2003, by permission of the author.

Sanders, Lynn. "Hardly Sporting: Don't Gut Title IX Until You Know What It Does." *Slate*, copyright © 2002, by permission of United Media.

Sheehy, Gail. "Four 9/11 Moms Battle Bush, *The New York Observer*, copyright © 2003, by permission of ICM for the author.

Sheikh, Irum. "Reading, Tracing, and Locating Gender in 9/11 Detentions." *The Subcontinental*, copyright © 2003, by permission of the author.

Shiva, Vandana. "Globalization and Poverty: Economic Globalization Has Become a War Against Nature and the Poor." *Resurgence*, copyright © 2000, by permission of the author.

Soueif, Ahdaf. "Arab Women Staying Alive." *The Guardian*, copyright © 2003 by Ahdaf Soueif, by permission of The Wylie Agency, Inc.

Steinem, Gloria. "Gender Smarts: Will Sex Ever Make Us as Smart as Race When It Comes Time to Vote?" *AlterNet*, copyright © 2002, by permission of AlterNet.

St. John, Phoebe and Masuda Sultan, "Raising the Voices of Afghan Women: An Interview with Masuda Sultan" copyright © 2004 by Masuda Sultan and Phoebe St. John.

St. John, Phoebe and Ellen Bravo, "Working Women's Lives and the 'W Effect': An Interview with Ellen Bravo," copyright © 2004 by Ellen Bravo and Phoebe St. John.

Susskind, Yifat. "War on Terror or War on Women? The View from Latin America." *MADRE*, copyright © 2003, by permission of *MADRE*.

Talvi, Silja J. A. "Women of the Promised Land." *LiP Magazine*, copyright © 2002, by permission of the author.

Vives, Olga, with research by Kristy McCray. "Latina Girls' High School Drop-Out Rate Highest in U.S." *National NOW Times*, copyright © 2001, by permission of NOW.

Voss, Gretchen. "My Late-Term Abortion." *The Boston Globe*, copyright © 2004, by permission of the author.

Williams, Patricia J. "Better Safe. . . ?" *The Nation*, copyright © 2002, by permission of *The Nation*.

The Feminist Press at the City University of New York is a nonprofit literary and educational institution dedicated to publishing work by and about women. Our existence is grounded in the knowledge that women's writing has often been absent or underrepresented on bookstore and library shelves and in educational curricula—and that such absences contribute, in turn, to the exclusion of women from the literary canon, from the historical record, and from the public discourse.

The Feminist Press was founded in 1970. In its early decades, the Press launched the contemporary rediscovery of "lost" American women writers, and went on to diversify its list by publishing significant works by American women writers of color. More recently, the Press's publishing program has focused on international women writers, who remain far less likely to be translated than male writers, and on nonfiction works that explore issues affecting the lives of women around the world.

Founded in an activist spirit, the Feminist Press is currently undertaking initiatives that will bring its books and educational resources to under-served populations, including community colleges, public high schools and middle schools, literacy and ESL programs, and prison education programs. As we move forward into the twenty-first century, we continue to expand our work to respond to women's silences wherever they are found.

Many of our readers support the Press with their memberships, which are tax-deductible. Members receive numerous benefits, including complimentary publications, discounts on all purchases from our catalog or web site, pre-publication notification of new books and notice of special sales, invitations to special events, and a subscription to our email newsletter, *Women's Words: News from the Feminist Press.* For more information about membership and events, and for a complete catalog of the Press's 250 books, please refer to our web site: www.feministpress.org.